BY HEART

VIKING

ROSEMARY

Elizabeth Smart
A LIFE

SULLIVAN

VIKING
Published by the Penguin Group
Penguin Books Canada Ltd, 10 Alcorn Avenue, Toronto, Ontario, Canada
M4V 1E4
Penguin Books Ltd, 27 Wrights Lane, London W8 5TZ, England
Viking Penguin, a division of Penguin Books USA Inc., 375 Hudson Street, New
York, New York 10014, USA
Penguin Books Australia Ltd, Ringwood, Victoria, Australia
Penguin Books (NZ) Ltd, 182-190 Wairau Road, Auckland 10, New Zealand

Penguin Books Ltd, Registered Offices: Harmondsworth, Middlesex, England

First published 1991

10 9 8 7 6 5 4 3 2 1

Copyright © Rosemary Sullivan, 1991

Printed and bound in Canada on acid free paper ∞
by John Deyell Company

Canadian Cataloguing in Publication Data

Sullivan, Rosemary
    By heart: Elizabeth Smart a life

ISBN 0-670-82629-4

1. Smart. Elizabeth, 1913-1986 — Biography.
2. Authors, Canadian (English) — 20th century — Biography.*   I. Title.

PS8537.M37Z85 1991   C813'.54   C90-095634-8
PR9199.3.S564Z85 1991

For my parents, Michael Patrick and Leanore Marjorie Sullivan, and for my brother, Terry

Sometimes a shaft of pain comes down out of a tree for no reason at all. Sharp, diagonal, sudden out of a landscape, it finds the vulnerable bit to pierce.

Happiness is not geometrical, but flows in from all sides wherever you look.

The Assumption of the Rogues and Rascals

Elizabeth Smart

Contents

Preface

I first met Elizabeth Smart in 1978. After reading her novel *By Grand Central Station I Sat Down and Wept*, I felt compelled to seek her out. Something about that novel, perhaps its bravery and its essential rawness, made me want to know the author. I travelled to her Suffolk cottage, the Dell, one bleak February weekend. The cottage was beside a gravel pit, which cratered the winter landscape so that it seemed as desolate as the moon: strings of man-made lakes crusted in ice, cranes rising from pits like strange pterodactyls. It was an eccentric, labyrinthine route to find the answer to my question: What had become of this writer, of whom little had been heard since the publication of her first masterpiece? How had she survived the pain of that book?

Elizabeth Smart, in gumboots and shaggy sweater, appeared at her gate to welcome me, and I was struck by the vulnerable, almost childlike figure she presented. Though her face was Audenesque, lined and lived-in, she was as candid and open as her book. Over wine and vodka we became friends. I remember her gestures: fingers threading blonde hair as if raking soil, her exclamations of "Good God!" in a voice mixed with glee and despair. And I remember her loneliness. When I asked her why there had been a gap of thirty years between the publication of her books, she remarked: "I had no place at the literary table. They would speak to me one on one, but I had no place at the table." I discovered that she did not mind my invasion of her privacy. She was pleased to know that people were listening, had heard. After that, I saw Elizabeth Smart a couple of times in London, and then we lost touch, until circumstances brought her back to her native Canada and our friendship resumed.

It never occurred to me in those years that I might come to write Smart's biography. When Catherine Yolles at Penguin Books approached me with the project, after some deliberation I agreed. Though I had known Elizabeth Smart, she remained a conundrum to me. Many accused her of self-absorption in her writing, yet she rarely spoke of herself. Her life remained mysterious. She seemed like an old Proteus, a shape-shifter who slipped through one's fingers and often refused to speak. She had reason, for the essential narrative of the life of Elizabeth Smart was, as I discovered, already there in her writing. She did not need to say more. "I have had my vision," she would tell me, and I have only now fully understood that she was not speaking of romantic love, which many have identified as her theme. She was speaking of what she called the law of pain. She would quote Kafka: "We need an axe to crack the frozen seas within us." She always insisted on disavowing safety; life was high risk and must be lived to its sharpest edges. She suffered much. In many ways, life had betrayed her expectations; it was messy, unaccommodating. But she never retreated. Smart lived in the moment, often with a wonderful roguish humour.

To thread the narrative of the life through the works has been fascinating. There is a quality of intoxication to Smart's life, as to her writing; she never let go. Her story has many compelling dimensions: she was born into a colonial culture where it was difficult to know how to get started as a writer; into a wealthy family where the expectations imposed on a dutiful daughter were to be a good hostess and marry well; and into a time when men were the writers and women were often muses who came down from their pedestals only to wash the dishes. She had four children and knew how the role assigned the mother emptied the writer's ego. She watched the male poet put his writing before any of life's other claims while her muse lived in "a female ghetto." She faced the dilemmas of isolation and silence. And yet what was remarkable about Elizabeth Smart was her "rage of will"; she "bashed on regardless."

If anything, the purpose of this biography is to redress the silence that surrounded Elizabeth Smart. When Smart is known, it is often in association with a vague romantic legend: as a woman who fell in love with a poet, had four children by him without ever having lived with him, and wrote one of the most passionate accounts of romantic love in modern English literature. But the real narrative of her life is more complex and compelling; it has to do with the experience of being a woman artist in the middle of this century. Smart was first and foremost a writer; she had too much respect for art to settle for anything less than the highest ambition. She would say: "It takes pain to burn through time, to turn a spot on the wall into the centre of the world, now and hereafter." Smart was often alone with her four children, often in poverty. She found little emotional or moral support for her writing, which, because it was experimental and far ahead of its time, did not receive the attention it deserved. She knew more than most about the pain of self-doubt. But she never regretted the early choices that determined the direction of her life. She could not imagine living without what she called "these female experiences," by which she meant love and children. She was fierce in her generosity, as in her disgust with the stingy or the boring, or those who cringed before the price life exacts for living deeply. She refused to make a distinction between her life and her work. She would have been shyly pleased to hear Elspeth Barker, George Barker's last wife, say of her: "*Grand Central Station* was a marvellous book, but as a human being, Elizabeth went far beyond it."

Many have been helpful in the researching and writing of this book. I would like to thank Michael Ondaatje for giving me the title. When one thinks of Elizabeth Smart, one naturally thinks of the heart, but anyone who spent an evening with her also remembers squirming when the inevitable moment arrived and one was expected to recite: anything would do, limerick or sonnet, but if one loved words then one had them by heart. I would like to thank Sebastian Barker, literary executor to the estate of Elizabeth Smart, for his support of my project and for the many conversations during which he readily discussed his gifted mother; Georgina Barker, for a two-year correspondence in which she candidly answered any questions it occurred to me to ask, for the generosity with which she has provided the photographs for this biography and for her invitation to her home in Cornwall, where she movingly traced the narrative of her mother's life; Christopher Barker, for his kind hospitality in London, for the right to quote from his mother's letters to him and for the photographs he provided for this book.

I would also like to thank Elspeth and George Barker. When I wrote to say I was researching the life of Elizabeth Smart, they immediately invited me to their Norfolk home. While George Barker remains sceptical of the art of biography—"I find nothing quite so contemptuous as the art of temporal judgement," he remarked—he spoke generously of Elizabeth Smart and has given me permission to quote from his published work. His letters to Smart he insisted, are a private matter, not available to scholars. Elspeth Barker spoke of Smart with an affection and eloquence that to this day move me. I would like to express my gratitude to Jane Marsh Beveridge, a woman as original as her remarkable sister, who invited me to Cambridge on several occasions, made available to me her excellent autobiography of childhood, "Four Horses, Sixteen Legs," and put up with my inquiries in several years of correspondence. I am also grateful to Russell Smart, Elizabeth Smart's brother, for his courtesy in Ottawa, and his prompt replies to any questions I posed.

To acknowledge all the people I interviewed and who wrote to me about Elizabeth Smart would take too long. Their words can be found in the pages that follow. However, I would particularly like to thank Charles Ritchie, for his wit and insight into the young Smart, and for permission to quote from *My Grandfather's House*; Irene Spry, for many lively conversations and for permission to quote from the papers of her late husband, Graham Spry; Alice VanWart, for the endless evenings in which we tried to unravel the complexities of Smart's life and for the invaluable work she has done in editing Smart's unpublished writings; and Didi Holland-Martin, for her shrewd insight into Smart's life and for permission to quote from her early letters to Smart; and Anastasia Wyatt-Wilson for her candour and for permission to quote from Jessica Barker's letters. I wish to thank Lawrence Durrell for permission to quote from his letters to Smart; as well as Jay Landesman, Smart's publisher, and Stephen Maas, executor to the estate of Willard Maas, for their permission to quote from Smart's letters in their possession.

I would like to thank those who have assisted me in my research: Thomas Friedman, for the readiness with which he interrupted work on his Ph.D. thesis to hunt for answers to my abstruse questions; Gail Martin of Ottawa and Preston J. Owens of Utah, who assisted me astutely with genealogical research; Claude LeMoine, Head of the Literary Manuscript Division of the National Library of Canada, for his wisdom in giving the appropriate home to Smart's papers and for his courtesy; Linda Hoad, of the National Library, for her gracious assistance; and, particularly, Lorna Knight, who catalogued the collection and never seemed exhausted by my endless inquiries. Thanks also to Sheila Powell at the National Archives of Canada; W.A.B. Douglas at the Directorate of History, National Defence; Shelley Cox, Rare Book Librarian at Southern Illinois University at Carbondale; Cathy Henderson, Research Librarian, the Harry Ransom Humanities Research Center at the University of Texas at Austin; M.N. Brown, Curator of Manuscripts at Brown University; and Diane Smith, Reference Librarian at the John P. Robarts Research Library, the University of Toronto.

I would like to thank the Canada Council, the Social Sciences and Humanities Research Council and The Toronto Arts Council for financial assistance in completing this book.

Finally, I would like to express my gratitude to my editor, Iris Skeoch—one could not ask for a better—and Mary Adachi, my copy editor. And to Juan Opitz who kept me "bashing on regardless"; he has the distinction of being one of the very few people Smart quoted in her notebooks by name. I believe she valued his opinion and support, as I do.

Rosemary Sullivan
August, 1990
Toronto

BY HEART

1   Personal Pronouns

Parents' imaginations build frameworks out of their own hopes and regrets into which children seldom grow, but instead, contrary as trees, lean sideways out of the architecture, blown by a fatal wind their parents never envisaged.

> Elizabeth Smart
> *By Grand Central Station*
> *I Sat Down and Wept*

Towards the end of August 1937, Elizabeth Smart walked into Better Books on Charing Cross Road in London. Browsing casually, she selected a poetry book from the shelf. Had anyone been watching her at that moment, the spectacle would have been intriguing: an attractive young woman, blonde, blue-eyed, smartly dressed, standing there as if transported. Outwardly she would have looked demure in a Harrods hat and a coat from Peter Jones, and had she spoken, the voice would have had the flat accent of a Canadian colonial. Certainly no one could have guessed either the intensity or the fierce will of this young woman, for, at the age of twenty-three, Elizabeth Smart was terrified of missing her life. In her hands, she had suddenly decided, was the book that would determine her destiny.

Nothing that had happened to her, no one she had met so far, satisfied the reaches of her imagination, and the longing to start was overwhelming. The stupidity of not devouring life, grasping it with both hands! She had written in her diary that summer: "Oh this unreality. God wake me up. . . . Living is unrealizable. These highly charged minutes with only a glimpse of the beginning of consciousness."

What she wanted most was to be a writer. She had written to Lawrence Durrell, the young editor of *Booster*, that the Canada she came from was "the most exhilarating, exciting, inexhaustable country in the world physically," but there were no people in it, no poets but "inarticulate" ones. Surely in London she could find what she needed. Love, she had determined, was the necessary catalyst to reach the creative edges of the self, but all the men she had met—and her admirers were legion—were too malleable. She wanted someone dangerous, whom she could not manipulate. She was stalking the muse, the demon lover who could crack the chrysalis; and her appetite was outrageous. Oh, for "time to breathe, to live, to enjoy, to revolt, to be vulgar, to philosophize, to digest, to be flippant, to be irrelevant, to feel, to know, to understand." When would it ever be possible to leap, "bellowing with jungfreud, into the arms of the infinite?"

And she read the book she held. The poem may have been "Daedalus": "The moist palm of my hand like handled fear/ Like fear cramping my hand/ . . . his comet face/Approaching downward . . . irresistible."[1] The words seared. On the spot she would have memorized them by heart, for she did not read books; she engrammed them. Who was this George Barker, so passionate, with such a roar of authority? She checked the biographical blurb. He was the right age. She said to herself: "That's the one." And she immediately began what she called her manoeuvres. She searched for Barker at parties, asking all her friends: "Do you know George Barker, because I'd like to meet him and marry him." And the young bohemian poet George Barker, already notorious on the London poetry scene, heard that a beautiful, rich blonde, an heiress, was looking for him with marriage in mind. He could dismiss this as besotted. Until he met her.

At that moment in Better Books on Charing Cross Road, without having met George Barker or seen a picture of him, Elizabeth's lifelong relationship with him began. She was already one-third of the way through her life, and everything that had preceded propelled her to this moment. To understand her is not easy, for she was a complete original: "I am the obsessional type. Which type are you? If you are the butterfly type you will never forgive my intensity." The imperative was to live, and she knew exactly what she wanted. The mysteries were located around three words—art, love, children. If anything, she was the female imperatrix; she rebelled against everything that would deny her female vision. To understand her isolation, her need, and her outrageous and brilliant determination, one has to go back to the beginning. It is an important journey, because in the process she was articulating what it is to be a woman. "Is it harder to be a man or a woman?" a friend would later ask her. "Oh, it is harder to be woman," she replied, "but it is also much more interesting."[2]

The story opens in Canada between the two World Wars. It was a peculiar moment in Canadian history that, in retrospect, has the odd sense of being both a false start and a new beginning. Canada was still, mentally and culturally, a colony, tied to Great Britain, and yet it had the cockiness of a young upstart. Great things were expected of this new country, and the generation who lived their youth in the lacunae between the wars grew up with an enormous sense of expectation. This would be their century. Elizabeth Smart was born on December 27, 1913. Unlike her literary predecessors in Canada, she felt it might just be possible to be a great writer. But there was always that schizophrenia: "Canada vs. the Mother Country." She called it "a fierce battle, a sad war." How, in this great emptiness called Canada, was one to start?

If the cultural pull that would determine the life of Elizabeth Smart was trans-Atlantic, her ancestral roots were entirely North American. The Smarts told their family history as stories, repeated like litanies and embellished at will. Elizabeth loved to claim that her great-great-great-grandmother was an Indian. The story started in the 1780s when a shadowy ancestor called Benjamin Baldwin married a Sioux chief's daughter, Ruth Paddock, in order to obtain ownership of Dutchess

County. No historical record of such a transaction can be located, and it seems to have mattered little that it was the Hurons not the Sioux who lived in the area of New York called Dutchess County.³ It was rich lore that Elizabeth would use to delight her own children. It gave a fierceness to her beginnings:

"You were an Indian, Mother?"
"Yes, darling, I was a Sioux."
"Did you kill any cowboys?"
"No, it was the English who killed me & burnt my village."
"How could they kill you, you're alive?"
"I know. But my great-great-great-grandmother was the Indian!"...
"It says in *Girl* the Sioux hated the English."
"Well naturally they did. The English were mean to them."⁴

When Elizabeth felt vulnerable, she would always call on what she described as the "insouciance of my Red Indian ancestors."

On her father's side of the family there was only one ancestral story. Russel Sutherland Smart was born in Winnipeg on June 20, 1885. When his mother died six months after his birth, his father, George Alexander Smart, absconded to Atlanta, Georgia, starting a new family which the Canadian Smarts were never to meet. Russel was brought up in dingy boarding houses in Ottawa by his maternal aunts, Auntie Tabb and Auntie Emma. Orphaned early, he had to invent himself, which he did with a determined ambition and intelligence that were remarkable. Of the Smart ancestry he was to say laconically: "The first Smart fought as a common soldier on the Plains of Abraham in 1759. He survived and that was good enough."⁵

All the stories came from the matrilineal line, the Parr side of the family. Elizabeth's mother, Emma Louise [Louie] Parr, had a flair for the dramatic and is clearly the elusive, complex, and difficult piece of the puzzle that made an Elizabeth Smart possible. She assigned Russel the part of Fifth Business; in most instances he was the brilliant, though invisible, facilitator of the plot.

The Parr stock was entrepreneurial. Elizabeth's great-grandfather Alanson Baldwin was an American, a pencil maker by trade, who owned a small saw-mill in Ticonderoga, New York. Drawn by the lure of wealth in the expanding forest industry in Upper Canada, he crossed the American border with his wife, Melissa Prior, in 1854. The town he arrived in, Bytown (renamed Ottawa in 1855 after the Outaouais Indians), would have called him part of the "American invasion." The influx of settlers suddenly expanded the population of the small frontier town to 10,000, and the dust from the saw blades, whining day and night, became so thick that the locals had to lobby for a road-sprinkler system. Baldwin made the best of the boom. Beginning with one mill on Chaudière Island, by the mid-sixties, he owned two mills, two steamers and fourteen barges, employed 150 men, and turned out 35 to 50 million feet of lumber per season.

When depression hit the lumber industry in the 1870s, Baldwin failed with debts of $65,000, and a yard full of market-ready lumber that could not be sold. But Alanson Baldwin was something of a local hero. According to *The Ottawa Citizen*, he had single-handedly saved Ottawa in the big fire of 1870 with the ingenious idea of opening the St. Louis Dam and using the full force of his mills to beat back the flames from the city.[6] Elizabeth took this piece of family lore to heart for, at the age of nine, she was to imitate her grandfather, "single-handedly" saving the city of Ottawa from fire by blowing out a match she found lying carelessly in the street. Perhaps Baldwin was also the remote genetic source of another characteristic. Called "generous to a fault," he gave timber to rebuild to the farmers from nearby Carlton who had been wiped out by the fire. "All right," he would say, "go to the yard and load up. Pay me when you can." The loads of lumber were never put on the books, and never paid for. Baldwin was already out of business by the time the farmers got back on their feet.

With Baldwin in 1854 came his ten-year-old daughter Kate. Elizabeth remembered her grandmother most distinctly for her secret pride in American citizenship. All her life she kept an American flag hidden in her dresser drawer among her underwear. Kate Baldwin married James Alexander Parr, who had been chief operator for the Montreal Telegraph Company before returning to his native Ontario, and settling down as a bookkeeper on Chaudière Island. It is likely he worked for the Baldwin Mill. The Parrs had nine children, seven of whom survived. Louie, Elizabeth's mother, born June 16, 1884, was the second-to-last daughter.

It was Granny (Kate) Baldwin and her sister Harma, like many Canadian matriarchs, who kept the family stories. Great-aunt Harma was the character in the Parr family and perhaps started the tradition of furious individualism that characterizes the Smart women. Harma was said to have been engaged seven times. Each time she was brought to the altar, she flinched, recovering at the last minute her fidelity to her first love, a soldier who had died in Libby Prison during the American Civil War. Each time, she dutifully divided her trousseau among the various cousins. Harma was a working woman, unusual in those days, an Ottawa civil servant. She lived alone in Ottawa with her housekeeper who was required to serve her mistress an elegant dinner each night. She was not wealthy, having invested her money with more daring than shrewdness, in mines and the new moving-picture industry. She lost most of it. Many in the family doubted the story of Harma's engagements, wondering who would marry such a sharp-tongued woman. "Poets!" she used to say, "I wouldn't give you 10 cents for a dozen of them."[7] While she may not have shared her opinions, Elizabeth loved Aunt Harma's fierceness: "She is an individual and alive—but not a person to live with."

Granny Baldwin was also the keeper of the family mementos. Most impressive was her treasured stereopticon, still in the possession of Elizabeth's cousin Gypsy Parr. The stereopticon held picture postcards of the Great War, portraits of wounded soldiers on stretchers carried through seas of mud. Granny Baldwin's youngest son, Clayton, had been killed at the Battle of the Somme and she kept his medals and cigarette case with its stale cigarettes still intact. She constantly reminded her grandchildren he had died for civilization and spoke of the atrocities of the German enemy. Elizabeth hated her grandmother's war propaganda and her xenophobia; all her life she would be disgusted by the idea that civilization could be saved by war.[8]

There was only one British ancestor that the Smarts laid claim to. On Elizabeth's first trip to London with her family when she was eleven, Mrs Smart's first priority was to visit the exhibition of Queen Victoria's doll house, famous for its hundreds of miniature rooms. The rest of the Smarts were intent on visiting the grave of their English ancestor, old Thomas Parr, in Westminster Abbey. The Smart children knew old Parr's story so well that they often repeated it like a play, each taking up a line of the story. Though buried in Poets' Corner, Parr was no poet. His distinction was that he had lived to be 152 years old. Born in 1483 in Shrewsbury, Parr was something of a rascal. Married at eighty, he was arrested for adultery at the age of 105 and was forced to do penance, wearing a white sheet in front of Alberbury Church, for begetting a bastard. He married again at the age of 122. In 1635 he was invited to London by King Charles to be exhibited at the royal court as a piece of antiquity. When asked how he'd managed to live under ten kings and queens, he replied that he'd simply changed his religion to suit the reigning monarch. He'd come "raw into the world and accounted it no point of wisdom to be broiled out of it." He was exhibited for some weeks at the Queen's Head in the Strand, but the "old, old, very old man" as he was styled, did not last long. The rich diet at court proved fatal to a man who had lived the simple and abstemious life of a husbandman. Parr died in 1635, having been the subject of portraits by Rubens, Van Dyck, and William Blake; and giving his name to a pill: "Old Parr's Life Pills" and to old Parr whisky.[9] That the Smarts were delighted to claim old Thomas as their ancestor tells us something at least about their humour, a gift that Elizabeth was to inherit. As a child she always claimed she was going to live as long as old Thomas Parr.

Though the Parr family might look back to heroic entrepreneurs, Indian princesses, and infamous centenarians, by the time Russel Smart met Louie Parr, she was living comfortably and conventionally with her family at 524 Besserer Avenue in Ottawa's then fashionable Sandy Hill. Louie was working as a clerk in the Land Patent Branch of the Department of the Interior. Yet, with Russel, she was to create one of the most entertaining and interesting families Ottawa had seen in a long time.

Russel Smart was by all accounts a man much loved but whom few knew well. His ambitious career is easy to trace. He had put himself through a practical-science degree at the University of Toronto (1901–1904), working as a packing manager in the basement of the local Woolworth's five-and-dime. He used to amuse his daughters by saying that had he stayed on at Woolworth's, he'd have worked his way to the top, and they'd all have been heiresses. He had, he said, lived in a tent outside Toronto and cycled ten miles to lectures. He was familiar with poverty. On graduation, he began extramural classes at Queen's University (receiving his B.A. in 1907) and joined the firm of Fetherstonhaugh & Co., Patent & Trade Mark Agents, taking charge of the Ottawa office. In the first year he doubled net profits from two hundred dollars to four hundred dollars, and with this promising business start was emboldened to court and marry Miss Louie Parr in 1908.[10] Always shrewd, he took his bar exams in Quebec in 1911, becoming a patent attorney, and then obtained a certificate in Mechanical Engineering from the University of Toronto in 1913. His skills were thus unique, combining law and science at a time when the demand for patent lawyers was increasing rapidly. In 1926 with his friend Mowat Biggar he created the firm of Smart & Biggar, Barristers & Solicitors/Patent & Trade Mark Agents, whose head office is still in Ottawa. He was to write several books on patent law, with Fetherstonhaugh and others, and to establish himself as one of the most prominent patent lawyers in Ottawa. From an orphan with no prospects, he became a man of considerable wealth, a prominent member of Ottawa's small government and business élite, and a lawyer with an international practice that sent him travelling across the Atlantic several times a year on legal cases.

The private man is more elusive. According to a family friend, the diplomat and diarist Charles Ritchie, the quiet centre of the Smart household was Russel Smart. "Plump, pink-cheeked, and bespectacled," he was a benevolent man. "He used to say that, when he left his law office, he put all thoughts of business behind him." Although he was not a great talker himself, he loved good rich conversation and friendship and gathered people around him. The Smart household became a hub for "broadcasters and civil servants, aspiring politicians and journalists, would-be writers and artists, young aides-de-camp from Government House in Ottawa and the more spirited members of the diplomatic corps. They came and went, declaimed and joked and argued. Many of them ended up in love with one of the sisters, sometimes with all three, simultaneously or in succession."[11]

Elizabeth adored her father. In the Smart family, she was to say "there was the feeling that one was the best there was. The terms now used—upper and middle class, establishment—don't really apply. We knew there were people richer, but we thought, 'They don't know how to use money; they don't have any fun.' We weren't allowed to mention money; my mother told us it was ill-bred. We laughed at the people who were rich and silly about it, who were boors and bores and frumps . . . [Father] would always use money in whatever way was demanded or wanted, if it was reasonable."[12] The Smarts were to become, as Ritchie called them, "an oasis in a cultural desert," a rebellious aberration among conventional stock, a place where one could discuss "books that shocked, pictures that were criticized, politics that were disapproved . . . Then we would turn to ridiculing the notions of social and sexual respectability, for respectability, now somewhat dented, was then securely entrenched." The tolerance was fostered by Russel. "About an idea," Elizabeth said, "you could always approach our father; he was truly unprejudiced. And there was the understanding that the mind must be fed." Ritchie described Russel as enjoying the play of discussion about him, "smiling tolerantly at outrageous opinions but without condescension, for he was one of those older men to whom the young could talk without censoring their sentiments." Russel was also a great reader and made his study available to his children. He was passionate about the theatre, and was at one point president of the Ottawa Drama League. Yet he remains curiously invisible. He was the backdrop to Louie's performance. After his death in 1944, his friend, the poet Duncan Campbell Scott would write to the critic E.K. Brown: "Too many of the veterans are leaving us. I shall miss Smart, he was a member of our little dinner club and the source of much vital talk there for he was, as you know, decidedly to the Left; I never knew anyone who was so generous to his family, maybe too generous." And on another occasion: "Peggy and I used to think that he gave a lot more than he got."[13]

In Elizabeth's own report, her father had always been someone on whom she could, privately, count. Publicly, he seemed to let Louie set the scene. The portrait of the father in *By Grand Central Station I Sat Down and Wept* may indeed explain things: "But from my father I had hoped for more. He could spread his mind out before you like the evidence of a case. But if he saw emotion approaching he smiled painfully, rocking in his swivel chair, hoping it would pass: 'Aren't you just a little obsessed about this thing?'"[14] Yet Russel was the source of the vast permission granted his daughters. "To speak to my father privately," Elizabeth would say, "I'd meet him at parties and arrange the rest of my life." Long after his death Elizabeth would write inconsolably: "All over and round the world there never was and never could be [another such as he]."[15] The wonderful if naïve assumption she had as a young woman that the world could be manipulated to her own desires came from foundations Russel had built. "It was a huge luckiness, but we never supposed for a minute that it wasn't ours inevitably."

It was Louie who was the complicated thread in the family fabric. To admiring young family friends like Ritchie or Graham Spry, later to be known as the founder of Canadian public broadcasting, she was a charming hostess. Ritchie described her as "a tall pretty-faced woman with an engaging warmth of manner, she enlivened the scene with a touch of the dramatic. She expected people to play up and was impatient of slowness of response."[16] Elizabeth could say of her: "She was quite a bit of an artist. Her talent for hospitality was instinctive, but her discipline about the details was masterly, learnt, strict—a great combination. Making homes, atmospheres, occasions appear spontaneous & no hard work, planning, organization, thought showed through the polished results."[17]

And Elizabeth's younger sister Jane could add that "her real gift was words. If she described someone, those words stuck to that person forever. If she said he was a skimpy little person, you could never see him in any other way. Even when her words were bitter and outrageous, they were said with such humour that you liked her."[18] That Louie was loved was eminently clear. She was humorous, energetic, and a lively companion.

But that Louie was a more complex factor, for her daughters in particular, was also clear. Her most extraordinary characteristic was an indomitable will. Jane would say of her: "She wanted to control the world; run it from her house like a private play. She collected people." Elizabeth would spend a lifetime trying to understand her mother. She concluded that Louie wanted to be a lady, "to escape vulgarity and the shameful world of the body." Louie was a peculiar mixture of romanticism and presumption. Jane felt that Louie Smart intended to rise above her Parr ancestors. Accordingly, she shunned Aunt Harma, explaining that Aunt Harma was a Baldwin, of whose Yankee spirit she disapproved. Yankees spoke of things like "guts and gumption," but she preferred "decency and decorum."[19] "I'm going to beat the Baldwin out of you," she'd tell her children. Curiously, she was not a social climber. She had invented her own form of climbing. She loved the glitter of Englishness, particularly Rhodes scholars (she herself had left school at grade eight). Her word of contempt for socially crude people was "gypsies." She wanted to instil in her children a "thing called character." If Russel was deeply democratic by temperament, Louie was not. While she could be generous, she "believed in the great class barriers. One had a duty to stay where God had been pleased to put one. Naturally she had been put at the top. . . . Any infringement, any sign of impertinences, of liberties taken and the claws came out."[20]

Louie had great expectations for her daughters. A girlfriend of Elizabeth, Bobby McDougal, remembers all the women in the family as "over-powered." "They had too much engine. They were all talented but they were prone to exaggeration and Louie backed them up." Elizabeth in particular was driven. "She had to have excitement. Any let-up and she'd get bored. She had to keep going. I don't know why."[21] The sympathy for Louie, who had her hands full, is evident. Still, the fact that seems clearest, and corroborated by all family members, is that when Louie didn't get her way, the emotional cost to everyone was high.

In her novella *Dig a Grave and Let Us Bury Our Mother*, which she drafted in 1938, Elizabeth fictionalized the courtship of her father and mother. It is the only portrait we have of the young couple; while not factual, it records what is perhaps more important: the emotional roles Elizabeth assigned to her parents. Her mother is the difficult, ambiguous centre; her father sustains the backdrop to the scene. Later Elizabeth was to say: "my father was taken over and fitted quietly into her obstreperous vision."

Why can I not explain or describe her? Could I reconstruct her yearning girlhood, with Emerson and Matthew Arnold in leather binding under her arm? My father took her in a canoe one day when they were twenty-one. They paddled softly up the canal under the weeping willows. She took off her great white hat and laid it across her knees, trailing her hand in the water. Her dress was white too, with a high neckline up to the throat, her long swan-like throat. She thought: He is looking at me, but I shall not let him know I notice.

"We have known each other for a long time, Miss Parr, would you allow me to call you by your first name?"...

She tucks her chamois leather into her bag. Her dreaming eyes strain after Emerson. "Be good sweet maid and let who will be clever." Did she make herself cheap to allow him the use of her first name? A little prouder, a little haughtier, in case. Her contrary skirts are reflected in the shadowed water.

"Will you take tea now, Miss Parr?"

"I am not hungry now, thank you."

Arnold! Emerson! Your ambiguous signals, your severe mistakes, bore these years for me.

She could spread sun. She could be a radiator of light. She smelt sweet. Her serenity could be like the wings of sleep, when it was in possession of her. Sometimes she sang lullabies and was a pillow against nightmares, toning and tuning all things that went on around her. Why couldn't this state last forever?

Her storms descended quicker and direr than typhoons, more deadly because her sun had opened your locked doors. You lay vulnerable, naked in the calm air, and the unexpected shock charred you, made you recoil, turned your insides to stone.[22]

Elizabeth has caught the intimate Louie Parr here, with her peculiarly Victorian romanticism, and her theatricality as a means of controlling any situation that might expose her vulnerability. She has also located something else, her mother's prudery, which Elizabeth spent her whole life in reaction against. All Louie's daughters felt the impact of their mother's sexual rigidity.

To characterize Elizabeth's relationship with her mother is essential, for she returned to its foundational memories all her life. In "Scenes One Never Forgets" she writes:

I am 63, the happiest person in the world.

But still I cry out at night, heard throughout the house, through several walls, still wrestling with infantile anguishes and anxieties.

"Mother! Mother! Mother!". . .

Desolate. Eery. Desperate.[23]

Childhood seemed to contain conundrums that Elizabeth could never solve and that she attempted to examine in her last years in many unpublished autobiographical sketches. Perhaps what was peculiar to it was its emotional dialectic: the pattern she describes of attention and withdrawal. The definition of love comes to us out of patterns set by our first experience. The extremities of love and despair seem to have been laid early in the imagination of Elizabeth Smart. It was the pattern she was to search for and repeat all her life. For Elizabeth, what characterized her mother was her "abandoning power." It set up a dichotomy between "pleasing mother and being myself." It also established her law of fidelity: she would never abandon those she loved.

When Russel and Louie were married in 1908, they settled at 515 Besserer Avenue down the street from the Parr family. Their first daughter, Helen, was born in 1909. In 1912 the family moved to 184 Cooper Street. A second daughter, Olive Walton Smart, died of meningitis at seven months on April 20, 1913. Elizabeth was born on December 27 that year. Given Louie Smart's temperament, the pregnancy must have been frantic. The child Louie was carrying, conceived before the death of her second daughter, would have provoked in her a state of solicitous neurasthenia, and been treated as the precious replacement of the life that was lost.

In 1915, when Elizabeth was two, the upwardly mobile Smart family moved to 15 Linden Terrace, a large three-storey brick house across from the Ottawa Canal. It had an imposing front porch supported by pseudo-Corinthian white wooden columns. Russel's law practice was growing and Louie was now beginning the life of comfort to which she felt she was entitled. The household was run formally. Domestic affairs were attended to by the cook, Rita, and the governess, Annette, under Louie's strict supervision. The children ate in the nursery when Russel was away on his frequent business trips. Otherwise they ate with their mother. Louie often spent her afternoons with aunts Edith, Jenny, and Florence, who were childhood friends rather than relatives (the latter the mother of Eugene Forsey, with whom the Smart children played). They would sit long afternoons in the drawing-room, Florence wearing her pince-nez glasses that hung from a gold chain, and gossip about the various cabinet ministers.

Louie's third daughter, Jane, was born at Linden Terrace on December 2, 1915. For Elizabeth the new baby's arrival was a traumatic event, displacing her as the centre of the world. Her record of this sibling rivalry from the perspective of years is amazingly raw. Perhaps Elizabeth was attached to it because it provided a private cryptography for the myth of a spoiled paradise. In 1978, she wrote notations to her childhood:

Born
Rejection
Despair
Incomprehension. Mouth hung open until 7 . . .
Hysteria of mother. Anguish. Fear. Birth of brother.
Unpredictable storms that shake the whole life . . .
Fear . . . terror . . . isolation[24]

Elizabeth had the writer's fascination for archetypal patterns. "One life is all lives." She was compelled by the eccentricity and arbitrariness of memory, the way certain early scenes recur and keep recurring. Further, the way they come as sensory images, giving the sensation that the part of the brain that lived those memories is still extant. In later life, she picked among the flotsam of her own past, looking for "clues to the origins of ancient storms, storms that still rumble ominously." There are several variations of the following anecdote that seemed to provide the code to her childhood: the laboured climbing of the narrow stairs, the folding of white socks.

I trudged upstairs, shooed by maid? nurse? mother?
Unwanted.
The baby slept.
I trudged on up, steps steep as Everest, revengeful, help-less, scouring the world for a small clutch to hold on to.
Where did I go? Rejected, up into the dark with difficult steps on two-year-old legs . . .

Weren't there any warm cosy moments? I must have known there could be, for I screamed and screamed and screamed at the top of the stairs . . . for my mother to leave her friends and gossip and cakes and teas and come.

But she never came. Or if she did for punishment, banishment into the huge deserted nursery, and the laborious folding and mating those thick white woolen stockings and placing them two by two in virtuous rows. . . . *Now* are you sorry? *Now* do you see how unjustly you abandoned me on that lonely landing?

Where were my sisters? Where were the servants?

What a mist that childhood is.

Yet it was that plump rosy baby, whose sacred sleep shooed me off, who found that her childhood had chewed away her life.[25]

Perhaps most fascinating about this memory is that it is an elementary illustration of how private and bifurcated reality is. Jane, the coddled usurper, described her own memory of infancy. Her bitter account is that when she was born, her mother put her in a basket (she didn't want another girl) and gave her to Helen, by then six years old. "Helen always took me as her responsibility."[26] Elizabeth's relation with Jane was never simple. It occasioned both ruthless competition and guilt. At sixty-three she was to reproach herself: "Now I ask myself, twisting & turning for my own survival, could I have taken full maternal responsibility for a little bewildered sister? I could have been warmer . . . more explanatory: a comrade, a teacher at least of what I knew. But I was secretive, cunning, bent on survival, devious."[27]

Both Jane and Elizabeth shared a bleak vision of childhood. Elizabeth felt that, on the whole, childhood seemed "about love & separation, love & longing, love & rejection, a stupor of love unsatisfied, the hopelessness of making oneself understood, helplessly bombarded by incomprehensible pain, the little comforts & jollities few & far between." And the pattern of a female solution was established early. Feeling rejected, she tried to please, to attain praise; "approval, a light or look in the eye, at me, at *me*, to give me a place in the universe, to confirm my existence, as I stood there shivering with doubt & fear, & nowhere to go."[28]

How do we account for such extreme stories? Clearly it had to do with Louie. There is the convenient notion from Freudian psychology that creative women are their fathers' daughters. But when the aggressive directing hand is the mother's (as in the case of Sylvia Plath or Jean Rhys) the psychological web seems even more intricate.

Why is it that the remembered scenes of childhood are often those of pain? Perhaps the traumas of childhood are devastating because the child is so undifferentiated inside that the hurt touches the whole of the self. Certainly the capacity for pain was one of the motive springs of Elizabeth's being. In later life she recounted a recurrent fantasy from childhood. "When I was a child I had a terror of [my mother's] head falling off. At night sometimes, when she was walking down the hall, her neck grew and grew till it broke and the head fell. Or she was lying across a bed with her neck stretched and her head fell off on the side. I was filled with fear. If her head fell off it was my fault. I could prevent it by loving her enough."[29]

There is no question that Louie loved her children, but love was seen by them as coercive. It was not unconditional: it was a vehicle for reward or punishment. According to her daughters, unless Louie's prescriptive will was met (if she wasn't loved enough), her hysteria could be triggered by anything when the time was right.

Yet this seems to assign blame, and, as Elizabeth was to conclude, blame is the least useful emotion in matters of the heart. It was Louie's very complexity that was one factor in the context that was to create her talented, unconventional daughters. Elizabeth's childhood was not, by any means, unrelieved gloom. She was a compelling, precocious, and imaginative child.

Elizabeth remembered an experiment she undertook when she was six years old. It is one of the moments in which we see the sensibility of the writer Elizabeth Smart first flash into articulate being. Though recorded in retrospect, the anecdote is resonant. The conundrum of what it was to be a thief suddenly occurred to her. How could she understand what it was to be a thief, a bad person, if she never stole? To know a thief from inside, there was no way to understand but to be a burglar. One day, she decided to sneak down into the pantry to steal six lumps of sugar. Nothing happened, not even a slight feeling of guilt. She ate the six lumps of sugar under the bedclothes. After this she stole regularly, but still felt unsatisfied. After all, sugar was one's lawful right. If she wanted to experience a dreadful sense of remorse, it was necessary to be really wicked. She proceeded with the experiment. One day in a hardware store, she stole a small one-cent bell. The remorse flowed. She felt a terrible unease. She was convinced that the hardware man knew and would shame her into confession. The coal man, the postman, the butcher's boy all knew and despised her. She began to toss and turn at night. No sleep, only nightmares of humiliation, her guilt written on every policeman's face. One afternoon when the house was deserted and quiet, she got the one-cent bell out from under her bed, crept out of the house to the garden and buried it as deep as she could. It was a great event. The shame and remorse disappeared. She understood at last the feelings of the burglar.[30]

At six she had learned instinctively the first law of the writer: the need for an exquisite sense of empathy. No understanding can come without actual experience. She would always be willing to carry any action to the logic of its extremity. She would always feel a lifelong kinship and sympathy with the outlaw, the outsider.

In the fall of 1920 when Elizabeth was seven, the family moved to Daly Avenue, briefly to 396 and then to 361. They were back in the familiar territory of Sandy Hill where they were to stay for ten years. It was Louie who was restless. Between 1908 and Russel's death in 1944 the family lived in nine houses. Louie loved to find a house and decorate it, but then she would become dissatisfied. She thought the place to which she had moved was the one to make her happy. Jane always felt that she never really formulated what she wanted.

While Elizabeth, at some moments, might feel the "little comforts and jollities were few and far between," there was much gaiety in the family household. Helen was just old enough to be assigned the role of big sister and Elizabeth and Jane formed an exclusive duo in childhood games. They were encouraged to read or were read to in the nursery by Louie or one of the string of governesses. Their favourite authors were Thornton Burgess and Sir James Barrie, most of whose books they knew by heart. Songs, rhymes, and quotations were a childhood habit. The nursery was decorated with panels depicting nursery rhymes: "Supposing a great big bugaboo/Stuck out his long sharp claw at you/Just supposing." Louie certainly had her hands full with her two precocious daughters running through the house at ages seven and five shouting: "Democracy, hypocrisy, debauchery and lies." Jane was to say that they didn't know what the words meant, but it entertained the adults. (It's amusing to think that these were the words they picked up in the family ambiance.) Elizabeth was very verbal, inventing neologisms: "olives were queevish" and witticisms: "Governesses are prim and proper like prunes and prisms."[31] Their governess Mademoiselle Sherier they called Mel.

The Daly house had a huge attic where the children played when Elizabeth was seven. It was at the top of steep angled stairs. "You had to go precariously along a little ledge to get to it. It was rough and dusty under the eaves with dark dead end nooks and dangerous uncovered floor boards." With the neighbourhood children they played "Sardines," a backward version of hide-and-seek; or dress-up with Louie's elegant Edwardian dresses, which progressively lost their glitter as bits of skirts were cut up to sew Christmas presents. After tea, the games would start. Elizabeth remembered "the incipient excitement, the imminent possibilities as the lid of the trunk was opened. The inspiration boggled. After a few minutes the imagination of quite shy children boggled too. When the staid fathers arrived to fetch them they were flushed & slightly drunk with their three dimensional dreams. The fathers glanced uneasily at so much life pulsating out of their docile offspring, vaguely apprehensive of the dangers of too vivid a vision of freedom."[32] The games always ended in orgiastic excitement, when, stuffed with pillows, the children would slide down the steep stairs on tin trays. Those too timid to try would be threatened by Elizabeth and Jane who would invent characters from the odd assortment of old hats, button boots, and garments to terrify the others.

But festive occasions could be trying. All her life Elizabeth said she disliked Christmases. The season was often spoiled by Louie's hysteria. She would get worked up at the thought of something looming ahead; when she was tired the most trivial things could trigger her underlying hysteria. A Christmas scene that seemed to repeat itself—Louie saying she would commit suicide, running to the bottom of the driveway, jumping in the car, and careering down the street through the snowy ruts—was fairly indelible. At such times Russel remarked curtly that Louie was a case for Freud.

There were two sides to domestic life in the Smart household. There was the formal household: Louie maintaining decorum. In good weather she had the children dressed in middies and skirts, with dickies and ties, and sent them off to Ottawa Normal School. At night they sat lined up on the porch and waited for Daddy. They would be sent to St Andrew's Presbyterian Church on Sundays, though Louie herself did not often attend. Louie liked the habit of display, ordering sleighs from the Launderville cabs to deliver presents at Christmas, with the three daughters dressed up in the white rabbit coats from Ogilvies. Her notions of decorum were exacting: she could complain of the cook—"I've told cook time and again not to serve the children two white things at one meal"—milk toast and junket. "Mother talked so much of politeness and decorum that we were confused about behaving at all," said Jane.[33] Yet, there was the wonderful Louie who indulged her children with taffy parties and charades. A childhood party at the Smarts was legendary, with elaborate masquerades and wonderful sweets.

But Louie could rip the whole fabric of reality into pieces with one of her scenes. In her autobiography, written from the child's perspective, Jane recorded a scene at Daly Avenue when Elizabeth was seven, shortly after the family had moved there.

> One day when Betty and I were getting dressed after our afternoon nap, Mummy came into our room. You could tell she was in a bad mood by the sound of her feet on the floor, sort of stiff and hard sounding. I guess Betty didn't notice because she answered back and was impudent.
>
> Mummy shoved her into the cupboard. Betty screamed and screamed and Mummy kept shoving the door, trying to get it closed. Then Betty started really shrieking loud, which was different and scarey, not like how she sounded at first so Mummy stopped shoving and let the door come open.
>
> Betty went on shrieking because her fingers were all bloody. They'd been caught in the crack of the door and squashed while Mummy was trying to shove it closed.
>
> Mummy started screaming too and hugged Betty and got bandages and peroxide and fixed up her hand. Mummy wrapped it all around like a big glove and Betty couldn't use it for days and had to be helped to dress.
>
> Betty didn't get any stitches though, just squashedness and blood and when the bandages came off, later on, her fingers were purpley-blue and yellowish and two of her finger nails came off.[34]

As an adult, Elizabeth continually returned to puzzle out her childhood. She understood its complexity—an initiation into love that was shattered. She had the courage to go deep into its entrails, to assume again the persona of the child in her effort to understand the childish guilt and longing. We see a child who is wilful, falling into tantrums of need. In an undated manuscript written in later years (though the anecdote is referred to as early as 1938), Elizabeth lives again the vivid agony of the child. She writes the anecdote as if from the child's perspective with such rawness and precision that it is clear that, throughout her life, she could fall back into this black hole of need.

She begins by describing her governess Mademoiselle Sherier: "She is bony and weak and her voice has no authority. My mother is away and the world is cruel and cold and there is only the boniness, the bleak snivelling ineffectualness of Mademoiselle." Mademoiselle falls "so painfully below my desire . . . Days have gone by and I have had no love. I am starving, starving." A battle is occasioned by Elizabeth's insistence on wearing an article of clothing the governess feels is too young for her: "Betty! If you don't stop crying I shall be obliged to put your head under the cold tap!" . . . "You are a rude, impudent, ungrateful girl!" Mademoiselle drags her to the bathroom and forces her head under the water. "The water runs up my nose, streams down my hair, I think I am really going to drown. I am terrified. I choke between my screams." Outraged, she decides to run away from home:

> I would go to my mountain, to my wild mountain where nobody could find me. I would live in the woods and build an enormous high spiked fence around my property. I would live on berries and roots. I would find my cat Mrs. Felix who was up there under the shed where she had kittens. She understands me! She was my true and only friend! She would have more kittens in the padded box with the strange smell and pale bloodstains and I would see it all and understand her tender motherhood. I would roam the woods and mountains like the wind. . . .
>
> I went downstairs to the kitchen and got some soda crackers from the frightened maids, who snickered timidly. I packed my brush and comb . . .

She marches off into the icy April weather but then begins to think of her mother who would soon be returning from New York with presents, and would find her child gone. Her heart would break.

> Oh dear God how terrible for her. She would rush like a madwoman tearing through the streets, tearing her softness, being run over by motors in her haste, and in the

woods, which she did not know, get lost, hurt by the bram-
bles, stumble on the tree roots, and break her neck, perhaps die! And it would be worse than all the unbearable
and terrifying family quarrels. I can't stand it. I can't stand
it. O God. She would break her neck running after me in
the woods.

I kept on walking, brooding all the time on my persecution. I couldn't turn back to be treated cruelly. All the way
up town, splashing unheedingly through the muddy pud-
dles. At the great hotel, lying on the wet sand I found a
match, still unstruck.

A match, unstruck! Dangerous!

It might catch fire and burn down the great hotel, perhaps the whole town! It was terribly dangerous! Perhaps
God had wanted me to save the hotel, the town, from
burning down, and so had sent me up here, to be a heroine. I, perhaps, was to save the town. This was my big
chance!

I struck the match and blew it out. . . .

It was nothing. Yet I saved the whole town. I am a
heroine . . .

In that moment she reinvents the old story of her great-great-
grandfather's heroism and saves the town from burning down,
as he had done before her. Also in her nine-year-old memory
may have been the familiar account of Louie's having almost
died in the great Ottawa fire of 1900 that virtually wiped out
the whole industrial section of Hull. Louie had been putting
clothes in her closet and when she turned round, they caught
fire in her arms[35]:

My heroism reconciled me to the world. It was notable to
suffer and to be brave in silence. . . . And Mummy!
Darling understanding Mummy! She would cry! She
would have hysterics. She might break her neck.

At the church I knew God had sent me up town to save
it from catching fire. He wanted to give me a chance to be
a heroine. And I had taken that chance. But such a heroine

could not bear to break her mother's heart. I could not bear it. I would go home and endure taunts and torture for her sake.

FOR HER SAKE.

When I opened the front door, smiling nervously, Mademoiselle, Granny, Jane, my older sister, and all the maids were gathered round, frightened and red-eyed.

They said "Hello Betty," kindly with relief.

I smiled and passed upstairs in peace.

But when my mother came home, I felt my love was too big and embarrassing. It melted me, and I was afraid. So when she came I went away and cried and hid under my bed, intimately with the stale smell and the startled dust.

"Don't you want to see your mother? This is a nice homecoming for me!"

I felt I was brewing the storms I dreaded, but could not help it. I loved her too much. She would cry and there would be a scene. But I could not help it. I stayed crouched stiffly under my bed, waiting.[36]

Years later, it amused Louie to recall the moment her child had run away from home, her tiny suitcase packed, and had saved the city by blowing out a match. Elizabeth has turned the incident into a literary anecdote, a carefully crafted reconstruction of a childhood memory in the strategy, if not the style, of James Joyce. From fact, she has structured a version of her childhood to account for a terrible sense of pain and loss, catching the melodrama of the child's world, defining its emotional spectrum. In this world of maids and governesses, she is alone. Her need is overwhelming: "Days have gone by and I have had no love." Everyone falls painfully below her desire. She wants the one she wants. It is her mother, who is characterized by her great "abandoning" power. She will recover her mother's love by her great heroism. Heroically, she saves her mother and will endure taunts and torture for her sake. (It is curious how the image of Louie's neck returns here.) Yet when her mother arrives, she cannot show her love. It is too large. It melts her. She is left alone, to endure rejection. This, then, was

Elizabeth's emotional heritage, as she saw it, and as confirmed at least by her sister Jane. A dependency on an idea of love. A legacy of overwhelming longing. A fiercely moulded will. A vision of heroism as secret suffering and a female capacity to internalize guilt. It is a walled-in solipsistic world. We spend decades trying to sort out the emotional inheritance of childhood. But as Doris Lessing has said, "The unfinished business of the past can be finished." Elizabeth would have to return again and again to the old wounds of childhood to heal them, to lay the ghost of the Louie in her head.

In Elizabeth's early childhood, the Smart family usually spent summers at Brackley Beach, Prince Edward Island. They would lodge at a hotel, with various aunts and cousins in tow, often Aunt Ellen from Ottawa and cousins Arthur and Kathy from Winnipeg. Russel would spend a short time with the family and return to his Ottawa practice. But in the summer of 1919, instead of vacationing at Brackley Beach, the Smarts rented Herridge Cottage at Kingsmere in the Gatineau Hills. In 1920 they returned and bought a property on the lake adjacent to Herridge Cottage. They called it the Barge, from the hull-like shape of the northern front of the cottage (though Louie used to say she thought the name appropriate because everybody was always barging through). With its wide prow of timber and glass, it seemed to be thrusting through the trees on the sloping cliff-like shores towards the waters of Lake Kingsmere below. Elizabeth always bracketed the murky years of childhood between the ages of two and seven. "I went in a dull dream from two to seven, punctuated by screams of rebellion, pathetic efforts at drawing attention to my merits. I dimly perceived adult doubts about me, suspicions that I might be mentally defective."[37] It's probably safe to conjecture that the radical change in her childhood life was the family's discovery of the Barge.

While the family moved through a variety of houses in Ottawa, the Barge remained a constant emotional factor in their lives. The original cottage was typical of the region: square in structure with a peaked red roof and totally encircled by a screened verandah. As soon as she saw it, Louie felt it would do. She had a west wing added, which included a large living room panelled in B.C. wood, with a huge picture window (the first in the Ottawa region) and high natural-stone fireplaces; the room was lined with books and had sliding doors into a dining room that could sit thirty. When these doors were opened for dancing, fires blazed from either end of the house. The house could accommodate large parties and had at least six bedrooms for guests. There were a pantry and rooms for the maids. Louie always needed a considerable staff: at the worst times, at least a cook, a maid, and a laundress who came once a week. She required everything immaculate, perfectly turned out. The chauffeur was housed over the garage next to the most imposing feature of the house, the semi-circular driveway that gave it its impressive entrance.

Though there were many tantrums as the house was being prepared—Louie, in her high scratchy voice complained that the work was shoddy: local workmen "had no idea what a gentleman's home should look like; I'll have to stand over them every minute"[38] and Russel soothed—the house that emerged was a tribute to Louie's talents. It took two trucks to bring trunks and furniture through the Gatineau Hills; "our precious possessions" Louie called them. Yet the effect produced was casual and comforting. Friends who had been there remembered the rattan furniture on the verandah and the beautiful view of the lake.

The holidays were always a benevolent time. The family would leave Ottawa at the end of May in the Model T as soon as the snow melted and the roads were passable, and Louie and the children would spend the summers there. Louie loved the Barge. It was only twelve miles from Ottawa in the adjacent province of Quebec; numerous friends visited, and she was constantly busy keeping the domestic machine of servants running or improving the house.

For Elizabeth from the age of seven and ever after, Kingsmere became her "loved recurring country." In the most profound sense, its landscape occupied her imagination, providing the image pool every writer needs at the foundational core of the mind. Her future metamorphic gift—becoming the landscape she described—was nurtured here for she laid claim to Kingsmere as her private cartography. Her initiation into nature was, as for all writers, a lonely, exalted time:

> The woods where I wandered ecstatically on the eastern fringe of the Laurentian mountains, made of hard huge beautiful very very old rocks of the pre-Cambrian shield offered the true the blushful Happiness. The spring-fed lakes were fringed with paper birch, quaking aspen, balsam. In April you skied through maples, up & down trails packed with sugary snow, while in thawed bits at the side Hepatica emerged among their livery, leathery old brown leaves, then pristine bloodroots, furled in . . .[39]

By temperament, her relationship with nature was mystical. Thinking back in later life she described her early ecstatic experiences: "Immanence of awe in a tree—could not stand the approach of revelation." At the age of fourteen, already able to articulate what Kingsmere was to her, she wrote a brief story called "The Birth of a Genius." Genius, she understands, is awakened in the hierophantic moment in nature. In her story a child "sits on the stump of the Mushroom Forest. He cannot leave; he cannot move; he is being told a secret." The story ends: "When a genius is born he is just as any other baby. But his real birth is when he is lifted up through the musical air of the Mushroom Forest."[40]

As a child Elizabeth was protective of her forest domain. "In my woods I hated even a messy stick moved, a stone thrown into the lake. All was perfect, immutable, decaying & growing at its own pace." And this occasioned fierce battles with her mother:

> Once . . . on a black & never to be forgotten day, my mother, with vague dreams of stately English gardens, had the woods near the house "underbrushed"—that is scraped & cleared of all the low delightful bushes, leaving

just the large naked trunks of maple, white pine, butternut, even their live branches had been lopped. When I saw the vandalism, I shrieked & cried & would not be consoled for 2 days. My eyes disappeared in puffiness. I heaved & shuddered with sobs. Wouldn't eat. Wouldn't move. They sent for the doctor in desperation (the noise I made must have been appalling). But never never could that bit of ground be restored to what it was. Eventually things grew, but not the same delicate balance, the secretiveness was gone forever."[41]

Another of Elizabeth's adversaries in her forest world was the future prime minister Mackenzie King. The year the Smarts moved into the Barge, King purchased Herridge Cottage, and much to their consternation began his career as a gentleman farmer. To create his "estate" he increased his tracts of land to include "The Farm" (in which he died); he also purchased the nearby cottage called "Shady Hill" (to prevent the sale of property to Jews "who have a desire to get in at Kingsmere & who would ruin the whole place.")[42] He razed much of the land, chopping down the pines and clearing the brush. He converted the pasture into rolling green lawn with beds of petunias, and paved the wild raspberry patches with flagstone. In childhood, Elizabeth used to run through King's property, knocking over his stone fence and leaving nasty anonymous notes. King came to stand for the "civilization" she hated. Certainly when King, by 1935, began to erect his artificial Gothic ruins amidst which it consoled him to stand in his knickers and tweeds, he became the butt of Smart family jokes.

Elizabeth's early days at Kingsmere were a wonderful adventure. There were the endless games with Jane, making bush houses woven from branches with their thrilling aromatic smells, building moss houses, hiding under the juniper bushes. They collected and catalogued flora and fauna from the numerous varieties in the Gatineau, while Helen took up birdwatching. When Russel would arrive from the city on weekends, there were the games of riding the running-board of the Model

T—part of the fun was that it was a conspiracy pursued out of Louie's sight—or being tossed in the juniper bushes. With Helen taking the lead, the children mounted theatricals on a wooden stage they had constructed, with curtains made from bed sheets. They would invite Louie and Russel, and often the poet Arthur Bourinot and his wife, who owned a nearby property on the lake.

In 1921, Louie had her fifth child, the long-awaited boy, named Russel, Jr. after his father. Nine years younger than Elizabeth, he was to be the treasured brother, the member of the family to whom she was closest. He shared her warmth and generosity of temperament, though not, perhaps, her daring. They played music together, and he would participate in her various publishing enterprises.

In the autumn of 1922, when Elizabeth was nine, she and Jane transferred from Ottawa Normal School to Elmwood, Rockcliffe Park. It was perhaps a measure of their social standing, for to Elmwood went many of the children of the well-to-do. Elmwood sits in the centre of Ottawa's Rockcliffe Park. It was then a pseudo-Tudor building with an imposing wood-panelled entrance hall, the requisite Assembly Hall with stage, and classrooms and dormitories for the mistresses and boarders. Behind the school were the tennis courts, which became a skating rink in winter. The British flag flew overhead.

It was certainly a good school, and quite traditional for the time in its pretentious attachment to Empire. The year Elizabeth entered, the school's name was changed from "Rockcliffe Preparatory School" to Elmwood, under the astute headmistress Mrs C.H. Buck. The school directory noted 111 students, roughly 25 of whom were boarders. The curriculum was good, including French, Latin, German, music, dramatics, art, Bible study, as well as sports, needlework, gymnastics, and dancing. One can tell something of the school in Elizabeth's time by the subjects of the school debates: "Resolved: That Coriolanus, in attacking Rome, proved that the Commons had been right in banishing him," or "Was the execution of Mary Stuart justifiable?" (the debate decided in favour of the execution). At the same time, there was a fierce attachment to Canada, which was perceived as the seat of British traditionalism in North America.

In 1923, Elmwood started the tradition of a school magazine, *Samara* (the winged seed or airplane man of the elm tree), so called because the magazine was to be a collection of literary fruits. It is rather charming, though the opening address by Mrs Buck indicates the degree of conventionality that directed the students. Quoting Dean Farrar, she writes: "If you would do great deeds hereafter prepare for them now . . . shew yourselves fit for them . . . But remember, that if the opportunity for great deeds should never come, the opportunity for good deeds is renewed for you day by day. Be something in Life; do something; aim at something; not something great, but something good; not something famous, but something serviceable—not leaves, but fruit."[43] The double-speak was laid early: the aim was not distinction but service, and appropriate female grace. "Ambition cast down," Elizabeth was to say later.

Though labelled "clever," Elizabeth adopted a camouflage of clowning at Elmwood. To capture popularity, not to stand out as a figure of painful fun, she strove to make the others laugh. Her effort was not to be a rebel but to try to conform as much as she could. She described herself as "hiding all I knew and my mad delight in learning." "Here the two-faced business begins." One of the things that irritated Elizabeth most about Elmwood was its colonial Englishness. She remembered Elmwood's pretensions and misplaced snobbery. It was full of British teachers who had failed to attain Roedean and decided that at least they could be top dogs in Canada. They taught "the honouh of the mothah countrih." When she was asked to write an Ode to a Nightingale when there were none in Canada, to study Rooks and Lesser Celandines (none either), she felt a "furious resentment." "At that stage my ambition was to sever Canada from the 'Mother Country.'"[44]

The material in the school magazine is appropriate to adolescent girls—much of it naïve and sentimental, full of schoolgirl wit. Apart from one unremarkable prose piece (1923) and a poem (1925), there is no work by Elizabeth during her time at

Elmwood from 1922 to 1929. However, in a schoolgirl spoof written in 1929 by her friends Elaine Meekins and Joan Ahearn, Elizabeth surfaces. Setting out in their private plane, the *Miss Elmwood*, the two hunt up school alumni ten years hence. They find their old classmates dispersed all over Europe: in London, Paris, Vienna, and New York, in various roles: an ambassadress, swimming champion, world-famous surgeon, leading London fashion designer, prize-winning novelist, actress, interior decorator. Elizabeth they find walking her children in an elegant pram down Ottawa's Laurier Avenue: "Betty Smart, taking her family out for an airing."[45]

At Elmwood, Elizabeth had become famous for "collecting" babies, as her sister Jane put it. Throughout her life, Elizabeth always pursued obsessions (whether writing, babies or gardening) with passionate intensity. Now she babysat for everyone, "collecting" babies, age one or two, and kept huge scrapbooks with photographs and cutouts of babies. (They were still around for Graham Spry to peruse when Elizabeth was eighteen.) Elizabeth later attributed this strange impulse to her powerful maternal instinct—other people's babies, birds building their nests. But Jane felt the obsession was a compensation impulse, a way of participating in households where there was less tension: "'Too much crying came from the Smart household,' said the neighbour Mrs. Fairweather." Elizabeth identified babies as a softening influence. Ten years later she would write in her diary: "Children make people flow—it loosens them, and expands them. Take the case of Granny's family. She married with nine children—and she is gracious and flowering. Great Aunt Pyra married, discontented with no children. Great Aunt Harma—spinster—hating the world and everyone—tight, always ill—liver and kidneys, sharp—unhappy—screwed up in herself—edgy—I love her—she is alive and an individual—but not a person to live with."[46] (It is interesting that she leaves her mother, with four children, off the list. Louie was not softened by babies.) It was a fierce dogmatism of Elizabeth's, established here in adolescence, that women needed children to be truly women.

Elizabeth began writing poetry at Elmwood. While nothing much appears in *Samara*, encouraged by a teacher who liked her poems, she published her first poem at age ten in *Junior Home*, an American magazine for children, and got one dollar for it. She was later to say, "It was one of the best paid things I ever did." She and Jane also kept journals that they called their "Personal Pronouns."

Elizabeth was a precocious and imaginative child. Beneath the surface calm raged extraordinary needs and she had to find ways to meet them. In the autumn of 1924, when she was eleven, she suddenly became ill and was forced to spend a year in bed. It was a peculiar incident. One morning while Elizabeth and Jane were waiting for the schoolbus, Jane managed to twist her ankle by falling from the wrought-iron fence that surrounded the Daly Avenue house. Dr Scott was called. At the same time, Elizabeth was complaining of tiredness—she felt too exhausted to go to school—and Dr Scott was asked to examine her. To Louie's shock, he diagnosed a heart murmur, caused by a leaky heart valve, and prescribed at least six months' rest in bed. The current wisdom was that "heart fever," unless treated by complete rest, would damage the heart for life. In a flurry of solicitude the house was rearranged and Betty and Jane moved into the large front bedroom. From her bed, Elizabeth directed the assembling of her Personal Pronouns.

Though Elizabeth's exhaustion may have been real, there are grounds for scepticism about the diagnosis; leaky heart valves were fashionable in those days. Her brother, Russel, commented years later: "It was a complete myth."[47] In thinking back to those days in a 1976 diary, Elizabeth herself wrote: "All I asked was a bit of attention from a furious Mom. But there was nothing there to justify that long interesting year." Elizabeth was completely invalided, unable to get out of bed even to go to the washroom. Correspondence courses had to be arranged. Elizabeth could no longer play piano, which she had begun to study at age seven, and a schoolfriend of Helen's, Katie MacLaine, was called in to teach her theory and the lives of the composers. To divert her daughter (Elizabeth was not an easy patient), Louie bought her three goldfish whom she christened Matthew, Simon, and Patrick Chopin Shumann Dolittle Smart.

One day that fall, Elizabeth reported to her mother that she had written a story called "Mosquitoes," which began "My Anthony, my Anthony, I am suffering in agony." Louie was delighted, and read it to all her friends. According to Jane, Elizabeth then wrote "Pudgy Baby" and she and Jane used to quote bits of it to each other till they had it by heart. She also began a serious study of flora and fauna, learning their Latin names and derivatives.

Elizabeth's juvenilia is witty and precocious. She had already read J.M. Barrie so closely that she had absorbed his satirical style, and the illustrations she drew to accompany her stories owe something to Barrie's *Peter Pan in Kensington Garden*. But her themes were entirely her own. Some of the stories are such raw fictions that we see laid bare the extraordinarily intricate mind of the eleven-year-old Elizabeth. Most poignant is "Heartless [or Pudgy] Baby."

> The woman came weeping into the room; her baby had just died yesterday. Died; really through her fault. Through her tears she looked at its crib, all fresh in crispy white, and, she *knew*, empty. But as she came nearer she saw it was not! In it was the dearest Pudgy Baby, kicking, and cooing and smiling. It was not *her* baby; she knew it. It was not even *like* hers. But though she said she would *never* look at another baby, this one, somehow, entranced her. . . .
>
> In a minute it was in her arms, and she was having her most perfect moment. Higher and higher grew her affection for it. She liked it. She *loved* it! She *adored* it!
>
> "What a cool breeze, I must shut the window," she said, laying the baby on the bed and going over to the nearest one. "My darling mustn't catch cold, Oh! no, that wouldn't do at all, would it, Precious?" She looked over at the baby—it had gone. Gone out the window—the Pudgy Baby was not there.

> Pudgy Baby laughed, as she alighted on a telegraph wire;
> she laughed fearlessly.[48]

Though others who have lost babies try to catch it to satisfy
their own needs, the baby escapes to nest in a crow's nest and
"play peek-a-boo with the stars."

For a child of eleven, this is a poignant story—particularly
the teasing push/pull of affection in which the orphaned child is
caught. The mother is revenged and the baby lives its fantasy of
escape, resisting the claims of others. For Elizabeth, with her
habit of collecting babies, the baby is already the perfect
moment. She retitled the story "Heartless Baby"—heartless in
seeking revenge through escape? From a collection of memories recorded in her 1978 journals, she gives the clue to the allegory by describing a childhood fantasy: "I shall fly in my
ghost-state to the window and watch them crying. I shall cry
for pity to watch their terrible remorse."[49] But here it is the
unfiltered vision of the child.

Louie would not have understood the complexity of her
child's feeling. By her own standards she was a solicitous
mother. When she travelled with Russel on his business trips,
there were always affectionate letters home. On board the
Cunard RMS *Berengaria* (April 16, 1925):

> We have a beautiful cabin. I shall draw you a picture of
> it. . . . The passengers appear a perfect rabble but there
> are many distinguished names among them so we may
> see."

From Hotel Ochen, Heidenheim (1 May 1925):

> The children here work very hard. They have to be at
> school at 7:30 and have much homework as well but they
> get a good education and they surely earn it. Do work at
> your French. . . . You have no idea how nice it will be
> when you travel, as I hope you may. . . . I get dreadfully
> lonely for you and I hate to think as I close my eyes
> at night that you are still out playing for you see you are

six hours earlier than me. I hope you are being my own darling girls.[50]

Louie liked to think that laughter and happiness abounded in the house, but control was always the issue. Love was the golden cup, held just beyond the fingers' reach till one learned to behave.

But Elizabeth's extraordinary need was already mitigated by her sense of humour. Her "mosquito" story is an amusing satire in which the mosquitoes, under the direction of their mother, Adelaide Mosque, who has had "a *very* thorough education, a rare and expensive one," learn Natural History: the mosquito heads the list of living creatures (since all creatures put themselves first) and man was only made for them to eat. In their scripture lessons they learn that Jacob Mosquitoesy was the first living thing on earth.

"We Intellectual Fish," by Chopin Shumann Dolittle Patrick Fish, is written from the fish's perspective. Lately the fish have noticed "one person who always stays in one place. (We have learned to recognize her as our mistress.) She lies on her back, but what puzzles us is why she doesn't go up to the ceiling like we do when we're sick. Even intellectual fish are puzzled sometimes."[51]

It is rather poignant that, now Elizabeth was in bed, she had the attention and control she needed, both from her mother and from Jane. One day when Jane returned from school, Elizabeth announced that she was founding the B.C. club (B.C. stood for baby club). Initiation involved writing two poems and making a miniature paper bag, which tasks had to be completed in a week. Jane duly completed her initiation. As president of the club, Elizabeth would dare Jane to enact certain schemes. One was to phone Elmwood's principal, Mrs Buck, saying she was Peter Pan, and if Mrs Buck was good she would go to Never Never Land. But Mrs Buck was so stern that Jane fumbled and blurted out who she was and was made an example of the next day. Jane could neither resist Elizabeth's dares nor refuse to answer her questions without fear of Elizabeth's ridicule. Even as a child, Elizabeth could impose her obsessions on others. At

least one friend, Joan Ahearn, was writing "baby letters" to
Elizabeth. They are clever. Joan had to assume the persona of
an infant and describe the uncomprehending and incomprehensible adult world from the perspective of her crib.

Elizabeth had rounds of solicitous visitors, who brought endless books. Previously books had belonged to the two children
communally, inscribed Betty and Jane Smart. Sometimes, if
Elizabeth had written the inscription, she wrote Bettyandjane
Smart, so that Jane complained she often felt her name was
"andjane." The new books were inscribed "Betty Smart hers
alone" or the "precise property of Betty Smart."[52] Elizabeth had
begun to withdraw into her own world, abandoning Jane.
Clearly given her own vulnerability, it was a necessary survival
strategy.

Jane describes how, in her autobiography of childhood, they
divided the world between them:

> One day when I rushed up stairs Betty was waiting for me,
> sitting up in bed with a list.
>
> She said, "I'm collecting flowers and birds and insects
> and stones and trees and stars and lakes and babies and
> little things and books and games and postcards and
> cigarette cards and samples and pictures of musicians.
>
> She went on naming every thing in the world until my
> head went dizzy trying to think of them all, then she said,
> "What are you collecting?"
>
> There was a long pause while I tried to think of some-
> thing she hadn't named. Suddenly it popped into my head
> like a poem.
>
> "I'm collecting people," I shouted with excitement,
> "People."
>
> There was a long pause while Betty took in what I'd
> said.
>
> It was strange because at that point I knew I'd won the
> game, so I didn't know why I felt cold and shivered.
>
> All Betty said was, "Oh."
>
> Ever after that, she left me my own age group and
> everyone younger, unless they were babies. She collected

most other people in the world and they were hers forever. The only ones she left for me were the ones with
bulging noses and twinkling hopes.[53]

For Jane, she and Elizabeth had been like Siamese twins with
only one ego between them, which they were to fight over all
their lives.[54] She always wanted Elizabeth's approval and it
never occurred to her that she threatened her. She could still say
late in life Elizabeth was a dramatic presence, stronger than
anyone she ever met. She obviously worshipped her and
resented her as well.

Helen's relationship with Elizabeth was simpler. She was the
older sibling, and easily benevolent. Much of the bond between
them was established in letters written from boarding school in
which Helen set herself up as something of a scamp for
Elizabeth to follow. She wrote from her private school, Miss
Edgar's in Montreal, to say she was playing Perseus in the
Latin production of *Perseus and Andromeda*: "I tear around
yelling illegible things in Latin and kill the dragon. It's really
very exciting." And advised her to learn Morse code because
she could signal with little dots and dashes, especially at school
during the lesson. She reported schoolgirl escapades—climbing to the roof after lights-out and down the fire escape to buy
sweets and cigarettes. "We all made merry till the small hours
and *didn't* get caught—pretty good work wasn't it."[55] Elizabeth
would later write: "Helen made everything cosy and fun for
me. She was wayward, rebellious, always had friends. One
thought of her out in canoes with courting beaus. But after first
marriage, [she] went home to mother and became very demure
doing all the things she hadn't wanted to do when she was
young."

Elizabeth returned to Elmwood. The heart murmur that had
sent her to bed for a year had improved. Helen wrote from Miss
Edgar's: "Isn't it fun to be able to walk again. Really you must
almost have forgotten how." "I've always felt very close to the
little mermaid of Hans Christian Andersen's story," Elizabeth
would later say. "Every step was painful because my feet
hand't touched the floor for so long."[56] But perhaps the illness

had done its work. While in bed she had read and memorized voraciously, and the episode laid the foundation for her impulse to write.

It was in the summer of 1929 at her beloved Kingsmere that Elizabeth started her various publishing enterprises. At the age of fifteen and a half, she produced a handwritten copy of *The Complete Works of Betty Smart* (author of "Wild Foods," "The Perambulating Notebook," etc.). The cover reads: "revised and reviewed by her and Not a Book for Children." It was published at Kingsmere by The Betty Smart Publishing Co. Ltd. All rights reserved. The introduction is wonderfully categorical:

> To begin with these works are not complete, and to continue with they are not works. But other people have made the same mistake, and therefore I am not an original sinner in doing likewise.
>
> In the beginning, hard-hearted reader, you should know that you will not like this book. But for you, that is all the more reason why you should read it.
>
> The satire in "The Land of Mosquitoes" has never been found out,and perchance never will be. But it is quite plain. "The Little House," H.R.H. [Hard-Hearted Reader] may not seem clear in its meaning, but you have been warned, and take your chance when you read this book.
>
> If you are one of the horrible type, that always reads introductions last, go on your way, for it is too late, and I cannot help you.[57]

The book contains thirteen prose pieces, written between the ages of eleven and fifteen. In them we already see that quality characteristic to Elizabeth: an original combination of romantic vulnerability and satiric wit. What is most clear is Elizabeth's delight in style. By fourteen she was already reading Lafcadio Hearn and Walter Pater; style was thrilling and the idea of publishing a book "delicious; the world opened up," so of course she published her own. Louie saved this material in a little trunk marked B. Smart. When she died, Russel kept it until Elizabeth reclaimed it.

Reading this material in later life, Elizabeth was astonished by her own sharp observation (it would always be hard for her to recognize her own talent). She particularly liked a story called "Patty Duh Fwaw Grass Sandwidges," which is a satire on the local "Women's Mission and Helpful Society" holding their church-basement monthly tea. "These were people I could hardly have had anything to do with, because ours was a rather flighty household."[58] Jane remembered the story "Mrs. MacPhail's Earrings" as based on a true anecdote. "Ella" is at church feeling religious when suddenly "her religious spirit flew away, her piousness went too." She has seen Mrs. MacPhail's earrings. "Forgive Ella's little pot (it is getting bigger) of hate; after all, dear lady, *you* do not see them all the time. . . . A raging tempest was raging in Ella in the peaceful church. But she got up and went out, because everyone else was doing that. . . ." The next day Ella has a victorious look of triumph, "because she spent the night pulling off Mrs. MacPhail's earrings! . . . Ella wanted Mrs. MacPhail's head treated in the same manner, but you have to draw the line somewhere. So I let the poor, dear, simple lady live."[59]

Elizabeth could already sense the hypocrisy that lay beneath much of the highmindedness of Rockcliffe Park, but she was not a rebel. "I always conformed," she said, "up to a point and quietly went my way. I don't believe you can fight against things. I follow all the rules unless it's absolutely necessary to break them." She had little gift for anger. In retrospect she would say: "I tend to go into paralysis rather than hysterics if something happens. I shiver and shake. I don't start screaming and making dramatics" (as, one might add, Louie did).[60] Clearly Mrs MacPhail's earrings became a convenient displacement for her "little pot of hate." And she finds relief in a dream fantasy of revenge. It is a sophisticated solution for a fifteen-year-old.

"The Little House" (written on February 22, 1928) whose meaning, she warns in her preface, may not seem clear, is a brief sketch in which the child tends the adult, obviously based on Elizabeth's need to save Louie by loving her enough:

The sun was large, and was melting into the sky, and the pine trees were silhouetted against it. The child was well on her way now, but she looked back, and saw the dear little house standing bravely out, as if *it* were not afraid of the dark. She thought of the mistress of the little house, the kiss, and a chokey feeling came up inside her.

"She's only a child, after all," thought the child.

It grew dark, and still, and the child went home. . . .

The end of this.

(Do you see the point? Ah! I thought as much.)[61]

Fear was a large component of Elizabeth's childhood. It had as much to do with her own temperament as with circumstance. All her life, Elizabeth seemed to lack a protective carapace. Unlike the little house, she was afraid of the dark; there was the fear that nothing was behind it, the fear that something was.

2 The Great Sexual Necessities

A woman's heart must be of such a size and no larger,
else it must be pressed small, like Chinese feet.
George Eliot
Daniel Deronda

We are so single without a mate. So pointless.
Elizabeth Smart
Necessary Secrets

Though Helen had been sent to a private school for girls in Montreal, and Jane was to follow, Elizabeth was enrolled at Hatfield Hall School in Cobourg, in the fall of 1929. With her went Sally Biggar, the daughter of Mowat Biggar, Russel's law partner. Hatfield Hall was run by Miss W.M. Wilson (B.A., London) and Miss W.M. Ellis (B.Sc., London). It had just opened that year with an enrolment of sixty-two students. High Anglican in orientation, it was under the tutelage of the Lord Bishop of Toronto. During the first graduation ceremonies, the Bishop of Ontario congratulated the school principal on "the founding of another school which had for its aim the threefold development of mind, body, and spirit, and where religious training would occupy an important place." And the school principal wrote a dedicatory poem:

Within Memorial House are busy workers,
No idlers, no mischief-makers, and no shirkers;

And all are happy as the day is long,
For life in harmony is one sweet song. . . .[1]

The students studied English Literature, Latin, French,
Physics, Chemistry, Algebra, Geometry, and History (Ancient
and Canadian). Academic standards were quite high. Elizabeth
would later speak a little German, French, some Spanish, and
write Latin. Sports included basketball, badminton, tennis,
golf, skiing, and riding. There was a school orchestra, and the
school often mounted dramas, ballets, and choral perfor-
mances. A photo in the school magazine shows Elizabeth playing in the orchestra at the All Saints' Day masquerade. The
girls are dressed as pirates and stand behind a cardboard ship.
The school could count on frequent lectures by professors from
the University of Toronto, as well as visiting musicians.
Cobourg was then a small town of ten thousand, sitting on the
edge of Lake Ontario in the heart of farm country, so that there
were frequent picnics and expeditions into the countryside.

The High Anglican orientation of the school had little impact
on Elizabeth:

> The Bible was always on top of the school books. But it
> was hypocrisy. I could see that. . . . You had to tie a pillow
> slip on your head before you went to chapel, you always
> got a black mark if your algebra was on top of the Bible;
> but this was not religion; one simply laughed at it.
> Meanwhile there were those five minute waits when you
> assembled in the assembly rooms . . . so I read the Bible;
> there was nothing else to read, and I was always so bored,
> waiting. The King James version, of course."[2]

For Elizabeth the notion of God was never moralistic. Her
appetite was mystical. In her mid-teens she was reading the
metaphysical poets, and it is to Herbert, Vaughan and Traherne
that we can trace the mystical vision that was an essential part
of the make-up of Elizabeth Smart.

At Hatfield Hall, Elizabeth developed the reputation of a

character. A school friend, Tibs Partridge, remembered one occasion when she showed up late for the usual school inspection. When she was asked to remove her shoes to see if her socks were clean, it was discovered that her socks were so full of holes she had bound her toes with tape. She was liked by her fellow students for her kindness (there were several stories of her turning up at the infirmary with gifts to comfort sick girls whom she knew only casually), and admired for the witty prose anecdotes she produced for the school magazine.[3] Academically she was an A student.

But the private drama was more compelling. Like any adolescent girl, Elizabeth had begun to be overwhelmed by what she called the "great sexual necessities." Once she had to leave behind the tomboyishness of childhood, she was at sea. She wrote in 1978:

> When I think of the Gatineau Country my heart lurches. But there are no people in my landscape, except enemies, desecraters, hunters, tree-killers, all profanities. . . .
>
> For what happened when I was out in the woods, on the mountain, remains the serious thing. People an extra. People more trivial. Lesser. And all to do with the great sexual necessities (that they all stumble over).
>
> I saw this coming with dread when I was twelve. What a tiresome diversion.
>
> If one could be 12 forever (pre-puberty I mean) & grow & grow, by-passing that 40-year boulder, one might get to know something.[4]

And she elaborated on this idea in a 1983 interview:

> On my 13th birthday I cried. . . . I felt then "I'm not going to be this wonderful, complete, in-control person that I am now, that I was at eleven or twelve." It is a terrible thing. Up until then I was just an observer of other people's emotions; then, around thirteen, you find that you yourself are vulnerable."[5]

As would any young girl, Elizabeth felt the dichotomy in the two-way pull—the need for love and for a ruthless privacy. Sex held terrors and privileges: the privilege of intimacy and affirmation for which she longed; and the power of rebellion. The terror and lure of sex lay in realizing that one was a taboo object. Elizabeth soon learned to be secretive, "having to camouflage books, read poetry secretly, pass ashtrays gracefully, be a Blonde." You could ski but you couldn't "moon about by yourself in the woods or people would think you queer." This was Louie's censure; to Elizabeth's familiar experience was added the element of Louie's prudery and fear of sexuality: "Men have this terrible desire." Louie wanted to keep her daughters innocent.

As the eldest, Helen bore the first brunt of Louie's hysteria. There were many physically violent scenes when Louie would wait for her teenage daughter to return from parties. She was afraid Helen would go to roadhouses on the way home, as many of her friends did, to snack after the dances. Louie would wait with a switch inside the front door and beat Helen about the legs as she ran upstairs. The eight-year-old Elizabeth witnessed one scene when Helen was twelve. Louie had worked herself into such a froth that she slapped Helen's face and tore off her dress, exposing her half-formed breasts. "Granny, mademoiselle, Jane, Russel and Daddy, and a lot of frightened maids watching. The darkened house for days after like a death."[6]

In 1931 (Elizabeth was then seventeen), Helen was the first to rebel. She was a student at McGill University where she had met a young man named Alan Swabey, a football quarterback. Knowing Louie would disapprove, Helen, already twenty-two, eloped with Swabey. With her usual uncanniness, Louie managed to phone the residence that night, too late however to prevent the "disaster." The family were furious, though eventually Swabey was taken on as a law clerk by the firm of Smart and Biggar.

When one thinks of Louie's pre-1939 Ottawa world, with its bizarre rules of decorum, her response was not surprising. She had accepted the safe constraints of that world and turned all her extraordinary energy into being the hostess. It had become her life; her role depended upon staying within the bounds of convention and her daughter was jeopardizing that convention. Louie refers elliptically to Helen's elopement in a letter to Elizabeth at Hatfield Hall. It is written with the by-now familiar manipulative sentimentality.

Sunday, midnight (Jan 19, 1931)

Dearest Betty,
I intended writing long letters to all my absent ones today, but this is the first lull since morning. As Jane and Helen have not sent a line since returning, I shall write to you first.

Your letter was so satisfactory dear and I read it over the telephone to Daddy in New York. It had the effect on him of wanting to create happiness in the hearts of his other two daughters and he volunteered that he would write a long letter to Helen. Daddy has always made the mistake of creating the impression with Helen that he approves her ways. As a matter of fact he has never quite approved. . . . There are queer influences at work with Jane too and I am very worried. I want to be wise and not antagonize her. How I hate the vulgarity and lack of restraint among the young people. I long to gather you all up and rush off with you to some far away beautiful country where evil is scorned and beauty and character—"sweetness and light" are the things worth striving for.

Helen's past four years are a nightmare to me. I waken in the night. Sometimes just panicky when I think about it. We must protect Jane at all cost. . . .

There isn't a mother in the world hardly who is not in anguish. Mrs. Hall and I had a talk—also Mrs. North and it's the same story everywhere. Mrs. Bate tells me she is putting the lid very firmly on her girls. And besides all their really messy indiscretions, being seen to have lost self control in every direction, I hear on all sides of their rudeness to parents.

You will say Mummy is riding her hobby again, but if you are honest with yourself Betty you will admit that I am right. The problem now is what to do about it. Can you help me?. . .

Tomorrow I am getting a new maid—a genuine parlour maid this time and highly recommended as entirely proficient in the arts of a parlour maid and also a capable valet and ready to take on the entire valeting of Daddy, even the shoes. I do hope she works out. Her name is "Inman." This of course is her last name.

I must go to bed now. I shall feel happy if you are helping on my side. I do want Jane to develop naturally and beautifully as she should. She has an exceptionally good brain and considerable talent, but she must build up character and practice more self control.

Good night darling. I love you.[7]

Louie seemed to live in a fantasy world entirely of her own invention. Her incapacity for self-reflection is remarkable. She was never implicated in the family traumas, so easily eradicated were the memories of those switches to Helen's legs, or Elizabeth's bloodied fingers in the closet. She was the one who created domestic tranquillity—the arts of the parlour maid, Daddy's perfectly valeted shoes. Later, as her anger towards her mother blossomed, Elizabeth would say: "The smug mother love walking around so self-congratulatory, so sure it won't be shot-at. Sacred, known to be sacred . . . committing acts of super-egotism under the guise of unselfishness, and with the approval of the world."[8] Louie could say to her daughters what she would never say to her son: "You don't know how to love," making them responsible for the emotional parsimony in the house. They would remember her penetrating resentful eyes. Elizabeth felt such an ambivalent mixture of love and resentment for her mother that separation would have to come by assault. To rip off the nagging fearsome mask, she would have to recreate Louie as a strange, almost Gothic fiction. So deep was the hold that she would have to dig a fictive grave and bury her.

Whatever Elizabeth felt about Helen's elopement—at eighteen she probably thought it romantic—much of her adolescent energy must have gone to sorting out the social world that had begun to engulf her, now that Louie had become one of Ottawa's most respected hostesses. Official Ottawa in the late twenties and early thirties was still a small provincial capital with a standard colonial élite. By 1930, its population had reached 127,332. The centre of gravity was the vice-regal court at Rideau Hall, residence of the Governor General; parties were a mainstay of existence and governing was done in between. In the monthly "Ottawa Letter" by Rideau in the pages of Toronto's society magazine *Mayfair*, the season was carefully recorded. There were three layers of notables to the socio-political power structure: the vice-regal court, the military, and Old Ottawa families, whose balls, weddings, European travel, and shifting fashions were dutifully noted. The royal calendar at Rideau Hall—the King's birthday, the coming-out parties, the ceremonial opening of Parliament, the Government House annual garden party—determined the focus, while the gaps were filled with dances at Christmas, musicals during Lent, skating and tobogganing on the Rideau grounds every Saturday afternoon in winter, with the occasional moonlit party thrown in. To the society people there were only a few places that mattered: the Minto Skating Club at Rideau Hall, the Country Club, the Seigniory Club, the Little Theatre of the Ottawa Drama League, the ski tows at Fortune, and the lake at Kingsmere. Here the overlapping circles of ministers, mandarins, Old Ottawa families, political advisers, and the new diplomatic set (until 1928 there was no Embassy Row in Ottawa) could be found arguing and gossiping across dinner tables, trading information in a city where information was as valuable as money. But even Ottawa was shifting slowly from the old to the new era and there was also a place for the band of established radicals who were the transitional generation (people like Eugene Forsey, Graham Spry and Lester Pearson, all Rhodes scholars and in the politics-as-public-service tradition).[9] "When I look back," Spry said, "it seems that we were always dancing. Always running off to a tea dance in Peacock

Alley at the Chateau or over at the Country Club."[10] One place the young men were welcome was the Smarts' home.

The Smarts were not Old Ottawa, like the Keefers, the Kingsmills or the Gilmores, but Russel, with his business and social contacts, was a member of all the requisite clubs: the Rideau Club, the Rideau Lawn Tennis and Golf Clubs, the Badminton Club, the Minto Skating Club and the Canadian Club. Russel and Louie gave their large parties at the Chateau Laurier or the Country Club, and the more intimate ones at Kingsmere or on Daly Avenue. Louie organized a quite astonishingly elaborate network of non-stop entertaining: afternoon at-homes, dinner parties, bridge parties, and dances. The Smarts figured in the pages of *Mayfair*: "Once more a dinner and dancing party—in honour of the Misses Clark [daughters of the British High Commissioner]—was given by Mr. and Mrs. Russel Smart. Their thirteen-year-old son, Russel, Jr., proved a great social success, that evening, charming his partners with his bright conversation and delightful manners!" or "Miss Beardmore dined with the Boals when they entertained before Mr. and Mrs. Russel Smart's dance for their daughters, Miss Betty and Miss Jane. This cheery party took place at the Smarts' summer house at Kingsmere. Nature was kind that night in supplying a large round moon and warm breezes. The fair-haired Betty wore white organdie. It is generally known that she plays the piano beautifully and writes a little."[11]

Though for the rest of the country these may have been the dirty thirties, Ottawa, as the seat of government, was essentially insulated. When the Depression did penetrate the city at the end of 1933 and 16 per cent of the population was on relief, most of the destitute were not Ottawa people but transients who had come to the city in search of work. They lived out of sight in crowded wooden barracks at Rockliffe Airport or in shack settlements at Brewer Park and the Lees Avenue dump.[12] For the Smarts the Depression remained theoretical. Politically, Russel could be described as a liberal, even if the elderly bachelor Mackenzie King, with his dog, his seances, and Scottish ruins, was a figure of fun. Many of Russel's friends were on the left, including Ramsay MacDonald, British

Labour Prime Minister, and Sir Stafford Cripps, his British opposite in Privy Council cases. And there were Ottawa associates, like the young Graham Spry, who thought, briefly, that he had converted Russel to socialism. But Russel remained a centrist and his business acumen assured that his own fortune was secure in the lean years. He told his daughters he never gambled money; he never bought on margin. Elizabeth could laugh in retrospect and say: "We were the three Smart girls. Everybody said we were smart because we didn't know anything about the cost of living."[13]

As hosts, the Smarts were among the best in Ottawa. Spry, who first met them in the late twenties, described them as "harbingers of the *coming* dangerous age of both Europe and North America, of the hastening age that changed art and literature, loving and living with a surge before and after the war. Kindness, pleasure, good rich conversation and friendship [characterized] The Barge or the Smarts' Ottawa home." At their parties "the younger men in the delegations [gathered], particularly the United Kingdom's Rt. Honourables and Lords and Sirs . . . a changing bevy of young Conservatives, Etonians, Harrovians, personal assistants and Knights, nobles and ministers." Affairs at the Smarts', according to Spry, noted for his wryness, were "small—10 or so for lunch, 20 or more for dinner, 100 for cocktails, 200 and upwards for dancing."[14] Later Charles Ritchie tried to remember what they had talked about on those long summer evenings on the screened-in verandah over the lake:

> There was a sense of release in the air, release from the tight small-town values that governed the Ottawa of those days . . . unorthodox opinions flourished. . . .We spoke too of our hopes for a different Canada, of the need for new ideas to break the crust of conventional thinking and of sterile political parties. . . . Our gatherings were not solemn seminars. People came from sheer sociability and for the schemes for amusement that always seemed to be afoot and of which Betty was often the instigator."[15]

A young British socialite, Didy Battye, visiting at Government House (she would later become one of Elizabeth's closest friends in England), often found herself at the Barge. She remembered it for its harmony and exquisite taste. "It was so friendly after being an English debutante. There wasn't the usual agony that no one would talk to you. Nothing about men and women. It was never a disgrace to be seen talking with another woman."[16]

Elizabeth began her induction into this heady world at the age of fourteen when she was escorted to her first dance in "combinations and smocks" ordered from England. She remembered the dances, the brunches on Sundays, the ski parties, bridge parties, the evenings her mother gathered people for readings from O.Henry. Charles Ritchie offers a portrait of Elizabeth at the age of eighteen:

> It was at an Ottawa cocktail party some time in the early 1930s that I first saw Betty Smart. I was standing about, glass in hand, talking the usual cocktail-party nonsense, when I saw a girl pausing in the doorway, looking around her with an expression of sly amusement, as though surveying a group of aborigines at their antics. She was extremely pretty, pink and white and golden, with the sheen of youth about her. "Who is she?" I asked. "Oh," said an Ottawa lady in sarcastic tones, "that is Betty Smart. Very intellectual, you know." There were two men with her, one tall, with a long, sardonic, humorous face, the other small and sallow, with a monkeyish look. "And those," pursued the lady, "are her bodyguard, Graham Spry, the socialist, and Donald Buchanan, who has something to do with art." I thought, "I must get to know that girl."
>
> When I went up to Betty to introduce myself, she greeted me with a marked lack of enthusiasm, and there followed a long pause. Then suddenly we began talking as naturally as though we had known each other for years. When she left the party accompanied by Graham Spry, she called back to me, "Come to see us soon at Kingsmere."[17]

Buchanan (who indeed had something to do with art; he was to become curator of the National Gallery) informed Ritchie that the Smarts were the centre of all that was interesting and stimulating in Ottawa. An invitation to Kingsmere would admit him "on probation to this charmed circle." Of the three sisters, each attractive and clever, Betty seemed to Ritchie the most original:

> . . . a creature of changing moods and contrasts. She could be gentle and charming, and then could turn disconcertingly to caustic frankness. There was a sensuous softness about her, yet she could change expression as though deliberately willing herself to ugliness, like a face seen in a distorting mirror. She was at home with children, and they responded to her fun and warmth. She loved poetry and knew every wildflower in the woods above Kingsmere. But she was no nature-loving dreamer. She had the stubborn will and intensity of temperament of the writer she was to become.

Ritchie did join the charmed circle and, like almost any man who met Elizabeth, was to fall in love with her. But it is Graham Spry who offers the best portrait of the complexities involved in becoming intimate with the young Betty Smart. Spry met the Smarts in September 1926 or June 1927, when a friend brought him up to the Barge. As each of the three Smart daughters reached the dancing age, Spry was selected by Louie to escort them to their first dances. She was sure he could be trusted. (After Swabey's arrival, Louie carefully warned him that they couldn't afford another impecunious son-in-law.)[18] He fell in love with each in succession. Helen was gaily sociable, and she and Spry were frequent dancing partners at the house parties of the young and marriageable, at the Royal Golf and Country Club, or at the supper dances at the Chateau Laurier. Jane he found more intense than Helen, full of varied talents. He remembered her as writing poetry, sketching and sculpting, and playing the violin, filling the Daly Street house with her exercises.

But it was Elizabeth who drew his attention. She was "well-proportioned, sturdy, and of medium stature . . . very blonde but not quite golden. Her eyes . . . a luminescent blue. She was a good swimmer, a trained but not skilful diver, and a superb dancer." Spry describes her as "the most original and talented of the three [sisters] . . . the best read and most intellectual and conversational, challenging, and in her own style, the most witty. Her reading, when I met her at 16, was already immense . . . . As a girl, she usually had a book in her hand. Her ability to recall and quote from memory accurately word for word was astonishing: she seemed to know every line of every sonnet of Shakespeare and no less the writing of the war generation and thereafter. . . . Her knowledge of ornithology and flora and fauna was intimidating."[19]

Elizabeth used to carry around the *Oxford Book of English Verse* wherever she went. When Louie took her to buy clothes, instead of watching the models she would be reading poetry. In later life she could still recite huge swaths of the book from memory. She rediscovered Shakespeare when she was seventeen (she had, of course, already studied him in school). It was Lear that excited her, and then she began to learn a sonnet each day. "I'd have a bath in the morning and repeat the ones I'd learned the day before, and learn a new one. Tristram Shandy was another passion, almost too exciting to read."

Spry fell deeply in love and found himself in a whirlpool. Elizabeth would put him in his place by calling him "Uncle Graham" (he was thirteen years older). When she was in Ottawa, they danced, swam at Kingsmere, walked through the Gatineau Hills or up King Mountain, and argued about books. In 1930, Spry, now deeply involved in setting up the Canadian Radio League that was to lead to the Canadian Broadcasting Corporation, moved to Toronto but continued to drive to Ottawa on weekends or to Cobourg when Betty was at school.

To be in love with Elizabeth was exhilarating, unlike anything Spry had known before. He felt she had a way of drawing forth what one usually obscured or ignored or had not known within oneself and that, as Spry accused her, one might regret revealing. On her side it was friendship. And it is she who offered him wise counsel. In a friendly letter she could advise:

What is it you want out of life? Not just solitary meditation. . . . There is only a certain amount that you can think
without stimulus. There are books of course, but even
books should be read spontaneously and when sudden
impulses come to you to read them. To read. On and on. If
you have real work and play which means friends and
exercise, which can mean any mountain, could you be
happier? Retire to think for three months, for instance,
near the sky and come back and fit your philosophy into
everyday things. Oh, think a lot, which means anywhere—in church, in the bathtub, at the office. . . . It is sad
to find out that you do not want to do the things you've
always thought you wanted to do. I think you need
friends. Doubtless I am wrong, but it is better to be wrong
than restrained. I'm not using a premptorily Oh, You
Know tone, I was just thinking and it may be something
different in a moment.[20]

She concludes her letter with the salvo: "Be good. No. Be bad and repent."

If Elizabeth could be a generous friend to Spry, there was another side he had to deal with. She had to push people to the edge. Spry's love, unreciprocated, must often have been tire-some. She was too young to know how to handle it. She would manipulate him: get her mother to invite him for afternoon tea, "I need you" and not show up till dinner; and after dinner play Poulenc or Mozart on the piano, and then petulantly refuse to continue. Spry remembered one anecdote that is revealing. She had asked him to go for a walk. "She dressed in her sloppy shoes that would not stay on, she gave me a cane, and then she would not go. . . . 'You are coming for a walk,' I insisted. We took the path along the stream that tumbles through Mackenzie King's property. The trees were arches, they formed an arcade, and the light seeped through . . . Betty grew mad in the light. She ran, she leapt, she sang, she danced; she frightened me.

'Horrible,' she said when she came to the chasm where the stream drops forty feet over the rocks." For Spry the night was perfect, all was peace and sanctity, an odd yearning. The next day, in front of Helen, Elizabeth asked: "What would you think of a man who walked through a valley in the moonlight and acted as if he were strolling down Sparks Street?"

After almost two years of loving her, Spry's reading of Elizabeth was shrewd. Trying to characterize her, he wrote in his diary: "Poetry. Complete surrender. And, a deeper, more massive, serious emotion. What a combination of qualities she has. Yes, unique, I love her, love them all, utterly now. She knows I do and it means much to her that I do. She said that in her way, she loves me and always will. But beyond that we never discussed more. . . . I too absurdly suffer the contrast between all she so often is and her temperamental vagaries; her taste for seeing how far she can go." Elizabeth could manipulate Spry out of his socks. "There were games. Little, damn wiles, little playings off . . . She's a scamp . . . anguish. Ecstasy. Then, all ending in a silly strategem."[21] The endless dances they travelled to could often end in scenes. Once, when she had wandered off with a young British lord, Spry lectured her in the car. She opened the door, threatened to leap out, and then flung her head on her arms and wept, or as Spry added, "pretended to weep." Both ended exhausted and humiliated. Though she might encourage her admirers, whenever Elizabeth found herself being fitted into some male version of what they wanted, her only solution was retreat. Spry was thirty-one and came to recognize his dependence on the "idea of Betty" he had created.

But while she tried to cope with the "great sexual necessities," Elizabeth's deepest emotions were attached to writing. She developed the habit of creating little books. Delicately made and printed by hand, one and one-half inches square and bound in cloth or parchment paper, they would be a forty- or fifty-page collection of her favourite poems. Some of the poems were illustrated by line drawings, or by a picture of a face or hand cut from a magazine. Spry described how she would hand the book to the receiver with a smile, a drop of her blonde head, and a graceful gesture of the hand. They were not love tokens but symbols of acceptance, recognitions of mutual affection. He also felt that the poems and their sentiments were tests of the depth of understanding that might be reached. He received three of them.

Apart from anthologies, the Betty Smart Publishing Company also did original works. One was a guide to edible wild fruits and plants of Kingsmere. Bobby McDougal remembered that on camping trips with Elizabeth one didn't bring food. Elizabeth would disappear into the woods for hours and come back with dinner—mushrooms, weeds, and nettles that would be boiled up into delicious soups. By this time Russel, Jr. was pulled into the publishing venture. In 1932, under the imprimatur Betty and Russel Publishing Company, they handprinted Russel's illustrated collection of "Moths of Kingsmere and Vicinity."

Spry's real role in Elizabeth's world was not as lover but as confidant in what had now become the private matter of writing. He genuinely admired and encouraged her, which became the source of a life-long debt of affection. Spry would set her essay assignments and she would write. One that survives is quite remarkable and shows her independence of mind. In a comparison of D.H. Lawrence and Katherine Mansfield, Elizabeth concludes that Mansfield is the better writer because she had absorbed all her pettiness, while he never conquered himself. "He hated much too much to be the universal artist . . . He is much too passionate. You turn away from him . . . you are sick to see him so exposed & painfully revealed."[22] Elizabeth was grateful to Spry because he helped to carry her through the blocks that came from lack of confidence: "He told me to write write write. 'There's no other way to write.' Fearing for me what I fear myself. How good. How good to feel he is to the rescue . . . he set the light of love of work alight and I was stimulated. Good. Even to write a tiny page about a bog is to feel fire such as I have not for ages. I *must will. I must.* I will."[23] "This panic, this blank, . . . sitting at my desk at Kingsmere in a catatonic agony."[24]

Living the social whirl of Ottawa was already taking its toll. Elizabeth knew that in her world writing was not a serious pursuit; she was expected to pass ashtrays and marry well. The split was agonizing. "Silence is safe. Silence is sympathetic. Silence breaks no bones." "Retreat, retreat into your true place & abandon the soppy, social bonhomie. Dare to be aloof & stern & uninterruptible."[25] When she was nineteen, her father bought her a two-hundred-acre mountain in the Gatineau Hills where she built her cabin "The Pulley" (named after the poem by George Herbert). There she could retreat to write. She painted the door and window frames yellow, and pinned up a copy of "The Seed Growing Secretly," a favourite poem by Henry Vaughan: "Be Clean. Bear Fruit. And Wait." She had begun to construct her writer's ego secretly and there were few conspirators to help her find her way.

3 Kissing the Dead Lips of Emily Brontë

No coward soul is mine
No trembler in the world's storm-troubled sphere.
Emily Brontë
[No coward soul is mine]

I shall say what I feel and I shall talk about myself unto
the last page, and I shall make no apologies.
Elizabeth Smart
Necessary Secrets

After the arduous matriculation exams at Hatfield Hall, Elizabeth graduated in the spring of 1931 with first-class honours in most subjects. Her tutors had remarked in her "Terminal Report" that her "deportment still requires a great deal of thought." She is "always original and interesting, but lacks a sound knowledge of the English language."[1] Elizabeth wanted to continue her education, and asked to be sent to England. Her father thought it a good idea and Louie felt that she should be "finished." "[Mother] believed that England was entirely filled with aristocratic families all with noblesse oblige and New England Puritan consciences."[2] It was decided that Elizabeth could study music if a good teacher could be found. After a summer at Kingsmere, Elizabeth and her mother set out to spend the winter in London. Russel went over a couple of times on Privy Council cases.

Elizabeth studied piano under Katharine Goodson and theory, harmony, and composition under her husband, Arthur Hinton. She was also taking extension courses in literature and history under the extramural study programme of Gresham College, University of London. Louie filled the time with sightseeing tours and social engagements: theatre, shopping, and visits to her British friends who included the Barrington Wards (editor of *The Times*), Lady and Sir Stafford Cripps, and Mrs Alfred Watt. When she could, Elizabeth slipped away. She wanted excitement: "I am sick of this Mayfair fashionable smart—socialness—*Tatler-Spectator*—jealousy—boredom—toeing the mark." There had to be another, vibrant life. She took to walking the secret underside of the city and wrote to Graham Spry:

> The radio is just playing the heartbreaking prayer, Yehudi Menuhin's. It . . . is most melancholy and forlorn. I played it all the night. Walked around London streets for a while, watching the people, old old men with beards and rags and sailors with roving eyes and jovial looking and of course powder plastic girls having to resort to tears when the sailors passed them by. Oh there were lots of them and they were the most interesting and there were still a few hopeful match sellers and even the whistling newspaper men and there were a lot of tight beaus in silk hats.[3]

Elizabeth found herself in the typical role of the daughter of the privileged, at loose ends being "finished." But she was a writer. She wanted more.

After returning to Kingsmere for the summer, Elizabeth was back in London in the autumn of 1932, this time with Jane and a chaperone, Susan Somerset, "a poor relation who had been foisted on Mummy because of her romantic conceit that all English except 'the wrong kind' were aristocrats." They were staying at the Basil Street Hotel, Knightsbridge. Elizabeth gives Somerset short shrift: "She tried to get 'eligible young men' to meet us, and could not understand that the reason we were in London was because we wanted to study. She died later and we always felt we killed her."[4] Elizabeth was to study music and Jane, painting. Privately, Elizabeth started to keep journals under the instigation of a friend, Bill Aitken (nephew of Lord Beaverbrook and to become Sir William Traven Aitken), who was encouraging her writing. Her first journal is entitled: "Journal of 1933—This Belongs to Betty Smart. A purely Practical Practice Book Recording Days Whether They are Worth it or Not. Of no Spying Interest!"—this for Jane or possibly for Louie.

Elizabeth was trying to decide what to do: she felt she had to choose between music and writing and by this second year, her interest in music had already begun to wane. "I couldn't think in music; I couldn't compose. I couldn't get beyond the base." She wanted to do something significant, something original—there lay "the entrancing life—the infinite delight in taking pains"— and she was certain that her gifts lay with writing. The problem was she had come to love Katharine Goodson, and didn't want to disappoint her. To quit music would be cheating, as if "I'd been pretending all the time and deceiving when she said she didn't take butterflies." She was afraid of being found a fraud.

> Katharine Goodson . . . kissed me. Asked after me and everybody. She doesn't love me like she did. She doesn't believe in me. She misinterprets everything I say. She misinterprets when I don't say anything. She disapproves of something. O I wish I knew. I wish I could get back.
> I love her too much. I am all dumb and embarrassed. . . .[5]

For Elizabeth there could be no simple relationship with someone she admired. It was always "getting back" to something that was perfect. But within the year, she had given up her ambition to be a concert pianist. The astonishing thing is that though she had studied piano for thirteen years and played very well, she rarely played again. No friend who met her after the mid-thirties knew that she had ever studied under Goodson, nor did her own children ever remember hearing her play. One might speculate that Elizabeth, feeling she had failed, kept this a dark secret.

Elizabeth thought of going to Oxford, and a private tutor, Mrs Paynter, was hired to prepare her for the entrance exams, but she didn't have the temperament for scholastic study. She was already reading the classics on her own and her journals are full of references to Homer, Virgil, Dante, Virginia Woolf, D.H. Lawrence, or James Joyce. She would wander down to the Tate or the National Gallery to encounter the Masters. Her responses were always intensely personal. Describing William Blake's illustration of Dante and Virgil approaching the angel guarding the gates of Purgatory, she could write: "There are mystical yellow and red lights and rays upon the water—and you can look into it and into it—and you feel a sacred feeling like the light of twilights and dreams when you were little. Strange, lost beautiful things and imaginings and forgotten inspirations."[6] She never took the entrance exams. One wonders what they would have made of her at Oxford.

Not sure where to turn she found herself falling into listless apathy, with sleepless nights of worry; into this vacuum of need walked the indomitable Louie. In her journal she describes a scene when Louie was visiting at the Basil Street Hotel. Elizabeth's powerful intellectual sophistication at the age of twenty was balanced by an equally powerful childishness, clearly provoked by Louie.

> Mummy and Jane both went to bed—I did too finally at 11. But I couldn't get to sleep—London was still making an awful noise there seemed so much worry over my head—I was hemmed in. I want to work more . . . and not go listlessly apathetically—I got scared. I wanted—like mad—O I do I do I do. But what was the use—I got scared. I said the "Though the Mountains be carried into the Midst of the Sea"—I think I will read the New Testament—I sat up. Jane's comforter was just in the shape of a black coffin. Don't be silly—be strong—don't let it run away with you. Why can't I have—if I want to? I lay down—shall I turn on the light & read—You're tired anyway. Then I heard someone opening my door. I jumped & sat up & said Who's there? Who's there? Who's there? & then Mummy said

"It's just me going to bed." & I said "O what are you doing Mummy & I whined what are you doing Mummy?" again and again. Then after a few seconds of silence she came in & caressed me & said she loved me & kissed me & lay in bed beside me & I with my head on her shoulder & a couple of tears came out of my left eye & rolled down my cheek over the lotion & they itched a bit. She lay for a while then went back to bed—& I slept because I might as well sleep as anything. But I said Hares first because tomorrow is the first of the month.[7]

One can imagine Elizabeth writing this scene with a certain amount of self-parody—"a couple of tears came out of my left eye"—but the need is real. Louie clearly encouraged this dependency in her twenty-year-old daughter.

Elizabeth sought escapes from the apathy that plagued her. One strategy was to visit her favourite author, J.M. Barrie, to whom she had a letter of introduction through Bill Herridge (Hon. William Duncan), her father's friend. That Elizabeth should have selected Barrie as her favourite author is distressing—he was not someone to be particularly helpful to her as an aspiring writer—but her attachment to him had much to do with Kingsmere, which Barrie's books had helped to make an elfin world. Describing her state as feeling "scared and elated by turns, and inadequate and unspeachable," with Daddy and Mummy "looking loving and joyously parental and soft and proud," and with Jane offering a smile and shy generous good-luck, she set off for Adelphi Terrace.

Sir James Barrie assumed Elizabeth was young, "obviously about sixteen" and he treated her kindly. They chatted about music, he saying he was not musical. "Neither am I they tell me," Elizabeth replied. Then they spoke of education, probably of Elizabeth's confusion about whether to go to Oxford:

He said he admired anyone who wanted an education and didn't think it spoilt anyone. He thought girls that went were better to talk to. He said, "But a clever woman never lets on she is clever. Whenever you hear anyone say 'That

woman is clever' you know that she is stupid. A clever
woman doesn't let you know." He said he had sent his
sons . . . to Eton and Oxford. He said, "I never had a
daughter but if I had I should like to keep her at home to
pour out my tea for me . . . But if she wanted to go I would
send her."[8]

More double-speak, but this paternalism is hardly surprising
from Barrie. He did offer vaguely helpful advice, saying that
"university didn't make any difference to writing—that just
came out of yourself. Perhaps you wrote all wrong according to
the rules—but that was your way and right for you."

Elizabeth was seeking direction for her ambition but she
received only conventional pieties. "I asked Sir James Barrie
what was the best education for a writer—he said 'To write.' I
asked Gilbert Ryle, an erudite philosopher at Oxford, how I
should prepare for my life. He said, 'You want your life to be a
cryptic sentence.' I asked Ralph Straus how to get started. He
said 'Read the News of the World.'"[9]

Desperate to get started as a writer, Elizabeth chose the route
most easily available to women. She fell in love with an artist.
It was a familiar history lived by most creative women before
her. A young man wishing to write finds a circle, and often
becomes the protégé of the famous writer. George Barker, at
about this time, was being taken under the wing of T.S. Eliot.
A young woman finds an artist/lover—a more dangerous
strategy. Nurturing her writing is not always the dominant
concern, and whose ego survives intact is not often in question.

Elizabeth began an infatuation with the British painter
Meredith Frampton. She chose the kind of man she could meet
in her social set. He was older, a father figure (who ironically
turned out to be a mother's son; she would later characterize
Frampton's "mother problem as like Ruskin's"). When
Elizabeth met him through the Allwards, Canadian friends liv-
ing in London, Frampton would have been about thirty-nine.
He was a well-known portrait painter, elected to the Royal
Academy, whose sitters included artists, actors, architects,
musicians, writers, administrators, a bishop, and the future

King George VI. His portraits are traditional in style with a curious combination of detachment and intense involvement. Not least attractive to Elizabeth was that his father, Sir George Frampton, was the famous sculptor of the monument to Peter Pan in Kensington Gardens. Elizabeth probably saw Frampton as her entrée to the world of artists, for it was she who pursued him. The infatuation is rather poignant in retrospect. A confirmed bachelor much attached to his mother, he was clearly flattered and fascinated by the beautiful young Canadian who had set her sights on him.

Elizabeth staged her campaign by asking Frampton to paint her a still life of a tree in Kensington Gardens near the statue of Peter Pan. She did not tell him which one, insisting he would know it when he saw it. The painting was never done, and the innocent liaison continued in a rather desultory fashion. Frampton explained that he had been immersed in a dark fog all that winter; after a period of work he had had a mild breakdown and had retired from life. Elizabeth wrote solicitously: "I understand your sadness and your sufferings, and I am sad for them, and I suffer for you."[10] As she returned to Kingsmere that summer, she was still not quite ready to give up, and sent him love, inviting him to Canada: "Here I am. Here I am waiting, still fresh, full of life." Later, appalled by her own daring, she asked him to tear up the letter and send it back. He did so but insisted he loved her candour—"English people pretend that they don't feel anything at all." She had made him feel young, which seemed not quite fair, since he had never felt young in his youth. He concluded: "Be happy."

In a letter back to Daly Avenue that February, she describes her liaison with Frampton. It is clear she is still being the respectable daughter, living out, as she was required to do, her mother's version of a romantic life, with the appropriate glamour of Englishness.

Feb. 2, 1933

B.S.H. [the Basil Street Hotel]

Dearest Mummy and Daddy,

. . . I never told you about the meeting in St. James Park

about 4 weeks ago—that lasted til 4 o'clock A.M.—did I? No. But you seem to have found out—I wouldn't feel safe at the North Pole. Now I shall give you the gory (or glorious) details. I was bold and bad enough to send F. a Christmas card with nothing but my name and a question mark. (I think myself, that this was quite chaste and as it should be.) He replied with a note which he delivered by hand . . .

So we each trembled in our separate spheres and waited for Sunday. It came. It was fresh and full of rain drops.

I put on the red dress with the green spots. It was growing dusk when I got to the bridge. He was there. Looking like an artist in a checked coat and his perennial umbrella. We went, very self-consciously to look at the tree— because he almost admitted that he knew which one it was. And I knew he knew—and he knew I knew he knew etc. etc. Then, after admiring the Pelicans and the emotional curves of the various trees we adjourned to the Criterion for tea—it was sprinkling rain quite prolifickly [sic] before we got there—and I dare say there was water all over my nose . . . [we] sat there until the seat beneath us grew hard in indignation. Then we sauntered out into the street . . .

We walked around London in the wet darkness & dim lights . . .

Well we walked until I had a blister on my heel—(I didn't mention it. I was stoic to a degree) . . . so F. said let's go for a drive. B. said O.K. again—even though he might erroneously think her a yes-girl . . . and then we drove for miles . . . But B. was not carried away & B. & F. behaved as though E.L.S. [Louie] was in the back seat. . . .

That's all."[11]

It's fascinating to think how Elizabeth had to play on Louie's innocence. She could report being out until four A.M., appealing to Louie's romanticism, without raising her fears. There was a thing called character. Elizabeth would later castigate herself for "the dishonest, dull, subterfugic letters I write home to my parents." This is neither dull nor dishonest but it is a performance. Clearly the best course was to flatter her mother and play up to her sense of the dramatic, within the boundaries of decorum.

But to Russel, she could speak more candidly of her relationship with Frampton, whom she identified with her father.

Feb. 16, 1933

Dearest Daddy,
. . . On Saturday I am going out with Meredith Frampton—that will be a "golden moment." He is so comforting and stimulating—why? Because he has ideas of his own—not educational ideas & he is a real artist all the way through. What is the best thing in anyone, I almost think, is silence. He is marvellous to be silent with—just sit & say nothing—you think a lot & you feel verra [sic] happy. Isn't that a rare gift? to be stimulating to another's mind without saying anything? Well, that's what he does to me & I feel bursting with content & exciting peace. O well—I will keep my head. I think he understands the country, too. He listens to the trees laughing in the wind in the right way. But of course I may be a foolish female carried away by imagination. *You* stimulate thought without saying anything. It was *you* who taught me to appreciate those things. *Selah*. . . .

Goodbye—Love Oh Love
Betty.[12]

Elizabeth was hurt enough by the abortive love affair to write about it three years later: "I'd like to go into the reality of the Frampton situation: whether in reality I was deeply affected by it, perhaps hurt." She could now see his "thinness and red hands," and the words that clung to his image were "juice," "tea," "umbrella," and his use of "one." But even this criticism she couldn't write without a sense of guilt. "It's his sense of delicacy, his sensibility and understanding that made me admire him—and are in fact what I always love wherever I find them."[13] In the end, Frampton was just one of Elizabeth's frustrated routes into the public world of art.

Louie Smart's expectations for her daughters were solidly bourgeois: she wanted them to marry well and she educated them for that purpose. There were the private schools, the comings-out, and the finishing touches, studying music and painting in England. When Elizabeth could report that she met Malcolm MacDonald, the Prime Minister's son, had lunched at Downing Street, and was to spend a weekend at Chequers, Louie was delighted. And when her friend Mrs Alfred Watt suggested taking Elizabeth as her private secretary and companion to Stockholm for the first international conference of the Associated Country Women of the World in June 1933, Louie was not only delighted, she paid the ticket and got Russel to donate funds to the organization. The trip was meant to broaden her daughter's experience.

Mrs Watt was the kind of woman of whom Louie approved, though she did not particularly like her, and Russel found her a bore. To Irene Spry, Graham Spry's wife, she reported outrageous stories of Mrs Watt, including that they had been asked to make a large donation to pay for her European wardrobe. Mrs Watt was a formidable Canadian character. Widowed before the First World War, she had moved to England where she helped to found a British branch of the Women's Institute and in 1929 was instrumental in founding the Associated Country Women of the World.[14]

In Mrs Watt's day, the ACWW seems to have been a somewhat ambiguous organization, perhaps more a social club than the political organization it was to become; the international committees were "never particularly enthusiastic about the idea of having an assembly of rural women in their midst." The executive adopted a benevolent maternalism towards its rural members, which was only to change radically after 1945.

Mrs Watt is remembered with some ambivalence by her associates:

A short, squat woman with a fine leonine head, rather short white hair, and, frequently, a fierce look . . . she had an ability to infect other people with her enthusiasm which really did amount to genius. She had an astonishing pertinacity and drive, a brilliant flair for publicity, and that streak of opportunism (common to nearly all genius and to many leaders) which can turn the most awkward situation to good account. Disappointments, snubs, rebuffs, recoiled from her sturdy little figure and left her still standing, rather aggressively—and still talking! Often enough her adversaries gave way, with bad grace, in sheer self-defence because, short of liquidation, there seemed no method of disposing of her. . . ."[15]

But Mrs Watt had no concept of work that contained drudgery. She disliked "chores" and detested routine, enjoying limelight and the stimulus of an audience. Elizabeth would find her, if not racist, certainly prejudiced, Presbyterian, and self-aggrandizing.

As with most conferences, the ACWW's first international conference in Stockholm was a round of social events. The welcome meeting was held in the Hall of the Academy of Music, followed by a reception in the Winter Garden of the Grand Hotel. It was reported in Canadian newspapers that both occasions were honoured by the presence of the Crown Princess. There were excursions after the conference to a model dairy, a domestic training school, and to the ancient castle of Skokloster. Elizabeth was very soon disenchanted. The trip proved another instance of having to perform in a false context and she found Mrs Watt impossible. "Always to be polite. . . . I thought a lot of evil thoughts. I mustn't think. A good description—'a cross old woman' it might jump out in a rage by mistake and I don't care I don't care. And snobbery and overbearing and insistent pride in personal distinction. And pettiness and sulkiness and aggrievedness. But no hate I felt. No hate at all. No bitterness. No resentment. Glory be."[16]

Clearly this is self-deception. The code Elizabeth established early was that she would never allow herself to feel hate, and her hatred was fierce. Perhaps this suppression was necessary to create the female persona of softness she required of herself, so that she would not be like Louie. Perhaps she recognized that were she to begin to plumb her "little pot of hate," all hell would break loose. She was not yet ready to be overwhelmed.

In the whole trip, the only relief she records is a brief spontaneous conversation in a pub after a walk up Mount Hausberg. "It was reviving. Oh for *definite* people to talk to! and to be wallowing in mind—I mean to have to use your wits to answer—to be exultant in the fray—K.M. [Katherine Mansfield] says 'the high luxury of not having to explain.'" After six weeks of Mrs Watt, it was good, if only for five minutes, to find sympathetic company in a pub in an incomprehensible language. By contrast, when she reported at lunch that she was reading *Lady Chatterley's Lover*, Mrs Watt replied: "I think it's perfectly disgusting to want to read a book my country won't allow."[17]

All of Elizabeth's energy during the trip went secretly into her journal. She was learning to reserve her deepest passions for writing. Without other writers to talk to she was infinitely confused, particularly about the problem of self-consciousness. She was afraid she was cheating, since authentic writing must be spontaneous:

> I looked at the queer lake and thought it is like something. . . . It's like a wet olive. That's good I said. It will go well in my diary. It is like a wet olive. It will be impressive. Then thought: I am copying Virginia Woolf. I am being influenced and "making phrases." I am cheating. I am not being myself—but taking her construction putting on a light meaning and saying O how original I am—and how apt. Then—isn't all this truth-speaking and self-analysis, isn't it all her influence or someone's—not your own? All this pretending to get at the core. It's not true, really. But then I thought as I scrubbed my back with a lint cloth and French Fern soap (brown and oval) isn't it permissible to be stimulated by people honourably, to be made more alert and alive and noting of things by others? To be shown and *taught*. Cannot I be stimulated by

Virginia Woolf and Katherine Mansfield (who is sometimes reflected in V.W.) and Mary Webb and Barrie and
the others? Yes, why not? To be my own original nature
self—to be the thing that is the strongest urge at my
depths—that is to lay all that down and laugh at it and
walk on a mountain alone—really alone in a wild place.
And not want to meet a soul. And that is really true and it
is the urge and the flame and it needs no fanning. Things
seem false if they are conscious. Conscious fun—nothing—revolting. Spontaneous they must be—bursting and
self-forgetful.[18]

So fragile was her creative ego, so strong the dichotomous pull
between the social world and the world of her imagination, that
to write would require a death. She records a dream she had in
Stockholm:

I dreamt all night of people getting married—Joan
—Rachel—Helen—and I dreamt of people dying and
lying in coffins—Mrs. Kirkhoffer—Emily Brontë—she
was wax—and Graham wanted me to kiss her dead lips. I
wanted to but not while he was there. It was very intense
this marriage and death—but not troubled.

O! I was happy when I woke. All the heavy dreary veil
was lifted and I was really awake again—after days and
days of semi-consciousness. The sun was lovely—it
didn't weigh you down.[19]

Writing was to kiss the dead lips of Brontë, but in private, once
the censors had departed. (Though Elizabeth was grateful to
Graham Spry, she sometimes felt he wanted her dependent on
him and worked to undermine what she called her "reserve of
fighting strength.")

In July she wrote desperately to her father:

July 27, 1933,
Braunlage Oberharz,
Germany
Dear Daddy,
I am going back to Canada. . . . It's the place for me. Jane

goes to McGill and I can stay at home. Anyway, whatever happens, I am going back to Canada & I should like to stay there. Jane must go to McGill—that seems to me natural & inevitable & the only right thing. Well, I suppose that's settled now. Really! I simply *can't* imagine or concoct the future—I simply *can't* think farther than today. (No *don't* tell me there's no such word.) But I do know that I want to be in Canada. I should be content to be "the comfort in the home" & pass ash-trays gracefully, as long as I can work, & I don't suppose anyone will stop me from doing that! . . .

With love from
Betty[20]

And she wrote to Louie two weeks later that there was no use going to other countries before you're "settled—like dough." "You must stay in your own country unless you want to be a loose vague dangling end." London was too fascinating. Elizabeth felt like a person drowning in its clutches; if she returned to England she would lose hold. It had been good, but now she wanted to be in Canada, at Kingsmere, among her mountains. Even if it meant, as she knew it would, being the angel in the house.

At the end of August, Elizabeth returned to Ottawa. The family had moved from Daly Avenue to the more impressive residence at 300 Acacia Avenue in the heart of Rockcliffe. But being at home was not the solution she thought it would be. In retrospect she wrote in her diary: "Jane and I have been miserable this winter—no use to deny it. Absolutely and utterly without the spark of life that comes with living. A great black heaviness was over us both. She at McGill and I here."

Certainly one factor must have been living in a household where the fragile harmony could be so easily exploded. Elizabeth describes one such crisis that arose from preparations for Louie's Christmas party that year:

We were all gathered together around my bed drinking

ginger ale and soft but pliable date cakes—and suddenly
J. [Jane] irritably referred to the fact that Helen Bradly*
had to be invited. It wasn't a minute before the storm
broke. The prop that holds up the sense of humour
flopped—the sanity—I mean saneness—snapped. All of a
sudden the irrevocable depths. Too late to be retrieved but
to run its course. Jane lying across my bed at the bottom—
"Well what of it?" Daddy smiling because he was upset
and yet optimistic. M. going deeper in and no hope for a
word to avert the already arrived—how can it descend
like a curtain all in a second? Hysterics. Then a walk outside by M. and a return to a striding up and down below
"Oh! Where can I go?"—and loud wailing void talk—like
a person in sleep stumbling along a path in an energetic
way—but unaware. [After this incident Jane and
Elizabeth retire to sleep] . . . M. came in—dead tired,
exhausted, and lined, but herself. She asked in a low tired
voice if Russel [her son] were in yet and went to her room.
I heard the bath water running. Later I heard her convers-
ing with R. from her window in Motherly sane, heart-
restoring tones and R. came in and said *S.O.S. Iceberg*
was good.[21]

Such scenes were to scar both daughters indelibly. When they
conjured Louie in their minds, it would be Louie pacing the
balcony, or lying in a heap on the bathroom floor. And most terrifying was that her hysterical outbursts were always triggered
by trivial incidents: they could never anticipate her rages and
the unexpected shock was terrifying.

But there was another cause of what Elizabeth called "the
neurosis," her profound sense of ennui. She was beginning to
hate Ottawa's social round: "Ottawa—the Sparks Street life—
it is really impossible. It gets you down. Ambition gets suffocated. People are so pretentious—if they are not sweet but
unconscious."[22]

---

*According to Jane Smart, this incident is to be explained by the fact that Bradly's
father was a dentist, and to Louie, dentists were unacceptable.

But such a life was not to be easily dismissed. Not only was it attractive, but it carried Louie's imprimatur. Elizabeth and Jane found themselves acting out a fantasy of social achievement orchestrated by Louie. In January of 1934 they were presented before their Excellencies, the Governor General and his wife, the Countess of Bessborough, at Government House. *The Ottawa Citizen* reported the coming out with its usual enthusiasm:

> Scarlet tunics seemed more in evidence than since pre-war days in the brilliant line-up of gold braided and be-medalled members of the guard of honour, honorary A.D.C.s, and aides-de-camp attending their Excellencies last night at the most picturesque drawing room in several years. There were 965 persons presented. . . . Statesmen may have just claim to first place in the sun at opening of Parliament, but even they must yield precedence on drawing-room night to the lovely young debutantes who make their first bow to society under such thrilling circumstance.
>
> Twenty-four were included in last night's lovely bouquet of winsome girlhood, a dozen or so daughters of the capital, others from Toronto, Montreal, and the Canadian west.[23]

Under a sub-article headed "Beauteous Canadian Womanhood Is Handsomely Gowned For Occasion," it was reported that "The Misses Betty and Jane Smart, debutante daughters of Mr. and Mrs. Russel Smart, were accompanied by their father. Miss Betty wore a blue crepe gown designed with a court train, and she wore a necklace of blue moonstones. Miss Jane Smart wore a simply designed dress of white tulle and the train of tulle was finished with ruchings." In the accompanying photos, Elizabeth, who had just turned twenty-one and was, in fact, already over the debutante hill, appears conventionally sweet and moony, whereas Jane's photo is a rather aggressive, pensive portrait, about which there was much talk among the ladies' circles.

In her diary, Elizabeth wrote simply: "I was presented at the Drawing Room on Friday night—and I quite liked the 'subservient' curtsey in the end, because I felt very lofty as I did it. D'Arcy [McGee] said, 'It wasn't fair to me to look as beautiful as I did.' 'Honestly Darling.' . . . It was a dreadful party."[24] Jane remembered only that she hadn't been able to find a bathroom and she had peed in her elegant dress on the way home to Acacia Avenue. Always more of a public rebel than Elizabeth, she was later to do a broadcast for CBC Radio lambasting the snobbery of the debutante tradition.

The problem for Elizabeth, it is clear, was that this life was infinitely seductive to her vanity. And she delighted in vanity. Vanity was "one of nature's ways to bind you to the earth . . . I took infinite pains before the mirror. Oh! It was fun." But the vanity stimulated is that of the beautiful sexual object, with all the attendant complications of sex. The man was a challenging test, a test of power and strength. Conquest was the focus. She could say of her date: "D'Arcy has presented me with himself. Therefore, in me, he was subsided. And he does not trouble me anymore." That she was a tease was not surprising: "As soon as they get to the point, I lose interest; honestly I don't want to be kissed at all (because it is so incomplete to start what is meant to go on) but I should hate it if they didn't want to." In fact, as close friends attested, Elizabeth was exceedingly shy, but like many beautiful young girls, she had learned that sexuality was an armour, a protective camouflage that gave her a way of negotiating the world to her side. "All pink and white and golden," Ritchie had called her. With such beauty it was hard not to create a persona to cater to what Elizabeth called "the world's veniality and vanity." In 1979 in "Diary of a Blockage" she writes that a young girl asked her what was it like to be beautiful. "It was embarrassing to be beautiful. It's comfortable to be old; it's so much more forgivable."[25] It was too easy to be seduced by the "siren comfort" that builds the trivial ego— Elizabeth expected attention. But she did not want to be a blonde, the recipient of every male projection; she wanted to be interesting. Charles Ritchie described how Elizabeth often deliberately made herself ugly, and Jane called her beauty "troublant"—it could fall apart in a minute. Often she had to whittle herself down at great cost to meet other people's expectations and she found herself living her ego at the level of the coquette. But she also felt smothered and manipulated and far from what she wanted to be:

> These are the sensuous days with the bang, now pushed back on high curls. Nothing but sensuousness seducing me, cajoling me, muffling me up in lazy luxury. That will to work is a faint idea, not an urgent immediate one. It is pleasant—no, it would be pleasant, but for the feeling underneath of time flying, of waste, of unaccomplishment, and the story of The Talents. This is the fight against the powerful, the irresistible, the compelling monster Sex.[26]

Elizabeth was engaged in a terrible battle for self-confidence. She was not satisfied by the easy flattery that came to the blonde. What was it that inhibited her? Clearly, it must have been self-doubt—"to go on vaguely, morbidly, unhappily, subconsciously thinking I CAN'T. Oh! Oh! Oh! And with a power of despair and resignation." The fear of criticism was strong. Too long a habit of being praised for the superficial graces only makes the ego more vulnerable to deep cuts. Misplaced female vanity, a female fear of appearing egoistic, was at the root of self-censorship. Though real stimulation and joy were in the work, one left them for something more feminine and humorous. In fact it was her own introspection and self-analysis that sabotaged her.

> I don't see anything clearly. It is all so unimportant. The clinking of cutlery as it is washed and the sliding of it away into drawers. I don't feel distinctly, minutely. It is so easy to sink into a kind of laissez-faire—even these words are bunkum and fit for nothing but the gutter. It is so easy just to sit and let the cat lick your feet, and the mind mess about idly. Nothing has significance. *That* is the neurosis that comes upon you as the result of living with other

people and not caring to fight them as they, in the throes of what Virginia Woolf calls "Sister Conversion," swoop down upon you with their stamping blocks and downright positive assertions of errors. O spirits of departed souls who have felt *urgently*! Send some help or at least the knowledge that what I have lost is not the most important thing in the world.[27]

She held desperately to her writing, as to a lifeline: ". . . anything and everything can be made into a joke or super civilized over, of course. Nothing matters here but producing the child— deformed, premature, blind or legless—but produced. I think it is death to keep it all in. . . . *There* is the joy to create, the love of pains and the striving, without which there is no life here. . . .The really mature thing then would be to take what I want."[28]

But that was the problem. What did she want? "How can you fight if you are not sure which is the thing you should fight? It is just me. No use to blame it on any but myself." The beauty she felt to be at the core of things kept its distance: "the beauty I know to be there—to be about me—but it cannot come and permeate slowly into each little cell, with a slow, complete and satisfying beauty. . . . Like a mother too tired to enjoy her baby—almost so tired she resents its intrusions—the spirit is tired." And she concluded that love would awaken the spirit. The man was to be the route to this beauty. "What he?" she asked herself. "*Any* he that loves."[29]

How could Elizabeth hope to sort out these conundrums? The vision of woman in love that the world offered was passive, submissive: the "swooning warmth of being loved." At twenty she writes:

I am going to be a poet, I said
But even as I said it I felt the round softness of my breasts
And my mind wandered and wavered
Back to the earthly things
And the swooning warmth of being loved.
Bright and hard and meticulously observant

My brain was to be
A mirror reflecting things cut in eternal rightness
But before I could chisel the first word of a concrete poem
My breast fell voluptuously into my hand
And I remembered I was a woman.

[Diary, November 18, 1934][30]

Yet there are always two sides to all our narratives: the surface story and the subtext, the embroiled emotions beneath. At one level Elizabeth was having a delightful time in Ottawa; she was the dramatic centre of a small sophisticated coterie. Charles Ritchie describes one of the social exploits she staged in May 1935. As she had since childhood, she loved to push people to the edge. To celebrate the spring solstice, she decided to orchestrate a happening which she called the "Revels of Bacchus." For Elizabeth, the world of myth was a real world and she determined to bring pagan ritual to staid Ottawa. All her life, she loved festivals. She saw them as "the rhythmic stops and gala days," "the periods that make the dance"[31]; they were indispensable mirrors to bring out unknown sides of the self. She sent out invitations to friends, with instructions as to their various roles. The festival was to include ritual dance, a sacred fire, music (*L'après-midi d'un faune* and Ravel's *Bolero)*, and the chanting of runic spells. For her guests Elizabeth made mead (laced with rye whisky and very intoxicating). Ritchie claimed there was talk of the "ancient fertility rite" of "spilling semen to fecundate the furrows" (though it was agreed this would be pushing things a little far). The site chosen was the ruins on Mackenzie King's estate at Kingsmere. While King eventually acceded its use, he wisely declined an invitation, though it amused Elizabeth that he got the reputation for having Bacchanalian parties anyway.

The gathering of twenty or thirty assembled at sunset: nymphs and satyrs, a Guards officer in his long underwear, draped in a tiger-skin rug borrowed from Government House. Ritchie describes Elizabeth miming "a series of roles, now a shy nymph, now a pursuing maenad." "By the flickering rays of the bonfire [King's] mock ruins looked like a grotesque stage set."[32] Jane remembers the event as being very wild, with couples disappearing to surrounding bushes for mysterious fertility rites. At dawn the survivors staggered home to the Smarts' house for eggs and bacon.

Canada was not the place for Elizabeth to find herself as a writer. Her set was too small, her world too insulated, she too easily dismissed, to find the support she needed. At this point Canadian writers were just breaking through the permafrost of colonialism. The poet Frank Scott in Montreal, with his wife, the painter Marian Scott, were one of the magnetic centres of the new literary movement. Elizabeth knew them, and described Scott as the most exciting man in Canada. Their movement was political and nationalist. Norman Bethune was a close friend and they were deeply involved in support for the Spanish Civil War. While Jane shared their enthusiasm and actively participated in the Spanish cause—she was known in Ottawa as a "Communist," and it was she who gave Bethune the ticket that got him to Spain—Elizabeth was dismissive of politics. Indeed one can say she was naïve. Though she had spent the month of July with Mrs Watt in Germany in 1933, Fascism meant little to her. She had even been amused that summer when her German escort Herr Writz was shocked and chided her for responding in kind to a Heil Hitler! salute in a Hausberg pub. She would always insist that the route to understanding even world movements lay not in understanding politics, but human nature.[33]

Scott's circle may have enjoyed Elizabeth but they could not penetrate her disguises. In retrospect, Marian Scott felt that she never really did the young Betty Smart justice. She had met her when she herself was struggling with painting and found her very pretty: a charming, rich, rather spoiled girl, and that was something she didn't have time for. She thought of her as living in a dream world. To the Scotts she was simply a member of her social class. A few years later Marian Scott would be astonished when Elizabeth brought them George Barker's books and said he was the one she intended to marry, though Marian Scott knew she had never met Barker. The persona

Elizabeth presented to them was of a young girl passionate about literature who, at a party, danced wildly, reciting Shakespeare. She hid the fact that she wrote, too timid to share her work. When she finally sent the Scotts a copy of *By Grand Central Station I Sat Down and Wept* in 1945, they were overwhelmed; no one had expected that Elizabeth would be the one to write a work of real genius. They read it aloud to each other.[34] In 1950, Frank Scott wrote to Elizabeth to say that he looked upon the book as one of the best achievements in Canadian literature to date,[35] and apologized for not having written her sooner.

Elizabeth could not find creative nourishment in Canada; she was already convinced that the real writers were in England. When, after long isolation, she began to rediscover Canadian writers in the late 1970s, she said she was moved to find how good they were, and intrigued to hear the echo in Margaret Laurence and Alice Munro of a Canadian voice that she recognized as her own. The long evolution of an indigenous literature from the mid-thirties to the sixties was not something that Elizabeth could find compelling. She was never good at movements. She had to find her own way.

4   The Stifled Moment

I've got to live. And the thing that is offered me as life
just starves me, starves me to death, mother. . . . I want
the wonder back again, or I shall die.
           D.H. Lawrence
           St Mawr

The being I am waiting for . . . "I create and re-create it
over and over, starting from my capacity to love, starting
from my need for it."
           Roland Barthes
           A Lover's Discourse

In the autumn of 1935, Elizabeth returned to London to resume
her social life and her classes at the University of London, this
time at King's College, where her courses included English,
Latin, French, Roman History, and Logic. She parodied her
first day in a diary entry under the name Yvonne Freshette:
"Read *Paradise Lost* by the gas fire in my blue negligée. . . .
Then Milton got sleepy & as I was too sleepy to go to bed with
him, I said Ah! I shall write my overdue article for the Country
Women [she had been asked to write up her trip with Mrs
Watt]. Thus ended the Great Initial Day of life in the outside
world."[1] It was not hard for Elizabeth to put any institution into
perspective. But she was lonely and still the people she met
could not satisfy the reaches of her imagination. She had

already linked the man and writing as the dual route to the same ecstatic centre.

That autumn she fell in love with Lord John Pentland, grandson of Lord and Lady Aberdeen of Aberdeenshire. There was a Canadian connection. Lord Aberdeen had been Governor General in 1893, and the family continued to visit Canada, often to see their friend Mackenzie King. But it is probable she met Pentland casually through her old friend Bill Aitken, who was Pentland's roommate. In December 1935 she spent ten days with Pentland and friends in Grindelwald, Switzerland, and the infatuation continued in London. There would have been trips to the country estate in Scotland, and that Christmas, Pentland gave her a Maltese diamond cross. He seems to have been a rather conventional and cerebral young man, formed by the Aberdeen tradition of high-minded liberalism and good works, and much devoted to his mother, Marjorie Pentland, who would later author a book about his overpowering grandmother. He would probably have been astounded to discover what Elizabeth could make of their relationship. To her poems or her gestures of love, he could reply: "I don't like being troubled."

Elizabeth was determined to live her mother's unlived life, to break all inhibitions. She wanted to go into life, to take what she needed. She had already established an ethic of ecstasy evolved from her own vision of natural mysticism: "Pride shouldn't be mixed up with love. [One remembers her portrait of Louie in her courtship days.] Love is large and permeating and accepting, like nature. It is not a calculated, civilized thing. It is not art, but religion—or it is nothing. . . . I worship worship the wild and my fierce humourless prayers are breathed secretly and intensely. Sentimental? No!! Cowards cowards cowards to hide behind words, to be afraid of a gust of wind. Oh the wild wind!"[2]

She invested all her ego in a vision of heroic love. Love with the whole soul, without reservation and control, with abandon and urgent desire, was to be the experience to crack open the self. It is a heroic vision learned from literature. What makes such ecstasy so heady is that the lover is made to assume the projection of all that is most desired in the self. But the headlong rush is also an escape from the self. Elizabeth's need to liberate her deepest creative resources was so profound that she had to evolve an ethic of love large enough to effect it.

If Pentland was a rather conventional young man, an appropriate product of his aristocratic background, in her diary he becomes someone who must be converted to her ethic: "I saw the delicate rhythm of trees on the horizon. If he could only reach that! Even that! After all, that is not the huge whole, but only an enviable suggestion. How, *how* can I possess the richness I find on the sky-line? Have I ever desired to possess his personality the way I desire to possess that little curving tree forever and ever?" She conceived of a love that would be a losing of self in the other, without boundaries:

> Oh! has this been weakness in me to get so specialized in man? Is the 'Understanding' a subterfuge? Because that is the greatest thing in the world. It *is* the world. It is God. I want an ecstasy — not a comfort. If I could love him and be faithful to him all my days, I would be made bigger by this compassionate step and understand all women in the world. I would love him more and more and be absorbed by the whole of him. I would be freed by him too and I would forget the small disgruntled ego.[3]

It was not for nothing that Elizabeth dreamed she had kissed the dead lips of Emily Brontë.

In modern Western culture, romantic love is a cultural artifact: the experience is one of the most seductive and consuming myths one can fall captive to. One might almost say it is the writer's first assignment: Neruda's *Twenty Love Poems and a Song of Despair*; Pasternak's *Doctor Zhivago*; Dante's *La Vita Nuova*. And for the lovers there are models to follow from Dido and Aeneas to Héloïse and Abelard, Romeo and Juliet, and Tristan and Isolde. Such passion has little to do with the reality of the other person who serves only as the hook on which to hang the myth. It is always astonishing, once the passion is over, to encounter the stranger standing there. But while the pendulum swing from agony to ecstasy is addictive, the dangerous component is that the projection must be reclaimed if the self is to survive such inflation.

Elizabeth, already heroic in her ambitions, was afraid to trust herself. "If I fall in the small-eyed gesturing fashion, all women of all time fall with me. Is it only a great ego and the female body demanding to be adored, stamping its petulant foot, insisting on homage, tossing its arrogant head?"[4]

For some male writers, love of this magnitude is the myth that releases the creative self; it is one of the few opportunities life offers to test the full range of one's being. Elizabeth understood this intuitively. (It would be inaccurate to say she had theories—as her friend Bobby McDougal said, she simply tried to be.) But while women are usually more than willing to take on the assignment, the man who serves as the male muse is much more wily and considerably less serviceable.

In John Pentland Elizabeth had not found the material for her myth. Not only was she too large for him, he tried to assert control. That Elizabeth needed John's support is clear. While she never lost her sense of the comic element of her melodrama (her diary of this year is called "The Stifled Moment or the story of my life by Belinda Blue a girl without humour"), she had much to fight against. Louie was always ready to sabotage her fragile ego. She wrote ominously in her diary that spring:

[The Basil Street Hotel]
March 6, 1936:

"I've hated you all day," she said. "You've been sneaking. You're the meanest little thing. You haven't done anything with your time. Any child could write the drivel you've written. Jane's put rings around you. She has a definite purpose. You've had your chance and you haven't done anything with it. You think of no one but yourself."

[Elizabeth closes the incident] When I finished Thurber I read Herbert Read's poems.

I must marry a poet. It's the only thing.[5]

One might take this scene as exaggeration, except that it is in

Louie's style when she was in one of her moods: pitting Jane and Elizabeth against each other, abetting the rivalry; attacking Elizabeth for indolence (though a writer was not what Louie wanted; she was never able to conceive of her daughter as a professional writer). It must have been hurtful to be accused of purposelessness, triviality, and selfishness, since these accusations Elizabeth had already internalized. The only solution was to marry a poet.

Elizabeth returned to Canada in March and began her first lengthy prose work, "My Lover John," a quasi-autobiographical record of her affair with Pentland, subtitled "a story of impotence" and written under the pseudonym Lorna Parr.[6] She was satisfied neither with the affair nor the story and one wonders if the pseudonym is a frustrated admission that she was still Louie's daughter. She sent the completed version to Graham Spry, although how receptive he could be to such material is questionable, but she needed response. She also gave the manuscript to her father, who remarked that while it was interesting, it was libellous, and in court he would not defend her.

At this stage in her apprentice work, Elizabeth made little distinction between autobiography and fiction. Her story has little plot and records the interior emotional life of the narrator, pursued at moments with an intensity reminiscent of D.H. Lawrence, whose work, according to Jane, Elizabeth had "engrammed."[7] What she seeks to define in her monologue is the nature of obsessive passion. And on this occasion she has not censored her anger. She writes in her story:

His own personal dignity must have been his staff, he cherished it at such enormous price. I remembered him always gathered together, his back to his fireplace, standing on his own ground, lights indirect, everything in meticulous good taste, no false notes but false notes for a purpose intended. I would rush into this room, flushed, eager, remembering things that never actually happened, but might have, between us, and he would confront me with this marble enigma of himself. What did he fear? Certainly a *stone* phallus is polite even in a drawing room.

"My lust was upon me," he would say with shame when natural waves too great burst through his fastidious etiquette exterior.

"Good," I would say without shame, but half-leering because of his disbelief in the body's morality; and he would experiment with my roundness and softness. But I felt the distaste of his spirit, still baulking against the shouting of his physicality. I could feel the terrible prostration of his dignity, urged onward by this vast vulgar Nature. His compulsion was mortifyingly, killingly humiliating to him.

Perhaps when the root of a first passion is frustration, it is all the more compelling. Elizabeth has taken on the role of Nature. She sees that John is circumscribed by the petty ego; she would free him by conquering his timidity. It is clear that Pentland's sexual distaste was at the core of the problem in their relationship. Elizabeth didn't have John's inhibitions. "Isn't the body the most wonderful instrument—the most wonderful plaything," she could say, though often she had to hide the profundity of her sexual longing.[8] The experience with Pentland only confirmed her loathing for good taste and fastidiousness.

The narrator is caught in an agony of compulsion and withdrawal. She wants, arrogantly, to redeem John; he, for his part, tries to tame, to dominate her:

The urgency grew. His ununderstandable, unapproachable, dominant personality began to obsess me day and night. He imposed a strictness, a discipline on everything with which he came in contact. I was limited, schooled, our meetings cut to once a week, or as a treat perhaps an occasional accidental or unprivate being together. This discipline piqued me. These tastes made me desire more.

But Elizabeth had not submitted. The impulse was really to convert John to her great understanding. The description in the narrative of their effort at sexual consummation, which would have been Elizabeth's first experience, is amusing if it weren't so poignant:

> "Not yet. Not here," I said, longing for the wet bracken, remembering the bushes of Virginia Water, and the slow secret decay of Nature's year. But he had not this longing for Nature, nor this identification of all good with her. But Nature's purification grows gardens on obscene rubbish. My supreme compliment to him was admitting him to my wild hill. I would take him to my Nature—that was the greatest I could say . . . I trusted absolutely to Nature's assimilative power. . . .

Though filled with doubts, Elizabeth persisted. The experience, as she crafted it into literature, is imitative in its Lawrencian syntax, and is certainly over-wrought; and yet its rhetorical extremism is matched by accounts from friends of Elizabeth's intensity. One suspects that she spoke little of this to John (she always preferred circumlocution to direct statement) but that John was in her emotional whirlpool is clear.

> "There's nothing else to do," I said, pressing the words like blood-drops from my overcharged brain. . . . At least I had the comfort of knowing my step inevitable. If fate had cornered me, the one road was easy enough to traverse. If there was no picking of life from death among similars, there was no misery in my surrender. The road might have certain pain, but if it was the only road, the pain was nothing, there would be pleasure in the bearing of it. But Oh! the agony of wavering indecision. . . .
>
> Then in the wet through these rows and rows of dim lamplit houses, through turbulent miles of inwardness, all things fighting together, all voices putting in their word, and the singing above all of the inevitable imminence of the Thing about to be.

When they do arrive at the seashore and find a hotel, the night proves disastrous, and was never to be attempted again. In the face of her intensity, John was impotent. Later, Elizabeth sent him a book on sex, "for which he thanked me sweetly, though trying to make a joke of it. But I am not sure that I didn't hurt him a little by this. His vanity." She thought that if it were only some small physical barrier that made these tortured misunderstandings, she could sweep them away by a "bold, and oh! brave move." It was always her duty to be bold. (Though this detail appears only in the story and not in her diary, it would not have been out of character for Elizabeth to have sent such a book.)

Nothing changes, of course, for the dynamic is set. Elizabeth is caught in an old rhythm: two beings in their own solipsistic worlds, each fighting with different weapons. "I often walked home alone along the wet deserted streets, feeling a kind of mother-consolation, seeing the world with an unbitter but melancholy resignation." Where the consolation and persistence came from was that Elizabeth was feeling the paradoxically comforting anguish of an old battle, that with her mother.

Unexpectedly, Louie came to visit. Elizabeth describes her in her story:

> She was balm, riches, luxury, strength. I felt remade because of her expensive talcum powder, and perfumes, her pretty underwear, her delicious warm extravagance. She had an unconquerable individual pride. She put back into me the excitement of expectation, the child-like delight in battle.
>
> She rented a large comfortable car and a chauffeur. She bought me a new and expensive fur coat, dresses, underwear, hats, stockings galore. She moved me into a large serene flat. She arranged for me to have massages to make my ugly legs a better shape. She made me have a permanent wave to sophisticate my wild and ingenoue [sic] hair. She ordered me a tonic. I began to revive.
>
> "John doesn't like me in black," I said.
>
> "Tush," she said. "What do I care what John likes?"
>
> Ah, did she dare? New worlds of possibility opened.
>
> "He thinks that common."

"Pooh! My taste is as good as his. That I should live to see a daughter of mine kowtow to a silly man!! Have a little pride!"

I began to perk up. An atomic vision of independence gave me new hope. With my new weapons I would challenge, I thought. . . .

I began to remember that there was a free life. My foolish prison was unnecessary. My unhappiness was self-imposed. My tempting mother seduced me too to this heavenly escape—I wavered towards it, half-hoping that the imminence of my departure would solve everything between John and me.

The "atomic vision" of independence that Louie seemed to offer was illusory; Elizabeth had simply succumbed again to her mother's orbit. She ends the story:

As I went up in the lift, leaving him below, he thumbed his nose at me. I knew then that he must be in despair, that he must love me. For it was a stroke of genius.

But it was too late. I was dead. I sailed home with my mother.

This, of course, is quite fantastic were it not ludicrous. Thumbing his nose at her, John is seen as heroic because it is her gesture: using pride as a weapon to mask despair.

Ironically Louie was probably right; Elizabeth had been completely and destructively dominated by John. On the boat back to Canada that spring she began to resent the cringing shape into which she felt he had forced her, appalled at her own humble acceptance of what she called his "too reasonable, joyless unnatural view of life." The regret lay in that she thought he might so easily have made her happy and didn't.[9]

"My Lover John" is clearly an immature piece—it so closely skirts the maudlin—still, it is an accurate account. This kind of love has to be built from the archetypes established in the personality and with intuitive shrewdness Elizabeth has caught it exactly. More important, Pentland was no help to her as a

writer. She wrote in her diary: "And he said that my poems—
or whatever other name better fits them—should be written and
then destroyed—either destroyed or sent as a letter to a
friend—to him! . . . Mayn't I, without too much conceit or
death-dealing self-love, arrange in order the heavy moments of
my life? Set my life out for myself without shame, without the
strategic self-depredation?—unnatural most unnatural idea that
I am bowing to I!"[10] Sadly Elizabeth could not easily dismiss
Pentland's put-down, nor see it as the product of a threatened
ego. She did not have the arrogance to presume that what she
wrote was important, nor indeed even that she had the right to
begin. The heady confidence of the child was gone. There were
the social expectations imposed on her as a woman. More
important, she could not win love by being the genius. George
Barker was to provide an exemplary contrast. He knew he was
a genius at sixteen (apart from the evidence of his obvious
intelligence, his mother had told him). All his lovers would
support him in this. When Elizabeth fell in love with him, it
was the way he went "from the sheepish and shame-faced to
the roar of authority"[11] that she delighted in. We love that which
we can least claim in ourselves. Elizabeth's struggle for authority was to be a brutal and protracted battle.

At the end of August 1936, Mrs Alfred Watt invited Elizabeth
to accompany her on her world tour to promote the Associated
Country Women of the World, again as her personal secretary
and companion. Elizabeth was not particularly enthusiastic
and, in her journal, called the pending trip a "detour" "because
it was only an excuse to put off for a little while longer the settling of my future. It is my long-winded excuse for never having done anything. An alibi, in fact."[12] Yet the idea of travelling
the world for six months must have seemed exciting, and she
thought she could handle Mrs Watt.

From August 18, 1936 to February 25, 1937, they travelled
through Canada, the United States, Hawaii, Fiji, Samoa, New
Zealand, Australia, Ceylon, Egypt, and what was then
Palestine. The London *Times* wrote of the tour: "In her world
tour, Mrs Watt was bearing a message from Her Majesty Queen

Mary to Women's Institutes of the British Empire," describing the ACWW as "a factor in world peace, an agency for better development of agriculture and home making, a missionary effort to enable countries where peasant and other country women are in a backward civic condition to become organized and so live better lives."[13]

Elizabeth herself described her work: "I did every conceivable job from ironing blouses and carrying luggage [Mrs Watt liked to save a penny, and it was a sore point that she put the heavy things in the hand luggage to avoid porters, and made Elizabeth carry the chamber-pots]; to intervening on her behalf, writing her letters and soothing people she had ruffled. I didn't get paid for this as it was called 'valuable experience.' I charmed people she antagonized against her own interests; I gave her affection when she made it difficult for anybody else to."

Elizabeth had two personas. Her friend Bobby McDougal would say after her death: "I knew Betty; not Elizabeth." Bobby thought that Elizabeth had a wonderful time. But to a closer friend Didy Battye, she reported that the trip was horrible. In one way it was a fulfillment of a personal nightmare—trapped like a fly in aspic, Elizabeth was back in the church basement of the Ladies' Helpful Mission.

Elizabeth hadn't the temperament for this kind of professional tourist travelling. "It is hard, in travels, to estimate the potency of a place. When a mind, teeming with half-followed ideas, [finds] no time to sort out and digest." In the Grand Hotel, Rotorua, New Zealand, she complains: "I've been looking at one of those Round the World prospectus pamphlets—it's vulgar and disgusting and sounds interminably dull. Dull, dull, dull."[14] While Mrs Watt thrived, she wilted.

At the interminable meetings (seventy-seven in New Zealand alone) Mrs Watt gave her speeches on the ACWW (which Elizabeth admitted were often inspired) and Elizabeth sold the pins, magazines, and books Mrs Watt was propagandizing. Occasionally Elizabeth also gave speeches on Canadian art or Canadian nature, and, at the social gatherings after, played piano, usually "To a Wild Rose," to the assembled

women. There were marathon days from nine A.M. until ten
P.M. being hero-worshipped by groups of small-town ladies.
She describes a typical evening in New Zealand:

> Change to red evening dress for dinner. Meeting in a
> Churchy hall. I sat on platform. So did the Committee,
> The Mayor, Mayoress, Girls' High School Repre-
> sentative, Women's City Club Representative, Women's
> Division of the Farmers' Union Representative, and they
> all welcomed Mrs Watt who spoke on "Women in
> Agriculture" with facts and notes. I played. A lady sang
> and two ladies duetted. Reception with tea, coffee and
> cakes at the hotel.[15]

While Mrs Watt might see that this "exchange of information
and forming of friendships" was foundational to creating an
"invisible and potent network," Elizabeth could not. One factor
accounting for Elizabeth's boredom was that she hadn't a political bone in her body. Though she had grown up in a household
that was visited by many of the significant figures in Canadian
and even international politics, and among her friends were a
number of young men who were to play crucial roles in
Canadian political life, including Lester Pearson, Charles
Ritchie, Eugene Forsey, Graham Spry, Frank Scott, and others,
Elizabeth disdained the political. Indeed, she may have disdained it precisely because it was her mother's world. Politics
was a social game of abstraction, played above the deep forces
that constituted true reality. It was a game for the social ego. A
friend in the British Labour party once remarked to her:
"You're not interested in politics. You're more interested in the
little things of life. Watching people. Not in the great issues and
underlying ideas," to which Elizabeth replied: "It's because
I'm only interested in the big things that I'm not interested in
politics."[16]

Elizabeth had not the rebel's capacity to leave Mrs Watt to
her own devices. She felt compelled to play along, and staged
her campaign of resistance secretly:

The point is I really am only interested in myself and the salvation of my own immortal soul. I thought that this six months' discipline would be good . . . I am the cat that walks by herself—and this experiment in administration, solicitation, and the way the world works is manifestly a mistake. . . . I wasn't made for their communal, citizenship, club world. . . . I looked at Mrs Watt in the midst of her country-woman gathering, making a speech, and I realized that you have to be slightly blind to *thoroughly* believe in *any* cause.[17]

Elizabeth was incapable of being satisfied by superficial encounters with anything, whether persons or the "indigestable sightseeing sight." There had to be intensity in each engagement, otherwise there could only be impotency and despair. "And I began to understand how, if I stood still for a while and listened and felt New Zealand, itself, the country, would come and permeate me, and I could love it, and start climbing hills again."

One source of consolation in her trip was her constant reading. "The poets are the most exciting thing I know—Auden, Archibald MacLeish, Conrad Aiken, Emily Dickinson, Spender, etc." While Elizabeth always castigated herself for her lack of discipline, the discipline she applied to her reading was rigid. Throughout the trip she kept a record of what she read and when, as well as her responses to the texts. "I simply couldn't make life mean anything all day—life or work. Nothing seemed new or exciting or worth the effort. But I found Hemingway good, and sane and his diary-style encouraging." Whenever Elizabeth felt catatonic, she made a list. She made lists compulsively, all her life. "Should I make a list, a resolution of willpower?" Elizabeth once wrote. "Would it rouse a slug?"

On this trip she discovered André Gide's *The Counterfeiters:* "I *adore* André Gide. There isn't even a dull or over-loaded sentence in the whole book—neither vagueness nor hammering. . . . [He] is alive in every sentence. He counterpoints and jumps but he always jumps at exactly the moment and to the exact spot you want to jump to."[18] It might be a description of her own future style. She was also revising the manuscript of "My Lover John," and writing poetry. From New Zealand she submitted poems to *Esquire*, including one titled "Poem Written in Spite of the Tropics." She kept a journal with the intention of publishing a record of her travels; by the end of February the manuscript would be seventy-eight pages. She also seems to have been sketching. One sequence of pencil drawings she called "The Dawn of Womanhood. A Biography of Symbols Showing the Awakening, Reaction, & Resignation of Innocence & the Inevitable Abandonment of Womanhood to the Moon."

To read Elizabeth's diary of this time is to read an account of someone sleepwalking. "Rich things happen every day. Rich thoughts tumble one upon the other," she reports. "Why can I not describe them?" Perhaps the explanation is to be found in the temperament of the writer. As a person and as a writer, Elizabeth had no interest in plot nor any capacity to describe character. Her gift, in life and art, was for the moment of intense feeling, what she would call the essence, the important core, the awareness to make the day alive.

With the kind of intensity Elizabeth had, she was open to continual manipulation by men who would not easily have been up to her ethic. She describes an encounter on the boat to New Zealand with a young man named Hall whom she calls "velvet eyes."

> He was cheaper and less mysterious today, but undoubtedly physically attractive to me. He can cause me violent overpowering moods and tears or utter unhappiness in a minute. What a fire, this sex! Never before have I fallen for a pair of velvet eyes and dark untidy hair and white teeth. . . .
>
> Is this business worth its trouble? Here I am sulking in my cabin for no apparent reason. What a destructive force until satisfied! What a consuming monster! Its thoroughness, insidiousness and subtlety astound me every time I suddenly see my puppet-like obedience to it.[19]

Elizabeth found herself in emotional conundrums of course, with Hall, and with a married man she met called Bill. "Is my alleged goal a self-deception? Is the eternal truth I tell myself I am seeking when I let men caress me, when I jump into the sea, when I dance and flatter myself by the flattery of men, is all this only devil's camouflage, worthless?" Her ambitions were Lawrencian: to evolve an almost mystical and indeed, for women, revolutionary ethic of love. She could speak of the beautiful abandonment of jumping back into the joyful pagan worship of the holy things of the earth. Though she doubted, she couldn't dismiss her "Pollyanna hopes and beliefs." "I honestly can't think [they are worthless]. Perhaps I am loath to leave my voluptuous pleasures, my conceited delights of the soul, my jealous aloof delights of the mind. Well, I can't know this. I can only go on following the strongest conviction, even if it is only a wolf in sheep's clothing."

When she could be herself, Elizabeth had a good time: she disappeared in Vancouver to have a wild spree on the town with local strangers, or later engaged in sexual contretemps with Bill or velvet eyes (though the affairs were never consummated; her first sexual experience was still two years off). But she found herself being fitted into the predictable double standard around sexuality. Elizabeth had a marvellous streak of sexual anarchy and though it attracted, it also disconcerted men and left her open to their censure, which she often transformed into self-censorship. At this stage, she therefore decided she was in pursuit, albeit clumsily, of eternal truth. She had broken with her mother's conventionality, but not yet with her high-minded romanticism.

Marriage might be a solution, yet she was afraid of the constraints of marriage:

On awakening: this terrible problem of matrimony! I don't want to get married any more. I dreamt I was married to John. First of all we were all at church singing hymns. Peggy and Lady Pentland behind. John was very sweet and helpful. But then I had to make an enormous bed for Lady Pentland and she didn't like the way I was making it.

It had piles and piles of extra blankets and things for
padding. I was trying terribly hard, but I couldn't please
her. John was somewhere in the background, sympathetic
but unable to do more.

How can I possibly marry and sign away my life?. . . .
Men, careers, one excludes all others forever. Where is
an occupation that embraces all things? And where is
a *man*?[20]

Elizabeth's "Pollyanna" belief was that there would be a soul
mate, "related to my species," with whom she could fulfil her
ethic of complete freedom, with whom she could live *and*
write. It was not necessarily an outrageous presumption. D.H.
Lawrence could write: "I think a man puts everything he is into
a book," and tell Jessie Chambers that he needed to be happy to
be able to write.[21] Elizabeth thought that the same ethic could
apply to her.

Sending Elizabeth round the world with Mrs Watt was like
sending Van Gogh to Tahiti with a United Nations fact-finding
team. It could not work. It was not until Ceylon that Elizabeth
seemed to feel completely alive. They arrived in Colombo on
January 6: "It was all so vivid, but so isolated from everything
else in my life. I hope it will not fade. These two weeks were
complete, utterly new, and utterly delicious. Nothing from the
past came dangling over."[22] The island with its scenery, its
food, smells, and colourful street life, was a revelation, and she
delighted in the Sinhalese people, whom she found cultured,
witty, kind, and proud. She began to recognize the racism of the
British colonials and found herself drawing apart from Mrs
Watt with her frequent references to the threat of Communism.
The ostracism of anyone who associated with the Sinhalese
made Elizabeth's blood boil, and she concluded that were she
Sinhalese she would be leading a red revolt.

Of course, with her new-found independence, she was heading on a collision course with Mrs Watt. "It was when we got
back, before dinner, that Mrs Watt's storm of abuse broke and
mutual aggrievedness came to a head." Elizabeth was thrown
into confusion. It was she who had failed.

The day of reckoning has arrived. My hand is trembling. Mrs Watt has complained of my rudeness, especially lately, which she says she can no longer stand. She has also mentioned my selfishness, and lack of sympathy. It is a blow, a shock. I knew I wasn't adequate. I could often feel her resentment, her aggrievedness. But I have in my own way, such as it is, tried to do the right thing by her . . . But I have failed dismally. I see myself in the hard, selfish, hateful light she must see me in—I have pursued a policy of compromise and *laissez-faire* too long. . . . I am a Philistine with whom *none* could live. . . . I prayed often and especially in the train behind the green curtains as I pulled out of Ottawa, that I would have the courage and the strength and the endurance to come through this with a noble character. Well, I haven't. I've failed.

(Poor Daddy! I've disappointed him again!) . . . Should I leave her at Port Said?. . .

When I started to write I wanted to gather my things and rush away out into the rainy night, but having argued myself into feeling it is *my* weakness and error and selfishness, I am inclined to take a less violent view of the matter.

But which way does my duty lie?[23]

It was all very well for Elizabeth to speak of duty, but this acquiescence to the need to please Daddy plunged her into self-disgust. Mrs Watt could be racist and self-indulgent, and yet it was Elizabeth who had failed in sympathy. One sees how deeply the middle-class standard of *duty,* the familial imperative of *character*, went. Clearly what was functioning underneath was an incapacity to believe in herself or in the importance of her own priorities, not surprising since she was an original and her ethic was new. The habit of being self-judgemental was so deeply engrained it amounted to self-sabotage.

I have grown so to love luxury and the flattery of social scenes and emotional splurges and soft soporific semi-sex that will anything ever happen to me?

I *think* so seldom. I *feel* so seldom. Mostly I just mope along. I'm cowardly. I'm stupidly polite. I try to make everyone like me. I'm willing to be mediocre and deny my God for the sake of peace. Can't I remember Huxley and Lawrence, Katherine Mansfield, Blake, Whitman, Spender, Eliot, MacLeish?

The split was agonizing, the self-rehearsals almost a form of spiritual flagellation. She *would* have her vision:

The world does it like this. The world will point at you and call you eccentric if you don't do it like this. Why don't you do it like this? Appease the world.

And, in appeasing, the vital years slip away, untaut, slack, loose, no use for chiselling the proper arrowy life.

Go my own way thoughtlessly?! . . . The delusion of self-expression? Surely I am sane enough to plot it into acceptable channels.

The urge of creative impulse? When was it ever so terribly urgent? I had quiet, peace; I had excitement and noise. When did I ever sit and write and write as I knew I should, as I knew I *must*, to live? But why have I been abasing myself lately? Denying my ego? Saying, "I must stop talking about myself. People will think I am conceited, or too introspective." What if they do? I am going against my own principles to deny my ego and its right of cockiness. I am trying to convince myself that I am nothing wonderful or mysterious or potentially great, when secretly I still hope and perhaps even believe I am. Ye Gods! I *should* believe I am.

This false mock modesty. Where did it come from? Being a sidling secretary? Toadying flattery to others?. . . Maybe it was extremes of vanity that killed the essential part of my vanity. The necessarily slightly self-deceptive cockiness that is the right, healthy, and natural sign of strident life.

Well, then, fat-head, I am a case. What is the cure? Something physical?—O *The Lives of the Poets?*"[24]

In Palestine, Elizabeth again seemed to awaken. After visiting the Women's League for Palestine, where Mrs Watt laid the cornerstone for a building, they travelled to Darania, the first Jewish communal settlement and visited a Girls' Agricultural College. Elizabeth was impressed with the college, with its life of outdoor labour, intellectual study, and communal ideal and requested to be able to return from London to stay for two months. She felt that the commune represented a real spiritual movement—the Jews returning to their country and roots: "Not once have the 'ideals' been hammered at me, nor have platitudes played any part in the explanations. What they say comes simply from the heart. There is no hypocrisy. You see, they really *are* an intellectual people with 'Torah' and music in their souls." Elizabeth felt exhilarated: "I can suddenly see the result of my six-month experiment and the things I have learnt on my travels. I am new-made. And I am pleased. O, if it can only continue!"[25]

An important encounter, not recorded in her diary, was her meeting with I.J. Hermann, editor and business manager of the *Palestine Review*, whom she met at the King David Hotel in Jerusalem. To him she gave the diaries she had been keeping and asked him how to turn them into a book. She thought of staying in Palestine, but again, indecision descended. "I began to dissect the reasons, and I came to a conclusion which is this: that I seek a mate, not a way of life. I must satisfy Nature before I invite God." She felt often "the hungry passion for children" and she was heading to London to find the one "related to my species."

She and Mrs Watt returned to England in February. At 8 Lowndes Street, Elizabeth picked up the threads of her life. It was to be a heady year, but still a year of waiting for life to begin. The relationship with Pentland was finally terminated, he insisting that he couldn't teach her anything or learn anything himself. Elizabeth felt cured and elated because the narcotic, the obsession was over. What replaced John was the will to work. "Free of my tyrant John. He is pleasant enough still to think about. I am free." She began to feel a new "or rather regained—independence of all people's mood."

Certainly her life was social. Almost immediately, there were innocent love letters from at least ten admirers. She was buying endless blouses, shoes, cosmetics, from Harrods, charging dresses to her mother's account at Peter Jones. She kept up a constant supply of books from Bolton's Library and periodicals—ordering *The Times, New Statesman, The Listener, Vogue,* as well as her Penguin paperbacks: "I love being in Europe," she used to say. "For 35 cents a week I can get all the literature I want and more." She took the occasional music lesson with Clifford Curzon, practising at the Hampstead home of Mike and Maryon Pearson, and resumed her extension courses in English literature at King's College, University of London. Her expenses, including the three guineas a week for the flat in Lowndes Street, were being paid by her father.

One new factor in Elizabeth's life was her friendship with Diana Battye, or Didy, as she was called. "From today I got the desire for Diana and her company. I thought I hadn't taken enough trouble to have women friends. Her life is so right, true and unvain. With her as a fortification perhaps I shall not even need John." Didy had been visiting at Government House in 1936 when Elizabeth first met her and was now a society girl back in London working in film and posing as a photographer's model under the name Doone Layman. She was a fascinating woman and it is not surprising Elizabeth would have selected her as an intimate among her round of friends. She was as dissatisfied as Elizabeth with the narrow constraints of her proper world. Though she found Louie a snob and Helen the straight man, Jane and Elizabeth, she felt, were terribly liberated. Elizabeth she loved for her capacity to turn everything into magic with a phrase. "Elizabeth was a free spirit, totally outrageous."[26] The anecdote she remembered best from her Canadian trip was going camping with Elizabeth in Quebec. They went to see a travelling circus whose main attraction was a dancing bear. Immediately they felt sorry for the bear who was a rather pathetic sight and Elizabeth decided the only solution to save it was to buy it. They brought it back to Government House in the back seat of Elizabeth's little snub-nosed Morris and hid it in a garage on the grounds. There was, of course, a small scandal when it was discovered.

After her world tour, Elizabeth seems to have been able to resume a regime of work. Even when she visited with Didy at her home, Billingbear Lodge in Berkshire, or with the Stafford Crippses at Goodfellows, Filkins, Oxfordshire, she kept up a pace of several pages a day on her work-in-progress, the travel book she called "Details of a Detour." Elizabeth called her manuscript "Details" because she could not find the overlying purpose, what she called "the meaning or epic pattern" so evident in Virginia Woolf's work. "I feel so loose and unknowing, just feelings, laziness, egotism. The labour, the labour, I must labour." She longed for direction: "O that I knew as my comfortable friends Yeats, MacNeice, Roger Fry, Virginia Woolf, A. Huxley, Spender, Auden, MacLeish, G.B. Shaw, etc."

May was a hectic month with preparations for the King's coronation. She was invited by the Coronation Hospitality Committee to a garden party at the Sussex home of Sir Paul and Lady Patricia Latham. There was the garden party at Buckingham Palace, and the endless at-homes: calling cards from The Countess of Bessborough, Eaton Square; Mrs A.J. Lascelles, St James's Place; Beatrice and Peter Spencer-Smith, St James's Place; Viscountess Trenchard, Eaton Square; Edward and Grisell Hastings (Eddie and Grisell, daughter of Lord Lammington, had been stationed in Ottawa; Elizabeth would later stay with them in Washington). There were also loving letters from a friend called Jimmie at the Prime Minister's Office in Stormont, Belfast. His parents were in the eighth carriage in the Prime Minister's Procession, just ahead of the King's. It is unclear whether Elizabeth rode in his carriage, but that she was in the full swing of coronation days is clear and no one was more pleased than Louie.

Her father spent a brief six days in London on a business trip in April and Louie, after hurried telegrams—"With you both in spirit" (April 19, 1937)—reported to Elizabeth on his return: "It was too wonderful to have Daddy home and have direct news of you. Daddy seems content with the daughter he left in

England. Your life sounds well ordered, a good mixture of work and play. . . . Much as I crave to see you I am very willing to have you stay over where life is richer and fuller . . . As long as you are happy and 'alive' you have my full consent."[27]

Jane Smart was always convinced that 1937 was Louie's greatest year. In Canada she could live vicariously her daughter's achievement—Elizabeth hobnobbing with the peerage and the political establishment. How seriously Elizabeth took the coronation is another matter. She may have played the sentimentalist for her mother, but to friends it was probably little more than an entertaining occasion for parties. Her friend, Jacques Bieler, could write from Montreal: "Glad to hear you're at the coronation. Glad to think there's at least one person there with a cool critical Canadian outlook, who will not be the least taken in by all the fanfare."[28] For friends like Grisell and Didy (neither was conventional), the whole thing would have been a lark. And soon Elizabeth was preoccupied with a bizarre incident that occurred shortly after Coronation Day. Didy suddenly disappeared after having had tea at the home of Viscountess Long. Scotland Yard was called in and the story filled the tabloids. A week later she was found, hysterical and sobbing, on the steps of the Regent's Park house of Lady Cynthia Asquith (her future mother-in-law). She was unable to remember a thing, but it seems unlikely that she had been kidnapped. More probable is that she had bolted from the trap she saw looming ahead, something Elizabeth would have understood.

Once free of John, Elizabeth had no lack of attention. It is likely that she needed to keep men on the hook. Charles Ritchie was writing from Washington, asking if he was a pre-Watt relic:

Feb. 16, 1937

Don't put me in limbo labeled old friend. Don't forget me. I don't forget that you are as beautiful as strawberries, that you know all Shakespeare's Sonnets, that you took surrealist photos before Dali, & that I was happier with you last

summer than I have ever been. I would say more but have
you not found some satisfactory ? my darling Betty.[29] ·

Or a bolder letter comes from a friend called Bill whom she had
met in New Zealand:

4 March 1937

Have you been leading lots more married men astray
since you left New Zealand? You really were good fun.

Good to hear that the candies I sent have added their
quota to your delightful body. It makes me feel I have a
right to—well, encompass what my hand can comfortably
hold. What do you think?

As a matter of fact, I do not quite understand you. It is
hard to find how much lovemaking there is in your body.
It's good fun trying to find out though. Your method of
handling a deux situation is most intriguing and I am looking forward to that walk in the Rockies.[30]

Elizabeth might have been amused by this letter. What do I
care, she may have said. "It pleases me to wiggle my seat . . .
Only sprawling vulgarity is authentic." Or she might have been
hurt at the presumption. In a 1936 diary entry she castigates
herself:

Think about dignity and pride wherein they are good and
proper and wherein they ought to be abandoned to the bigger attribute, generosity. But *anyway*, never be coy,
coquettish, or flirtatious in a physical way. Never egg a
man on to be physical. If he wants to leave, say goodbye.
This has always been a principle yet why have I abandoned it at times? Anyway, it defeats its own end. From
now on I must be *mental* until I find myself a proper mate.
However, may that be soon!

Because my days of virgin *hauteur* are at an end, even
as my youth is at an end—the days of Graham when I
could scorn what I thought was his meek self-deception.

Now I am grateful for a little kindly feeling. That's just my mistake. I ought to be haughty again, self-sufficient, and independent as I was, listening *only* to the inward voices.[31]

Very few of Elizabeth's relationships with men seemed not to have been amorous. She won them with her charm: "I was glad of my physical womanly charm and rejoiced to own such a powerful and easy weapon." Jay Hermann, who was corresponding from Palestine about "Details of a Detour" was won to her side on these terms:

I have already written to you that I am very happy to be your gardener, saviour, friend, guide—and I say now lover. The good news that you are free and saying it with so much gusto—you are free and ready to become enslaved and that is as it should be.

My blood pressure reaches high peaks at the prospect of having you here again. I think you are a girl with a tremendous amount of talent—but it requires a tingy bit of tending and gardening—since you insist upon using that word.

Despite the obvious condescension, Jay did take Elizabeth seriously as a writer. Apologizing for his delay, "I wanted to give your child undivided attention," he offers a detailed criticism of the manuscript. Part of the problem, he felt, was that while she as narrator was interesting and vital, the people she met were of little value.

May 15, 1937.

[Your book] must continuously arouse curiosity and interest. You defeat the object by giving staccato chapters. Many of the chapters are, in relation to the story as a whole, pointless and irrelevant even if they in themselves are good. Don't mind if I repeat myself here when I say that after 78 pages I do not know where you are heading and for what purpose. Nor do I get any cohesive picture of that part of Canada you traversed . . .

There is no doubt about it. You can write and where you fail it is in experience that will come with more writing.

My love,
Jay.[32]

It is unclear how much of Jay's advice Elizabeth used. She eventually abandoned her manuscript, perhaps finding it too unwieldy. She would need to invent a new prose form to contain her vision. But Jay gave her confidence of a kind. Though he confessed he had taken her up rather flippantly as a beautiful blonde, he found that she was the real thing and advised her not to allow her talent to run to waste: "If a person has the natural grace to pen and pencil so regularly thoughts and grave pictures out of the void and space and express feelings and poignant lines of poetry, then I say that person has to be beaten into an author."

On June 11, as she did each summer, Elizabeth sailed for Canada, spending the summer months at Kingsmere. She returned to the U.K. in August, travelling tourist class on the *Empress of Britain*. (In those days the crossing took eleven days; she had already made it about twenty times.) Her sense of frustration that nothing was happening to her was overwhelming. It was this August that she walked into Better Books on Charing Cross Road and found George Barker's poetry. On August 30, 1937 the first mention of Barker appears in her notebooks. She was reading *Janus* (1935), *Poems* (1935), and *Calamiterror* (1937) and was hunting down his poems in all the small magazines, including *New Verse, Life and Letters, Twentieth Century Verse,* and *Horizon*. It was now that she checked the biographical blurbs and discovered he was the right age, and decided he was to be the one. But, though she searched for Barker at parties, he was to remain a chimera that eluded her for three years.

That autumn, she decided to study theatre. The French avant-garde director, Michel Saint-Denis, had just immigrated to

England to open his Academy in Islington. It was an exciting experiment. Following the Stanislavski method, the two-year course included classes in breathing and voice, in calisthetics, reading from texts and improvisations, as well as lectures in the history and theory of the stage.

Sir Peter Ustinov, who was also a student at the Academy, offers a rather painful but revealing portrait of Elizabeth.

> Here, at drama school, I was for the first time exposed to the permanent presence of a veritable battalion of girls, all dressed on the first day of term in black bathing costumes—all that is, except one, a Canadian girl called Betty—I will refrain from identifying her further—whose black costume had not yet arrived, and who crouched among us in salmon-pink bloomers and a bra, looking like a Rubens nymph who had wandered into a sinister witches' coven by mistake. . . . I felt for the wretched Betty, crouching like Susannah in her salmon-pink lingerie on the first day of a new life for us all. It could not have happened to a less fortunate victim.[33]

Not until 1989 did Ustinov discover that the Betty he referred to was the author of *By Grand Central Station I Sat Down and Wept*. It never occurred to him that the timorous girl he had known could be the author of that book.* At the Academy he had categorized Elizabeth as one of the many girls who had no serious ambition to be actors; they were just filling in time, keeping out of Mummy's hair. The Betty he remembered was not easy to know. She seemed very secretive and provoked no gestures of curiosity. Seemingly friendless, she behaved like a squirrel, and gave the impression she had no experience whatsoever. She remained in his mind forty years later when

---

*Smart's sister Jane pointed out that the Betty of Ustinov's autobiography, *Dear Me*, was Elizabeth. When this was mentioned to Ustinov, he was astonished, because he had never connected the author Elizabeth Smart with the Betty he had known in his youth. When shown photographs of the young Elizabeth, he recognized her instantly. (Author's interview with Peter Ustinov, Toronto, October 21, 1989.)

he wrote his autobiography because she had provoked his compassion.

> Whenever we had to read from classical texts, she was invariably selected for the interpretation of amorous or, what was worse, suggestive poetry by the saucy giants of the past, and even discreet references like "the sweet disorder of her dress" caused the unhappy Betty to stammer and to giggle, turning a deep accusing red, and casting a veil of embarrassment about her. Her calvary came in a play of Beaumont and Fletcher when her partner in a dramatic text was supposed to say "Then will I pay a visit to the Low Countries," in a thinly disguised reference not to the Netherlands so much as to the nether reaches of the human body. This was too much for poor Betty, whose convulsive giggles eventually turned to bitter tears. I hope she is happily married, far from the coaxing reach of libertine poets, for she helped me to realize that my problems were negligible compared with some.

According to Ustinov, as a teacher Saint-Denis was dedicated to the theatre as a priest is dedicated to God, and something of a minotaur assessing human sacrifices offered up for his own gratification. Elizabeth was always assigned the suggestive parts. Ustinov thought of her as "poor Betty." She made herself indelible in his mind in one of the exercises in which they were to imitate animals: she "trotted around, an elk from her native plains, entangling her antlers with imaginary thickets and being hunted by erotic braves." He, on the other hand, played a salamander, and dozed comfortably in the sun for three whole months.

By temperament, Elizabeth was secretive, interested in neither power nor display. Out of her literary element, she was inhibited. No one at the Academy knew she was writing. In retrospect Ustinov could imagine that "we must have seemed awfully young to her. She must have been in training for something. If one is ambitious, one does things of that sort to stimulate senses one knows are there but dormant." Connecting the writer and the young student, he imagined her as "very romantic, a kind of Charlotte Corday in the secret service of romantic love. If I'd been what I am now I would probably have been absolutely fascinated by this strange creature, though at the same time I would have been frightened by her intensity." Ustinov felt that it also mattered that Elizabeth was Canadian. The Canadians kept to themselves; they were slightly exclusive. They felt different because Canada had not yet made an impression on the world. "There were hidden elements others were not to know, others who were in what appeared to be the mainstream. Such things have changed now that Canada has an identity."[34]

Ustinov was right about a number of things. He characterizes Elizabeth as the inevitable victim of male erotic projection (already he sees her as within the coaxing reaches of libertine poets though he knew nothing of her search for Barker). Far from being the vamp, among the student actors she was shy and inhibited, terrified of others' judgemental opinions. As in her earlier days at school, she kept hidden all she knew. It would have been inconceivable to them that this same young girl was about to break into the full strength of her creative powers as a writer. All Elizabeth ever admitted of this time was that, according to Michel Saint-Denis, she had absolutely no dramatic talent, and that Saint-Denis didn't like her. She was a couple of years older and he liked the women young and malleable. As with her musical training under Katharine Goodson, Elizabeth kept her theatre days private, and after her death most friends were surprised to hear she had ever studied theatre. Her real life went on outside the school. One of the people she met was Vanessa Bell (though not Virginia), from whom she purchased a painting. One day that spring Elizabeth disappeared from the Academy, as she had arrived, without explanation.

© Georgina Barker

Elizabeth's mother, Louise Emma Parr (around 1902).

© Georgina Barker

Elizabeth's father, Russel Sutherland Smart.

Elizabeth with Granny Baldwin, and sisters, Helen and Jane.

Elizabeth, age two.

The Barge, at Kingsmere in the Gatineau Hills.

"Betty" Smart, debutante photo, around 1935.

Elizabeth with Lord Pentland at a London club in the early thirties.

Mrs Alfred Watt on her world tour, 1933.

Jean Varda, in Cassis, France, 1938.

Alice Paalen in Mexico.

Garden of Los Cedros y Begonias, San Angel, December 1939. From left: Alice Paalen, Cesar Moro, Pierre Bral, Eva Sulger, Jeanne Bral, Wolfgang Paalen.

George and Jessica Barker, Sussex, 1939.

*One of the convicts' huts at Big Sur, California,
1940.*

*Portrait sent by George Barker to Elizabeth
(around 1942).*

© Georgina Barker

Elizabeth Smart in California, after meeting George Barker.

© Georgina Barker

George Barker, Elizabeth and Georgina at Willard Maas's penthouse apartment in Brooklyn Heights, 1941.

5   Dig a Grave and Let Us Bury Our Mother

Who am I angry at? Myself? NO . . . It is . . . all the
mothers I have known who have wanted me to be what I
have not felt like really being from my heart and at the
society which seems to want us to be what we do not
want to be from our hearts.
                    Sylvia Plath
                    The Journals of Sylvia Plath

Sometime in the spring of 1938, Elizabeth met the Greek col-
lagist Jean Varda at a party. At the age of forty-four, Varda
(called Yanko by his friends) was already well known as a
flamboyant and innovative painter with the reputation of a
bohemian-philosopher. He had all the arrogance and presumption that Elizabeth found most seductive in artists, since she
lacked it herself. According to his fond mother, Varda was, at
fourteen, a portrait painter worthy of hanging in the Louvre.
Born in Smyrna and raised in Athens, he joined the movement
of surrealist and Dadaists in Paris before the First World War.
In 1931 he settled in Cassis on the Mediterranean in a crumbling twenty-room mansion rented from a British lord. His
"mansion" became a carrefour for itinerant and indigent artists,
including the famous—Picasso, Braque, and Miró.

At the party a plan was struck—Elizabeth was invited to
accompany Varda and his friends to his home in Cassis. They
were all artists and the idea was to work. The friends included
Julian Trevelyan, a painter, and his wife Ursula, a potter; Ruth

Beresford and Roland Pym; Michael Wickham, a photographer, and his wife, Tanya; and Simonette, a painter and Varda's girlfriend. Elizabeth had been searching blindly for years for people who shared her "nervous system," as she would have put it. It seemed as if she had at last broken through the barrier and life suddenly opened with possibilities. Varda had exactly the temperament that could excite her, and he lived the life of artistic permission she had been seeking.

As was her habit, she wrote the account of her trip into a six-page manuscript called "For the Little Cassis Book."

When I sat down at the window waiting for them to come, I thought they would never come. I could not believe anything could ever happen to me, except what I laboriously pulled out of myself, by dry pain, alone. I was dressed in black, sober and ugly. For the death of my past? Or, as Ruth liked to say, "mourning for a future?" I don't know. I sat on the window sill poised. My past was finished and discarded. What if they should never come and I should have no future? Could I sit on my window sill, the narrow ledge of the present, eating apples forever? For I believed they *could* not come. Like gas, I thought life would not "take" with me. . . .

How shall I describe what Varda was to me then? He terrified me and yet I knew he was good. He was like an element. He was a wild manly gale. He smelt of brown earth and grass. But he had satyr's eyes. I knew no conventions would restrain him. Virginity to him was a fruit to be eaten . . . But I believed still nothing could happen to me—the power of the cold eye, the biting tongue. I was going to France to work. All these people were my stimulating friends. Women and men.[1]

For Elizabeth, who had been longing for "time to breathe, to live, to enjoy, to revolt, to be vulgar, to philosophize, to digest, to be flippant, to be irrelevant, to feel, to know, to understand," Varda was a revelation. Anaïs Nin could write of him to Henry

Miller: "Yes, I saw Varda, at parties. Loved him. See him as you do, a free, lusty and joyous man, a poet but a real man, very youthful, and his love of women is a relief after so much disparaging I see around me. He turns them into myths, poems, collages, delights of all kinds."[2]

Varda was, by most accounts, a delightful mythomaniac who collected people and turned them into a collage signed "Varda." Henry Miller was enthralled with his vitality. For him Varda was a *saltimbanque* who did everything with ease, never knew a dull moment, and had the delightful vigour of an animal:

> To Varda, women gravitate as naturally as bees to the flower. He enchants them, as Orpheus did of old. He clothes them in fitting raiment, tells them how to dress their hair, suggests the flower or perfume they should use, teaches them the use of their limbs, what stance to take, and whether to bound like an antelope or canter like a palomino. He endows them with all the graces. He also instructs them obliquely how to listen, or how most effectively to resemble the various musical instruments which he accumulates about him like weeds.[3]

To be equal to Varda's ego (even he could blush sheepishly at his own mythomania) one had to be formidable. Any gathering was a composition chez Varda. One did not have dinner with Varda. It was the "Festival of the Iniquitous Baptism," or the "Banquet of the Discordant Muses" (one remembers Elizabeth's Festival of Bacchus). At Cassis he loved the spontaneous party, when his puppeteer friends would drop by and he dressed the women as his own collages called possibly "Flowers Trapped in a Labyrinth" or covered them in coloured paper cut-outs: blue rhomboids, orange triangles, purple parallelograms, green trapezoids, lavender pentagons. Varda lived the myth of the artist, confident that reality would always be malleable to his great capacity for metamorphosis.

Elizabeth and her new friends travelled to Cassis by car, stopping in Paris to visit Varda's friends Alice and Wolfgang

Paalen. Paalen was also a surrealist painter and his wife Alice, a poet and painter who had been Picasso's mistress. They were simply part of the landscape now, though both were to become essential to Elizabeth when she later visited them in Mexico. For Elizabeth, the days were full of new worlds: sympathy, emotion, and an intoxicating excitement of the brain. "Varda in changing shapes and colours moves in and out like a tune on the radio which fades and grows sometimes disturbingly loud."

At a party in Paris, Varda made his first overtures. He backed Elizabeth against a wall and said: "'Take Care! Take Care! I am Oriental. I will not be played with!' It was like a sudden thunderstorm. His wild insistent pressing, his tears, his emotion." She was afraid. That Varda was disturbing in a way no other man had been is clear from the dream she records in Paris.

May 9

I had a dream last night and it contained all terror and despair. All things converged. From my two old and from my one strange new world the seeds came, more forceful than in their own wearily-beating day.

Varda symbolized the new. Always, in times of doubt and emotion in my dreams, I walk down Elgin Street* in a snowstorm, the whole world shrouded in a sort of pale twilight. The lights from the Roxborough† shine and it is always towards that that we are walking. There we part. But I feel that I am wrong to part—to send away thus—I am strangling and wondering which is true. He turns, hurt, proud, shut up, and goes down the lift—or up. Last night he lived up on the next floor. It was an open lift. I repented. I grew desperate to dispel the hard knots he was creating. I rushed to stop the lift and my hand got squashed.

I went into my flat. It was huge, and the glaring lights above shone on the ugly furniture, some of it in dust covers. I am full of remorse now for I see the sin I have committed against a gentle suffering man. Suddenly I love.

*Elgin Street, downtown Ottawa.
†The Roxborough Apartments, where the Smarts often stayed in between residences.

Then (dreams collecting always from the secretive dreariness of the day before) I look for a place to remove my tampax. There is a large room on one side behind, full of packing cases, and amongst them a toilet with a brown seat. I go towards it and sit down, bare. Then I look up and to the left are iron bars and all the girls from the LTS‡ holding the grating looking in and suddenly there are workmen all around. I rise quickly (perhaps pulling "T" but somehow later it reappeared in) and leave this cement floor place.

I am about to remove T in the dust-covered drawing room when Mummy and Daddy and Russel and Jane arrive and I am in an agony of guilt. I try to explain why I am in Paris. They believe me and love me. The room is filled with adolescent boys, friends of Russel's. This I remember made me draw some conclusion; I forget what.

Later though, Mummy fell over the banister and I just caught her in time by the tip of her coat (my black coat with the safety pins) and Daddy helped me draw her back. We kissed her, Daddy and I, but all the time Daddy was really kissing me, passionately. Mummy's face was red in patches marked off by ridges like a rose garden. We flattered her. She beamed. Our flattery saved her just in time but I remember the fact that it did utterly sicken me.

It went on for a long time, full of terrors and doubts and despairs. Varda always appeared walking by sad in the distance. . . .

I woke up in the middle of the night and I was terrified and trembling. It was still pitch dark. I was afraid. I was alone. I was in a strange country. Unknowns surrounded me. A baby bewilderingly came out of the womb. My feather mattress cover was on the floor. I drew it up and around to be the ultimate comforter.[4]

Though it is presumptuous, indeed foolhardy, to affect to psychoanalyze a writer's dreams in retrospect, one can see that this

‡ London Theatre Studio—one remembers Elizabeth's sense of exposure there.

must have been one of those exact informational dreams, recording with archetypal precision the dynamic of Elizabeth's psychic life. Certainly the terror of sex with Varda is patent. It involved guilt and blood; betraying father-lover; abandoning an ambiguous safety, the mother with the face of a rose garden, who must be flattered. It meant a terrible birth, into the loneliness of the self.

The people Varda had collected around him on this trip were all young British bohemians. Varda's current girlfriend, Simonette, was to say, "We were all rather good at falling in love with everybody. We were gypsies in a kind of way, all painting."[5] Elizabeth made a lasting impression on her. Simonette found her enchanting: "She was lovely, strange and mysterious." And generous. Though Varda's *castle* was spectacular, no one had much money. The arrangement was that each in turn provided the food. Elizabeth was known as the best off and Simonette as the poorest. "Betty's day came before mine, and she would always buy much too much food so that there was some left over for me." But most indelible was her memory of going for a walk with Elizabeth and she remarking that she was determined to have children by George Barker. "Betty hadn't yet met him but she felt that, no matter what Barker was like, the children would all be wonderful poets."

Early in their Cassis stay, Simonette broke with Varda, having fallen in love with someone else. Varda turned his attentions to Elizabeth, and though she may have anticipated and even hoped for this, she was at first disconcerted. Simonette said they would quarrel over who slept on Varda's floor (it seems that in her memory he was always careful to be short of beds). Elizabeth tried to use Simonette as protection, but Varda was not to be dissuaded. The pursuit began in earnest and, in fact, became violent. Simonette described Varda as "difficult, coarser than us. We were all well brought up and didn't do that kind of thing."

Elizabeth's stratagems for some semblance of control were astonishing. One day the group, having decided to go by boat to Martique, stopped at a run-down café for lunch and ordered a bottle of wine. Elizabeth refused to drink, saying even one drop would make her ill. To test her they gave her some wine in a glass of water and she immediately fell under the table. The others left. Not sure whether Elizabeth was pretending, Simonette returned two hours later to find her still under the table. Still puzzled by the incident fifty years later, Simonette wrote to Elizabeth to ask whether she had been faking that summer of 1938. The letter was returned. She did not know Elizabeth had died two years previously, but her curiosity is a measure of the hold Elizabeth could have on one's imagination. If Elizabeth was faking, she had stamina; she was certainly not going to be found out.

Yanko persisted. His salvo was: "On the thirteenth you will be mine." After Simonette left he assigned Elizabeth the room beside his, assuring her there was a lock on the door. The lock, it seems, was on the outside. The first day in her room, he attacked her. She bit and fought like a wild animal and they scuffled on the dirty floor. "Face fear. I faced fear. Ah well. Flowers must fruit."[6]

Unlike the account of the unsuccessful night with Pentland, Elizabeth's description of her first sexual experience is indirect, though the motif is sacrificial: "We walked up the road, up the hill, up the path to the haunted house, up to the stone altar among the pines. The nightingales warbled, the moon shone—the mountains of rock were bulwarks. We sat on the cold stone of the altar, all the time the nightingales trilled around."

But on the 14th she records the incident in retrospect in her diary:

May 14

There was a question mark in the sky only it was backwards.

There was a pine tree and the rest was blue. This is all. This is the key.

The yellow eyes are glaring at me without melting.

"*D'ou viens-tu Bergère?*"

From the beating of the heart O! like a pulse of the sea, uncontrollable, for a vision upwards through the thorns.

Should I have expected these tearings of the flesh by the way? For the *toiling* I had set my teeth against. Rip! Rip! The disobedient flesh and on top at last a soiled remnant gasping its goodbye. For me, these visions are a consummation worth the world beside. All I would give away and accept fiend's puny jeers. Then that unspeakable largeness wipes away those cloistral pickings of the nose, less than my sporting with the eight-day long Atlantic.

You see, even now, through tears just defeated, comes the balm, aerial souls of pine.

This is enough, and the upward mingling of the sun. . . .

Out of these rocks comes the saving essence—and by saving I mean no blasphemous poster on the summer road, but an overwhelming force of spirit that may be fierce wanting, by an uncondensed and unadulterated throe of upward desire, enter, enter the body and purge. O glorifying! O glorifying with a full full sweep of conscious space, as they say before leaving us no word, less than no word . . .

Yet the rocks tower above. Yet there are elements unfaced. My death to dare before I reach those green top trees, I attain the world, to drink in forever my overflowing metaphors.[7]

Elizabeth had fought sex a long time; it was so powerful. When she did submit, it was to a colossal mystery. Out of these days in Cassis, she emerged a writer. She had found the rhetoric of metaphor to contain her vision, surrealistic and sustaining. What is remarkable is the way she weaves the banal—"the cloistral pickings of the nose"—and the apocalyptic. There were still elements unfaced in this unspeakable largeness. She would dare.

She wrote to Graham Spry from Cassis: "I am so happy. It is so sunny. I think I shall never come back." "I feel shut off by time & distance & cash from the whole wide world. Days slip by. But I've written several poems & ten new pages of John . . . Life is cheap & pleasant here & I can work at last unhampered."[8]

And she wrote to her family:

June 4, 1938:

Dearest Mummy and Daddy,

This is an *ideal* life, and I see no reason why I *shouldn't* finish *both* my books. It is a life from which every possible inessential has been removed—even some I always used to look upon as essential have become quite unnecessary. We live well, in spite of spending about $2.50 each in a week . . . [There are] fresh Jerusalem artichokes, cherries from the tree in the garden . . . Soon figs and apricots will be ripe. We sail a little, we swim a little, we walk . . . we work . . . My bed is a folding camp which is very warm and chaste & smells of fresh hay. . . . [9]

In August Elizabeth returned to her beloved Kingsmere as she always did. She expected to be back in Paris that autumn, but the coming war conspired to keep her in Canada. She did not see Varda again until he came to Ottawa the following summer (he was in New York for an exhibition of his paintings) and their relationship resumed. But the extraordinary impact Elizabeth had on him is clear from a letter he wrote to her in 1941 after she had left him to pursue her relationship with George Barker. He saw her as a predestined creature, rampant on myth, and more powerful than he in pursuing her visions.

May 10, 1941

My dear Betty,

. . . I have had such nightmare, I would see visions of you after you left me that used to make me shake and scream in the middle of the night. In these dreams you appeared like in those monstrous profiles you used to scribble of yourself, the eyes were blank, without sight, you were always beside precipices, with an inane smile you were offering a flower to anybody or nobody. You were stark mad and shapeless.

. . . enough of the past. I quite understand you had to take a blind attitude towards anything concerning me. You had problems of much greater concern and immediacy. This attitude you took of me as the tough unbreakable guy who is always surrounded at the crucial moments by life, friends and opportunity to solace him was perfectly natural. . . . The fact is that your belief and the belief of any woman who preceded you proved true. Virginia came along. . . .

Yours cannot be a happiness as I could offer you. I knew all the time it will all seem insipid to you. You are of the type of woman who from Aspavia [sic] to Eva Sulger must needs dedicate her life to somebody. Not for any immediate palpable measurable happiness which your kind scorn but for some fulfillment which I guess although I don't quite understand. It is good luck you have found your dedication . . .

Well, dear Betty, I suppose with predestined creatures like you not a tear is wasted. It all goes toward the perfectability of the soul into [sic] which you believe.

Yours most affectionately,
Yanko.[10]

He asked whether she would like him to send on the collage he had done of her. In his portrait Elizabeth seems a comet trailing long nebulous trains, as though she were an erratic member of the solar system.

That fall of 1938, at the age of twenty-four and for the first time in her life, Elizabeth found herself grounded; her father, anticipating the war, refused to finance her return to Europe. Being stuck in Canada came as a shock. Although she had been in the south of France at the height of the Spanish Civil War, she was not compelled by the war that fascinated so many writers as the last stand against Fascism (she never wrote of it in diaries or letters). She must have known war was coming. Russel was not being particularly prescient in anticipating danger. Although

Chamberlain had signed his pact of appeasement with Hitler's National Socialists that September, there were many who understood with a kind of fascinated fatalism that Hitler's fantasies of a Greater Germany included not simply German-populated areas as he claimed, but the whole of Europe. Already people scanned the skies for the bombers that would announce the Second World War.

By temperament Elizabeth was a pacifist and she was appalled by the way people in Canada seemed ready to embrace the war frenzy. She felt their righteous indignation was a mask: a death-drive had been loosed and history was now in the hands of fishmongers. She would later write: "O Führer of self-love and self-hate, whose false moustaches fooled us into thinking he was not us: where is your twin enemy with the terrible banner of peace?"[11] In September she wrote notes for a poem expressing her disgust at the predatory lust for war:

> "Honour above life" says the complacent wife 3000 miles
>   from death . . .
> And the gaunt dreamers in their disturbed garrets
> Disaster-provoking eyes
> Seeing really, as they have seen so often in mind
> Bombs hurling from the skies . . .[12]

Many seemed relieved that the waiting was over and the doom had at last begun.

Had she had money of her own, Elizabeth might have found her way back to France that fall. Now she had to make do with Ottawa. The Smart family had again moved, and were renting Coltrin Lodge, an impressive house with sculpted gardens and columned entrance in the heart of Rockcliffe Park. Louie had reached the peak of her social ambitions; they could now have parties grand enough to require the attendance of the Rockcliffe police to direct traffic.

Suddenly Elizabeth was at loose ends. She felt (or imagined) pressure from her father to be out of the house, married, or earning money. Louie was still imposing the same domestic tyranny. In October Elizabeth went to visit Jane in Toronto and received the following missive from Louie:

9 Oct. 1938

Just a hasty note from Kingsmere where Daddy & I escaped to today as the town house in its state of confusion was too much for us . . . The new parlour maid is gentle, pleasant, & so far completely useless and there is going to be some severe regimentation before the present staff are much use to me. Also there seems to be so many odds & ends missing including a dozen silver dessert spoons. It's so upsetting to my mental peace. . . . Really I think ineffectual and untidy people should be banished to muddle along together in some south sea island & not confuse & make life hard for people who are trying to make life pleasant & orderly for themselves & others (I know you will enjoy this as reminiscent of Aunt Harma). There is a terrific amount to be done & the expense staggers me, so I feel for Daddy & all our sakes. I must try & get things running nicely & give him some kind of reward for all he is spending.

Mother[13]

P.S. Daddy & I sat behind four of your contemporaries at the Don Cossacks & we agreed that whatever the faults of you two—you are bigger & better & more beautiful in every way than those four so realize we shall have hopes for you.

With France behind her and the Cassis manuscripts piling up, Elizabeth felt the need to do something professional. She also wanted to become financially independent, with the idea of returning to Paris or New York. Though she felt journalism would interfere with her writing, with her usual alacrity she plunged forward. On December 12, she got a job on the staff of *The Ottawa Journal*, writing feature articles for the city editor, light editorials, placid accounts of women's activities for the women's pages, and social notes. It wasn't a solution to her financial problems. The paper paid her $2.50 a week on the grounds that she was living at home and didn't need the money. And still she had to buck Louie's efforts to control her life. She worked mornings and evenings, which interfered with dinner parties and Louie's social engagements. Louie would try to keep her at home saying: "Stay in bed, don't go in," bringing up wonderful breakfast trays to seduce her; she felt working on the *Journal* wasn't quite the thing to do.[14]

Elizabeth spent days (and nights) writing up female temperance meetings, missionary societies, and sometimes wild flowers, Douglas Fairbanks, Jr., "The Price of a Debutante" or the "Opening of Parliament." It was a lark and she enjoyed much of it. Her pieces were provocative, amusing, and sometimes outrageous, as when she suggested that a maypole be constructed in Connaught Place to celebrate the impending visit of King George VI. Mackenzie King could lead the Royals in the maypole dance.[15]

One of Elizabeth's friends among Ottawa journalists was a young woman called Muriel Flexman who had come from the west to work for Canadian Press. She remembered Elizabeth doing cartwheels in her crinolines on Parliament Hill when they visited the Press Gallery. "She simply felt she had always wanted to do it. She could do anything. How many of us can?"[16] Flexman saw Elizabeth as dramatic: "She liked an audience. It was not exhibitionism; rather she needed a foil, someone who was up to her and could stimulate her, could back her up. She knew what she wanted." In Flexman's memory, she seemed to have had a different part every day:

> One time we had an hour off. It was the first day of Spring and Betty decided we should go in search of the first flower, the hepatica. We were walking in the street and a friend came by in a car. Elizabeth hailed him and asked to borrow his car for an hour. I was astonished. It wasn't something I could do. We drove to Kingsmere and Betty climbed out, peeled off her shoes and stockings, and climbed the hill; I followed in my heels. She was

marvellous about wild flowers, knew each flower and its season, and knew whether it was native or an immigrant.

On one occasion Flexman was invited to dinner at Coltrin Lodge and found Varda there visiting from New York. He seemed dark, wild, and dramatic in style. Elizabeth was dressed as a June bride, all in white, and the room was set for a wedding—with silver candlesticks and white lace. Varda gave her three flowers: a red tulip, a blue hyacinth, and a yellow rose, the primary colours, and placed them on her head. It seemed to Flexman as if he were trying to bring her down to earth. She didn't seem to mind. "Betty was dramatic and spontaneous, fierce in her desire to live life to the fullest. I only knew her three months and yet I savour having known her."

That January Elizabeth began sending poems to Lawrence Durrell's Paris magazine, *Booster*. Though several were accepted, they were never published. The magazine died that spring, but a friendly correspondence with Durrell continued. In an early letter she asked Durrell's advice about other magazines to which she might send her poems, and told him whom she liked among the poets: "I've read nearly all Auden and MacNeice and I like them very much. Spender too I found very exciting when I discovered him, but lately I've been disappointed. (I don't like politics. I think it's as bad to get so emotional about how to run a country as to get hysterical about the housework and hipped on the housemaids' idiosyncrasies). . . . About my favourite younger poet is George Barker. He excites me most, even when immature . . . I liked a woman I discovered in the only copy of *Delta* I've seen, called Antonia White."[17]

The reference to Barker was an offhand remark, but Barker was a needy friend and Durrell saw an occasion to help him. He had concluded Elizabeth was wealthy and gave her Barker's address, suggesting that he would be willing to sell manuscripts. With twenty-five dollars Louie had given her for clothes, Elizabeth bought her first Barker manuscript, a poem "'O Who will Speak from a Womb or a Cloud?'" which appeared in Barker's collection *Lament and Triumph* (1940):

Not less light shall the gold and the green lie
On the cyclonic curl and diamonded eye, than
Love lay yesterday on the breast like a beast.[18]

One can imagine Elizabeth's reaction to this, her first Barker acquisition. Barker, like she, was in love with the rhetoric of language and the mystique of poetry. "What is poetry?" she wrote in her diary. "Poetry is life moving, terrible & vivid. Look the other way when you write." It never occurred to Elizabeth that any relationship would be possible with Barker other than to love him. It had long been clear, since the days she first read Barker in Better Books and let it be known that this was the poet she would marry, that Barker would be the *He*.

Still, what she wanted from Durrell at this point was advice as to her writing:

Jan. 15, 1939

Dear Mr. Lawrence Durrell,

You're quite right about my technical equipment flopping on me. I've made the most desperate efforts ever since I can remember to get discipline, even to going around the world with the most arrogant old woman I could find. I suppose I've always hurles [sic] myself in the wrong direction. But what *is* the right direction? . . .

"Is it stodgy up there?" Well, worse, probably. It is the most exhilarating, exciting, inexhaustible country in the world, *physically*, but there are no people in it, no poets but inarticulate ones . . . All the people who might have been poets go into External Affairs and never speak again. Ottawa is full of happy married couples, snobbery and caution. It is a place to live a pleasant life if you want to be pleasant and nothing but pleasant, but if you even mention poetry they say you pose. . . .

[People] think of poetry as a namby-pamby dressed in a badly-fitting, beige chiffon dress, rather than the kick in the pants it really is—as real and immediate. . . .

Canada I adore but I'll die if I have to live here. It's like a huge mine full of gold but I haven't even got a chisel—only hands. O it'll take *hundreds* of years. I spose we'll have to start to decay (being now raw and green) before things will begin to happen. . . .

I hope you have fun in Greece and time enough to read this History of Canada and Autobiography of

Elizabeth Smart, spinster.

About age—25, two weeks ago, but slow to rouse, like the elephant.[19]

On June 6 Louie, who had travelled to London with Russel on business, was writing to Elizabeth at Coltrin Lodge. "I imagine that you are keeping home beautifully and liking it. Do keep up the training of the little maids. They are such good material to work on & they mustn't be spoiled when I get back. I wish Daly could see how the brass on this side is polished. However, I feel they do their best."[20] Perhaps this was the final straw. Desperate to get out, Elizabeth picked up her life and, on July 6, fled to New York where her sister Helen was living. "The vast towers—the life, gaiety—here now colossal life. England dead in a winding sheet. Canada not yet conceived." Again she had to muster all her strength against the censors. She had been warned that New York was glittering and cruel—a young woman could never stand it. "Thus the elders wag their heads and point their fingers and cluck-cluck, and little ambitious girls in home towns decide, after all, they had better marry the pimply persevering suitor from over the way."[21] But she found it was easy. She just boarded a bus.

She got a job doing publicity for the J.B. Neumann and Nierendorf art galleries, and on the advice of friends went to Powers photographic agency to try her hand at modelling. She also took a stack of manuscripts, including "My Lover John" to a New York agent. The agent handed them back, apparently shocked that such a young woman and seemingly proper and well-behaved, could write a novel about male impotency. Lawrence Durrell had suggested she try to find an American publisher for George Barker's new book of poems, starting with New Directions. He also offered to ask Henry Miller, then in Greece, for advice as to where Elizabeth could send her own manuscripts and suggested she send some poems to Desmond Hawkins. By this time he was disabused of the notion that Elizabeth was rich. "Are you writing anything?" he asks. "Running away from home is not all jam, young woman, and starving don't go with writing poetry unless you are unusual. So don't starve and do write, and keep out of evil ways as your mother father and brother would have you do. And if they ask you whether you believe in Chamberlain do not murmur under your breath 'The yellow-bellied Birmingham rat.' It gets you nowhere. Just sigh and say 'As for me I'm neutral.'"[22] Elizabeth wrote back to castigate him for his paternalism.

She also wrote to Henry Miller, ostensibly asking for advice about how to obtain his out-of-print books. He replied that he would be keen to meet her, as Durrell had spoken of her and liked her letters, but not to send him her manuscripts. He hated the job and was no good judge of other people's work anyway. He told her to just keep writing her books, that was the only important thing.[23]

There were many downs in New York when Elizabeth felt vulnerable and useless. There were no chains to bind her and she felt that she was floating in a great ocean all alone. As it had been once in London, her terror was that she would be submerged. Moments of consolation came from the attentions of others. She speaks of two male friends: "From their two pairs of eyes flow the most buoyant doves into the huge empty stadium of my ego." She needed what she called the "petrol of flattery." There was an emptiness, a hole in Elizabeth that she had, desperately, to fill. There were good friends in the city, including Marian Scott, Jacques Bieler, and the painter, Pegi Nichol, who had taught her at Elmwood and of whom, one might add, Louie did not approve. (Of Pegi, Louie had said: "She is completely selfish and temperamental and undisciplined. The more I see of the 'arty' life the more I think that they give small return for the confusion they create.") As always, Elizabeth had a good time, but she wanted to arrange the threads of her life: "See what may come! Home in dark cafes! . . . The desire of other people! The rich curiosity. What can be done to outlet it? make it into a world?" New York was a beginning.

Yanko came to New York, and his presence revived her. He was the one stable thing her eye could pin its giddy focus on. Though Elizabeth had learned to negotiate her way through the world with charm, she was, according to her sister Jane, deeply shy. In the social world Yanko was her buffer. Again she concluded: "I see love is the second most searched for after the first cruel thrusting forth. I can only live, in its warm envelope, expanding, breathing, like a live, blind thing, more blessed than the embryo for it *knows* its own bliss. Be my surrounding cloak."[24] The notion of love as a womb, a birth, was an obsessive image for Elizabeth.

On September 1, while Elizabeth was in New York, Hitler's panzers rolled into Poland. Two days later, France and England declared war, and on the 10th, after a week of purely formal neutrality, Canada followed. Fifty-eight thousand men joined the Canadian army that first month. Elizabeth wrote in her diary: "The ghoulish aboriginal rites over the air of Hitler's 'Peace or Destruction' speech. The clapping and foot stamping like a tom tom's beat, gathering hysteria. All in the six o'clock grey dawn. Helen crouched over [the radio] . . . a long drawn out terror." The World War that was to kill millions had begun, and was to be the backdrop against which Elizabeth pursued her ethic of love.

In New York, Elizabeth had not escaped the long reach of Louie. On October 9 Louie phoned from Toronto—hysterical. Any time her daughters seemed to be slipping from her control, she had the intuition to obtrude. Elizabeth was not home and she poured out her bitterness to Helen: if Elizabeth were going to marry Yanko she might just as well commit suicide; Elizabeth would have killed her, etc.; Jane had brought up the subject of marrying her current boyfriend D'Arcy Marsh; she had a cold and the war was getting her down; it was all impossible. Elizabeth's reaction was predictable: "I am glad I was out. But way below I am afraid she may catch me and drill her fierce bitter will into my escaping life, and I am troubled by her and for her."[25]

Louie need not have feared for the moment. Elizabeth had no intention of marrying Yanko. He did not meet her expectations of complete love. In fact, Elizabeth had understood something about Yanko:

> For I say to my friends, O you should meet Yanko. There is a man that knows how to live—who can greet each day as a new day, who loves, who gives, who can receive. He is gay and happy as a child, he enters every fun, he fills other people with gaiety and happiness, YET the tragedy grows on his face.
>
> Is the hiddenness—the impossible-to-be-disclosed hiddenness—the tragedy? That even he cannot know, cannot, will not, could not bear to tell himself, and so it is written on his face?
>
> This is the wall. And though the wall's softness, the tender gesture, comfort the weary head, the spirit weeps. I cannot uncork my wine into the unknown bowl.[26]

Elizabeth was in fact being honest to her own myth. She felt love was plunging to the depths of self, not for the sake of the other, but under the absolute compulsions of the self's own directive. "He *must* devour me. Minute by minute pouncing on it ravenously. Not for my sake—because he loves me so much he wants me to be happy—For his own sake—*Only* because he is compelled." In Yanko she sensed a fear that kept him frenetically moving. By Yanko's own admission, his ego kept him afloat and free of any disaster. There would always be another woman whom he could put into a collage signed Varda.

At the end of November, after resisting the idea of going into advertising copy-writing in New York (she wasn't quite ready to settle down), Elizabeth decided to take up the offer of the Paris friends she had met, Alice and Wolfgang Paalen, to visit them in their new home in San Angel outside Mexico City. She was desperate for some kind of anchor: "I have lost my polarity. Since about a year I have been dizzily revolving, jaggedly, convulsively, or being stuck stagnant in some miscellaneous pocket. The hectic *Journal* life kept the issue at bay . . . But now . . . I am indeed floating in the great ocean alone."

She left New York on *The Siboney*, November 24, 1939; many of the passengers were European refugees fleeing to a neutral Mexico. Again Elizabeth was escaping—alone, alive at last. For the first time she travelled steerage—"here I was taking the vomiting body of humanity to my bosom." Trapped in her own psychic battle, Elizabeth could be romantically cavalier about her fellow passengers, identifying her escape with theirs in her diary: "I said smiling when I had to lie on the canvas cot, and they vomited on all sides so that it splashed right onto my face, and the stench was everywhere, O I am in the thick of it. I love love love this my humanity, my people, themselves. It was so good—I was so escaped I smiled all over and said not one man am I expanded to, but all men and all women . . ."[27] The refugees fleeing Nazi persecution were simply a symbol.

Perhaps Elizabeth might have had the opportunity to know the refugees as individuals and to be sensitive to the tragedy of their fate, but, true to form, almost as soon as the boat sailed, a cable arrived from her family fowarding the fare for first-class passage. A steward was dispatched to steerage to collect her. At the time, she wondered if it was Helen or her father who had cut short her fantasy of escape, though in the story she was to write about the trip, she makes her mother the culprit. Again she was caught—pleased at the attention and comfort, but knowing its cost—"Can I sustain my great adventure in this familiar comfortable isolation? Cherished and guarded, my work is double—to break through the misty clouds that lull and ease, and to translate when I get there."

The hold her Ottawa world still exerted cannot be exaggerated. She captures it perfectly in an image from a dream she was to have shortly after. She dreams of running from Yanko:

I packed things, some red crêpe paper. Then everyone gathered sitting on a highly polished floor, a scene like school, only the head mistress (Mrs. Birch) teacher's house, also half the governor-general and diplomatique. Some teacher asked me a question and I looked to answer, but I had on a hat with a veil pulled so tightly that all my features were squashed together. I tried to pull it off but it was too well tied.[28]

The Siboney travelled via Havana and Vera Cruz. From there she took the night train to Mexico City and was in San Angel on December 2. Although it began inauspiciously, the trip was to alter everything. For a woman of Elizabeth's temperament, it was only another woman who could help her to sort out the devastating mother archetype she carried in her head. There was a part of her that was still slightly afraid of women. Alice Paalen would change that. Once she had left behind Yanko, Elizabeth was at last free to listen to the movement, the things around her, and "*not* only hear the loud ticking of the man's psyche beside me."

6 Music and Sappho's Girl

Eros once again limb-loosener whirls me sweetbitter,
impossible to fight off, creature stealing up.
Sappho
LP, fr. 130.
Translated by Anne Carson

To me, Sappho, you are like the lotus unfolding.
Elizabeth Smart
Necessary Secrets

The Paalens lived at "Los Cedros y Begonias" in San Angel at the centre of an exuberant artistic life. Austrian born, Wolfgang Paalen had emigrated to Mexico in early 1939, probably fleeing, like many, the impending conflagration in Europe. He was a surrealist, and when Elizabeth arrived he was in the midst of organizing, with André Breton, the first international exhibition of Surrealists in Mexico City.[1] The Paalens' friends included Diego Rivera, and the Peruvian painter and poet, César Moro; there were also artists at a nearby colony at Lago de Chapala. As Christmas approached Elizabeth was caught up in a social whirl. She went with the Paalens to Diego Rivera's birthday party. She found him warm and benevolent, and delighted in his house with its layers and cubbyholes on the outside, and the rooms within crowded with Mexican sculptures and his own portraits. She met his second wife, Lupe Maria, and his mistress, Navia, though not Frida Kahlo, since

128

Kahlo and Rivera had recently been estranged. Much later, when she came to know her art, Elizabeth would regret having missed Kahlo. She may have seen in Kahlo's life, curious parallels to her own.

But more important than any of these social encounters, it was as if at Los Cedros y Begonias, Elizabeth had walked into exactly the right pattern to jar her own sensibilities awake. The Paalens lived in a *ménage à trois* with a Swiss friend, Eva Sulger. The domestic arrangement intrigued Elizabeth. Paalen, the artist, was the centre around which the women moved as satellites. Alice was the muse, the one to consult for advice about work, and Eva the handmaid, "the attentive, humble one, waiting for orders, service, rebuff."[2] All four were working: Paalen was painting, reading Nietzsche and studying astronomy—the house contained a tower and telescope—and he was studying books on mathematics, space, and time. Alice and Elizabeth were writing poetry and translating each other's work (as Christmas presents, Elizabeth made miniature books of her poems). Eva too seems to have been writing poetry.

Elizabeth was fascinated by the dynamic in the household where the man had two women "like a pair of crutches." Eva was quite straightforward in her mind. She was the conventional groupie and had attached herself to an artistic household, her childhood discipline in self-denial leading her to accept the minor role—sweet but with a "face like a skull and her shoulders huddled and she always thinks of things to be done, and sees about them, and does the dirty work and worries . . . her feet like whipped but faithful dogs."

In many ways, Paalen also conformed to his artistic set, and it is interesting that Elizabeth is rather ruthless in her portrait. She saw Paalen as proprietorial and intolerant, needing the women to keep fears of his own inadequacies at bay. "Today began with the knots in the stomach—Paalen's voice with the damning note in it for all who did not agree—dictating and damning. Alice tried to put forward a view but he called it not thinking clearly, childish, not seeing before her nose. . . . I wouldn't dare venture out to get that scathing rebuff, and she only ventured timidly."[3] Elizabeth searched for images to characterize him: "suddenly the distant train steel shrieked like a trapped woman and afterwards the masculine pursuing whistle, low, predatory, sure." It's as if she were thinking of Paalen when she later wrote of:

> The frail disgruntled geniuses [who require devoted attendants] . . . and grind them into the ground in the course of using their help, ignoring their needs, telling them, convincing them, that their greatest possible glory is to be a handmaiden to the Muse of a genius.
>
> When I was young, I scorned such geniuses, I despised their miniscule gifts, colossal egos, out-of-touchness with the suffering of others.
>
> But still. I see their need, now.
>
> There must be a more elegant way of creating confidence for yourself—the safe ground on which to stand and tremble.[4]

Paalen predictably attempted to induct Elizabeth into his coterie. And Elizabeth, predictably, was half-caught. Paalen flattered her—he claimed he had fallen in love with her in Paris and had been sick for a week. But she felt a loyalty to Alice—which he dismissed as Christian and bourgeois—and she recognized that his pain was vanity. He said he wanted women to be drawn to him irresistibly, because they couldn't help themselves. Though this was not far from Elizabeth's own ethic, in Paalen she saw it as a weakness that longed for tyranny since it included all women. His advice she also saw as manipulative: "He said if I wanted a pleasant happy life, Yanko would be fine—But if I wanted to accomplish something, the facility was dangerous—I must be unhappy to create. He spoke about his *ménage*—said he couldn't bear to have the intimacy of two and with three he could be alone in a crowd and that would be better." "Can I have no avenging whip?" Elizabeth wrote in another context, but it would have been welcome here since, though she saw his callousness, she still had to struggle with what she called "insinuating motherhood," the impulse to respond to a perceived need. "I will not be deceived. I was a mother to my mother. I am scarred with my passionate sympathy, my abortive tenderness, and I will not yield," she wrote in her fictional reinvention of the moment in the novella *Dig a Grave and Let Us Bury Our Mother*.[5] As the man leaves, the female narrator feels "Knives cutting me, thrust in my stomach, mother, woman, watcher clawing like wildcats in the bed." It is the hereditary line of the mothers that dictates passivity, responding to the man's needs against the claims of the self.

But it was Alice Paalen who was to be what Elizabeth would have called her personal drama. It is questionable whether she knew an objective Alice Paalen, for Paalen functioned as a mirror onto which Elizabeth could project elements of her own psyche. Elizabeth knew this clearly, as she wrote in her fictional account: "I am in the enemy I fight, like Jonah in the belly of the whale. There is no escape yet from that umbilical cord that winds round me like a hangman's noose."[6] It was essential to understand Alice Paalen as a vehicle to understanding herself.

Alice Paalen was clearly an unusual and gifted woman. Anaïs Nin describes her to Henry Miller:

> I met her today at an exhibition. She is striking in appearance. Tall, dark-haired, sunburned, she looks like a Mexican-Indian woman. But she was born in France, in Brittany. Her smile and her expression are dazzling, dazzling with spirit, wit, life. She has some trouble with her hip or leg, which makes her limp. Her paintings are completely drawn from a subterranean world, while her descriptions of Mexico are violent with colour, drama, and joy. . . . She talks interestingly about Picasso, whose mistress she was at one time, and who delighted in withholding pleasure from women.[7]

At one level, Alice Paalen's liaison with Wolfgang Paalen was not hard to fathom. In fact it is the familiar rationalization that draws most intelligent women to subordinate themselves to the artist. Paalen needed her and the thing that drew her to a man was to be needed. Paalen might be dictatorial, intolerant, and thoughtless, but on the other hand he was one of the most intelligent, really intelligent men she had ever known. (It seems almost a rule—if the male artist speaks of his lover's beauty, a woman speaks of her lover's genius.) Alice clearly gave Paalen's work priority over her own. She explained to Elizabeth: "He is one who should paint all day and write all night—he was not made for a normal pleasant life with other people—he hated most other people and was always terribly tense and full of new ideas." Paalen, she concluded, must have an unhappy life, and as her life belonged to him, why should she not have an unhappy life too. Elizabeth records Alice's rationalizations in her diary: "It was hard and lonely, to have cast off all belief and safe holds as Paalen had—it was not easy—it made him unstable—it was terrible to live with—but she flattered herself she could help him." The other side of the relationship was that Paalen provided the necessary catalyst to Alice's self-confidence—encouraging her to write poetry, criticizing it. When the towers of her belief in Paalen crumbled, she would become ill, all her own confidence gone.

Elizabeth didn't question the need to be needed. In fact, she writes as if in explanation: "You see, you see her true goodness—her always humble always questioning soul? She needs to be needed—and Paalen called me adolescent when I said I wanted to help Yanko." The basis of the tragedy was not Alice's subordination but Paalen's misuse of Alice's goodness. He, Elizabeth felt, had not the courage to live up to Alice's level: "Her fingers caress life's pulse. Life flies by him and he grumbles because he feels a draught."[8] Imagination, not intelligence, were what seduced Elizabeth. And she was certainly not ready to look at the unequal dynamic of power on which the symbiosis fed nor at the self-destructive element of such goodness.

A more immediate drama had to be played out. Alice Paalen was a poet, beautiful, unconventional, and exotic, with experience vastly different from Elizabeth's own sheltered life. In her, Elizabeth encountered for the first time a woman with whom she could be completely open. "Your beautiful palace, Alice, I could walk into it wide-eyed and innocent and betray no one. Bringing too the most far and secret boxes of my heart and my distrustful soul." Elizabeth immediately translated the encounter through mythological references. She was right to do so since the friendship was played out, at least on her side, at the deepest psychological level. It was both Sapphic and narcissistic. "Alice," she wrote in her diary of December 18, will be "the world's lover-mother. She is all tenderness. She could not hurt." Elizabeth knew she could trust Alice in a way she could, as yet, trust no man.

The attraction between the two women was erotic and Elizabeth was at first the passive recipient. She wrote in her diary:

> She leans over me as into a pool, tender, her hair falling, her eyes eternally smiling, but like jewels smiling, their smile cut out eternally and unchangeable, her mouth too stretched and smiling the eternal smile, a woman taking pleasure in a dream. And her whole smiling face, with its dark falling hair is like a reflection in a pool—her glance smiles on, only the water makes it waver and tremble. The smiling gaze penetrates, is unceasing.[9]

The beautiful narcissistic image is wonderfully precise. Elizabeth knew that she, as the reflection gazing up into Alice's face, was gazing back at herself. Not through a man could she discover herself, but only through a woman.

Before there was any physical consummation of the erotic attraction, Elizabeth records a dream about her mother:

December 20

> I dreamt a long dream of Henry Miller and his friends and of escaping and indoor swimming pools and then my mother and a flock of sexual babies and Neumann—my mother had liked the preliminaries, not knowing or suspecting where they led, but when she came back from Neumann's she was terrified. Neumann had tried to put his hand under her dress. She said Look! and she lifted her skirt and showed me how she had sewn her underskirt

together into a kind of below-the-knees bloomers, with great untidy stitches in sailor's strong thread. She was defiant, but I touched her face and it was as hard as stone, petrified with fear. All over she was hard lumps. I was filled with compassion for her terror arisen from ignorance so I sat her down sprawled in a chair and told her to relax—"Now your toes," I said, and she relaxed her toes—and I went all the way up, being careful, I remember, not to mention any delicate parts (don't say "thighs," I remember I said to myself—change it to "top of your leg"). Gradually she thawed out and I went away to a cafeteria to get something to eat.[10]

She had already transmuted the liaison with Alice in the depth of her own psyche into an encounter with her mother. The mother she incorporated had to be soothed—the fear of sexuality; but also the mother image sets up the predictable dynamic—the frenzied desire for escape and the desire to comfort. She was indeed, as she would later put it, at twenty-six years of age about to give birth to her own mother.

She wrote in her diary on December 25: "I am hiding something. Did you know? Why am I hiding it? It is not shame, nor even a sacred secretness. It is something only the body's language can say, oiled by the strange tides of mysterious passion." Clearly, the relationship had been consummated. She tried to find lyric expression for the experience: "Monday night peering peering into womanhood—grasping new worlds, pliable like seaweed stretched and floated."

The two escaped from the Paalen household and went to Acapulco for a week, convincing Wolfgang that they must go because of Alice's ill health. At Calete Beach, Alice found other lovers, but the intimacy and revelations continued. Elizabeth felt exhilarated and wanted to work. "I want to work at some definite work so I can measure my accomplishment. But since my mother forgave me, and I could feel some tenderness again, I am no longer possessed by her and my dissipated forces embrace the wind. Fiercely free the concentration till and willy-nilly pearl is born. *Think.* "[11] Within a week she left the Paalens' for Hollywood to join Yanko, and though she had helped with the arrangements she missed by five days the opening of Paalen's First International Surrealist Exhibition of Surrealism at the Galeria de Arte in Mexico City, which, it was said, half of Mexico attended.

While she was at Los Cedros y Begonias, Elizabeth had started work on what she called her "Mother Book." She had first to struggle with the form since she felt the traditional novel was devious—hidden and indirect. She wanted a new form to accommodate the raw moments, raw thoughts—poems, notes, diaries, letters. Prose like Anaïs Nin's *House of Incest* came to mind. Elizabeth was enthralled by Nin, by her capacity to convey "the feeling of naked, terribly condensed and understated truth—her feeling of every moment bursting to capacity with awareness of itself.[12] She was evolving her own style and Nin gave her a kind of permission to believe in her own instincts. "She dares to speak." The two writers were in some ways remarkably similar. *House of Incest* takes from surrealism a style of collage, a juxtaposition of moments. There is no narrative as such, but a recording of experience at the level of archetype or dream, carried through the power of the image, and much of the experience, as is clear from Nin's own diaries, is autobiographical. The theme is also daring—an exploration of incest. But Nin's novel, though heralded by friends like Miller, is not entirely successful. In fact she had not Elizabeth's metaphoric splendour.

In *Dig a Grave and Let Us Bury Our Mother* (the title from Blake's *Tiriel*), Elizabeth, at a deep intuitive level, knew exactly what she was doing. It is constructed like a poem, by radical juxtapositions rigorously managed. The majority of it is taken directly from her diary entries, moments of intense perception, a world on the edge of imminent revelation. The power comes from the archetypal movement of the narrative beneath—the encounter with the mother archetype. The failure comes from the ineffectualness of characterization.

Elizabeth tells the story of the triangle: "I am staying with friends, a man and two women; it is a *mariage à trois*. All is warm and stimulating. They are Europeans, concerned with writing, painting, ideas. They bolster my freedom. I revel in the airy cut-off kingdom of Ruth, Peter, Maud." These narrative sutures are clumsy and flat. Elizabeth couldn't figure out how to get the story told, a problem that was to be solved easily in *By Grand Central Station I Sat Down and Wept*, which is a dialogue, from the *Song of Solomon* the form natural to the theme of love. But she did understand completely her archetypal theme. Where the novella elaborates on her diary is in the exploration of the psychological dynamic between the narrator (Elizabeth) and Ruth, based precisely on Alice Paalen.

In her novella, Elizabeth offers a stark outline of the life of Alice Paalen that does not appear in the diary, and her identification with Paalen becomes understandable. Ruth's childhood and youth are a string of tragedies that Elizabeth details: tuberculosis in the bone after a fracture at age three; after six years, emerging from a cast with one leg six inches shorter; a fracture to the second leg so that she is left with only a slight limp; pregnancy at sixteen, a brutal birth, telling no one, certainly not the beloved mother; her mother's death soon after; the hated father and his lover; poverty; working to keep her child in a home; its death at nine months; a string of lovers who attracted her pity; the lover who kept the revolver under the pillow whenever she threatened to leave him. Into this confusion, Peter (based on Paalen) brings peace and security. He gives her another sort of liberty. "He had freed her from all the ghosts of her frightful childhood and adolescence."

How much of this is Elizabeth's invention and how much is accurate are unclear. She may have been amplifying the biography, but that she perceived Alice's experience as a starker mirror image of her own childhood traumas is clear. Alice, with her great absorbing sympathy, was the apogee of suffering womanhood:

Then her smiling face, bending over me with the falling hair. I, listening, listening, gathering the rare essence, waiting for the full revelation.

Her eyes though—she was *all* woman. She was wo-manhood. Her eyes then were worn, tired, sad, deceived, full of bitter knowledge, love, all the wonderful and dreadful things that ever came to woman. Her eyes like this, naked, were my mother's eyes, terribly terrifyingly near—eyes my mother had after her long scenes of hyste-ria and crying, of pacing up and down the verandah, wail-ing in her uncanny voice: "I am going insane! I am going insane!" or moaning as she lay soft and whale-like in a lump on the bathroom floor.

But all the while that Ruth's naked eyes peered at me, her smiling dream mouth floated above me like the moon, smiling, smiling, tender and soothing and sure, the lips of wise love, knowing their rewards, but insinuating, like a snake, and poised ready to strike. . . .

How can Ruth, who calls herself all animal, who makes love to anything loveable in sight, and knows that women are to be loved before all else, and my mother with her sexual fears hidden in her leather-bound Emerson, have the same passion-wracked face? How can the worn-out eyes, criss-crossed with bitterness and knowledge that they have been deceived, still see and desire to be the image of the tender one, smiling forgivingly at the death-blows given by the child? . . .

Ruth, Ruth. I will be your mother. And with the consol-ing kisses receive again my mother from your lips. Not to her womb again. But she into mine. I am hiding the thing that haunts me in my womb. But my womb is as large and as forgiving as the world. I walk complete and free, the giver of life. . . .

We are in the erotic caves, warm, damp, fold upon fold, the caves, bigger than the mind can hold, they hug the mind, enveloping, sinking it back, burying it in rocking softness.

Or with my mouth I swallow myself and her.

It is my mother I swallow. It is the repellent flesh of my mother I embrace. The ogre is in my bed. For living pity's

sake I am kissing the one I fly from. It is a wailing child. I
am older than the world, older and stronger.

Pity rips, seeing the agonized need. Those flowery
women with dewy faces in the morning. Those prostrate
women in their great forsaken meadows, with their daisy
chains, woven like Penelope's, rejected and scattered
about. That coming they awaited, no more than a blind
beast's bounding on the grass. Gone by! Flashed like a
storm! Their terrible urge was to give! . . .

Are you happy? Are you happy? Yes, we say, weeping
with an unhealable woe. The palms weep too, and in the
north the pines. And the wind howls.

But my mother is in my womb.[13]

Elizabeth was enacting a ritual, her vision Blakean: "Love or
lack of love that twists the world and rules both heaven and
hell." Through Alice, she could recover tenderness for her
mother, seeing her fear. She could take her mother's stunted
life and give it birth, and not be trapped by the mother in herself. Elizabeth believed that, essentially, Louie battled the vulnerable body because her mind refused to know her desperate
primitive need. It tore the heart to see her bitter need, yet she
turned that into a frenzy to hurt in revenge. Her violence and
hatred bred violence and hate. Outrageously, brilliantly, swallowing the female lover, Elizabeth swallows the mother and
gives her birth. The ethic would be that of the womb—acceptance of life. In the face of suffering and betrayal, she would
have the courage to love, to walk "complete and free, the giver
of life."

In Hollywood Elizabeth soon lost faith in her novella. It was
to become one more abandoned manuscript. It had begun as the
"Mother Book," to be told from Louie's perspective: "As I tell
her life from her angle, let me break in with my own wail all the
time, as if a mourning spectre." But then the doubts set in: "I
must rend the Now . . . I want each word to be essence, irre-
placeably and authentically the only note. Mummy can only be
a book about now, with Mummy as a recurring note slowly

revealing its source. More (NOW) would be drudgery or cheating. And I am too happy (praising the lord) for that. My island of harmony![14]

But the book and the love of Alice Paalen took her to another level of insight. Thirty-seven years later she could write: "But I forgive my mother. Alice presented me with the pity . . . the murderous act of stepping resolutely into my own life. Hearing, trembling with, her cries, her frantic unfair efforts to sabotage me, but going unflinchingly on. . . . So I forgave my mother for causing the passionate love I had for her, for casting me out of Paradise."[15]

The intensity of Elizabeth's response to Alice Paalen was certainly a product of her own psychological need for an exorcism. It was also mutual. Alice could write longingly to Elizabeth in California:

> You cannot know that you came to Mexico for me. That great fresh blonde wind that scented the lilies, that carried the song . . . that left its great blue suspended above my eyes (and there are traces of your eyes in the air that continued to live after you were gone), the house is still perfumed with your presence. If I am on the divan in the livingroom, I feel the cruel lack of your coming to be beside me, and thus I learn the desolate lack of your vitality so that I now feel in a sort of Sahara.[16]

But already Elizabeth had come to fear what she called "Alice's tearful articulate love." Once consummated, the passion reverted to affection. (The letters from Paalen continued until 1942.) Perhaps Elizabeth was frightened by claims Alice seemed ready to make. Alice was not the solution, in part because love with a woman did not bring with it the mystery of the child. Elizabeth still believed she could forge a love of epic dimensions that could fill her desperate need. She looked to the poet. The George Barker she had invented from his poetry loomed as a solution. While at the Paalens' she could write in her diary of December 14:

George Barker grows into a long dangerous image and is woven among the undertones. . . . But O the excitement is in the for instance: "Wondering one, wandering on." "I penetrate the valleys bringing correct direction." It is the complete juicy *sound* that runs bubbles over, that intoxicates till I can hardly follow (and the recurring lines in "Daedalus;" "the moist palm of my hand like handled fear like fear cramping my hand." OO the a—a—a—!)[17]

It is clear that Elizabeth was in love with the language of the man. Barker was the Voice to pour things out to (not of course simply the ear). He was to be the muse. In Mexico, she had articulated her vision of herself as "nature's instrument. A key that fits no other lock, a plant that can only be fed from one source." Her greatest gift was her natural mysticism. Sometimes she could feel that when she listened she became space, and then it was wonderful to be alone. "The expansion. Even the love of man is only a remedy for man. A crutch that will be easily forgotten in space." But she affirmed, in the core of her being, the womb. She was the female vehicle to nature's fulfilment. Even in a mystic moment her response to nature was female. There are few descriptions of nature that are so compelling, and she has caught exactly the strange raw openness of the Mexican landscape:

"To give back electricity to the moon."
My hand in the moonlight criss-crossed with a dead tree's shadow. A hand, seen for the first time. So strange I trembled.
The moon draws me like a magnet—my head up hung to it, my legs and arms dangling like marionettes.
Or it charges me and I leap like a shorn sheep. The moon forced my mouth open and my teeth and entered me as I lay shaking on the brittle beige grass. Like a baby forcing the womb open its electric globe forced open my mouth. It was in me. Then I noticed how each single star in that enormous wideness had pinned me here and there ("my blood gathered in points"). So I was strung on a

clothes-line sagging only where there were no stars. One
star moved in a tripping glide like a housefly on the ceiling. The moon's pulse shakes more potently than the roar-
ing machines at the power plant. The glitter glues my eye
not dazzled but bewitched. Who has been my lover like
the moon or possessed my eye? One finger went numb; I
drank the creeping cold like a caress. But the moon rivet-
ed me. Barking dogs, men's mumbles in adjacent court-
yards, far booms, but only I spread out on the grass by the
moon, taken entirely, made its element.

I can never realize the *strangeness* of the moon, the
potency, the *gloriousness*. When I see it I want to shout, to
leap—Why did nobody ever tell me? If anybody has ever
seen the moon why don't they go around talking, raving,
being astonished about it? So exciting. So mysterious. So
appallingly beautiful. It's a miracle, an inconceivable
splendour? Why is not the whole world buzzing with
wonder and consternation? How can they exclaim over a
soup bowl—and miss the moon. MISS IT ENTIRELY
because some poet made a whore of its name, but a plati-
tude. But even then, the exclaimer over the soup bowl, the
platitudinous poet—can they not REMEMBER? A hun-
dredth part of that wild incredible phenomenon should be
like a double dose of intoxicant drugs. It is a power plant
terribly charged—and too much moon could easily kill
me with shock.[18]

The mystery of the moon, the mystery of birth, of sexuality. To
dare to be exposed, utterly undefended, raw and reactive before
the great sweeping mythic organic forces. This Elizabeth
would aspire to. She would celebrate her femaleness. She
would affirm the authority of the womb. She felt there would
be no struggle between her instinct to be related to the beloved
and to stand alone and for her own depths. As long as she had
the courage.

In Los Angeles, as Elizabeth picked up the threads of her life
with Varda, one of the things on her mind must have been the

recent marriage of her sister Jane. She was sorry to have missed it. Trying to explain to Alice Paalen why she wanted to be there, she had insisted it was not for the social trimmings but for Jane—"Jane, what she must be suffering and feeling to be put through all these paces." Jane had fallen in love with a charming, madcap Irishman, D'Arcy Marsh. Though he was a drinker, she assured her close friend, the writer Joyce Marshall, that her love would be enough to save him.[19] She had wanted to elope, for the truth was she was pregnant, and the two had asked Russel's permission to marry, but without explanations. Suddenly Louie was involved and a huge wedding was afoot. Preparations were spectacular: a trousseau of laces stitched by the nuns in Montreal, and an endless parade of dressmakers. Helen wrote to Elizabeth that at the trousseau tea, all Jane's underclothes were "spread out in view like an Egyptian general."

Yet, whatever drama was happening at home, Elizabeth's first thoughts were of George Barker. While in Mexico she had continued her correspondence with Lawrence Durrell. He had suggested that she contact Anaïs Nin, and also explained that "George Barker, as far as I know, is in Tokyo by now; bad luck missing him, he is such a sweet and sensitive person, always shying away and twinkling off into the deserts of his own private life like a bushman's totem. A difficult, painful man, much in need of air uncontaminated by Englishry, which pervades and destroys."[20]

Through the auspices of T.S. Eliot, Barker had been offered the job of Professor of English Literature at Sendai Imperial University in Japan. Eliot had taken Barker under his wing, having earlier arranged financial backing for him—under his directive six people were donating ten shillings a week towards Barker's support. When the Japanese job came along, Barker accepted it because it was "admirable to have an income." He also recognized that war was just around the corner and had decided he would object conscientiously, but going to Japan seemed a better solution.

Barker left for Japan on November 18, 1939. No doubt it must at first have seemed exciting—a foreign university post in the Orient for an impecunious poet who had never himself attended university. Barker's inaugural address to the university is full of enthusiasm. Soon, however, he found himself on the "spiritual rocks"—he was at a provincial outpost, teaching students not particularly interested in literature, and among professors who had reconciled themselves to the backwaters of scholarship. He felt the Europeans had the dead-eye glare and lifeless flesh of people whose nerves were shot. They were "cupidity-mad" and he considered none of them entirely sane. From almost the day of his arrival he was calculating his departure. Certainly Barker was appalled by mediocrity—always confident that he belonged among the great. But Japan too he found "monstrous." As a consequence of the ten-year war with Manchuria, the army was running Japan. Wherever he went he was followed by a policeman in white gloves. He also found the Japanese, at least in Sendai, uncleanly, and he complained about the smallpox, the lavatories, and the language. He found he could not write.[21] On February 2, 1940, he wrote to Elizabeth that he was going absolutely nuts in Japan and that unless he succeeded soon in crossing the Pacific, it would be curtains not only for him but for his poetry. Though he had never met her, there was, he said, no one else to whom he could appeal. Out of the blue of their unacquaintance, he asked that she rescue him and send two tickets. In return he offered his gratitude and the unpublished manuscripts of his private journals.[22]

It was not surprising that Barker should appeal to Elizabeth. He thought of her as a rich patron (she had bought a manuscript), and he followed the ethic that it was the poet's right to expect support. Privately, he prayed that God would loosen the hand of E. Smart. It was also characteristic that when he felt restless, Barker expected others to rescue him. He had the grace to add that if Elizabeth couldn't send him salvation, the potential friendship should not be jeopardized. He'd make it across the Pacific even if he had to do so on skis. It was his outrageousness Elizabeth loved since it matched her own. The shock was the request for two tickets. It was the first intimation she had that Barker was married. George, she said later, "had always been very cagey even misleading about his private life, so that the biographical material in anthologies etc was very slight and unrevealing."[23]

Elizabeth immediately rallied and began a campaign to get George Barker to America. April 13: "All day and all night I wrangle ways to rescue Barker from Japan. . . . The promise I blithely made him (and WILL keep) begins to be a centre of radiating apprehension sending shivers from the bottom of my spine."[24] For Elizabeth, the campaign was a heroic one. "April 29: Writing and lonely in my 'little room.' But more than a nun's glee."

She wrote letters to everyone she knew to be interested in literature in Canada and the U.S., well over a hundred people. One by one, her begging letters were returned or worse, ignored. Of course, she turned to her family. When she asked her father for three hundred dollars for Barker, he replied that he couldn't send anything because he was already borrowing to pay his income tax and added: "I have not all the facts but it does seem curious that Barker should look to you for this (he managed to get to Japan). I can't quite go all the way with you about the poets and writers. Some of the greatest of them have been able to maintain the usual human contacts & some of their deeper understanding has come from their relationships with human beings."[25] Russel did, however, send an affidavit of support that the American Consulate required before issuing visas for Barker and his wife, again suggesting to Elizabeth that George Barker's difficulties might be exaggerated and due to a new environment or temperament. "If the latter it will follow him everywhere." He warns her that he has not mentioned sending the affidavit to Louie, and not to refer to it when writing, "not even to me."[26]

Louie was much more virulent. She criticized Elizabeth's changed sense of values: "This passionate desire on your part to assist a British poet stranded in Japan seems so far to outweigh your interest in a very vital human problem in your own family." Though she said she had read Barker's work and found him able, there was no reason for Elizabeth to be the one to go to his rescue. She claimed that Russel even saw humour in the situation—the last time Elizabeth had mentioned Barker it was with a desire to get him from England. This, of course, was shrewd on Russel's part, since the heroic dimension of rescuing Barker from Japan only added flair to a long-held fantasy—to have him for herself. Louie warned Elizabeth that her father had no use for poets who couldn't stand on their own feet. With her usual thoroughness she went on: "What would it matter to the world, honestly, if some of these moderns were never heard from again. What the world needs from them now is character—*being* and if necessary *doing*, but not crying out for someone else to shoulder their burdens as well as his own. It isn't playing the game."[27] Such rhetoric was guaranteed to strengthen Elizabeth's resolve.

In fact, Jane's wedding had left the Smart family in a state of crisis. In February Louie discovered that Jane had been pregnant. Soon fury turned to sentimentality. "Poor little Jane." "I understand her. I understand emotionally. She was deeply in love with D'Arcy and her idea was to have him at all costs. He was behaving badly and she with her mad generosity gave all."[28] Even six months later she could still write: "The whole dirty mess is never out of my thoughts." D'Arcy was to blame. "He dishonoured Jane before the world and he cheated us into having a wedding and getting presents out of our friends."[29] It was neither in Louie's temperament nor in the conventions of her generation to examine the implications of her daughters' situations. There was some consolation, however. Helen was in Reno seeking a divorce. Her marriage with Alan Swabey (whom Louie complained had more the manners of a commercial traveller than of one descended from a long line of DeBretts) had broken down years before and she was about to marry an American surgeon, Averill Stowell, of whose family Louie thoroughly approved.

Russel, predictably, was much calmer. He felt that Jane was happy, but was hurt that she had not told him, though in fact she had asked his permission to marry quietly and he had insisted on informing Louie who turned it into a grand occasion. The crisis seems to have increased his intimacy with Elizabeth and in March he was writing with candour:

I do not think we are really so far apart. Life has forced many compromises on me & I have been unable to select & hold resolutely to one pattern, as you feel able to do. Living of course is the principal thing & my main concern for you is that you should have all the life that is possible...You have chosen to enlist with what Winnifred Hottby called "The Runners," those who in art or literature seek out some new world for their generation. It is a proud band & I do not think you will fail for lack of finding a word to deliver . . .

I still think your judgement of your mother is harsh. She is often right but obscures her rightness by ill considered or even violent invention. She is more in the control of her feelings than anyone I have met. Perhaps I took the easy way in building my defenses & not matching violence with violence. But in the early years I had a good many things to do & it seemed the only way to get them done. She might have been happier with someone whose spirit matched her own . . . [30]

He ends his letter by encouraging her to get on with her writing and offers his continued financial and moral support.

In fact, the toll on Russel of sustaining the household seems to have been increasing. He writes: "I am not becoming disillusioned, only a bit lonely as friends and others do not seem as close as they once did." "Each year adds some painfully acquired knowledge and less interest in repeating exhausted experience. The law of diminishing returns always works," but he adds stoically, "there are always fresh crops to harvest."

Throughout the family drama, Elizabeth kept her distance in California. Though she continued to live with Yanko, the relationship was deteriorating. It was clear that their temperaments were at cross purposes, too different for the dance to continue—Yanko complaining that he couldn't work, that Elizabeth didn't take care of the domestic world adequately. "I just become the valet. Doing errands. The room is a suntrap full of stagnant heat like an oven," he reproached her. Is it my fault he can't work? she countered. "I always swore housework would never become an issue with me—an obsession substituted for living. Even is it better to live in filth than empty resignation preparing for *something* that never arrives." She was sitting in on Bertrand Russell's lectures at U.C.L.A., and taking dancing lessons. "Choose between dancing and me!" Yanko demanded. Yanko, she felt, was a kind of litmus-paper presence colouring all her feelings, sights, and reactions; it was not her self, in fact, the artist in her that was demanded. And yet, whenever Yanko left for an exhibition of his work, Elizabeth felt abandoned.

> Even today, before he left, I could say, "We must part, it is time we parted." He grabs at life, he talks with his mouth full, he rushes, full of only his own purpose, hither and thither, my threadlike life is smothered. He never hears anything. But Oh the minute he left—I could have thrown all my belongings and ambitions away and rushed after him not to have to face the empty room and the terrible empty bed where he will never come again, and the whole of big empty Los Angeles which I have to face, which I shall look at for the first time with my own eyes not his. Till now it was he only I saw and heard and explored.[31]

Elizabeth was terrified of being alone. Alone she sank into apathy. The only solution was to write.

> Why don't I write the terrible heavy blanks. I open the book, I stare. I say, there's nothing to write. Catch the disease and dissect it to find the cure. . . .
>
> One thing that deflates me here is the impossibility of *communication* with anyone. No language, no look of the eye to see your meaning is caught. . . .
>
> All my life I fight the glazed eye, the lethargy. I insist I am independent. I *will* the sitting down at the blank page to write. I say I have no need of people; I can pull out the vital thing myself if I am strong and moral enough. But I go flatfootedly up the hills, blearily eyed searching for my vision with a dead heart . . .
>
> "Write the blanks," I said before. This evil, this sin, so

monstrous in its descent—its jellyfish anatomy so known,
so stale. It is just the flight of all delight, mystery love—
unambiguous bones left but invoking less than any earthly skeleton or a lead grey day. A pall, a drugged relapse
into a state of nonexistence—no pain except the fatal
knowledge that life is embracing me and I cannot feel
her touch. . . . I slip the vital hours into penny slot
machines—to pass time, to start my stuck wheels only
love can oil.[32]

Elizabeth believed that more than sexual passion what she
wanted was "cerebral exploration." George Barker was the
solution. "If George Barker should appear now I would eat him
up with eagerness. I can feel the flushed glow of minds functioning in divine understanding and communication."
Elizabeth had every reason to trust that Barker would be
responsive. The chemistry was already articulating itself in his
letters of gratitude that she had undertaken to save him. A
friend of Elizabeth's, Temp Fever, then with the Canadian
Legation in Japan, had shown him a picture of a blonde glory
who was either Elizabeth S. or sunrise over the Rockies. Barker
had a suspicion from the beginning of his correspondence with
Elizabeth that something was afoot. He was to say later that the
first thing he fell in love with was her name.[33]
   In an effort to gain money for the Barkers, and consistent
with her emotional extravagance, Elizabeth went so far as to
engage as a maid with a Mrs Kennedy but the job lasted only a
few days. She made the mistake of asking her employer to lend
her money for the Barkers and was promptly fired. In the end,
she was able to raise only a third of the money from friends.
The rest came from Christopher Isherwood who had a lucrative
job as a script-writer in Hollywood. She did not know
Isherwood but wrote to him. Isherwood replied: "I'm glad you
wrote to me. I'm a great admirer of George Barker's
work . . . Unless something unforeseen happens, I hope to have
the $200 within a few days. I would like very much to meet you
and Barker if he comes."[34] Isherwood sent the money, but it
didn't arrive. Desperate, Elizabeth rushed over to see him with

Barker's letters and telegrams. Concluding the money had been stolen en route, Isherwood only replied: "Well that's too bad, isn't it" and gave her a second lot.

Barker wrote to his brother that he'd just been given the continent of America by an American who admired his poems and that they would be in Los Angeles that summer, and sent Elizabeth his new book of poems as a gesture of his gratitude. She responded that she had done nothing really and was grateful he was coming to America, ending her letter: "I can't think of a welcome worthy Columbus. But it's yours if you can think of it."[35]

Already the heroic terms of the relationship were established. One dimension of its power, probably the most compelling, was to be its literary rhetoric, reminding one of La Rochefoucauld's axiom that we love as we do because we have learned from literature. Neither having met Barker, nor having seen a picture of him, Elizabeth was in love with his language: "Barker's new poems arrived and I say O how ashamed I am to have thought *mine* were poetry, for he alone says *exactly* what I wanted to say, and even the very word sounds I was wanting to utter and the same elastic bounding back. That is my maddening injury. His are all true. Mine limp and labour. But when I opened the book my excitement made me too impotent to read. My head ached with too much greed. My eyes were glazed with wanting too much at once."[36] Elizabeth had encountered her muse, her double, her equal; a man who could, like her, "leap bellowing with jungfreud into the arms of the infinite."

Throughout that spring, the relationship with Varda continued rather limply. At the end of May, Elizabeth and Varda moved with some friends to an artist colony at Anderson Creek on Big Sur. The artists were living in shacks left behind by convicts whose forced labour had been used to construct the Carmel–San Simeon highway three years earlier. It was a spectacular setting. The cottages were perched on a cliff, a thousand feet above the sea. Jack London had gone there in the old days and Robinson Jeffers lived nearby; Elizabeth used to say you could almost see him brooding on his cliff. Henry Miller would describe Anderson Creek six years later as a region where extremes meet, a region where one "is always conscious of weather, of space, of grandeur, and of eloquent silence."[37] The coyotes howled at night and mountain lions ranged the far ridges. The landscape was prehistoric and apocalyptic. "Last night in the starry sky there was a terrifying black rainbow, tubular and snakelike," Elizabeth wrote in her journal as she began to articulate the landscape for the new novel she planned to write. She was excited by the possibility of a new form: "Prose, please, prose for a while, straighten out the rushing-water excuses—say, This is my whole duty. Don't take refuge in the automatic formula poem," she castigated herself. She wanted a prose as metamorphic and mysterious as the landscape and found herself writing passages that would eventually be incorporated into *By Grand Central Station I Sat Down and Wept*. Much of what was to become Part Two of the novel was begun before she met George Barker.

The colony at Anderson Creek consisted of about ten people. Elizabeth described them as a wonderful grab-bag collection. All were Europeans: English, Dutch, Greek, etc., painters, a musician, a philosopher, a man who studied rattlesnakes. One was a Spanish philosopher called Jaime who had come in on mules before the highway was built and had horses that his young daughter rode naked and bareback. They rented the shacks for five dollars a month, organized a shower from the stream, dug garbage pits, and generally worked at their art.

While Anderson Creek may have been isolated, Elizabeth was very much aware of the war that was consuming the world around her. The Europeans among whom she found herself agonized endlessly about the fate of Europe, and when news of the fall of France in June 1940 reached them, they were in tears. They were anarchists and it was to become clear that, as aliens living on the West Coast of California, they had not escaped the scrutiny of the F.B.I. Even if the U.S. was still isolationist, the country was jittery.

Louie's disturbing missives continued to arrive from Ottawa, and now they had a new theme. She began to complain that Elizabeth wasn't contributing to the war effort: "Do you feel that your writing is sufficient contribution to a troubled and war worn world? Is there still a reading public for abstract ideas? If so, I'm afraid I don't know them."[38] And she complained about the effete and decadent crowd in California: "There isn't much to be said for saving one's skin and pouring out one's erotic emotions at a time like this."[39] She herself was doing Red Cross work, helping out in a tea room and tuck shop to raise money for Canada's soldiers. By June she had found a new campaign. Ottawa had begun to fill up with English refugees, mostly children from London sent to Canada to escape the blitz. She was committed to opening her house to one of these children, whatever the sacrifice involved. Taxes were a burden, she complained, and she envisaged the possibility of having to move into one of the small houses they rented out to tenants, and having to do with one maid. "But it's a relief to get to the point where we can really help—what a world and with traitors in every camp, but right is bound to prevail." "As you have seen by the papers, Princess Juliana is living in Ottawa." (Louie was happy to remark that when the Princess played tennis at Government House, she picked up her own balls.) "Dorothy German has Lady Ann Hemloter's children living with her. The English accent is going to have a fine tempering influence in the little Rockcliffe public schools."

If Elizabeth needed an explanation for Louie's enthusiasm, her father provided it in a letter in July: "Refugees are to the fore & there is great competition to get children with social kudos. Dorothy German has scored by getting some of the Cavendish family & the Colemans have the grandchildren of Lord Maugham. . . . We called H.V. Hodson but his children are going to Australia. Also tried the Barrington Wards. I expect that some way or another we shall have a couple of them on our hands soon." Elizabeth had obviously felt the need to defend herself since her father adds: "Everyone is not carried away by patriotic fervor here. In fact the knitting and bandage rolling has died down. There is no particular virtue in this. I think I understand your position. 'They also serve who only stand and wait.' You must ultimately be judged by the value of what you do. If this is good, all will be forgiven."[40]

Elizabeth's disgust at the war frenzy expressed in *By Grand Central Station* finds a root here. Louie's war work may have been sincere, but in the frenzy over refugees she was cultivating her own snobbery. The war served to stimulate what Elizabeth had called her belief in the great class barriers. "A strange vanity," Elizabeth had mocked—"that one is born superior, cannot but be superior, whatever one does, however one lives." But Louie's admonitions hardly fazed Elizabeth since she was, at the deepest psychological level, preparing for what was to be the great transformative moment of her life.

July 4

Last night I dreamt about the Barkers—it was all very awkward; it was Kingsmere, and Mummy was there, and not enough beds unless I slept with Yanko which was impossible. And the MacLaines were there and the woods were a refuge. I took the Barkers but especially Jessie [Barker's wife] who was small and sweet and rather silent up to a great cliff to see Anderson Creek. It was several miles above and very steep. She said, "This way down?" and I said, "Yes, but be careful," and she smiled and leapt down. How could she? She didn't seem to know she would be killed. At the bottom she was bloody and smashed. George was on a camp bed bent over. I tried to take his hand. He said, "Leave me alone." I wept. He was softened. I found a little fat man, elderly; he said "I don't want them to see me cut her throat." I ran to Jessie. She was still limply warm and alive. There was a horrible blue-bloody line around her throat. I said to the man, "You're only a dentist. Wait and I'll go and get a surgeon." I ran out into the road. It was paved and bordered with cedar trees. Some people went by in a Rolls-Royce dressed for guests to a wedding. They were disgusted at my torn clothes and bare legs. I was afraid to ask them. But I did. They didn't understand. I went distractedly along, under the cedar bushes, I ran back. I told the dentist he had better operate, everybody was going along to the wedding. They all had harassed faces and said it was an outrage my being allowed onto the highway. George was always in the background, tender, grave, sympathetic, tall and thin with a smooth pale face. Jessie must have recovered for later there were flowers in the sun.

But in the first part Mummy was predominant, and George and Jessie I had to keep in the woods. When I was on the Kingsmere verandah, I said why didn't I remember his face when I saw it?[41]

In this frenzied and terrifying dream, Elizabeth anticipates the coming scenario with extraordinary precision. The future had its own logic. Subconsciously she already knew she would have to sacrifice Jessie; and with the ironic prophecy of dreams there would be no wedding. George was faceless—she still had not seen a picture of him—and she would carry this over to her novel. One of the extraordinary things about *By Grand Central Station I Sat Down and Wept* is that the male character is never objectively described. When asked about this, Elizabeth replied: "Of course he is faceless; the *he* is a love object."[42] The book is not autobiography, a personal account of a love affair; it is archetypal. The experience recorded is the ecstasy and the agony of passionate love.

7   Oh My Canadian!

What is it men in women do require?
The lineaments of Gratified Desire.
What is it women do in men require?
The lineaments of Gratified Desire.
William Blake
Miscellaneous Poems and Fragments

When George Barker and his wife, Jessica (née Woodward), stepped off the bus in Monterey on July 6, 1940, they were walking into a scenario whose dynamic had already been set. Elizabeth would write in *By Grand Central Station I Sat Down and Wept*: "I am standing on a corner in Monterey, waiting for the bus to come in, and all the muscles of my will are holding my terror to face the moment I most desire. . . . Behind her he for whom I have waited so long, who has stalked so unbearably through my nightly dreams, fumbles with the tickets and the bags, and shuffles up to the event which too much anticipation has fingered to shreds."[1] When asked by her editor Alice VanWart in a candid moment decades later to describe her exact reaction when Barker stepped off the bus, Elizabeth said: "He was all wrong." He was lanky, bespectacled, and unsophisticated.[2] But if, momentarily, he was not the image she had fabricated in her head, the *frisson* quickly passed. George Barker was to be the *he*. Elizabeth was in the headlong rush of

154

passionate obsession and Barker was mercurial enough to receive her projection.

Elizabeth said she had been surprised that the Barkers, having landed in Vancouver, had immediately come to Monterey. She found them a cabin at Big Sur and thought, briefly, that the three of them would be just friends. But the relationship with Varda ended abruptly and by the last week of July, George and Elizabeth were irrevocably entangled in a love affair that was predestined by an extraordinary matching of personalities. Elizabeth was later to deny that the relationship was romantic. It was, she said, "realistic." "You get into a state where you fall in love . . . The fact that I was madly in love with the English language and with poetry may have given vent to my feelings."[3] Elizabeth was little able to resist the hydraulic rush of passion: "Under the waterfall he surprised me bathing and gave me what I could no more refuse than the earth can refuse the rain." In his diary of July 23, Barker too was overwhelmed: "The harmonics of all music and the mathematics of suspension bridges cannot equate the angle of this head as it leans to one side under the summer of its own coronals . . . Oh My Canadian."*

George Barker was a poet who could call California the "unimaginable continent where everything is possible."[4] It was the vast permission he demanded from life that, for Elizabeth, was most seductive. This was, seemingly, a man who did not cringe before life, who lifted irresistible fists and was not to be tied by petty conventionality. The relationship was, as Barker called it fifty years later, "a great love affair."[5] The bond was erotic (the chemistry brilliant), and it provided the cerebral exploration she so ardently desired, for Barker, unlike Yanko or any man she had met so far, had the imagination to meet her passion.

It is strange how such love is even physically transforming. From the moment she encountered Barker, Elizabeth left behind the persona of Betty Smart and became permanently

---

* This is the only quotation Barker allowed from his unpublished works. "Diary of George Barker," NLC; BOX 62, F2.

Elizabeth: "Elixirelizabeth" George would call her. The delicate face of the debutante was gone. She wore her blonde hair loose, in a golden corolla, and, in photos from this time, her face holds the insouciance she claimed from her ancestors. George too was transformed. The mincing look one can occasionally see in earlier photos went, as did the spectacles, as though through Elizabeth he claimed his own erotic authority. Both were young, twenty-seven, and both were engulfed. Such passion always seems an assault from without by a force too great to fight off. One staggers under the pressure of Eros.

But Barker was married. The role inevitably assigned to Jessica was that of saint and martyr. At Big Sur Jessica played the wife, carrying the luggage and chopping the wood while the poet composed and Elizabeth typed the manuscripts. Elizabeth's guilt towards Jessica was enormous: "On her mangledness I am spreading my amorous sheets." But such passion could not be denied. In a chronology of events that Elizabeth later wrote for a script based on *By Grand Central Station* in 1980, she describes the climax of this love. It is not clear whether this is factual, but it is psychologically accurate:

> It is George who must make a decision. That night, as they sit around drinking in the local tavern, he is utterly charming and charismatic, but avoids any serious attempt to solve the problem. Instead the evening turns into a nightmare; he tries to pick up a soldier, who is AWOL, lashes out at both women and ends up by getting into a fight with the other customers. When they return to their cabin that night, he comes into Elizabeth's room, made up as an Assyrian, and makes love to her.
>
> "And this, though shocking, enables me to understand, and myself rise virile as a cobra . . . to assume control."[6]

Both were caught in the dilemma of desire: the paradoxical Janus face of romantic passion. From the time of Sappho, romantic love has been ecstatic torture. All proportions disappear and the loved other becomes a vocation, almost a fetish. One is filled with longing, needing to possess the other to fill an emptiness, hating the loss of self as one runs to embrace that loss. Excess and madness become a strength. Simone Weil calls it hanging between hunger and repletion. For both Elizabeth and Barker, it was the other's extremism that each loved. To Elizabeth, this love gave her the authority to be fully herself—and her passion was marvellously hermaphroditic. "[I] rise," she wrote, "virile as a cobra . . . to assume control."

Who was this George Barker who had walked into Elizabeth Smart's imagination? In an image of Barker she held in her mind, she describes his childhood: "We see young ragged boy riding home-made go-cart in sleazy part of London. Then wandering in Battersea Park in mist. Poor. Prickly. He scribbles away."[7] It mattered to Elizabeth that George Barker had invented himself from the least likely material.

George Barker was born on February 26, 1913 in Loughton, Essex, though the family moved shortly thereafter to London. His father, Colonel George Barker (the title was affectionate), had been a soldier with the Coldstream Guards. His mother (Marion Frances Taaffe whom they called Big Mumma) was Irish Catholic from Drogheda, of which port her father had been pilot. Barker grew up in a huge tenement block in Chelsea—the family, three sisters and a brother, living in three rooms. Childhood he remembered as a general time of absolute horror and mess, the "spectre" of poverty that hung over them worse than the "spectre of war"—his mother pawning her wedding ring every Wednesday and his father returning at evening to the flat, unable to find work. We watched "the soul of a proud man / being slowly and mercilessly torn out of his / body and thrown to the dogs in the gutter. His children knew / that the last glint of this pride somehow or other / slept in the army pistol he kept under his pillow." [8] Barker disappointed his father by taking up the trivial occupation of poet. His mother, however, was behind him, and Elizabeth was to envy this. "Big Mumma's love, though selfish in its way, was more loyal [than Louie's]. She was proud of the writing, the books, and didn't attempt to read, interpret, understand. She simply exulted in the achievement." [9]

Barker described how, when he was thirteen or fourteen, Big Mumma managed somehow to take enough money from his sister's salary—and she probably also hawked the china—to buy him a huge second-hand typewriter from Selfridges on which he managed to bang out his first poems. "When I was fifteen or sixteen, I had discovered that I was a great poet and this was such an embarrassing discovery that I had to make it apparent to everyone or otherwise I would have felt I was cheating. So I affected a great long blue cloak down to my ankles and a huge Spanish-style hat so that I looked exactly like the advertisement for Sandeman's port." [10] Through a brief correspondence with Middleton Murry, he discovered David Archer's bookshop on Parton Street off Red Lion Square where the young poets gathered. The day he walked in on Archer, he found him looking like a strange crucified figure on a ladder: "Be an angel, hand me that hammer," and Barker was inducted into the fold. He must certainly have been one of the impecunious young poets who found little match boxes with ten-pound notes mysteriously tucked in their pockets when they left the shop. He was advised to send poems to Walter de la Mare who gave him an introduction to T.S. Eliot. Eliot admired his work, and at twenty-two Barker's third book, *Poems*, was published by Faber & Faber (he had already published *Thirty Preliminary Poems* and the novel *Alanna Autumnal*). Faber poets had been upper middle-class, public school, and Oxford or Cambridge men. It wasn't easy to break the blue line from the universities to the London publishing houses, and Barker was the first to do it. He was also the youngest poet to be included in Yeat's *Oxford Book of Modern Verse*. His was the first generation, including David Gascoyne and Dylan Thomas, to have been educated in state schools. Barker went to Marlborough Road School, a Dickensian school at the top of the road with 2,200 "ragged-arsed urchin boys and 2,300 girls." Barker called it "lovely and tough." He then attended Regent Street Polytechnic where his remarkable intelligence was recognized. He was never to forget his class origins. Barker's route to rebellion was much more easily mapped than

Elizabeth's. He found the support where it mattered, from his mother, from the Jesuits who took his education in hand, and, most important, from other male writers. Ambition was not cast down.

Anyone who visited the Barker household in the forties described it as a remarkable menagerie. By then the family had moved to 23A Stanhope Gardens in South Kensington, the house Elizabeth would have known. It was a Victorian terraced house, and the Barkers, whose finances had improved considerably, had the first two floors. One walked up the stairs leading from the ground-floor hall, through the kitchen-scullery, and the official, little-used dining room—where a large Aztec-style canvas painted by George's brother, Kit, hung on one wall—to the large sitting room decorated in Chinese style: dragon-painted vases, screens, and peacock feathers. There the Colonel, currently employed as Butler to Gray's Inn, would sit with his port and cigars, samples presented by the shippers who supplied his employer's cellars. Barker senior was quintessentially English: formal, he drank little and was the embodiment of decorum. But his rages, because they came unexpectedly, were terrifying. A friend of Barker's, the poet David Wright, describes him:

> He was one of those people who, when their wrath is up, do not take thought but add cubits to the stature. Though he never spoke to me except with kindness, and once even advanced a pound note against the security of a very post-dated cheque, I have seen the person of the old man tower with the towering of his dudgeon, literally fill the kitchen-scullery where the family did most of their living, till his head appeared to bump the ceiling. If the bad mood were on him you could feel it two rooms away: an emanation capable on occasion of stretching beyond the house itself. . . . I have heard that his apocalyptic rages were characteristic of his father [a Lincolnshire farmer], who at midnight when the drink was on him would go into his yard and wrestle with the cattle.[11]

Big Mumma, who was most often to be found holding court in the kitchen, was the old man's dichotomous opposite. As Irish as he was English, she was, as Wright described her, as "solid as mother earth, gregarious, generous, but not soft." "If she had a fault it was that of being too magnetic a mountain."

One didn't remember cooking in the Barker kitchen, but the cup "o'tay," or the bottle of gin. Big Mumma would accept all and sundry, waifs and strays, the more the merrier. Irish to the bone, she could recite hundreds of poems by heart and loved hilarity. As Barker wrote in one of his finest poems, she was the centripetal force of warmth and light in the household:

> Irresistible as Rabelais, but most tender for
> The lame dogs and hurt birds that surround her,—
> She is a procession no one can follow after
> But be like a little dog following a brass band.[12]

Among Big Mumma, the daughters and the hangers-on in the kitchen, the Colonel couldn't get a word in. He didn't like the people coming in and out; he wanted his privacy, and withdrew into his own isolation. Or he erupted in rage, often against his sons who were not of his cast of mind. They had disappointed him with their painting and poetry, all very well as entertaining diversions but hardly promising pecuniary security. Barker resisted his father's values all his life, though he was to inherit his unpredictable rages. The family called them "Islandic": insane, lurching around, smashing things up, totally deranged."[13]

To understand Barker, one looks to the father. He was terrified of his father, whom he considered inflexible and profoundly authoritarian, of a stern militaristic mind. He flew from his image and all he stood for. Even when Barker was middle-aged and the Colonel was dying, he refused to visit him. When his last wife, Elspeth, insisted he go, he returned two hours later, claiming the car had broken down. Not until he wrote the moving "At Thurgarton Church" "(To the memory of my father)," first published in 1971, could he understand "the godfathered negative" that controlled his father's life:

Desire above all to live
as though the soul was stone,
believing we cannot give
or love since we are alone
and always will be so.[14]

In his youth, Barker's driving imperative was to flout every moral standard for which the Colonel stood. His first novel, *Alanna Autumnal*, was a direct, flagrant account of incest between a brother and sister. When Eliot recognized his talents and published him, he set out on the career of being George Barker, of being outrageous. With the moral climate of the thirties, he couldn't afford moderation or toleration.

Certainly it is difficult to make a clean break. There would always be two sides to George Barker: the man of marvellous intelligence and wit who loved to provoke and play, who loved to control the moment and create delight, the one Elizabeth called charming and charismatic; and the man who carried his father's rages within, when his mind could turn poisonous and nasty, and the rage was almost a state of possession, from which he would either emerge crying in agony, or have forgotten the next day. There was also the man filled with guilt, a guilt nurtured in Catholic metaphysics and often focused on an incident from adolescence, when in a game of fencing he accidentally blinded the right eye of his sixteen-year-old brother, Kit.[15] It was usually women who were on the receiving end of Barker's anger. Barker repeated his father's authoritarianism in his attitude towards women. He was afraid of being devoured; the slightest suggestion of it and he ran. This of course was not unusual among creative men. Polymorphous in his sexuality, Barker served not woman but the white goddess.

In the mid-thirties, Barker was already something of a legend as an improvident bohemian poet and brilliant talker in the London pubs. Maurice Carpenter described him in 1934 as "an imperious young man with a roman nose, a sensual rather feminine mouth . . . a beautiful profile and flashing eyes . . . We immediately took to one another, he assuming the role of bully, older brother, brilliant expositor, intimate cajoler, and I the listener, admirer, sufferer and mirror, though I was in fact two years older than he was."[16] Wright said that Barker, "for me and many was a magnetic legend, like Byron; a mysterious absentee in America, from whence he had returned, bleeding from wounds and wives." Like Dylan Thomas, Barker's locus would always be the pub, where by some "form of ESP or telepathic tocsin," friends and disciples mysteriously assembled. "One would find George Barker, tartan-shirted, slightly hunched, standing at the mahogany counter in the middle of a mob of poets and painters, similarly summoned, who would have come, as I did, to listen and participate in some of the best talk in London, comic and profound, passionate and humorous."

Of Barker, one can say one thing with assurance. Convinced of his own talent, he had made a commitment, from which he never wavered, to dedicate his life to the vocation of poetry. He was "married to poetry," as the writer Paul Potts put it. A vagrant in life, "the only place where he has a fixed abode is in the poetry of this language."[17] He had, in fact, the tunnel vision of the artist, the capacity to dedicate himself wholly to one objective. For Elizabeth, herself so scattered, this capacity to believe in himself was grounds for deep admiration. The dedication carried with it a proviso: Barker loathed the "professional" poet and anyone who prostituted himself to the practical demands of life. He once told the wife of the poet Karl Miller that Miller should be kept in an attic and fed on buns and be made to avoid conventional jobs so that he might concentrate on writing. "That boy has a tiger in his loins." Though George Barker never had any money, and was often extremely poor, he never courted the writing establishment and was to find himself progressively isolated. But the large talents, he felt, were always "locked out." "Nothing could have been harder than living as a poet when I did," he said.[18] There were many temptations to play the professor, and risk one's talent drying up. Instead he improvised; when he needed money, he could always write advertising copy for John Betjeman at Shell Oil.

Like those whom he called the true poets (his favourite predecessor was François Villon), Barker willingly made himself a student of catastrophe, a veteran in the school of appetite. Barker's "malady is an ingrowing soul; his virtue that he has diagnosed it. His prescription is—Excess: he will rage himself out," as the critic Hugh Gordon Porteus put it in 1934.[19] Life was dangerous, high-risk; the poet had a tiger in his loins. He rode it outlandishly and with great humour. But of course those who tried to ride with him were at great risk. Elizabeth did not realize that if her cosmos was directed by the god of love, his would always be directed by the demons of his art.

When George Barker met Jessica Woodward in his late teens, the relationship had a profound effect on him. He could write in his notebook that he had never known anyone to absorb him into her as she had done. Yet there was her self-control, her "Englishness." Jessica, who was four years older than he, became pregnant and they were married in November 1933. Petrified of her parents, especially of her Irish Protestant mother, whom she thought would kill her if she found out, she gave the baby up for adoption, which, of course, became a constant source of grief. The portrait of Jessica one might gather from her letters is of a rather shy, self-effacing, clinging woman dedicated to Barker and his work. Barker used to say that she was the Geraldine Chaplin character in *Doctor Zhivago*.[20] The marriage was good, but the sensibilities were not matched. Clearly Jessica hadn't Barker's energy. It may only have been a matter of time, but Barker did love her and, before he left her, would be trapped in paroxysms of guilt and moral paralysis. Elizabeth must have been unlike any woman Barker had met before. She was tantalizingly beautiful; he presumed rich or at least with access to money; she shared his fierce intelligence and passionate commitment to literature; and she was absolutely and uninhibitedly sensual. She could meet Barker on every level.

Elizabeth, George, and Jessica left Big Sur on September 27, heading for Los Angeles. What Jessica was told is unclear. She had intimations of disaster, but it is certain that she did not know what George's intentions were since he did not know them himself. Elizabeth believed that George had declared unequivocally that he loved her, presumptuous of course in the face of a marriage that had lasted seven years. In Los Angeles, the trio found Jessica a place to live and Elizabeth was put up by friends, a Mrs Witchner and her lawyer son Milton, (the Wurtles in *By Grand Central Station*). Elizabeth only knew of George's equivocation in retrospect: "George vacillated between the wife's place and mine, saying he was getting things fixed up for the wife, and it was only humane etc. Pity etc. No doubt he was telling her the same about me."[21] George and Elizabeth started out for New York on October 7. There was talk of visiting D.H. Lawrence's shrine in New Mexico, but they managed only three nights on the road, staying in hotels under assumed names like Mr and Mrs Henrik Van Loon, before the wild spree was over.

In the autumn of 1940 the United States was not yet at war, but the country was jittery and obsessed with the idea of Communists, spies, and Fifth Columnists infiltrating their shores. F.B.I. officers were stationed at all state borders. As they crossed the Arizona border, Elizabeth and George were stopped. George was immediately under suspicion: a British citizen of draftable age who claimed to be a poet and was meandering across America would appear an ingenious cover to the F.B.I. The two were initially arrested under the Mann Act, an archaic act designed to apprehend gangsters. If an unmarried couple were caught in a motor car crossing a border and the woman was under twenty-eight, this was grounds for an arrest. As Elizabeth put it: "You could fornicate in any state legally, but not cross a state line for the purpose." The penalty was a thousand dollars or six months in jail, which gave the F.B.I. time to pursue evidence against the criminals. George was released. His papers were in order, and his fortuitous habit of using fictitious names in hotel registers meant that fornication couldn't be proved. But it was discovered that Elizabeth had entered the U.S. illegally. She had crossed from Mexico; by chance her passport had not been stamped, though she had thought nothing of it at the time. She was held in prison for three days, and while she made light of it afterwards, the ordeal was harrowing. The agent who grilled her about her past and demanded an explanation for the months she had spent in the

U.S. took sixteen pages of notes. The federal boys, as she called them, were serious. Though a three-page F.B.I. file exists on Elizabeth Smart, to this day it cannot be released in the interests of national defence. One might speculate that the F.B.I. had been keeping careful tabs on all those Big Sur anarchists on the Pacific Coast.[22]

As she refused to implicate Varda to corroborate her story—a woman alone in California writing was not a credible explanation in 1940—Elizabeth had a hard time of it. When she spoke of love for Barker she was called a religious fanatic. Finally Mr Witchner telephoned her father who then telephoned the ambassador in Washington and her papers were forwarded. She was released into the Witchners' custody in Los Angeles. George meanwhile had returned to Jessica.

In mid-October George and Elizabeth set off again, this time by train, managing to make it to New York where they stayed with Elizabeth's sister Helen. They were both broke. With wartime restrictions on cash flow, Elizabeth was not receiving her usual allowance from her father. She returned to Ottawa at the end of October with the idea of raising some money, and attempted to sell her two-hundred-acre mountain and her cabin "The Pulley" in the Gatineau Hills.[23] It was clear that, completely in love, she would do anything for Barker.

To Elizabeth in Ottawa Barker poured out all his passionate love in letters of high and randy rhetoric.[24] To her sexual challenge he could rise like a new-made Priapus. She was the one who shook the mystery of life in front of his face like a St Catherine towel. Everything and everywhere seemed suddenly inhabited by elixirelizabeth. Finally, the wild erotic Elizabeth had found her catalyst. It was Barker's talk, erudite, passionate, and outrageous that held her as it would hold many. For Elizabeth he would always be one of the "sexy ambiguous poets." She loved his humour. Who else could be at once profound and humorous?

Russel and Louie were of course relieved to have their daughter home and even amused as she turned her prison ordeal into entertaining anecdotes. But Louie wanted to know about the "poet" person. When Elizabeth told them she was in love, she found no sympathy, but now the old arguments about loyalty and decency and adultery had no power. She wired George the fare to Ottawa. When he arrived Louie refused to have him in the house; he found a room in the sleazy side of Hull and they met furtively in cafés. It did not escape Elizabeth that the city was a metaphor of her state: on the Ottawa side the spires of Parliament and the posh Chateau Laurier hotel with its chartreuse-green roofs and respectability; on the other the E.B. Eddy match factory with its smell of wood and sulphur and the French poverty of Hull where at least the liquor licensing was freer. Only Hull would accommodate her love for George.

Barker was not lucky in Canada. On one occasion he set out impulsively for Montreal with Jane's husband, D'Arcy, who was a journalist working on a story. Police had been posted on Montreal's bridges, on the look-out for German prisoners escaped from the northern P.O.W. camps and heading for a neutral United States. Again he was stopped and arrested for having no registration card; he spent a night in jail as an unexplained alien before Elizabeth could rush down from Ottawa with his passport. This time she thought she had left family and trappings forever. Putting up in a cheap Montreal hotel, they managed several wonderful nights together. But George had other problems on his mind. He was ill with throat trouble, a recurrent problem from childhood, and he was thinking about Jessica. They returned to Ottawa, and at the end of November he left for New York, probably explaining that he had to sort things out with Jessica. He sent a telegram from New York on November 23, saying that he had made everything dandy and sending love.

But everything was far from dandy. Barker had been less than candid with Jessica. He had written to her in late October, and on November 7 she wrote to him in Ottawa from California, complaining that she had not heard from him in a month and that her friends expected her to have a breakdown any moment. "If I had a home to go to and a Father to fight for me it would be different, but as you know I had not a soul to turn to . . . I may mortgage my soul at any moment to come to you.">[25] The explanation he offered to reassure her must have been ingenious as she wrote to him shortly thereafter:

Honestly Gran I think you have been framed in the best possible manner and the chance of your getting out of Ottawa without becoming irreparably involved is horribly remote. I don't think that you realize for one moment the sort of person you are dealing with and with her father, a lawyer also obviously playing against you and you believing that you should be grateful and kind, the only hope for you is to speak your piece and just run. It is not pleasant for me to just sit and wait while they play their little games with you, and considering that both our lives can be ruined by them so easily, you must realize that I am scared and you should be also. His lies to me are understandable only if you have let him believe that you are or will be Elizabeth's lover, or that she has told him so. And do you realize that he, in his position, can possibly fix it so that you cannot get your visa for weeks—and in that time anything could happen—and also he might be able to prevent you getting money to me. For God's sake, Gran dear, don't trust any of them for even the tiniest thing. . . . From the way you spoke this morning I am convinced that you do not suspect anything underhand, unless of course you had someone listening to you. I think it is possible that if Elizabeth has convinced her father that you are necessary to her happiness and that you really love her, he will do anything in this world to keep you there, so that you will eventually agree. I do not say all this out of sheer prejudice, but I have met so many people in Hollywood since you left and if only half of the stories are true, she has lied and intrigued in so many places for things and people far less important than you. . . . I also think that you have played into their hands in the most incredible manner, from the moment you left here without giving me your forwarding address. Do try and realize Gran that I am only trying to preserve something that was good for so many years and more experienced people than you can be and have been convinced of the truth of things that are untrue by the hysterics and general art of Elizabeth. . . . People gape when I am introduced to them as your wife, as you are Elizabeth's poet and genius from Japan and I apparently rose like Aphrodite but from the Pacific.[26]

But theirs was a passionate love neither George nor Elizabeth could abandon. Elizabeth could no doubt convince herself, as a woman often does in this situation, that the marriage had broken down and Jessica would be better off without Barker since it was she, Elizabeth, he loved. On November 24 she slipped down to Helen's in New York, and met George, later claiming that this was the glorious day on which her daughter was conceived. She was soon back in Ottawa waiting for Barker to join her. Letters flashed back and forth. Elizabeth wrote: "I wish desperately you could come up for Christmas but if so what about poor Jessica? It would be awful to be alone in N.Y. . . . How would you like to live in a fishing village in New Brunswick or Nova Scotia? But I have lots of plans for working things out if only Daddy would talk to me. He just avoids me & I've lost all my weapons of persuasion."[27]

Calling her his absurd blonde Pocahontas, George proposed that he emigrate to Canada and wondered what they could do about Jessica. She could not simply be abandoned in New York, which was too formidable a place for someone of her background. Elizabeth responded by proposing a job for Jessica in Canada. Jane would help, though if Jessica were to come to Ottawa, she would have to say that she was with them when they were stopped by the F.B.I. since the story was abroad and she would inevitably be asked. The problem was George. Elizabeth could get her old journalism job back, but a draftable Englishman couldn't get a job in wartime Ottawa, and furthermore they couldn't live together. Ottawa was "too small—you don't realize how everybody's sighs & breathing are known around town almost as soon as committed." Only the Canadian wilderness would be for them. "Would you like to go right into the wilderness?" she asks.

As for me I'm dying, I'm dead. There's only one remedy
for me & now it seems as impossible as unattainable as
distant as a weekend in Mars. I'm the madman batting his
head in *every* direction, & not even finding a place to begin
filing for liberty. I'm doomed too & it's even problematical
that resuscitation will work at all. I say O well I'm only
getting back what I gave Jessica only hers was 1000 times
worse for hers had no future. But there are no wells of *anything* in me not even pity. I'm not even sorry for myself.
I'm dead that's all . . . I can't live here because I can't live
here with you & I can't live without you or meeting you in
cafés in Hull or while Jessica is out for an hour . . . [28]

Barker was trapped in indecision. At one moment he could
write to Elizabeth that his life was hers and they must not pro-
long minor martyrdoms. He would be ruthless, immoral if necessary, and break with Jessica. But then he found himself
paralyzed by pity and could not leave her. The impulsive hasty
trips continued: after Christmas George came up to Ottawa;
they spent New Year's eve together; in mid-January, two weeks
in Montreal. Elizabeth again thought it was forever, but George
went back to Jessica in New York and she motored up to
Ottawa alone. George was ill and ended up in a New York hospital with tonsillitis.

By now Jessica herself was impatient. She wrote to Elizabeth
on January 14:

I'm so sorry I have been so long in writing. We have been
completely frozen at the cottage and capable of very
little. Gran has taken in the New Yorker articles which
are very good I think, and we hear about them tomorrow
definitely.

At first he swore he had not mentioned divorce and
eventually admitted it but because it was unfair you being
in Canada etc. etc. But you probably know the kind of
thing. It is unwise to believe anything unless you also
hear it from me and vice versa don't you think? It's all

perfectly foul and ghastly and I'm sick to the marrow in my bones.[29]

But Elizabeth had not given up. She wrote to George on January 17. She was sick with a cold:

> These very surroundings induce my deepest moronic mood. I can never remember why we aren't together. My love to John who is brilliant enough to see what an immoral bastard you are. . . .
>
> What do I see when I glance at my hands but the blood of your testicles so indelible & nostalgic? I gaze like Lady Macbeth or hide my guilt when I hear someone coming. It's enough to hang me on.[30]

She thought of them living in Nova Scotia, though that was problematical, since she felt they must use assumed names. If they were found out in wartime, they risked a prison term, and they might be taken for spies, living on the East Coast for no apparent reason. But she wanted to believe it would be all right: "Let's go and be randy in the Bay of Fundy."

War and subterfuge were to be the backdrop to all their encounters. On January 18 George went to Harvard where he had been invited to give the Morris Grey lectures. He stayed briefly with Frank Scott whom Elizabeth had told him to call. To get herself down there was more complicated. Elizabeth wrote to Frank Scott asking if he would pose as her uncle. She needed him to write to her a letter inviting her to visit and indicating that he would send her the funds as she couldn't legally get money out of Canada. Marian Scott remembered Barker as a character who delighted in shocking. They were horrified and amused when he told them that "If England should fall, think of the wonderful elegies the poets could write." He became the occasion of an oft-told anecdote. Barker had been the last straw for their French Canadian maid, drinking the orange juice she had meant for other guests. She had a nervous breakdown, and was found catatonic, her arms stretched out in the form of a cross. Clearly the breakdown had nothing to do with Barker but it was the kind of story people loved to attach to him. Marian Scott only remembered George and Frank talking, with her and Elizabeth on the sidelines.[31]

By late February, Elizabeth was clearly pregnant. She always said: "I deliberately set out to have a child. I was deliberate about all of them."[32] With what she called the "huge luckiness" of her childhood, Elizabeth had never learned to worry about the future. She thought only of the next step. In retrospect she was amused by her presumption, confessing that she expected a marvellous woman would turn up, Scots or Irish, to help her. "She wouldn't mind if she didn't get paid and she'd look after me. But she didn't turn up, I'm afraid." A decision had to be made. She wrote to Barker on the 24th: "I'm not running away from you because god knows that would be an impossibility since you are what makes my blood continue to flow, but I'm not in the right shape to stay in Ottawa any longer so I'll have to leave & soon." She could not tell her parents: "There will certainly be difficulties about keeping the remainder of my life secret but if I go into wild & inaccessible enough country and cover my trail with enough lies & alibis & appear back home every so often to reassure them, perhaps there will be a solution. But I am absolutely determined that they shall never know or have a chance of anyone telling them. I do owe them that at least."[33]

The problem was where to go. She thought of the Bahamas, but gave that up, anticipating she might have difficulty in getting the right papers to bring the baby back into Canada. She couldn't get an affidavit to live in the U.S. She thought of England and wrote to External Affairs to request permission to go to Great Britain. The response was turgid. It was brought to her attention that an Order in Council of June 4, 1940, prohibited women, other than women employed in the armed forces or public service of Canada, and children under the age of twelve, from travelling to European war zones.

She was still unsure of George:

The fact though, the terrible fact probably is that you can, & can never, leave her. So if you can't, you can't & if you

can't I won't ask you to. If you don't belong to me how can
I want you even though I am dying for you? . . .

Don't think I'm not bleeding from every pore. I'm only
lucky to be able to hypodermic myself & cover over every
gape so that I can feel nothing cold or hot or pleasant or
excruciating. . . .
I do love you more than anything else in the world or
the world. That's not the trouble or rather perhaps that is
the trouble. E.[34]

She told George she had decided to leave for Vancouver in
early March. He joined her in Ottawa and they left by train for
Vancouver on March 3. It was a romantic trip. George remembered the train passing through the Rockies, the dining-car
table covered with glasses, and the way the light hit the glass
and sparkled out of Elizabeth's face.

In his *Dream Play*, August Strindberg wrote: "Oh the agony of
ecstasy and the ecstasy of agony. You look for love outside
yourself when love is your very nature." Part of the addiction
of love is the pendulum swing between pain and longing so that
the ordinary is inflated to a level of dramatic intensity. There
are not many states in which one can live so intensely, and few
people would forgo it. Yet the subtext beneath is a distressing-
ly familiar pattern. Barker vascillated between the two women,
trying to placate both and using every subterfuge to do so. They
in turn became enemies. Jessica, trapped between dependency
and outrage, saw George as the victim. Elizabeth, the other
woman, waited in agonies of loneliness. The truth was that for
Barker writing took pre-eminence. Passion was heady material
but the moment it became consuming he would lash out or
retreat. But what had begun for Elizabeth as projection turned
into love. She knew Barker was the catalyst for her to reach a
heroic version of herself. "Alice [Paalen]," she had said, "presented me with the pity. George gave me the courage to break
the surface bonds, to face the murderous act of stepping resolutely into my own life."[35] She had found something she could

fight for aggressively, unequivocally, totally against the world's terms. In love she found authority, and she would write her book. But she also had to spend years learning how to release herself from the projection without sabotaging the love, to accept Barker as a vehicle rather than the end.

The relationship was unique. These were two powerful writers. Along with the painful ecstasy of the push/pull tension of love was the high rhetoric of its articulation. Elizabeth wrote letters to George in her notebook to which he responded, and out of her side of the correspondence, Elizabeth would later extract pieces that would be part of the exquisite mosaic that became *By Grand Central Station*.

For Elizabeth love was an irrevocable involvement, because in encountering Barker she had at last walked into the full dimensions of herself. On September 21, 1940, a little more than a month after the love affair with Barker began, she wrote in her diary:

God, come down out of the eucalyptus tree, and tell me who will drown in so much blood. I saw her face coming out of the mist by the dying geraniums. . . .

On her mangledness I am spreading my amorous sheets, but who will have any pride in the wedding red, seeping up between the colossus thighs whose issue is only the cold semen of grief? . . .

But it is not easing or escape I crave when I pray god to understand my corrupt language and step down for a moment to sit on my broken bench. Will there be a birth from all this blood or is death only pouring out his fatal prime? Is an infant struggling in the triangular womb? I am blind but blood not love has blinded my eye. Love lifted the weapon and guided my crime, locked my limbs when the anguish rose out of the sea to cry Help and now over that piercing mask superimposes the cloudy mouth of desire. . . .

Cut, the rocks breathe their accumulated gases and the greedy castor tree casts them up and down the canyon that is so in love with tragedy.[36]

There are few modern writers who have so exactly caught the apocalyptic power of great passion. It has made her raw, unlayered skins, shocked her awake and into attention. The brilliance of the language is its metaphoric energy, so that the human and the organic are intertwined. Never are we so alive as when submerged in the agony of ecstasy and the ecstasy of agony. Elizabeth knew the intoxication would disappear, therefore she wished "urgently to articulate it . . . *This* in that hour moved me to tears and made a gaze through the dining-car window a plenitude not to be borne."[37] And she turned this love into a vision. All around her were the insane and twisted passions of war; she herself had been victim of its ridiculous paranoias. She saw war not as an objective phenomenon of historical process, something that somehow happens, but more as a collective neurosis that rises out of warped human emotion, almost as Freud would have it, a compensation impulse for unlived life, a negative and impotent drive to death. Love, with its impulsive courage, could recover the vision of plenitude. "All flows like the Mississippi over a devastated but grateful earth which drinks unsurfeited, which raises a praise to deafen all doubters forever, to burst their shameful inadequate eardrums with the roar of proof, louder than bombs, screams, or the sobbing of remorse, and stronger even than the spilt blood's poisonous tides."[38] Over the following months she crafted her vision in extracts in her diary.

She understood that Barker was the occasion for her new-found authority. "With George has come an ability to count out all the distracting faces in the street. Therefore and only to explore within, or build them again but better in the more becoming mind."[39] The vacuum of need she had felt at core was at last inhabited. Love for George provided the still centre, the emotional focus that freed her to write.

There were still detractors; Barker's friend in New York, Gene Derwood, the wife of an acquaintance, Oscar Williams, advised her that she should not want to be a poet because George was and she could never be as great as he. (This was a hurtful memory Elizabeth returned to all her life.) She felt unable to articulate her protest but was now sure that what she had to write had not been written before. She had found her voices.

Elizabeth had begun *By Grand Central Station* before she met Barker, but it continued under the stimulus of the encounter as a dialogue, which, from the *Song of Solomon*, has always been the exquisite form of the love poem. Barker was reading and annotating her diaries, and the letters she wrote are carefully crafted as vehicles to convert him to her heroic vision. She could quote his own words back at him: "Only Love can with a great gaze stop." And ask, "But where is love?" "Crucified over five hundred miles. Stretched out in the snow over the dilapidated country where only the birds are at home and they only for six months of the year." Love was what "he staked all for, all he had, ungamblable." [To this Barker appended a marginal note that he had bloody well not.][40]

Addressing Barker as "my bastard, my weather, my indicator pulse," and the one to unstick "the glue of my mother's clutch. Can Freud explain why it is stronger than the North East wind, reason or pre-Cambrian rock?"—she writes:

> But will you forget when you hold your so vulnerable head between your hands that what we are being punished for is not just that sea of peace we achieve when you call me You Bitch but the Cause (my Soul). . . . Do you see me as the too successful one like a colossus whose strong thighs rise obliviously out of sorrow? Or all female who devours and grabs? Or strong & invulnerable with my greed? If you think these things there are your sins, not the blond saplings with blue eyeshadows leaning toward you in the print shop.[41]

But the letters are not always at this high level of rhetoric. They could be playful and nasty:

> Dear George Barker,
>
> I am a little girl 27 years old. Will you support me for the rest of my life? I would appreciate this.
>
> Yours truly,
> Elizabeth Smart
> R.S.V.P.

To which George responded by asking why the bones of Christ he should. She was too heavy and he needed support himself. Elizabeth countered:

Dear Mr. B.

I hasten to inform you that my figure still has willowy spots as I only weigh 136/163 yet all odds against me. If you cannot support me you will miss a good thing. This is a tip from a friend.

Yours,
E.S.[42]

When she appealed to him: "Take me," he replied that he would take her for a ride. On another occasion, finding a blank page in the midst of one of Elizabeth's powerful prose monologues, George wrote that he was in a dirty hotel bedroom, more or less reclining on a friend of hers, and writing to her. His hands, he assured her, held only a pencil. Elizabeth countered:

Dear Lamb: Please forgive my bawdy friend George Barker for bothering you with irrelevant details of my amatory pastimes. I trust you do not feel I have trespassed too far in promising you my friend in the midst of such pursuits. These latter, I may say, I have found to be life's chief balm, though often like the rest of my undignified race, trying to disown them by rationalizing the superiority of things less inextricably woven with the undiluted flesh. Arguments that glisten with authority in the midst of formal ceremonial or forced chastity have less chance, I find, of surviving the sensual floods, than the stars have of outshining an equatorial noon. Do you, dear Lamb, not agree?[43]

And then she adds with wonderful outrage: "Fuck this bleeding friend. Balls and shit to this friend and all my hate. E.S." Elizabeth was no wimp in this love. She may have delighted in George's humour and outrageousness, but when he pushed too far, she fought back.

George and Elizabeth found themselves in Vancouver together. Though there was ecstasy, cheap hotels were the backdrop to their love. Barker spoke of wretchedness and no cash, of a land where there is no one to talk to and nothing ever happens. He was restless. He wanted out. Elizabeth was too intense. He would mock her, saying cheap hotels were not romantic, just dirty. But having no money never bothered Elizabeth; she understood her privilege: "Having once had money you don't really feel poor, just that you haven't had money for a while. Real poverty is the relentlessness." To George poverty was not romantic, it was debilitating.

Barker vascillated between ecstatic affirmation and cruelty. When he felt that he was losing himself to the passion, he could resort to misogyny. The easiest thing was to accuse her of infidelity. It was she who had sabotaged this love, because he couldn't forget or forgive her former infidelities. He would not forgive her Yanko, or promiscuous encounters on Mexican beaches, which he admitted were nothing more than the afternoon frolics of a bitch in the dust but now were daggers in his heart.[44] She would throw at him his promiscuous past, but George had no problem admitting and even flaunting his own licentiousness. She, on the other hand, was always on the defensive, having to convince him that nothing before had mattered.

Elizabeth could never fully perceive or perhaps believe the nature of the power struggle. Her brother, Russel, may have come close to the truth when he admitted to liking George but finding him weak. He felt that his sister made George feel inadequate. "In George's eyes, she had everything: she was rich, beautiful, and she could really write."[45] But Elizabeth, of course, was willing to abandon all these gifts for George, since *he* was the poet.

Barker was trapped in his own gods. He felt great passion: glorious, blind, irresistible; he felt guilt. He was certain erotic love inevitably destroys and consumes those it ignites. He used his Catholic misogyny to explain himself to himself. Sin and betrayal are inevitable. George could enter easily into the Catholic philosophy of pessimism, but how to sustain an idea of the good? But in sexual terms, one might counter banally: SIN for men is also Safety in Numbers. By vascillation, he could avoid a confrontation with himself. One might say that George was, unlike Elizabeth, always in control of his own misfortune.

Looking for an out, George sent a telegram to his friend John Fitch, insisting that he come and bring Jessica, without of course mentioning Elizabeth to her. John Fitch arrived, alone. Elizabeth was shocked, realizing his sudden arrival had been prearranged. On April 3 George set off in Fitch's big red Buick for a joy-ride down to Big Sur and across America back to New York. When Fitch asked, "What about Elizabeth?" Barker replied: "Oh Elizabeth knew this was going to happen."[46] In her diary the next day Elizabeth wrote:

> It is not possible that he will not return. I sit here on one elbow hourly expecting his tight peremptory tap on the door. Each time the inefficient jangle of the elevator gets into motion, I start up. Will this monster stop at my floor and disgorge my miracle? I hurry back from a half-finished walk up the street. Are there any telegrams?. . . I see a car with a tall radio aerial—this is the grass of hope that grows indomitably over my eyes. . . .
>
> I know that perhaps tonight his mouth like the centre of a rose closes over John's mouth burning with apologies of love like a baby at the breast.[47]

She felt she was going crazy, her brain rattling like a dried pea, unable to sleep for the dreams of corpses hidden in ice. There was no firm ground to stand on. With her own ethic of excess, how could she fault George's extremism—the poet was, by definition, an extremist. At last knowing her abandonment, she wired ahead to New York that Jessica had telegrammed for cash. "Why return. I definitely resign. Have wired sister to give her something."

Now, her only preoccupation was to find a place to have her child in secret. She looked on the map, circled it with a pin and plunged. The pin pierced Pender Harbour, a rough logging and fishing hamlet on the Sechelt Peninsula in British Columbia. It was inaccessible; boats only sailed twice a week. On April 5, carting her parcels and boxes of books, she boarded the steamer from Vancouver to Pender Harbour, a six-hour journey to travel sixty miles.

In Pender Harbour, Elizabeth rented an old disused schoolhouse opposite the landing at the mouth of the harbour (she still had her seventy-five-dollar dress allowance from home). She painted the door yellow and placed a sign above it: "The cut worm forgives the plough." She cultivated her loneliness, avoiding the prying sympathy of the locals who watched her pregnancy and scrutinized the letters at the post office that came addressed to Miss Smart and to Mrs Barker, the name she went by. She knew nothing about practical matters. Her trunks were full of evening dresses and books, and on her first day there she went to the local store and ordered ten pounds of tea. One day the Mounted Police came to her door to investigate the new arrival. They found her harmless—"a religious maniac." She had pasted up pictures of Madonnas, Christs, and bits of Blake and Ecclesiastes cut out of paper on the window frames and over the doors.

Meditating the full reach of aloneness, she walked the harbour—a stark landscape, rocky, moss-laden, with beautiful red-bleeding arbutus, an archipelago on the blue strip of horizon where one expected the gods to step down to the ground— it was the mirror of her psyche. She went into the town and bought an old wind-up Victrola so that she and the child she was carrying could listen to Mozart. She read Wordsworth's *Prelude*, Rilke, Auden. She felt the child's head bump her stomach, and continued to write the memorial that would "scorch and bleed the uncaring the inattentive world." Fearing she would die in pregnancy ("You always think you'll die when you give birth—it's something atavistic—I wrote a will before each labour"[48]), she wanted the book to be her testament. Meanwhile she wrote letters home to her family, describing her wonderful life in the primitive wilderness. She had told them she was working on a novel.

Elizabeth did find one close friend, Maximiliane Von Upani Southwell, a cultivated Viennese woman twenty years her senior who had moved to the outpost with her fisherman husband and ten-year-old son. By the time Elizabeth met them, he was an invalid and they were living on the dole, but with immense elegance. When Maxie first visited Elizabeth she picked up a well-thumbed copy of Rilke on the kitchen table and said: "I see we shall be friends."[49]

But Elizabeth again found herself waiting for George: "Forty days in the wilderness and not one holy vision." The letters continued. He claimed she was cold about his going. He was hunting up Jessica, daunted to think what might have happened to her, and proposed that once things were settled, he and Elizabeth could go to England in September. He suggested that Sebastian, as they had come to call the baby, could be left in Canada, or would she rather he remain in British Columbia and never write another word? He had only one poem to show for the ten days spent on the Before Christ Coast. If Elizabeth would understand him, he implied, she must understand that the chaos of his life was synonymous with and justified by his vocation to poetry. He was also clearly having money problems, trying to get money owed him by his publisher. On May 22 he sent a telegram from Winnipeg; he had bought a through-ticket but to save money decided to turn in his airline ticket and come the rest of the way by train. He wrote that at the moment he possessed eighteen cents and the hotel cost two dollars a night. In the morning he would either be arrested or evicted. But he would get there.

The signals from George were so complicated that it was as if she were caught in a maelstrom. On receiving the telegram, she rehearsed his betrayal, trying to imagine an explanation and an exit:

No I will not allow him to wreck my life or turn bitter and broken because, after all, he was only certain of loving me for perhaps three days or weeks. I will not say it was any less because now his incredible capacity for what was surely unnecessary deceit to both of us knocks everything from under me, entirely dissolves me so periodically. Of *course* he can love us both, but why be so to us both? We're both good people. We can understand. We might even both rise to hard demands made on us to love (the abstract I mean). Or must he be the all things to all things (both of us, who make the circle whole)? But I don't invalidate even the moments when I was most deceived. . . . nor can I cease loving nor will there ever be another who was all the things I wanted so completely and the only one destined. . . . I could slit my throat from ear to ear better than know he stayed for melodramatic reasons concerning the world's favourite story of the too-well too-lightly loved and left with child. No one has done any wrong. It was all worth while. . . .

The worst thing is the deceit. Even she who sees the offence itself so large (but then, to save herself from total wreck she was able to make *me* the monster) minds the deceit most. "My dearest love—you reign empress in my heart—you totally reign my mind." "Dearest Elizabeth I am all Elizabeth my head my heart my hand." [from Barker's telegram.][50]

But if George betrayed, she would chose fidelity to the vision. She found herself decorating the schoolhouse with dozens of silver tin cans filled with yellow flowers for George's arrival. He came on May 28 and stayed exactly one month. Saying that he was getting a divorce from Jessica and promising to be back before the baby's birth, he left June 28. He did not return.

Elizabeth resumed writing her novel, which she constructed meticulously like a mosaic, selecting fragments from her diaries, adding new material. The first chapter was written last. She remembered the "agonizing boredom of finishing [it]. Part

One . . . seemed so thin & boring I thought so it must seem to all."[51] Being very pregnant, she found it tedious checking through the Bible for the bits she wanted. In her isolation she could not, of course, know how fine her book was. The last chapter had already been written before she arrived at Pender Harbour, on one of those previous occasions when she came down from Canada to see George and he didn't meet her at Grand Central Station as planned. "He probably met me the next day," she once remarked. "One needn't be too accurate about this, as it's not . . . history, but fiction." She made the narrator and lover nameless because the story was not personal. Her theme was the "thing never said but always done, the saying invariably abandoned for the being. Which is, in truth, the simple fact of being a woman overpowered by voices of blood each time she rises to speak her piece. And love that gives, compels her to adore being devoured surrendering to a destruction that of course causes her to be born again, but obliterates all private ambition and blinds her eyes and her heart with images of unborn babies."[52]

The book was completed two weeks before her child was born. While she could not celebrate her child to her family, she was able to write to her mother to say her book was done: "I'm really pleased with it. I'm going seriously into the business of getting it published . . . I've done what I came to do." Shortly before the birth she moved in with Maxie. On August 26, she felt the first pangs of labour. Mr Reid, a local fisherman, rowed her by boat to the Mission Hospital. She wrote in her diary on August 27: "All day doing nothing but the hoola hoola in the hospital. It was sunny & beautiful."[53] Georgina was delivered the next day at 4:10 P.M.

The miracle she had been imagining since adolescence had finally devolved on her, and though she was alone through it it was still a "very great joy." Elizabeth had lost none of her obsession. She created a historical record for Georgina, as she was to do for each of her children. She returned to her lists, describing the birth, who attended, who visited. One week before the delivery she had written to her child:

A LITTLE NOTE FOR SEBASTION BARKER OR, IN HIS ABSENCE,
FOR GEORGINA ELIZABETH BARKER.

This is my last will & testament written by me in my own hand, in a mind sound but sad because it so nearly witnessed the maturity of a miracle but missed by a hairsbreadth. But. I have written about that in my book.

It is to my child I wish to make my apologia, for George Barker surely will know by now I was created only to deliver him. If he didn't have quite enough courage to be sure of this before it was too late I don't love him any less. But to my child I owe some explanation, though I still think it is worthwhile being born. I hope he will not mind being a bastard. Surely it will help him to avoid the bores, the snobs, the petty, & the afraid. And even when he looks at my life let him remember that truly there is nothing worth anything in life but Love—all kinds & for all objects, but never less than total. Let him have my books & my records. It was Dido's lament he heard in the womb. I hope he will know more about music when he is 6 than I do now & know how to *listen*. Let him have all his father's papers, & the records, & the books & MSS. Let him know that there wasn't a moment ever when I didn't want him. Let him love both men & women in all ways, but from an excess, never a fear of love.

I kiss you Sebastian or Georgina Elizabeth & forgive me if you don't like being born, climb mountains, sit in trees & read Quia Amore Langueo, or swim across a mountain lake.

Your mother,
Elizabeth Smart
Thursday, August 21st 1941—at Pender Harbour, B.C.[54]

Barker was now desperate. To his letters Elizabeth responded with anger or silence. And she stopped sending him bits of money, at which he protested—if she refused to send him money, he would simply steal it or get it out of her sister Jane or go crazy. In his rage, he claimed to have gone to an old boyfriend of hers and knocked out two teeth. He insisted she could not slip away from him. In September he sent her a sequence of five love poems, celebrating Georgina's birth, and written as a dialogue in which he assumes the voice of Elizabeth.

Barker was attempting to come west. His editor at Macmillan could write a mutual friend Willard Maas that he looked like the wrath of God and was on the verge of pneumonia. While Barker attempted to assuage Jessica, scrambled for money, and dealt with the draft board, he found one final hurdle that was insurmountable. His application for immigration to Canada was summarily turned down. On September 19 F.C. Blair, Director of the Immigration Branch of the Department of Mines and Resources wrote:

Dear Sir:

Your letter of the 12th instant reached me on the day on which the Minister considered and dismissed your immigration appeal. I regret to have to inform you that this closes the door on your entry to this country. It is unnecessary that I go into any detail regarding the matter beyond pointing out that our officer reported that you intended to remain for a few days as a guest at the home of Mr. Russell [sic] Smart who lives in one of the suburbs of Ottawa and that Mr. Smart was paying your transportation to Vancouver. I got into touch with one of Mr. Smart's daughters who informed me that you were not to be a guest in her father's home, that her father knew nothing about your coming and would not receive you nor would he provide your transportation to Vancouver or elsewhere. I gathered from the conversation that you are far from being a welcome guest in that home for reasons which you probably know as well or better than we do.

It was also observed that when our officer asked about funds in your possession that you mentioned $40.00 which later on you were unable to show. We already have

on our file a great deal of information about Elizabeth
Smart and her illegitimate child. I would strongly advise
you to remain where you are without any further attempt
to enter Canada, at least until after either you or your wife
secure a divorce. If then you are interested in coming to
Canada, write and let us have the facts and we will let you
know if admission can be approved.[55]

It is likely that Barker was following Elizabeth's advice in
using Smart as a sponsor (her letters were full of P.S.'s on how
George should secure his entry permit—"Under no circumstances WIRE Jane—it might ruin everything—it is too dangerous. Use AIRMAIL only."). She could not have anticipated
that the director would phone Coltrin Lodge; from the
response, the sister who answered the phone was probably
Helen. And the Director did not mention what Elizabeth later
learned to be the subtext of the letter. Louie had used Russel's
influence with immigration to have Barker refused entry to
Canada on the grounds of moral turpitude.[56] Louie knew Barker
was married: she did not know that Elizabeth had had his child.
The Director was obviously discreet. While they kept a file on
Elizabeth, he did not mention to the Smarts the existence of the
"illegitimate child."[57]

Nothing could have sent Elizabeth more strongly back into
George's orbit than this letter, which he surely reported to her.
The law and the forces of sanity were yet again dictating her
life. George, whatever his weaknesses, was the true pole
towards which her being inclined. His very wildness, his willingness to pursue his desires, guaranteed his integrity.

By November, Elizabeth was contemplating coming east.
Her father was ill. George was living in a cottage in Nyack on
the Hudson, and had suggested he was unable to give her his
address because he wouldn't be there long and to write to him
in New York. In fact he was with Jessica in Nyack. But he was
clearly worried that he was losing Elizabeth and wrote placatory letters, asking when she would step off the train in Grand
Central Station, for now there was nothing else to keep him in
the continent of America except her coming. She had sent him

the manuscript of *By Grand Central Station I Sat Down and Wept* and he responded with a marvellous twenty-page critique. Barker had always affirmed her writing. He had called her the writer through whom the Atlantic continent would find its articulate voice, the one upon whom Virginia Woolf's genius had devolved after her death. Now he wrote that *By Grand Central Station* was the first true native prose poem in English, the thing he had tried to do himself in the novel *Alanna Autumnal*, that the French succeeded in doing because they combined intellectual passion and spiritual reserve. The sensuality of words, the ballet of semantics in her novel were tremendous. He knew of no one writing in English with a more fluid fountain of pure sensuality. He was astounded by her authority. He had only one reservation: sometimes she lost the narrative feel under the glut of metaphors exhibited for their own sake. He couldn't quite see what happened towards the end. But the letter is a passionate affirmation, spoken with humour. Her book had body: feet, legs, and my god! genitals. He made suggestions about certain metaphors that didn't work: he could—inspiration was a bitch and he had her phone number. He wanted to sit with her and discuss this creation, her youngest daughter. He was certain Emily Brontë, Héloïse, George Eliot and Virginia Woolf would be the pallbearers at her funeral. In his opinion, she was the only poet born on the continent of America since Whitman. It was heady praise and Elizabeth needed it.[58]

Elizabeth left Pender Harbour on December 7, putting Georgina in the care of Maxie. It had been "3 months of anguish & despair and running through the bushes & then off in a boat, leaving Georgina a tiny figure in Maxie's arms."[59] It would have been heartbreaking for her to leave her three-month-old baby but she was looking for her daughter's father, and must have been terrified at her own father's illness. When she arrived at Grand Central Station, George failed to meet her, and she had to go to stay with her friend the painter, Pegi Nichol. In her diary she recorded cryptically that she had spent two horrible days at the cottage in Nyack with George and Jessica.

She arrived in Ottawa on December 24. It was a hellish time, with George phoning and asking her to marry him. At the end of her diary in 1941, she records: "This was a very sad year for ES—it was spent mainly in having Georgina & the very great joy of it was turned into the most unimaginable sorrow."[60] It was not the book but the child that was her miracle.

8   How Many Miles to the Gallon to Babylon

*All our desires are contradictory. . . . I want the person
I love to love me. If, however, he is totally devoted to me
he does not exist any longer and I cease to love him. As
long as he is not totally devoted to me he does not love
me enough. Hunger and repletion.*
    Simone Weil
    Gravity and Grace

Suffering is a mistress I cannot deny.
    Marcel Proust
    Remembrance of Things Past

Probably through her father's influence, Elizabeth managed to
wangle a resident's permit for the U.S. She went to Washington
in mid-January, staying with her old friends Grisell and Eddie
Hastings—he was a captain of the British Navy on duty in
Washington. Her plan was to find a job and bring Georgina,
who was still in Pender Harbour under Maxie's care, to
Washington. She took the first job she could find, as a filing
clerk with the British Army Staff punching holes in telegrams
and arranging them in chronological order. She moved through
the ranks from file clerk to mail clerk to confidential mail clerk.
Soon she got a job at the British Embassy, in the office of the
Minister in Charge of Information, Harold Butler. Ten days
later Butler's personal assistant shot himself, and she asked
him: "Why not make me personal assistant, as I'm going

cheap?" He did. As she described it, her job was to reply to the bores to whom he had to be polite, cut down his radio speeches without giving him too much anguish, and fend off the importunate self-important.

But beneath the posh job, the bizarre anguish of her life continued—she became ill with eczema, which the doctor put down to worrying. And George persisted in what had by now become the charade of divorce. He was trying to explain what had gone on in the cottage in Nyack. He told her that in spite of what Jessica had said over the phone (and could you blame her if she omitted certain aspects of the truth?), he was in the process of being divorced. He said that to have subjected Jessica to the anguish of having said as much when she was actually there in the room would have been diabolical. He also proposed that he and Elizabeth accept a job under the Quakers, rehabilitating a town destroyed by earthquake near Mexico City. George told her that he was working without rest because there was no time left if he was to earn the plaster cast in the museum of national biography. He asked her to send him a ticket to Washington as *The New Yorker* was procrastinating and he had only forty-three cents. He went down to Washington in early February.

But Elizabeth's life still had some of the old sociability since many of her Canadian friends were in Washington. On a trip to New York she finally met Anaïs Nin[1] and Lawrence Durrell, who reported to Miller that she was a blonde Viking type. She kept up her professional writer's life, trying to get her manuscript published, and in February wrote to Louie that *By Grand Central Station I Sat Down and Wept* had been accepted by Colt Press, a small experimental press in San Francisco, and things were looking up. Perhaps she had used her contact with Miller to approach the publisher, William Roth, since Colt Press was about to bring out Miller's *The Colossus of Maroussi*. If Roth thought of publishing her book, it came to nothing. Very soon the press had difficulties and closed down.

Elizabeth's greatest concern was how to manoeuvre to get Georgina to Washington. There were problems with Immigration. She was asked to prove that Georgina was her baby and that George was the father.[2] And suddenly, things were far from good at Pender Harbour. The Southwells' son developed a serious inflammation behind one eye and was ordered to Vancouver for an operation. Maxie had to go with him and had no choice but to place Georgina in a foster home for two weeks while Immigration procrastinated.

In the midst of this confusion Elizabeth still felt that, at all costs, she had to keep the secret of her child from her parents. She finally arranged that Maxie would put Georgina on a plane in Vancouver. The question was who would meet the plane? Elizabeth feared that if she did her parents would find out; there were many eyes in Washington. It was decided that her friend Grisell Hastings would pick up Georgina and a story was concocted for the purpose. Georgina was to be a British subject whose mother had died in British Columbia, and who was being returned to her father stationed in England in the British War Service. But when Georgina arrived on March 5 on an American Airlines flight, there was a big stir at the airport about the mystery baby, and reporters showed up in droves. The passenger list identified the baby only as Georgina Elizabeth; airline officials couldn't clarify the issue. The stewardesses told their stories of Georgina's flight: she had slept well and eaten her formula. Grisell was grilled but wouldn't explain the mystery. There were rumours. Was she royalty? nobility? since Grisell was the daughter of Lord Lammington. The story with photos made the headlines the next morning in the *Washington Times*: "LONDON-BOUND BABY PASSEN-GER IN PLANE PROVIDES MYSTERY AT AIRPORT HERE: INFANT ENDS ONE STAGE OF MYSTERY JOUR-NEY" and in the Baltimore paper: "EARL'S DAUGHTER MEETS MYSTERY BABY."[3]

Georgina was spirited to Helen's home in Baltimore. Russel, Sr. was visiting at the time and was told the elaborate story of the dead mother and soldier father. The moment he looked at Georgina he turned to Helen and said: "Is that your baby?" But he kept the secret. It was to be another two years before Louie found out. Soon Elizabeth had come down with measles and the doctors ordered her to stay away. Georgina was suddenly ill with an ear infection and Helen had to hire a night nurse. She

sent a solicitous letter to Elizabeth in Washington and a telegram also arrived from Jessica wishing Georgina well.[4] Finally
on the 6th of April, the doctors declared Elizabeth free of con-
tagion and she was allowed to collect her baby. The cost of hiding Georgina must have been high since motherhood was what
she had waited for. Unable to celebrate her child publicly, she
used to visit baby shops in Washington just so that she could
talk about children.

By now Jessica had resumed her correspondence with
Elizabeth. April 4th Good Friday:

Dear Elizabeth,

I am here as I have just received your letter and walked
out on a party to write this and think away from Gran. Of
course he has been living with me all the time and happily and very passionately (this because from your letter it
counts more than anything with you) and he is finished
with you and is just forgetting the last remnants of you etc.
etc. He has been quite angelic and done so many things
that mean great effort for him and I was and am convinced
that he loves me. I telephoned him because I had read your
letters, including today's which is a masterpiece I think,
but Gran said you refused to be convinced as you did not
want to be. Also I was not to get in touch with you as you
would lie to me. The arrangement now was that we should
ask you down and he would tell you in front of me, so that
I would be convinced for all time.

I know he loves me Elizabeth and I believe now what I
first believed. That he enjoys sleeping with you but does
not really want to live with you. Obviously he could have
been living with you all this time if he had really wanted
to do so and he says that all the lies are to prevent me
going from him and it must be true. After all I have left
him once already. But you pursue him Elizabeth and
apparently you would rather ruin his life than let him continue being happy with me. . . . You certainly have made
your mark on our lives my sweet.[5]

But by April 13, Jessica left George again. She demanded money for the rent, telling him she would not take money from Elizabeth's friends, but preferred "to borrow from the males I pick up not your lady for me. . . . You certainly have made things as unpleasant for me as you could. But it does not matter, really, now."[6] Jessica had no intention of picking anybody up, but it was a perfect ploy against George, who could be manipulated by jealousy. He responded that all his nightmares had come home at last; he insisted he was completely in love with them both.

On May 20, Jessica seems to have given up the fray. She wrote to Elizabeth: "I'm not going to write a long letter—I think that the important thing is that I become more and more convinced that Gran will never be able to say that he doesn't love you. . . . Jessica."[7]

Perhaps the way to understand George Barker is to recognize that, unlike Elizabeth or Jessica, he lived his life as a dialectical challenge, balancing between the passions of love and art. Addicted to guilt, torment was the element he cultivated. He often felt like a victim with Elizabeth and Jessica standing over him as spiritual detectives, about to arrest him for any false feeling. Elizabeth was Cleopatra, Jessica the saint whose sanity invites degradation. He often spoke of returning to Catholicism; it provided a route to absolution.

Anaïs Nin met Barker in October 1941, and describes him in her diaries:

> George Barker comes, with his dilated Celtic blue eyes, his brilliance and accuracy of mind, vivid talk, electric and fertile . . . [he] is now living in the Bowery, in the most leprous, festering part of New York, a street lined with Gorki flophouses, with sour-smelling bars, with doorways in which sodden and decrepit alcoholics lie asleep, as eroded and distorted as the lepers of the Moroccan ghettos. His wife [Jessica] is ill with tuberculosis. He looks at moments like a fine trapped animal trying to scale the walls of his cage.[8]

Barker and Nin often talked of Catholicism and of guilt, with Nin insisting that Catholicism "gave us more guilt than absolution, more crucifixions than resurrections." It created masochism. To which Barker replied that that wasn't the religion's fault. "If we repeat [the crucifixion] over and over again, it is because we did not accomplish it totally, wholly."

To help Barker financially, Nin suggested he join her circle of erotica. Nin, along with Miller, Robert Duncan, and other friends, was writing erotica to order for a rich businessman, though the collector, as they called him, always complained that the writings were too literary and wanted them to get to the point. Nin supplied paper and carbon, and protected everyone's anonymity. The idea of Nin's being a madam of a snobbish literary house of prostitution-writing appealed to Barker's sense of humour and seemed more inspiring than begging or borrowing money, or cajoling meals out of friends.

Barker delivered a manuscript in December. "George Barker is terribly poor," Nin wrote.

> When he comes, he is like a man sitting on a drill. He vibrates as if he would explode. His eyes are like blue porcelain washed by the sea, his words staccato, like a typewriter. He wants to write more erotica. He wrote eighty-five pages. The collector thought they were too surrealistic. His scenes of lovemaking were disheveled and fantastic. Love between trapezes. He drank away the first money, and I could not lend him anything but more paper and carbons. George Barker, the excellent English poet, writing erotica to drink, just as Utrillo painted paintings in exchange for a bottle of wine. I begin to think about the old man [the collector] we all hated.[9]

Nin tried to sort out her impressions of Barker and one sees why Elizabeth loved this young poet.

> He is so quick, so sharp, so focused, vital, electric. A taut mind and body, throwing off sparks. Turbulent. His wet Irish eyes, mocking with that caressing slant towards the

cheeks which indicates voluptuousness. At first I did not like his flippancy, his disguises. But when he said: "What can one do when one is removed not once, not twice, but a hundred times from one's real self?" at that moment I liked him, understood him.

We talk with suppleness, clarity, swiftness. Images appear spontaneously, a search for heightened living. His body is all keyed up for it. I am sure he makes love the same way with nervous, feverish activity, as if a current of electricity were speeding through his body.

But Nin had misgivings.

A visit from George Barker. He is wildly propelled by tensions into sudden animation, restlessness, nervous buoyancy, spirited but shallow. His writing has the same sparkling but false tones. It is not emotion but a kind of brain fever. It is as if only the maximum state of tension keeps him alive. When the Westerner suffers from this electric short circuit he does not have the relief of the primitives, to dance all night, to drum until they fall to the ground. In George Barker it is agitation.[10]

Nin is of course being rather pretentious with her cult of primitivism, but she has caught something of Barker. Sometimes one suspects from his letters and poems that his emotions become rhetorical, an intellectual and literary performance— not that Barker didn't feel deeply, but that he did not have the courage of feeling, and rather used cynicism, or a pendulum swing from self-pity to self-aggrandizement to escape the logic of emotion. It did infect the writing, which is often brilliant, intellectually exciting, but occasionally emotionally untrustworthy. Barker's true voice, as in his poetic sequences *The True Confession of George Barker* or *Villa Stellar*, is a Byronic deflationary wit, painful in its vision of emptiness.

While Elizabeth was engaged with sorting out her life, Barker was busy with his work; this was an extraordinarily creative time for him. He was collaborating with the New York avant-garde film-makers Willard Maas and his wife, Marie Menken, on a film called *Geography of the Body*. Experimenting in the fusion of verse and film, the three filmed details of each other's bodies with a dime-store magnifying glass taped to a 16mm camera. The sound-track was a surrealistic poem written and recited by Barker, in which allusions to exotic and mystical travels, synchronized with images of ambiguously defined zones of the body, evoke the body as landscape and geography.[11] The film was to make a considerable stir when it appeared in 1943. Barker was also submitting poems to *The Nation*, where he sometimes went to find a typewriter to type out poems, and his *Selected Poems* came out with Macmillan in New York. He was twenty-nine, at the beginning of his career, and he was frantic to be under way. He continued his intermittent visits to Washington.

In a hotel in Baltimore on November 9, Elizabeth's second child, Christopher, was conceived and the event carefully recorded in her journal. That December, Jessica also became pregnant. Before she was finished with Barker she wanted her own children. George told his friend Willard Maas it was the least he could do for her. She was to have twins.

Elizabeth was now desperate to leave Washington. Her pregnancy was becoming apparent and she knew that if she did not get away in time, she would never get an exit permit. With great difficulty and much string-pulling by her father and Graham Spry in London,[12] she finally secured a job as a junior assistant specialist with the British Information Services in London. With her papers at last in order she waited for the chance of a boat. She had to be ready to leave on a few hours' notice and warned her family that she could not get up to Ottawa to say goodbye.

Nevertheless, she had Louie's blessing. Louie thought her motives in going to England were patriotic and she wrote enthusiastically: "It's all very exciting! I understand your wanting to go & am quite in sympathy provided you can be of use in the country . . . There is one thing I know & that we as a family share & I wouldn't say it if you were not going into the danger zone. We have *guts* & we can stick it & if the worst

happens, I know you will not be afraid. The only fear I would
have would be falling into enemy hands which would be much
worse than death for any woman—especially a young & pretty
one."[13] Louie's fear was not entirely neurotic. Many Canadians
saved from sunken Allied ships ended up in German P.O.W.
camps. She asked Elizabeth to take Russel, Jr. (now stationed
in England) his Victory vitamins.

Elizabeth would say in retrospect that in fleeing to England
she was putting the Atlantic between her and George, but she
had every expectation he would follow her. She wrote to him
on February 15 insisting he come to Washington:

My dove, my duck:

. . . I will buy some tulips and we will have fried chicken
and I will give you a lecture on the nature of morality and
the anatomy of truth and the susceptibility of god . . . I
love you more than ever every minute like a pair of Cuban
thingummies that you rattle with bobbles on them. i cried
when you made me that happy because I would so much
rather die while it is like that than have to go from what is
all i want to what is more than i can bear a cold storage
hell from which i am always afraid i may not be resur-
rectable. Have you considered the possibilities of connection between resurrection and erection—res—a thing,
erection:-resurrection or conversely, es plus erection
equals resurrection for you. But O supposing this ety-
mological mathematics doesn't lead me into
heaven? . . . Georgina is fine and . . . will have a fit of
hysterics if you don't come . . . I am a little worried about
Christopher though because he hasn't had enough attention or any proper prenatal mystics performed. Light a
candle for him, and since he is now floating in my inward
sea, a prayer for all little barkers at sea. . . .

Thence went into the arctic but nevertheless said: what
is stronger than vitamins and more recuperative than two
weeks in Miami? and answered & said: It is the seed my
soul, which cometh out of the mouth of George Barker in

a moment of love into the Elizabethan meadows which ben set to clipp em unto. . . . please say you COMETH for otherwise my so recently fattened cheeks will wither & deflate themselves with powerfully sudden & disastrous results.[14]

Before sailing for England, Elizabeth managed to spend three weeks in New York, staying with Willard and Marie and seeing George. On March 25, with Georgina in tow, she embarked on the *Tyndareus* for the three-week crossing. During the war, passenger and cargo boats carrying essential supplies always travelled in convoys protected by gun ships. Forty-nine ships left New York and were joined by another eighteen in Halifax and St John's. By mid-ocean they were accompanied by an anti-submarine escort of thirteen gun ships. The crossing was extremely dangerous. Ships travelling in convoy had to deal not only with the rough North Atlantic weather, but with the hazards of navigating in close proximity to other ships while maintaining radio silence. On the nights of the 4th and 5th of April the commodore of the convoy, Admiral Sir C.G. Ramsey, RNR, who was travelling on the *Tyndareus*, reported that visibility was phenomenal. Conditions were perfect for an attack—the northern lights functioned like director beams. On the 4th three ships were torpedoed and sunk; the following night thirteen attacks were driven off by the escort. Four stragglers lost the convoy and were sunk in the crossing. The *Tyndareus* was torpedoed but survived.[15]

It is a measure of her desperation that Elizabeth would have set out, pregnant and with a young baby, on such a dangerous journey. Certainly she wanted to protect her parents from her infamy and she dreaded the consequences of Louie's discovery of her "illegitimate" children. But she may also have wanted to get George to England, away from Jessica. One can imagine the terror of moving in a war convoy under blackout with the German U-boats lurking in the open seas. She had no illusions, having left behind both her and George's manuscripts so that they would not be lost if she went down. When the torpedo hit the *Tyndareus*, she almost welcomed it. She would write later in *The Assumption of the Rogues and Rascals*: "I escaped by a hair's breadth the torpedo that seemed at the time to be a friendly if banal ender of my story. When the alarm sounded, I waited, with my daughter strapped into my lifebelt, full of relief, a kind of wicked joy, that I should be offered such an effortless way out of my pain. But that was not to be."[16] The subtext to this was that, shortly after leaving New York harbour, Elizabeth suddenly knew in her bones, though the evidence was slight and had been carefully withheld from her, that Jessica was pregnant with George's child. In retrospect she was glad to have survived the attack and wrote to Marie Maas that she and Georgina had escaped by a miracle.

When one tries to understand Elizabeth Smart, one sees that this obsessive passion fits into her cosmos. Her world was egocentric. She could sustain a private reality if she could be heroic. The very fact that George Barker could resist her with such sustained intensity guaranteed the hook. She could win him to her conviction. She would "*not* be placated by the mechanical motions of existence" . . . she would not tell herself that tomorrow would be more reasonable, nor "be betrayed by such a Judas of fallacy: it betrays everyone: it leads to death. Everyone acquiesces: everyone compromises. They say, As we grow older we embrace resignation. But O, they totter into it blind and unprotesting. And from their sin, the sin of accepting such a pimp to death, there is no redemption. It is the sin of damnation."[17] No, Elizabeth could say I want the one I want, the one dictated from all eternity. She could bear the pain.

It is curious that, in relation to men, women learn two things: to be the desirable object and to live for another. The erotic impulse to power is acceptable; but the naked impulse to power—I am the genius—is not. In fact, she chose a strategy that came easily to gifted women in her world. She could win value by attaching herself to the genius: Barker, at the age of twenty-nine, already had the literary world's attention; it was easier to believe in him than to believe in herself. But in addition to being an artist, Elizabeth was driven by a second imperative—that of the womb, since for her motherhood was an erotic and sexual triumph. One might wonder if this indeed made her most dangerous to Barker. All that was male in him wanted to resist that maternity that would absorb him. It was not for nothing Barker admitted to Elizabeth that he was essentially adolescent—he had Big Mumma behind him. Barker believed in a neat cosmos that bifurcated the world into strict divisions: "man living in relation to the absolute, cursed by a sense of the ideal; woman living entirely in a world of relationships."* He would chose his ideal battle with poetry; he would not be drawn down into that female chaos. There he would lose himself.

Elizabeth landed in Liverpool, now five months pregnant, with Georgina on one arm and her trunks of books and clothes in tow. When she showed up for her job at the British Information Services, she was fired within two days for "procreational activities." The Ministry was not about to take the plight of a pregnant woman into account. She visited George's family, and they were kind, saying it was too bad she hadn't met George ten years earlier. Her major problem was where to live. Her old friend Didy Battye, now Didy Asquith, invited her to join her at Scarlet-sub-Edge, Stow-on-the-Wold in the Cotswolds. It was there George found her when he arrived in England on June 15.

Didy was living at Hinchwick Manor, a magnificent estate owned by an aunt and uncle. The Asquiths had given her the stone cottage attached to the stables, which were then used only for storage. It was small, with bedrooms upstairs and a huge airy loft, and a large room with an old iron stove and fireplace below. The children remembered going to the manor in the mornings for cocoa, but in adulthood couldn't remember its rooms. Michael, Didy's husband, was a naval officer and absent on duty so that Didy was alone with her young daughter Annabel. She was pleased to have Elizabeth join her.

* Patrick Swift in *Homage to George Barker*, p. 61. Swift explains that, in Barker's view, the sexes are divided by their ethical positions and quotes Barker being typically outrageous: "I have always been astonished that women are allowed to enter churches. What conversation can they have with God?" When I asked if he still affirmed this "ethical distinction," Barker remarked: "I think it's very true." (Interview with author, April 29, 1989.)

Didy believed that the time at Scarlet was the happiest for Elizabeth. Life was simple. Elizabeth had impeccable taste, and even without money, could turn a room into an occasion, with flowers and candles. George was often there. Didy liked George, although she was intimidated by him and would later write to Elizabeth: "Probably because I have a huge admiration & respect for, quite apart from a real affection & I still feel a bit shy of him in a way one does about superior beings."[18] They would sit in the kitchen before the fire, or out on the lavish grounds of the estate beside the stone pool and sing "Foggy Foggy Dew" or "When I Wear My Apron High," or recite poems: "Quia Amore Langueo." Though it was wartime, life in the Cotswolds was still pastoral. They would take the long walk up to the lake through the rambling hills covered with wild bluebells, with the black-faced lambs frisking in the pastures. It was as close to Kingsmere as Elizabeth might have wanted. Each time George left to return to London* Elizabeth suffered, but she thought he was still with her, and the times in between were happy. She spent her days waiting for her second child, sewing clothes for Georgina, always with elaborate smocking, and began her project of producing an exhaustive bibliography of the works of George Barker. If she didn't "husband" his works, who would? She could make the life of some poor scholar at the end of the twentieth century easier.

Elizabeth was being encouraged in her strategy of how to get George by the Maases in New York. She called Willard and his wife, Marie, The Informers. They kept tabs on George for her. In July Maas wrote to her:

My Dearest Elizabeth:

. . . I *do* believe in the possibility of everything like platitudinous rivers running at last to calm seas.

---

* It is sometimes difficult to determine when Barker lived with Elizabeth. When asked how long they lived together, Barker replied: "That's a question I can't answer. I don't think we lived in the same house for years. It was one of those queer things. It was rather like an actual animal. The affair itself moved around. It wasn't anything except a pure love affair." (Interview with author, April 29, 1988.)

By this time you will have received my wire and by this time surely the resurrection has taken place. One thing, and already I suppose it is too late for advice, I was convinced of those last weeks George was here and that was that he did love you and that the way to hold him, since he desires most to hurt those he loves, was to be firm in your demands. Your silence was terrific and made him make, I am sure, decisions he would never have made if you had acted differently. All the weeks since you left were filled with madness for him, and mad inexplicable actions . . . he must have been going through some self-crucifixion, since he seemed to have put his fist through a window . . . you will learn, my darling, that only firmness and hardness, coupled with your expansive desire and love for him over it all, will save him, and now I know surely that if he is to be saved you must do it. . . .

Now, it would seem to me, is the time for final actions. The knockout blows and the block busters and the round the clock raids on George . . . according to George he gave Jessica a child to do the one decent thing he could do for her before leaving her (which may be a subtle rationalization beyond my understanding). In any case he should be taken at his word. . . . Victory is yours—don't throw it away. . . .

Oh if you see him kiss him for me and make love for all sad lovers the world over—if I knew that were true, life would be a hell of a lot more bearable . . . Willard.[19]

Elizabeth gave birth to her first son, Christopher, on July 23 at the local hospital in Moreton-in-Marsh. She loved the hospital. A little cot was provided so that she could have her baby with her all day, and she found the conversation of the other seven women in the ward fascinating. They were local women, farmers and cottage women. But George was not there. He sent a telegram to the child saying "Forgive me" and to Elizabeth, "You are really clever." In an exquisite little book she later composed with George's help called "Xtopher's Book" she described his prenatal adventures. The book was a kind of diary and album, with descriptions of Christopher's genealogy and blood line, narrative details of his birth ("he weighed ten pounds when the dirt was washed off") and photos of those who welcomed him into the world.

> Christopher Barker was conceived one afternoon in a hotel in Baltimore on November 9, a date with special meaning for his mother. Prenatally he went to work with his mother for the British Army Staff in Washington, then to the British Embassy, and travelled to work each day by buses which took an hour. He suffered innumerable pre-natal shocks including a two months estrangement of his parents which began with some violence on November 28th; a suicide perpetrated in his mother's office; three weeks of fury in Brooklyn Heights; a transatlantic voyage with torpedos and emergency alarms; 3 cleansings for Scabies; 2 days at the Ministry of Information; the bumping of his 35 pound sister and her sitting on him in buses, tubes, & trains; dismissal from a house at which he was visiting; reunion with his father; air-raids of a mild sort; homelessness; love, jealousy and boredom; rations and the English attitude to pregnancy. Saint Christopher and Christopher Columbus guard this Christopher Barker; whether he carries Christ or looks for islands that aren't there; may his extra-big toe and his athlete's heel and his shoulders that stuck in the vagina come in handy.
>
> When Christopher was severed from the umbilical and laid in the basket, he said, in a loud pleasant voice, "Da" which is, so be it.[20]

She has entitled a telling photograph of herself and her two babies, with George significantly absent, "The Unholy Family" and listed as Statistics: "Christopher's father is a poet and there is none better alive this day in England or anywhere else." It was as if the text were written in stone: the father of her children was a poet and poets by definition are absent. When George, in his own hand, added a list of the "Professions of Forebears," of himself he wrote: writer and cad; of Elizabeth:

poetess and courtesan. In a disturbing addendum headed by a drawing of skull and crossbones, Elizabeth has added: "When Christopher was 5 weeks old . . . he got a twin half brother and sister by his stepmother Jessica. . . . 'But thereof came in the end despondency and madness.'"

Elizabeth wanted a home. She did not want a husband in the conventional sense. She never affected a ring and admitted only to stooping so far as to change her rationing card for the greengrocer. But she was not content with George absconding. With children, she had become the captive, while George remained free for his work. Still she believed there must be some way to win him. She tried cajoling. A week after the birth of Christopher she wrote to George:

Darling George:

Where are you & what are you doing & are you very unhappy & harassed & if so why don't you write & tell me all about it since who's supposed to be your helpmeet but me? . . . If it's the bloodhounds or the beautiful pilot or the gay paraders or the tigers of regret or whatever there must be a use for me since my love's not sporadic & periodic but like milk which if not sucked swells up till the breasts are footballs & has to be expressed by force.

Christopher was circumcised today . . . When I think he's my son I feel all nice & cosy but when I think he's *your* son, I feel so pleased I cry.

Please come & own him & me. Or if you can't come yet, then write us your instructions for the conduct of our hours, and lives.[21]

There was no way Elizabeth could figure out the right strategy for George. One might wonder if there was such a thing for him as an objective world with its claims. Barker felt that his deepest obligations were to his own writing. It was the lifeline he could hold on to while frenetically and inadequately balancing the broken pieces of his life. He resisted Elizabeth's love as possessiveness. He was sure of her and could afford to be high-handed. At some level he always believed she could take care of herself; after all she had her father's money. He wanted the women in his life to be there as adjuncts, not as the central theme. What is curious perhaps is his own refusal to let go. In fact he continued to hold on to Jessica. After his departure he sent what money he could and peremptory missives to report on his son. She could write to him as late as August: "Don't you think it's possible that you have changed so much that we aren't the same kind of people any longer? But I mustn't get churned up mister dear or think too deeply now or I don't sleep."[22] Her situation must have been abject. She was worried about hospital expenses and where to stay after the child was born. It was also true, however, that she had become a *cause célèbre* in New York, and many friends rallied with support, some certainly because they believed Barker had behaved like a cad. (Willard Maas reported that Peggy Guggenheim was subscribing a fund for Jessica.)

Jessica knew Elizabeth had had a second child, but Barker insisted it wasn't his, though she hardly believed him. She gave birth to twins, Anthony Sebastian and Anastasia Clare Barker, on August 27. It was not easy for Jessica to give up George, or perhaps the nostalgic version of their lives before Elizabeth had entered the scene. She continued to believe it could be recovered post-Elizabeth. And perhaps, too, she had so long been the handmaiden to George's poetry that the cost of losing that rationale for her life was high. She continued to write to him about his books and to discuss whether to dedicate his new poems to her children or to T.S. Eliot.

George saw Christopher for the first time on August 9; he had returned to Scarlet to collect Elizabeth and in mid-August they moved back to London, staying briefly with George's family until they found a room at the top of a house in Coleherne Road SW10. They were to stay in London six months, and the repetitive pattern of their life was becoming clear to Elizabeth. George was as frenetic as ever, busy about his literary contacts. No doubt the young writers like David Wright must have been delighted to have him back. He wrote afternoons at his mother's in Redcliffe Square, and Elizabeth often showed up at the end of the afternoon for a drink. She met friends like David Gascoyne, Dylan and Caitlin Thomas, Clement Davenport, and Tambimuttu, editor of *Poetry London*, who was interested to hear she had written a novel. She wrote hurriedly to Marie Maas to send her manuscript of *By Grand Central Station I Sat Down and Wept*. There would have been nights at the pubs in the environs of Old Compton Street. Money was scarce. Barker had been turned down for military service. It seems that none of Elizabeth's Canadian friends in London liked George, and an old friend who had contacts in the Ministry of Defence had George called up several times, but each time he was dismissed as not the right material for service. Had Elizabeth known of this chicanery behind her back she would have been furious. Barker was confident Elizabeth's friends had intervened and effectively prevented him from getting a job. He complained he was living off the dregs of journalism.

Elizabeth found herself more and more alone, waiting for George. In an October letter addressed to his mother's home but not postmarked, she pleaded her case. George, she accused, had done the one thing that could possibly assail her, by which she meant her babies. She was discovering that having children breaks down one's privacy and makes it impossible to write. But she added: "I know with ALL my heart that it has merely paralysed me, and that if you *help* me, I will soon be able to walk, & to run, & to fly, as I used to do quite easily at the mere idea of your little finger." She insisted he was her true love and her husband "no matter how many wives post you their midnight dreams."[23] If he decided she must be seen in public in black serge & spectacles, she would comply.

But Elizabeth knew she was trapped in paralysis. She could not write and her diaries are filled with unsent letters and fragments of writing:

> I am corsetted by fear. I can't move. I am mad with fear. Fear has driven me mad. I am afraid of the wind, the empty house, the air raids, burglars, lunatics, ghouls,

catastrophe, sudden appearances, disappearances, death. I am most afraid of death.

He can get me but I can't get him.

Do I want to record these days—these purgatorial days which I forget even before they are gone?

George—you must do something. I CAN'T stay alone in this house for so many hours. I AM GOING MAD.[24]

The relationship with George had fallen into bitterness and recrimination. She felt he found in everything she did ulterior and reprehensible motives. If she washed her face, it was for the wrong reasons. She seemed to be living in the radius of his hate, ignored, abused and insulted. George was not above taunting her with Jessica: that noble creature so good in herself that she couldn't believe in the bad motives of others. Elizabeth carried on her own private dialogue with Jessica. In her diary she wrote: "Balls to you, Jessica, with your astute line of the abused. The reason you manage him so cleverly is because you don't love him. He's *your* husband, and *your* honour is at stake. You like the pose of the faithful wife. Besides you anticipate prizes. (Now you're being vulgar, Elizabeth. O, then, will the psychoanalyst judge? No, he will say: Tell me what you are afraid to tell me: Well, mother said I must never call anyone common.)" She must continue to be a lady. She watched George trying to make "all his lies true by posthumous actions."[25] It is almost a relief to hear Elizabeth's anger: "You ignore me and the children but if Jessica gets diarrhoea, it moves you to an elegy."

Elizabeth had reached the point where she knew she must salvage her self-respect, or what was left of it. She knew that she and her children were supernumerary and for her own and their sakes she must get out altogether. She could never finally submit, as perhaps Jessica had done, to George's control. Jessica might be willing to carry coals and wash floors and nappies and sweep and sit up alone night after night for the occasional glimpse of George, but not she. She wanted equality, not the one-sided game. Didy remarked that she and George fought. "He couldn't domesticate her. Not George, but the idea held her."[26] "I am bitter & very angry & full of hate & revenge," she wrote, and yet as soon as she sat down to write a list of the reasons she must leave, the pencil was writing a love letter. Without love Elizabeth believed she would be dead.

9   Marginal Notes,
Never the Text

Es tan corto el amor y tan largo el olvido
[So short the love, so long the forgetting]
Pablo Neruda
Twenty Love Poems and a Song of Despair

If only we could all escape from this house of incest,
where we only love ourselves in the other, if only I could
save you all from yourselves, said the modern Christ.
Anaïs Nin
House of Incest

After what must have seemed a considerable respite, suddenly
the drama at Coltrin Lodge in Ottawa resumed. Elizabeth's
father wrote to her in October to say that Louie had discovered
the existence of Georgina. While Louie was staying in
Baltimore with Helen, Tommy, Helen's son, had blurted out the
big secret. Louie had asked him if he remembered the little
English refugees Geoffrey and Elizabeth Ann and he replied
that he remembered Aunt Betty's refugee. Louie's intuition
was quite sufficient to draw the right conclusion. Russel's letter is unrevealing: he says that Louie was on the whole sympathetic to what Elizabeth had been through and added that if
Elizabeth was happy that made up for nearly everything, since
that's a goal few reach. He and Louie were well and were gain-
ing some perspective on the "hot and bothered years" when
their children were growing up.

Elizabeth wrote to her mother: "It is such a blessed relief to me that you know about Georgina. The greatest weight on me always was that it would hurt you. And I am so grateful, too, that you have been so marvellous about it." She insisted that the tone of happiness in her letter was not a subterfuge. "It is heavenly to be in England which is still a fine and private place where people are expected to be individuals and where nothing ever happens bad enough to prevent a cup of tea."[1]

Louie replied on January 21. Louie's letter is compelling. She did love Elizabeth and was hurt for her; she was also deeply concerned over Georgina's illegitimacy and responds with her usual sentimentality: "It isn't my hurt that matters. I am only hurt because you have hurt yourself and that beautiful little child—She looks like a little flower escaped from some garden in Paradise—If only she hadn't escaped. I don't blame you darling & certainly I don't judge you. I just don't understand."[2] She wondered whether Elizabeth's friends knew the situation or whether she had told them the refugee story, and asked if Jessica was still alive. If not, she should marry George, even if she left him immediately after, so that the child could have a name and a place. "It doesn't matter now what any of us suffer if we can make it up to her." Characteristically, the letter goes on for another two pages to detail her social life and her trip to Florida to visit Helen's in-laws, where she didn't take kindly to the coloured help and the outrageous wages they got for doing so little.

One wonders how Elizabeth responded to this letter. She was probably deeply relieved. Louie could rally, could support, was sending Christmas presents, and Elizabeth was grateful to have her love. That sentimentality ran through it like a fault line, always rendering her love problematical, was to be taken as the territory. And there yet remained a second hurdle. Now was the time to brace herself and tell Louie about Christopher:

Dearest Mummy,

I don't know how to tell you what I want to tell you because I am afraid it will distress you perhaps more than anything: I mean that Georgina has a brother because I didn't want her to be lonely. He is fine & looks just like Daddy . . . I have dreaded telling you about Christopher (after Christopher Columbus because he crossed the Atlantic prenatally looking for a new country) because I feel you may find this even harder to understand and perhaps you don't know how much I mind hurting you & know it is your distress that assails me when I have nightmares or get sick . . . [Graham] said "one got over" such things as love . . . He had once been in love with me for 7 years. . . . It's hard to point out why comfort, either mental or physical, may not be the supreme goals of life, no matter how nice they are if you can get them. . . . I have now got things in order & my life functions properly.[3]

It's strange to realize that in Elizabeth's relationship with her mother there were many similarities to her relationship with George; she had always the placatory, apologetic, needy role in love.

This time, though Louie was shocked, her support must have been a heart-breaking relief: "There is no denying that your letter was a pretty bad shock to your father & me & it is hard for us to see why you have elected to live your life this way. Also it is an ache to feel that we can't acknowledge your children as our grandchildren. We don't judge you dear. However mistaken you seem to us to be we recognize that you have shown tremendous endurance & courage & that makes our hearts ache & makes us yearn over you continually. . . . Why darling did you have to do it all the hard way. Anyhow, never doubt that you have our love and sympathy."[4] Russel immediately cabled Elizabeth increasing her allowance to two hundred dollars a month to "keep the wolf from the door." Again Louie suggests that George divorce and marry her, and wonders whether the children are known as adopted refugees or as her own. Louie could not know how absurd this question sounded in the context of war-torn London. She mentions that she sits beside a bowl of fresh violets, her thirty-eighth Valentine from Russel (they had been married thirty-six years). Whether this was intended to hurt, it would have been a painful stroke for Elizabeth in her loneliness. Many of her accusations came, typically, by indirection. She could write of Russel, Jr.'s new girlfriend Cecile: "He doesn't sound the least bit blinded by infatuation but just sanely and soundly in love with her." Or comment that she felt no anger or resentment but simply wondered where they had failed Elizabeth that she took a wrong turning. Yet Louie ends the letter with a declaration she was to stand by: "Realize that nothing will ever change our love for you. It doesn't rest on what you do. You are part of us."

What she was telling friends may have been another matter. Her old Ottawa friends the Osbornes were to visit Elizabeth and her two children in London and report back that the children were loveable. Mrs Osborne wrote to Louie: "As for that nasty word taint, forget it. It's just laughable. I'm sure they're both immaculate conception children."[5]

Elizabeth was struggling with the usual problems. She had found a little Regency house at 9 Hammersmith Terrace, Chiswick, with French windows and a garden overlooking the Thames. The house was cold and drafty, and barely furnished, and Elizabeth had to stoke the boiler herself and carry hot water upstairs in pails, but it was the first home she had ever had and she was thrilled. The problem was she could only get a one-year lease as the owner wanted it back. She tried unsuccessfully to find a couple to live in and share the rent. Briefly she had a part-time job doing research half-days in the library and a woman across the way came in to help, because, she said, Elizabeth was "a brick," tackling the home and children alone. But she wrote to her mother that things had gotten impossible with George. "Everything about George and me is so difficult and painful I find it almost impossible to write about it." She begged her mother not to listen to fresh details of her "sad story," and to "forget everything that is heartbreak. Everything is but I try to ignore it because after all what can you do but keep your eye glued to the hopeful." She begged her not to be hurt as "hurting you is the worst hurt of all."[6]

Elizabeth again wrote to Marie Maas, requesting that she send her manuscript urgently because it would give her an excuse for being herself on the days when she didn't feel "like being a chattel."[7] She couldn't get a full-time job yet, as she knew the children needed her too much. She had applied to put them in Anna Freud's nursery but was refused because Freud was only taking the children of the poor. Later she would put them in a government nursery in Knightsbridge for three weeks as she searched for a new home, and contemplated a job at the BBC, but it was a disaster. They were in a terrible state when she got them back; they had lost weight and Georgina couldn't speak for days. Georgina remembered Elizabeth saying they were in strait-jackets when she came to pick them up. She swore she would never leave them again.

Within five months Elizabeth was on the move again. London was traumatized by air raids, and her street was hit heavily by incendiaries. A time bomb was dropped on an adjacent house but luckily didn't go off. There were nights when fire-bombs slashed the street. She remembered sitting on the steps of her house with the poet David Gascoyne, she with her two babies in her arms and he reading her Baudelaire as people ran with buckets of water and the flames leapt up. They were astonished when it was all quiet and they found they were not dead. It was decided the children must be taken into the country and George suggested that they go to his sister's cottage in Devon. The plan was that Elizabeth would look after her children while his sister took a holiday.

The conditions in the cottage were as usual primitive: no sink in the kitchen; the water was brought up by kettlefuls from the coal scullery. But though it was cold, it amused Elizabeth that Oliver Cromwell had once planned his campaigns from her room, and for the first time she felt the village gave her the chance to know all types of English on an equal footing. But she soon found herself alone with five young children, doing all the shopping and cooking. She even had to haul in the washing each night, as sheets reflected in the blackout. She wrote to Louie: "I have chilblains, but I feel I am doing a large job. I think the housewives have the most miserable time of all with never a moment off." She longed to get back to London to pursue the job at the BBC that Charles Ritchie wired was still open. And yet she told her mother: "You ask me what I am going to do with my life. What I would like to do best is to live quietly in the country with George & have a lot of babies. But if that isn't possible, get an interesting job and have a 2nd Best life. It really all depends on George I'm afraid."[8]

Within two months, Elizabeth moved to Gloucestershire. She had found a small house in Condicote, one and a half miles from Didy at Hinchwick Manor. She was to stay there a year; it was the first time she had anything like a permanent home with her children. Elizabeth's life had always been shaped by a habit of impermanence: the hotel room, the temporary lodgings, the sense of being on the move. Safety had never been her concern. She had always sought intensity, no matter what the cost, to escape the web of convention that reduced one to non-life. But now, carting her children from place to place was exhausting and she must have longed for a home.

Condicote in 1944 was a small stone village of perhaps twenty houses encircling the village green, with one church and one local pub. The post-box, which she must have visited often, was elevated on a stone platform next to the red call-box. The smell of wet hay from the adjacent farms hung on the air. Elizabeth rented the bottom half of a house called College Farm surrounded by an eight-foot stone wall, and just off the village green. She had one large room with a fireplace that provided the only heat, and a paraffin stove for cooking. There was no plumbing but she and the children could take a weekly bath at Mrs Pilkington's. The owner of the house, Mrs Foster, was available to cook a mid-day meal and do the washing, and her fourteen-year-old daughter, Georgina, helped to look after the children. She was Elizabeth's idea of the perfect nanny— big-bosomed, patient, and competent, and Elizabeth felt lucky, with every other mother she knew crying out for help. She also knew she would have to get a full-time job eventually and wanted the children to be slowly accustomed to having a minder.

Nothing had really changed. Elizabeth continued to be able to draw her allowance, though intermittently war intervened and the cheque didn't arrive or the money didn't go far. She was always in overdraft at the bank. She made clothes for the children, decorating them with beautiful smocking. She would complain that George often managed to get money out of her for the pubs; she didn't mind for herself but it was taking money away from her children. The indignities and discomforts of poverty never bothered her. She could fill the house with wild flowers and make nettle soup when she had to. But George was sending money to Jessica. (He never gave money to Elizabeth, always insisting she had a wealthy father to back her up.) Since the crux of every matter for George was cash, she felt she was losing the power struggle.

George shuttled between London and Condicote, but she felt he was now spending all his time plotting to get to America, hardly the foundation for a peaceful domestic life. Her diaries become records of the children's illnesses, the toing and froing by bicycle between College Farm and Hinchwick, details of christenings, or anger at George who wanted her to sweep the floor when she had been thinking about her sick child—a bare record husked to the bone as if Elizabeth were paralysed. "I realize that I am afraid to say the important things & therefore there seems little point in this book, except as an exercise in description of daily domestic tasks. Perhaps one thing will lead to another—or the truth will emerge from the omissions."[9] She was discovering what she would call "woman's lot." It was woman's fate to be the one counted out, the loser, the humiliated. "Can I be a writer whose tale is heard when the statistics are sifted?" she wrote. "This morning I hit Christopher in the face with my fist because of George's letter, because of landlord's bills. It is unfair. I am crying from guilt, despair, humiliation, love, being the one left out."[10] And she wrote a list of the famous in drawing rooms, everyone from Barker, to Dylan Thomas, Connolly and Djuna Barnes, and herself excluded.

She was sad and tired. Georgina Foster, whom they called Big Girl, took care of the children in the mornings, but Elizabeth could not write. She spent her time on her Barker bibliography, writing to friends and publishers for copies of books and articles, or obsessively crafting little facsimiles of Barker's books, and also composed "A Guide to Barker's

Babies," a narrative of directions to Big Girl explaining the chores of looking after children. Elizabeth had herself learned from a book and her knowledge was by this time thorough.

On May 19 she was mending her blue-striped dress and preparing the children for a picnic when the postwoman arrived with two telegrams, one for Mrs Barker, one for Elizabeth Smart. "They're both for me," she said. One was from Mr Harvey at the bank saying her father had died on the 18th, the other was from her old friend Bobby McDougal saying how sorry she was. She was bewildered, too shocked to believe the truth. She recorded the event: "I cried but then began agitatedly getting the picnic things together, & crying. And thought, all one can do after all *is* to cry. It doesn't seem *enough*. But I tried not to give myself time to realize it because I didn't want to collapse at the picnic or have to tell the others."[11] Characteristically, Elizabeth nourished her grief in secret. To trauma she responded not with hysteria but by withdrawal. She became comatose. Beneath her grief at her father's death lay guilt since she believed she had failed him. He had been so optimistic, and she had wanted him to be proud of her. "There is never & nowhere a time for such a word." The same day a form came for George from the American consul to emigrate to America to "join his wife & children." "The evening by myself was horrible," she wrote simply. George was in Condicote but it seems she didn't tell him until the next day, when she had word that her brother, Russel, was coming up from London.

Her father had been ill with ulcers for years, but he was as stoic as his daughter, and none of his family realized the severity of his condition. He and Louie were spending the weekend at Kingsmere when he began vomiting, at regular intervals, the brown blood called coffee grains that is the sign of hemorrhaging in an ulcer patient. Neither he nor Louie recognized the crisis, and only after he became very weak did they call a doctor. He was rushed by ambulance to Ottawa. His veins had so contracted that it was at first impossible to give him a blood transfusion. When he finally did respond, he was too debilitated and died within three days. His last words to Louie were to beg her to stay with him. Only one of his children, Jane, was at his bedside. Both Russel and Elizabeth were stranded in England; Helen arrived for the funeral, which was an impressive Ottawa occasion. Russel had been admired and loved. Louie was devastated. She castigated herself for not having told Russel how much she had loved him. "He used to say sometimes that I didn't think he had achieved. It was only in fun, but I wish I hadn't missed so many chances to praise him."[12]

Russel, Jr., still on active service with the Canadian Forces, came to see Elizabeth and George in Condicote after his father's death. He was clearly worried about Elizabeth and wrote to her on the heels of his visit: "I know your vast capabilities . . . but like me, you are capable of falling into a psychological rut where myriad of petty routine details demand your unceasing attention." He found her situation on the brink of the primitive, and with all the children, the routine seemed a hundredfold more conducive to despair than his own situation in the army. He warned her that her mind craved expression not repression; she needed something creative, and he encouraged her to pursue her efforts to get a job with the BBC. "Unless he was pulling a fast one," he wrote, "George also sees this point, for he certainly agreed verbally."[13] He wanted to see her committed to some diversion that would lead to a happier state of mind. To him, she had not seemed happy for some time.

With Big Girl around, Elizabeth had some freedom again. She would get a lift with Mrs Pilkington into Moreton-in-Marsh to buy food, and she soon mastered the art of shopping with government stamps. To get milk one had to get coupons at the clinic, which had to be stamped at the post office, and then one had to find a shop that wasn't closed at mid-day. It became clear rather quickly that if you drank a lot of tea and coffee, you would have to do without soap. At night there were dinner parties with Didy, evening rambles in Didy's car, a trip with George to Stratford, a children's fancy-dress party on the common on Salute the Soldiers Day. The village was full of evacuees and encampments of trainees in the hills but apart from the constant rationing, the Cotswolds passed what was called a benevolent war, its pastoral quiet only disturbed by the planes passing overhead. On June 6, 1944, Mrs Foster knocked on the door and said the invasion had started. The planes zoomed and circled and bayed but it came to nothing. George continued to come down from London but Elizabeth felt he did so only to get away from the bombs. She wondered again if she would have the courage to leave him.

Elizabeth wrote in her diary in July: "Nothing will ever be right till *he* wants more children, not necessarily per se, but necessarily & because of the nature of love."[14] The rationalizations and conundrums she was able to weave are remarkable, and perhaps only explainable as obsession. She had been obsessive all her life. She had always wanted babies. She once said in a radio interview: "I found it necessary to have these children. For the first one I went far away from my parents, because I didn't want to embarrass them. And then, well, I just felt I had to have some more so I went on having them as quietly and inconspicuously as possible."[15] She had always thought of seven and in 1943 after Christopher was born made a list: Jane was to be born Xmas 1944; Sebastian spring 1946; and Bartholomew (or Domenick or Benjamin) autumn 1947. As Simonette Strachey indicated, she had sought Barker out for this purpose. Whether in Elizabeth's mind babies had to be the product of love or love produced babies is unclear. The act of love, she would often say, "becomes two-dimensional when Eternity hasn't even the remotest possibility of entering the bed."[16] While Barker may have shared her idea of eternity entering the bed (as an early letter castigating Elizabeth for using contraceptives makes clear), for him the idea of conceiving children was a poetic idea. As usual, for her it was real. That Barker now wanted no more children was a desperate sign.

What still confused Elizabeth was the presence of Jessica. Jealousy, tragically, if typically, keeps one in a state of shadow-boxing with phantoms. She thought the battle was to win George from Jessica, and did not yet see that the ambiguity lay in George himself.

I know I know I know he is only trying to keep the situation OPEN for Jessica so his misrepresentations (I mean lies) will work out. O Hell O Heaven O horror & he expects me to take this merely marking time & call it love & be willing. Of course I can't really write in this book because he reads it & takes offence throwing up continually the fact that I wrote "I am going to leave George." I know I am not a wise woman or I could wait wisely or say nothing & never want to see his letters or know to whom he writes or what he does in London or how he feels about J. But it is 4 years since we met & it is still as messy if not messier than ever. The trouble is, for me, that there is always hope. I.e. either J. is a wonderful woman in which case a triple situation might be possible, or she is not, and he might eventually realize it.[17]

Perhaps she was thinking of the Paalens, but Elizabeth had had nothing but contempt for that situation. She had seen then "how the frail disgruntled genuises require such persons and grind them into the ground in the course of using their help, ignoring their needs, telling them, convincing them, that their greatest possible glory is to be a handmaiden to the Muse of a genius. . . . There must be a more elegant way of creating confidence for yourself—the safe ground on which to stand and tremble."[18] But was that not the situation in which she found herself? She could not see it. She sought instead to censor her jealousy, not to nag her man with uncomfortable questions. And she wrote to Marie Maas that "things have been bad, but now they're good because we have bitten our love on every side & it's still a good nickel. And when we have a fight & part even for 24 hours it's awful & I have to admit that even if he has quintuplets in every village in England & sleeps with his mother & the whole U.S. airforce I can't help it. I love him."[19] She concluded that the only solution was to accept the fact that George loved two women; it was possible to have divided and still true loyalties. If one faced the fact head on, one could avoid misery. George was divine, marvellous, and undoubtedly a genius, and made other men look like "tissue paper." "I do think also that George would be much happier if he *either* declared that willy nilly he had 2 wives & we must all accept it whether or no, or *else* that he chose one or the other. It's his fatal desire to *make* us each believe we are the *only* one that makes the mischief. Naturally we want to believe it & he goes out of his way to convince us. O well. Pray & be patient."[20]

But in tougher moments she understood George's domestic politicking. "Naturally he wants two women. Who doesn't? And seeing he's got me safely in a little nest, wouldn't it be the other that he would be straining his ingenuity to reconquer?" It constantly astonished her that he was capable of making Jessica, (or, alas, her) believe anything; for instance, that though he was spending a couple of years with her and having lots of children, yet what he really wanted and needed was the other. She would never find the commitment she wanted from George. In August she conceived her second son. She wrote to Marie that George was angry because he thought the new baby might "influence Jessica adversely." He told Elizabeth she had "stolen it." She explained abjectly to Marie: "I simply can't help wanting babies if George looks at me erotically. Perhaps it could be psychoanalysed away, but only if the love could be too & then what'd I be—Peter Pan, Medusa or a really nice hermaphrodite?"[21] She asked Marie to send photos of Jessica's children.

What Elizabeth may not have realized was that Jessica was finally withdrawing from the fray. In January she still held the faith and could compliment George on his new book, *Eros in Dogma*, which George dedicated to her twins. (When Elizabeth read the dedication and threatened to leave, he simply told her he had been provoked to it when she had made him angry.) Jessica thanked him for the loved familiar poems that "go singing through my heart and always will," and wondered how Mr Eliot felt about it, or more importantly, Mr Barker; whether the bad things were wiped out by it all. It was something they would have to discuss when they were both much older and wiser. She missed their laughter. For better or worse she would always be amused by him. She sent him the twins' birth certificates since there was talk of her bringing them to London and wondered how "Leechie" (Elizabeth) was doing. Was she packing her bags for the job George was hoping to get in Madrid? But in February it occurred to her that travel would be dangerous for the twins. "They are my life and the best thing that ever happened to me and I would sacrifice anything or anybody for them." Jessica was still Catholic (she liked a mutual friend John Coleman because he "had religion" and clung to what she called her innocence, claiming that the sexual imagery in Auden's verse went over her head until it was explained to her). In the whole catastrophe she was the victim. In May she wrote a stinging letter:

> Since that glorious day in Big Sur I have implored you to stop lying but still you go on and send me further from you with each lie. I hear from people we know in London that you are still seeing Elizabeth—I never thought otherwise—and fighting most of the time. And it is not your "enemies" who send news but people who like you and are really concerned to see you wrecking yourself. I am very sorry for you and I think it is a pitiable situation but I know that it will continue as long as Elizabeth lives. You haven't the strength to break with her forever and if you attempt it she will track you down again and as you refuse to tell the truth there is no one that can help you, least of all me. I did everything possible to help you when you were here and suffered every possible hurt and indignity in consequence but you went to England and left me knowing she would be there and what would happen. There will be another child and so on and so on. You've just got to realize Gran that one cannot go on having another chance and another indefinitely. You both took the "gilt off the gingerbread" for me for ever and I am never never going to enter it again. Elizabeth is too animal for me to be able to cope with and you are probably a physical and mental wreck and I am sick of nursing you back to normality to run off to Elizabeth again. I can only suggest that you be as happy with her as you can and

forget me. I am already responsible for two lives and that is too much. Bye bye Mister dear and do send me poems for publication—the cash would be extremely helpful.[22]

In a second letter she wrote: "I doubt if ever again I shall have the patience to live with an adult. You say you are shot but believe me you don't know what that means. And as for love—which I don't believe in any longer anyway—I just don't have the energy." In July she turned down the American Consulate's offer of a passage to England. *I will not return*—certainly not until after the war. I have nothing to return to and the longer the Atlantic is between us, the happier I shall be. And that is definitely that. There is no need for us to discuss it again. . . . Be happy and for God's sake stop telling such fantastic lies." Jessica meant what she said. There may have been future equivocations, but the relationship was finally over, though Jessica never divorced Barker. She exacted a promise from him that he would never try to contact the children. To them she simply said that George had gone off to do a reading at Harvard one evening and never returned. They understood quickly that questions would not be answered and didn't learn for decades of the existence of other Barker siblings. Certainly, Elizabeth was never mentioned.[23] When she died in 1989 of Alzheimer's disease, Jessica was still Mrs Barker.

Elizabeth wrote her New Year's resolutions for 1945:

1. Keep a Diary or Daily Notebook.
2. Keep Accounts & *never* spend more than c20 a month in living (& partly living).
3. Keep the children prettily dressed always.
4. Keep Everything *Clean*.
5. Answer all letters within 3 days.
6. Keep bowels open.
7. Have a baby. [a check mark appears against this entry, with the addition "Sebastian 16th April 1945".]
8. Learn to play Chess.
9. Write Canadian History Book.

10. Acquire a Radio, Piano, Dulcitone, Harpsichord, Clavichord, Gramophone or other means of obtaining music, & teach children to listen.
11. Translate Canadian Folk Songs & acquire all available books & information on them.
12. Make a final decision about George, if he won't about me, & stick to it. The years roll on & the freezing wind.[24]

When Louie realized Elizabeth was to have a third child she was thoroughly shocked and wrote with vituperation: "How can you ask for my blessing on so wrong a deed. I can't think of any line of reasoning by which you could think it fair and right to go on having children."[25] There was a grave moral issue: her children, being illegitimate, would be "handicapped," and an economic one: her allowance, which had reverted to one hundred dollars a month after her father's death, would be too little to feed three mouths and she would hardly have the freedom to earn money from writing. And then the blow: her father, because of her irresponsibility and lack of decency had died a broken-hearted man. Louie was disconcerted. Elizabeth had now become the talk of Ottawa. She assured Elizabeth that, though she would continue to help, Russel would be her priority; he would bring honour to the name he bore and deserved her sacrifice. She tried platitudes: a house built on sand cannot stand; one can't cheat the fundamental laws of living, etc., but she knew they wouldn't work. Louie's censure had never really stopped Elizabeth pursuing any of her obsessions. Her mother now started to send baby clothes for the new child, onto which Elizabeth carefully sewed Barker's name.

Her brother, Russel, also wrote to Elizabeth to say he found her logic hard to understand. He could speak of Louie's "fury letters" as being exaggerated but she had logic on her side.[26] He warned her that her allowance was not secure if Mowat Biggar should die. He accused her of amazing optimism and advised her to set about the idea of securing independence and taking responsibility for herself should the need arise.

The truth was Louie felt she was poor. When her husband's estate was probated, she found she owned only Kingsmere and 361 Daly Avenue. Russel left an annuity for Louie of $8,000 and an allowance for his three daughters of $1,200 each. However, the whole was subject to taxation and Russel, Jr., concluded that Elizabeth's allowance would be $100 a month. (He, being the boy, was left nothing until after Louie's death, though he was to take over his father's firm.) Now Louie insisted she would have no surplus funds to come to the rescue of her daughters. She decided to sell Kingsmere, and though Elizabeth wrote to beg her not to—"It is my true home"— Kingsmere was sold to Graham Spry for $10,000. Elizabeth did not complain, but with Kingsmere gone, she must truly have felt she was in exile.

But soon Louie had her own reasons to ask for Elizabeth's blessing. She had dropped her widow's weeds and decided to marry John Stevenson. That it was only a year since Russel's death seems not to have bothered her. Stevenson, who was a correspondent for the London *Times* in Ottawa, had always made a threesome at Kingsmere and was constantly a part of the Smarts' life. Often Russel, Sr., suffered his presence. He had admitted to Elizabeth that at times Stevenson's influence had not been good but one had to deal in the rough with people. The friendship pleased Louie and Louie got what she wanted. When Louie was named a co-respondent in John Stevenson's divorce from his wife, Ruth, and Ottawa tongues buzzed, she only laughed and said it was ridiculous. Though many believed it was an affair, it seems unlikely.[27] Louie was a Hedda Gabler, more attached to attention and control than to passion. But this time she had surprised herself—marrying a man whose divorced wife was still alive should have been unthinkable (her familiar harangue was that second marriages are first cousins to prostitution) and it even occurred to her to wonder if she was now doing an Elizabeth. John, she wrote, was an adoring lover and sent her wonderful letters every day. He had said that if she wouldn't marry him, they could live together. "It is really almost like a miracle to be nearly 61 & to have someone so much in love with one & so devoted & that someone so brilliant & so delightful a companion. I'm afraid the other widows are going to be very envious."[28] She was assembling her trousseau and preparing to live happily ever after.

Elizabeth, more than enthusiastic about the relationship, wrote Stevenson tips about courtship: he needed a little poetry, a few flowers, and lots of flattery. She congratulated her mother: "Glad you have JAS [as the family called him] to keep you in good spirits, as if he were the parent and you the favourite daughter." Curiously, Elizabeth still saw Louie as the child who needed care and attention. She was later to say that Stevenson won her mother but was never allowed to share her bed nor type in her house.[29] Louie was married on December 27, 1945.

Louie wrote to offer Elizabeth another fifty dollars a month and Elizabeth refused. Louie was furious and must have written one of her typical letters, for Elizabeth's response was firm:

March 12, 1945

I don't grudge anyone anything they have. . . . I said I wouldn't take the $50 because I thought you couldn't afford it and I don't want you or anyone else to make sacrifices for me, no matter how willingly. I have chosen my life & I am quite prepared to take all the consequences & though your gifts & help are always terribly welcome . . . I don't want to feel I am an encumbrance to you, & I certainly don't want to have a few more comforts at the expense of yours. . . . I can live on my $100 quite easily until I am ready to take a job. . . .

I *never* indicated that you or any of your friends in Ottawa had the minds of tradespeople. . . .

I know you would give me the clothes off your back if you thought I needed them. Please believe . . . that although I have many difficulties to contend with, I am contented with my lot and that nothing I do is done either irresponsibly or without thought. I do depend very much, though, on having sympathy from you, even if it is impossible to understand one another. I only hope that you believe that even if you can't see any rhyme or reason to my behaviour. I have reasons which seem good to me, and that you believe in the sincerity of my motives—or failing that, just give me a faint benefit of the doubt & continue to send me your love and blessing. . . . Anyone with children is very much tied & usually quite exhausted. I am very lucky to have the help I have.[30]

Elizabeth was trying to find a way to "bash on regardless." Though she had resolved to make a final decision about George, she could not. Instead, she was teaching herself to live in a state of "expectationless neutrality." The world was changing. The war was winding down; by the close of 1944, France had been liberated and everyone was awaiting the end. London was a pocked and dreary landscape; one in five houses had been bombed, many friends had died. She and Didy began to fantasize escape. "Didy and I often plan our imaginary trip across Canada with all our brood," she wrote to her mother. Their ambition was to have a caravan and be independent and self-sufficient. She tried to turn despair into cynicism instead of a weary "moaning-groaning." In April, awaiting the birth of her child, she wrote in her notebook: "The Pear tree is blossoming and George is lying. I must think about the soul to whom I am about to give birth":

Whether or not I am in love now I neither know or care. It is not my concern or my necessity to enquire into anything which if it exists at bottom is too esoteric to be dissected. But the abstract (love) & its size & shape cover me enormously: whether love can endure & if women must always be abandoned. So that the vulgar figuration of the good woman as weeping & the bad woman as smiling have both a tragic foundation of fact. George has led me to a long & tedious contemplation of this dead-end tragedy. But soon I shall be taking to labyrinthine ways—with my bambino on my knee.[31]

She had found a new theme: whether it is the fate of women to be hurt, to be counted out of the fête. "I must put it all down for the drowning women to whom no one has ever thought it worthwhile to speak," she told herself.

On April 16 Sebastian was born at the Moreton-in-Marsh Cottage Hospital. That night Elizabeth had left the children with Didy and met the 6:57 train from London carrying George and Sue Asquith. They took her to the hospital. Hard labour started at ten, and the baby was born at 11:30. The doctor missed the birth—he had been waiting in an adjacent room, but hearing no noise, had concluded nothing was happening. When he entered, the nurse was already cutting the umbilical cord. Elizabeth wrote of the birth: "The exhilaration was all missing." Two days later, still in hospital, she received the proofs for *By Grand Central Station I Sat Down and Wept,* which was finally to be published by Tambimuttu. As had happened once before, the child and the book came together. Elizabeth took her three-week-old baby down to London for V.E. Day, with her two youngsters and Big Girl in tow, but Big Girl had never been out of Condicote before and cried all the time from homesickness. With George and Didy and Michael Asquith she milled among the euphoric crowds at Trafalgar Square and Buckingham Palace and watched the bonfires and firecracker displays. They stayed at the Barkers', but the house was so crowded and the difficulties of arranging for the children so exhausting that she was soon back in Condicote. The war was finally over, and that was relief of a kind, but her own domestic confusion hadn't abated. She wrote to her mother that it was hard "to make a home from a couple of Penguin books and a mattress." Big Mumma had sold all George's things when he went to Japan because she said she hadn't thought he would ever come back, and they had virtually nothing of their own.

The most exciting prospect on the horizon was the long-delayed publication of her book. Barker, by his own admission, had had nothing to do with its acceptance. His only involvement, he insisted, had been that in 1941, when Elizabeth had told him her initial title, "Images of Mica," he had cringed. "Anything would be better," he had said, "even a line like this," and had picked at random the sentence beginning: "By Grand Central Station I sat down and wept."[32] Although Elizabeth resisted most of his other editorial suggestions, happily she took his advice on this one.

Tambimuttu, already infamous as the editor of the magazine *Poetry London* and of Editions Poetry London, knew a great book when he saw it. Elizabeth delighted in Tambi: he was a personality, a Soho fixture. On his arrival in London he had fostered the legend that he was a prince from Ceylon; princes didn't carry money, and he was famous for his capacity to get money out of other people. He started *Poetry London* in a basement room furnished with a collapsible camp-bed and kitchen table but was soon able to find a string of backers that included the publishing house of Nicholson and Watson. He had a brilliant editor's eye and published, among others, Kathleen Raine, David Gascoyne, Henry Miller, Anaïs Nin and Vladimir Nabokov. Every night, summer and winter, he was to be found in the pubs of Soho, wrapped in his blue melton overcoat buttoned to the chin against the British cold, surrounded by his group of supporters. It was he who coined the phrase Sohoitis: Soho was a dangerous place. The threat was not knife-fights but its seductiveness: one could stay there day and night and get no work done, ever.

Elizabeth's advance for *By Grand Central Station* was twenty-five pounds. If indeed she got the money, it was probably all she ever saw from Tambi. He was often seen going around the tables of the Wheatsheaf, carrying a bag or hat and asking for donations for destitute artists. If the alms flowed properly, he would seat himself and the artist at a table and, with all-dispensing benevolence, buy a round. The starving artist might get a Scotch egg. But if Tambi was an amusing scoundrel on financial matters, he was extremely generous in his schemes for poetry.

By Grand Central Station came out in August. Helen Scott, an editor at Editions Poetry London sent the contract on August 24, saying "I like the idea of doing this after the book is out!"[33] It was wartime, only two thousand copies were printed, and, because of paper rationing, the text was squeezed into fifty-eight tightly packed pages. Elizabeth was to confess in a 1977 interview for *Vogue* that she had had high ambitions for the book. "I wanted to see if I could write a book—this sounds boastful—as considerable as something by Jane Austen, the Brontës, or George Eliot."[34] In fact the book disappeared quickly. The first review appeared in late September in *The Sunday Times*. It was only ten lines, but called the novel "an exciting and original book, half-way between a novel and a prose poem. Too often writers of poetic prose lose their sense of form, but Miss Smart's love story has a beginning and an end. This book is recommended, not only for its passionate, sensuous use of language, but as a moving soliloquy on love and the contemporary world." L.A.[35] Elizabeth did not know who L.A. was but she was pleased, and sent the review to her mother, warning that she didn't expect all the reviews to be as good as this. They weren't. The anonymous review in the *T.L.S.* called the book "curious outpourings" and remarked that the "actual incidents were washed away in a flood of self-revealing comment and analysis." "Miss Smart has considerable skill in expression and a gift for poetical phrase which is occasionally arresting; but her heroine's self-absorption is so intense that it produces a revulsion of feeling in the reader and leaves the impression that the author has wasted a great deal of poignancy on a trivial and undeserving subject."[36]

However, the formidable Cyril Connolly reviewed it favourably in his magazine *Horizon*. *Horizon* was the best magazine around and in the same issue were poems by Dylan Thomas, George Barker, reproductions by Marcel Duchamp, and a portrait of André Malraux by Edmund Wilson. Connolly called it a prose experiment on a familiar theme, "a violent and adroit piece of home-wrecking" though the narrator wins the reader's sympathy because after all she's telling the story and she isn't spared the consequences. But he found the telling fresh, revealing "a genuine gift of poetic imagination, a fine sincerity, and a deep candour in suffering which does not degenerate into self-pity." Connolly complained that the novel needed another six months' work; "the magnificent humourlessness of the *Venus toute entière* . . . blinds her to the moral

situation and also to all general comic or ironical attitudes."
But "with the hit-or-miss night-minded school of writers to
which Miss Smart appears to belong, there never is another six
months. . . . Nevertheless this first book is full of promise and
belongs to our time."[37] The book was discussed among friends,
admired in small circles and disappeared. If Elizabeth hoped
that the book would be the route to her own "labyrinthine
ways," she was wrong.

By October Elizabeth had set herself up permanently in
London. She was living in a Chelsea basement for which she
paid twenty-five pounds and looked after the flat of the tenant
above. George was more or less absent. She had barely enough
to live on, according to Jane who kept tabs through Canadian
friends, and was trapped washing baby clothes and pushing prams, though Jane felt she herself was more distressed
about the situation than was Elizabeth. However, Elizabeth
desperately wanted a job and was looking for something in
publishing.

Ominously, in December, Jane began to report on Louie's
reaction to Elizabeth's book. Louie wrote to Jane that it was the
"erotomania" of an undisciplined young woman who was a
disciple of Henry Miller, and that she had burnt her copy. Louie
had learned that six copies of the book had been seen at
Murphy-Gamble's, a local dry-goods store in Ottawa; she
immediately rushed down, bought, and burnt those books also.
Louie was always thorough. She then approached her friends in
External Affairs and requested them to ensure that the book
would not be imported into Canada. She could call in old debts
incurred in her days as a great Ottawa hostess. Whether it was
officially banned will never be certain, but for decades the
book was effectively kept out of Canada.* Louie's real complaint about her daughter's book was that the few lines in

---

* Though an official directive to prevent the importation of *By Grand Central
Station* may have been sent through External Affairs to Customs and Excise, as
far as is possible to tell, no records of a formal nature survive. Under wartime censorship many publications were banned; however, the lists of which books were
banned were regularly destroyed. Smart did send copies of her novel through the
mail to friends in Canada.

which Elizabeth describes the mother held her up in an unfavourable light. Her vanity was piqued.

It never occurred to Elizabeth that the book would hurt her mother, so that when the attack came in a letter, it must have been a shock. Louie began her letter by increasing Elizabeth's allowance to $125 a month (reminding her that money was always a bribe) and then the tirade followed:

> Thank god your father does not know that you are reduced to living as a char in some man's basement. What he did know completely broke his heart; and even admitting it as you once did, you could then publish a book to be read widely in Ottawa writing down your father & me & practically holding us up to scorn or revealing the most sordid details of an erotic "love" episode, to complete our sorrow & humiliation. The conclusion of the whole thing is very logical & how you could have expected it to end otherwise is not compatible with sane thinking. The only redeeming thing about the whole affair as far as I know it, is that you have shown the most marvelous fortitude & endurance & courage. If only these fine qualities had been put to a better use earlier in life, how different the whole story might have been. Sometime I would like to know from you if, taking all the sorrow & suffering & tragedy into account, you feel it has been worth while.[38]

Louie also complained that Elizabeth had used them. They were a "source of supply" that made it possible for her to indulge every whim and know that she would be helped out. She showed neither respect for them, nor self-respect nor indeed self-interest.

But Elizabeth was not to be sabotaged. She had already returned to an old consolation, one might say the only one, apart from her children, left to her: writing. Resuming her old habit of mosaic composition, moving entries from one journal to another, she began again to rework actual events into poetic fiction. Thirty years later, the material would be incorporated into *The Assumption of the Rogues and Rascals*. In her June

1945 notebook, one finds the moving entry: A WOMAN OF THIRTY:

> I picked these roses because they looked so disgusting waiting there desperately wanting the bees to come & fuck them.
>
> On this lovely afternoon what is left of my youth rushes up like a geyser as I sit in the sun combing the lice out of my hair.
>
> For it is difficult to stop expecting ("What my heart first waking whispered the world was") even though I am a woman of 31½ with lice in my hair & a faithless lover.
>
> It is June 17 but the sun keeps going in & I have been frustrated too many times to be able to withstand its uncertainty. Who can I talk to? Who can I be angry with? To whom can I show off my brilliance & my newly brightened eye or the cynicism I have made out of my despair instead of dreary-moaning-groaning?
>
> Last night the pressure of my captivity & helplessness made my brain reel, so that I felt dizzy & faint. Rats & rabbits die of indecision when an experiment forces them to be forced two ways. Why shouldn't I die at the insolubility of my problems & the untenability of my position?
>
> I need a house, a husband, money, a job, friends, furniture, affection, someone to look after the children, clothes, a car, a bicycle, a destination. Who is there for me? I see now I was the one-too-many. I was the mistake. The circumstances in which I find myself are marginal notes, never the text. It will revert to the simple narrative, what it was when it started, before I entered, far far too positive of getting my just share.
>
> In the thick hedgerows, the summer flowers like distant cousins, get on with their rapturous lives that have nothing to do with me.[39]

Now thirty-two and looking back, Elizabeth felt she had betrayed her gift: "Once I leapt bellowing with jungfreud into the arms of the infinite. I have not done that which I was to have done." She knew she had a subject: the women who are counted out, to whom no one thought it worthwhile to speak, but she felt inhibited. One factor was certainly George Barker. Throughout the notebooks are Barker's extrapolations: i.e. "elucidate"; "No good god too much nature"; "paragraph explaining what follows" etc. Elizabeth felt inhibited by George: "You are reading this book & censuring my secret heart. You are editing my too passionate prayers."[40] Barker probably thought he was being helpful, but Elizabeth was caught in a dilemma common to women writers. Like Hilda Doolittle, for example, struggling with the maestro Ezra Pound, it would take Elizabeth decades to admit that Barker's presence had become restrictive; she feared his censure, and her terror of failing to meet his severe literary standards did not contribute to facility.

Still Elizabeth's mood was not always *Sturm und Drang*. She could also laugh at herself. In 1946 she started a draft of a cabaret song called the "Grand Central Station Blues":

By Grand Central Station I saw down and wept
Because of the date that you never kept
By Grand Central Station I sat down and said
Being in love is worse than being dead.

Boo hoo hoo hoo
choo, choo choo choo
Wish I could lose
These Grand Central Station blues.

He was bad
But I loved him like mad
I have to cry
Because that dirty double-crosser said goodbye.

[Chorus] Boo hoo hoo etc.

I cry and cry and cry
Cause love and all its trimmings is a great big lie
I cry all night and I take a train at dawn
Lovers' meetings end but the journey goes on.

[Chorus] Boo hoo hoo etc.[41]

While Elizabeth felt her entrapment with three babies in her arms, she knew George would neither let her leave him nor stay with her. In May 1946, Rosie, her fourth child was conceived. Elizabeth wrote simply in her diary: "I thank God I am pregnant and nature has control." On May 31, George sailed on the *Kaveena* for Montreal and the U.S. He was tired of living in London. It was time to resume his American literary contacts. It was also time to think of Jessica. He had begun to write to her again, and though he received letters written in vitriol, he consoled himself that at least the sensation of daggers was contact. He wrote to Willard Maas requesting him to tell Jessica he loved her and fantasized living with her in a small house with a garden in the United States, away from oppressive England. He also asked Maas to look for an academic job for him.

But Willard Maas considered himself a special representative for the Elizabethan dynasty, and from him Elizabeth heard what was going on in New York. George was still infinitely mysterious, being as usual involved with acquaintances of the moment, and with a whole flock of projects under way, which included *Of Love* (a novel, later to be called *The Dead Seagull*) and *Jerusalem* (an historical novel partly completed). Maas was having him record poems and songs. But he reported that "no one seemed to take [George] as seriously, at least not his hysteria," which he felt George produced because he thought it required. Jessica had left for Missouri a week after George arrived. Maas was not kind, saying that he thought Jessica was, if anything, "a little disappointed with his return, for she would see an end to this great martyrdom which brought to her aid half of literary New York." George, he said, spoke endlessly of Elizabeth, with bitterness but mostly with love, and always with "a desire to get back, as if there, if nowhere else, was something he had not found changed."[42] George also spoke of the children, whom it is clear that he adored, after his fashion. Barker wired back to Elizabeth in England that Jessica was obtaining an annulment.

It is not to be doubted that Barker was indeed in turmoil. In his diaries, he could write with self-disgust of his incredible cruelty to others and saw a parallel between a devastated

Europe and his own devastated existence. He wondered what on earth he was pursuing or who was chasing him that he should travel so maniacally between England and America. What was this frenzy of immigration? He *must* make a decision.

In September, while Barker was still in the U.S., Elizabeth decided to move to Ireland where she felt living would be cheaper. With the influx of people still returning to London after the war, house prices were now out of her league. Through friends she found a house: Ballyrogan House, in Arklow, County Wicklow. Barker arrived at Shannon airport on September 20. The meeting could not have been felicitous. On the 27 she wrote a farewell letter to him thinking she was ending the relationship.

27th September 1946

I do not think that I want to lie down in your crowded bed for bouts of therapeutic lovemaking. Loving you, I see no beauty in lopsided true love. It really is in sorrow & not in anger that I say: I do not want you any more because *I simply cannot bear it*. It isn't only the unfaithfulness. It's the loneliness, the weeks & months of being alone, really cut off from you, receiving perhaps a postcard saying I fuck you as you pause for breath in fucking somebody else. It would have been better if I had married before I met you, because then you could have given me a few months of fulfilling attentions which is all, apparently, that women need, & then I could have returned to the someone who, possibly, would have cared for me. For you do not want the responsibility even of love & by this responsibility I do not mean either money or guilt.

I realize that if you had cared about me the small necessary amount you would not have left me alone with so much pain, but would have contrived to find some other way of doing what you had to. This is the depths & the final & the end of my misery & degradation & if I say goodbye to you now I will be able to keep from being bitter because I am so grateful to you for your last few moments of frankness.

Dearest George, I will NOT give up the belief in true love or if you will romantic love—IT IS possible I KNOW. I never *wanted* anyone since you. IT IS possible to cometh to rest in someone—but you have not evidently had enough pleasure & power. Maybe I want the middle-aged things now. I've had my fuck, but I've lost my Love. My womb won't tear me to pieces now, maybe, but my heart certainly will. Goodbye. Elizabeth.[43]

George's immediate response was bitter: he complained that preferring an extra-marital orgy certainly demonstrated the depth of the romantic love she must feel for him. Why hadn't she saved him the seventy pounds and told him not to come back from America? But soon he was writing another letter to say that he loved her as deeply and painfully as ever and that only the cemetery could release them. Their problem was cash-lessness. He was going to the Authors Society to see if he could get a bursary so that they would have ten pounds a week between them, and he would look for a job in America. He asked her not to harangue him in letters. His muse was sulking, because he had not paid her enough attention. She was jealous of Elizabeth.[44] Both were still locked in their separate dependencies and desire followed on the heels of recrimination.

But by December, Elizabeth had hardened. She complained that he denied the existence of herself and the children to acquaintances, and that he was interested in her sister Jane, to which he responded that her remarks were as hysterical as all her violent speculations. It was impossible to go on feeling romantic about a woman whose only successful affair was the one she had with herself. He was tired of her lectures on moral perspicacity that came out of her colossal sense of intellectual superiority.[45] Elizabeth, however, was most bitter about money, not for her own sake but for the children's. On one occasion George failed to deposit a cheque for which she had been waiting in her British bank.(He could never really believe she could

be desperate about money. There was her family behind her.)
On the strength of the deposit Elizabeth had written a cheque in
the village of Arklow. When it bounced, her credit in the local
stores was cut off and she had to turn to her old friend Bobby
McDougal in London to come to the rescue. Her bank warned
her peremptorily not to issue further cheques unless she had
funds in her account.

With her credit dried up, Elizabeth had to move. She found a
small sea cottage in Hillcrest, Roundstone, in County Galway.
By this time she was living in extreme poverty. The stone cottage was directly on the beach protected by stone cliffs, so isolated that one hardly saw other families for weeks on end. She
and the children had to walk miles for water—two buckets a
day had to do for drinking and washing up. There were times
when food was scarce, and, calling upon her old skills as a nat-
uralist, she would go out to collect nettles which, when made
into soup, tasted much like spinach. The children were amazed
to see their old enemies turned into edibles. Roundstone was a
poor village; everyone had lice in their hair and had to have
their heads shaved and painted with gentian violet. Yet
Elizabeth kept the children beautifully, still making their
clothes by hand, covering them with smocking. The older children remembered Roundstone as a wonderful time, running
wildly across the moors with the moor ponies and jumping
across the bogs. Elizabeth often spent her evenings making
small handwritten miniatures of Barker's books.

In January she wrote to Marie to say that George was there
with his brother Kit, but "I am very old now & care very little
what he does." There was little food and no electricity. "We all
sit hungrily in the dark & think we are going mad, which I dare-
say we are." "I'm very tired, tireder than Ireland, more irritable
than England & more derelict than the unrehabilitated continent."[46] George, who was waiting for proceeds from a play, proposed to take them all to the U.S., but she doubted the six of
them could afford to live there: "It's not as easy for a Mother &
4 as for a Lone Wolf." She asked Marie to send her some CHIX
nappies. "It would make life BEAUTIFUL to have some—it
would be better than Romance, Sex or even Conversation."[47]

When Rose was born at home at 4:03 on February 18, she wrote to Jane that she was glad the baby was born in daylight. She had run out of candles and it would have been a daunting feat to give birth in the dark. The district nurse delivered the baby. Local friends came to visit, and the baby was wet-blessed on the forehead by an Irish peasant woman. Rose was put in the scrubbed coal scuttle when she was born because there wasn't yet a cradle. Elizabeth wrote of the birth: "Excitement but not exhilaration." George, Elizabeth wrote, did not see Rose till she was six and a half months old.

Elizabeth did not appeal to Louie for help. It was Louie's fantasy that her daughter had settled into a nice clean farmhouse where things would be done for her. She was busy relocating the Kingsmere furniture in the new cottage at Murray Bay that she and John were leasing. It is interesting that, though John came to England at this time to visit his mother who had had a stroke, Louie did not accompany him.

At the end of June Elizabeth decided to leave Ireland since the rent on her house was to go up for the summer trout season. Her mother offered to pay her fare back to London. Elizabeth spent a frantic night in Dublin trying to cash a cheque and then herded her four children and an Irish nanny onto the evening boat. With Jane's help she had found a place to live in Essex.

Jane had met the English writer Ruthven Todd, then living in New York, and discovered he was willing to rent out his house, called Tilty Mill House, in Duton Hill, near Dunmow, Essex. Todd was already known in London as a good poet. He had written an excellent book on William Blake and an allegorical novel called *Over the Mountain*, one of the first English books in the neo-Kafka manner. It was arranged that Jane would pay the rent of one pound a week, plus fifteen pence extra for the furniture, in U.S. dollars; it was to be a present from her with no strings attached except those imposed by Todd: that Elizabeth be especially careful of Todd's valuable library and, particularly, of his extensive collection of Blake. The house included linen and had nine rooms, indoor lavatory, fireplace, and gas heaters. There was no electricity, and candles and oil lamps had to be used. A woman called Mrs Legerton cleaned the place and Fred, the miller, was available to chop wood and keep the water pumped, which services were to cost one pound a week. Louis MacNeice lived next door, and the nearest pub was The Rising Sun in Duton Hill. It was an hour's ride from Liverpool Street Station in London to Dunmow. Elizabeth contacted the local taxi driver, Graham Brown, who was to drive her out to the house.

When she arrived, it felt like heaven. The farmhouse sat at the end of a long bumpy track with a sloping meadow, highland cattle, an old water mill and millstream, and lots of buildings full of pigs. The walls were festooned with roses, the yard with mauve poppies; there was a white picket fence and even window frames. Inside, the house was a jumble and it felt a little like opening up Pompeii: the floors scattered with letters, chequebooks, wood shavings, spilt bags of nails; children's drawings, magazines, thousands of books, manuscripts, notebooks and posters heaped up higgledy-piggledy. In cupboards clothes had mildewed and the moths flew out when she opened the doors. She immediately sorted the manuscripts and letters in the attic, arranged the magazines and books in chronological order, and settled down gratefully. With a home at last, she knew she had found a way to bash on regardless.

George Barker, Elizabeth and Georgina, New York, 1941.

Condicote: Village fête during "Salute the Soldiers Week," June 3, 1944. From left: Sebastian (Friar Tuck), Nanny, Didi Asquith (a pirate), Didi's daughter Annabel (Robin Hood), Elizabeth (an Austrian), Christopher (Julius Caesar), Georgina (a Balkan), Alfreda Irquuhart (a Chinese).

© Georgina Barker

Leaving Ireland "with all our worldly goods," June 1947.

© Georgina Barker

Elizabeth with her children. From left: *Sebastian, Rose, Georgina and Christopher, at Tilty Mill House in 1948.*

Michael Wickham, Elizabeth (centre) *and Shirley Maiden, at Tilty House, 1949.*

Elizabeth's children, Tilty Mill House, July 1949. From left: *Rose, Christopher, Georgina, Sebastian.*

The Soho crowd at the Mandrake Club, spring 1951. From left: *Robert Colquhoun, Marsh Dunbar, Robert MacBryde, Bobby Hunt, Oska Wood, Peter Dunbar, Elizabeth and Sydney Graham.*

The Roberts at Tilty Mill House, 1952.

© Michael Wickham

Elizabeth at Tilty Mill House,
(late 1940s or early 1950s).

Photo supplied by Georgina Barker

Elizabeth with Tambimuttu and Georgina at a party, 1971.

*Poster advertising a reading for the
National Book League, 12 May 1977.*

Rose Barker at age seventeen.

Elizabeth in her sixties.

Elizabeth with George Barker at Bintry House, Norfolk, in the late 1970s.

Elizabeth with children at the Dell. From left: *Jennie Kember* (seated), *Alice Kember* (on lap), *Elizabeth* (centre), *Christopher Barker* (standing), *Clare Barker* (Christopher's wife, seated), *Lydia Barker* (on lap), *Rufus Deakin* (front, centre), *Leo Barker* (front, right).

© Christopher Barker

Elizabeth Smart at kitchen table, the Dell cottage, Flixton, Bungay, Suffolk.

10 The 97 Positions of the Heart, Lying Low

To tell you the truth, I've been driven so hard by life that I feel nothing. Through these years it is not my mind that grew numb, but my soul. An astonishing observation: it is precisely for feeling that one needs time, and not for thought. . . . no time, no quiet, no solitude . . . off to bed, which means lying in bed with a book . . . The books are good, but I could have written even better ones, if only . . .

Anna Tsetsaeyva
Notebook

If thou wilt ease thine heart
Of love and all its smart,
Then sleep, dear, sleep. . . .

Thomas Lovell Beddoes
"Dirge"

Elizabeth was grateful for Tilty Mill, but she again found herself isolated in the country with four children (the youngest only six months old) and a young Irish nanny. She had little money, though as she had written her family earlier, she was rather good at cutting down her wants. She felt old. She was thirty-four.

In an effort to take charge of her life, she went up to London to look for freelance work. She sold her first article to *House and Garden* that autumn and returned to her notebooks, writing a little more of *Rogues and Rascals*. To make a bit of money on the side, she sewed and sold children's smocks. She continued to keep a vague log of George's appearances. He came on and off, at two-week intervals, staying for two or three days, until January 1948 when, Elizabeth wrote, he left by taxi with all his bags and a stormy face.

For George things had clearly changed. He had completed *Book One* of *The True Confession of George Barker*, perhaps his finest sequence of poems, and was still working on his novel, *The Dead Seagull*. Elizabeth reports that he went to the south of France with "Cass" in July 1948. Cass was a young woman he had met in Soho, the girlfriend of the artist Bruce Bernard.

Didy Asquith wrote that she had seen George in Paris; he still talked of Tilty as a haven but said that he had decided to leave Elizabeth alone. His friends had advised him it was better to leave the children alone as well. The truth seems Elizabeth didn't really want George at Tilty.

In 1948 a friend of Elizabeth's past surfaced. She had asked Julian Trevelyan whom she'd known since 1937 if he knew of someone who could take photographs of her children for a fashion magazine. Trevelyan suggested the idea to Michael Wickham, a photographer who had been a member of Varda's entourage on the trip Elizabeth took to Cassis in 1938. By now he had left his wife and was living in London. Wickham went down to Tilty Mill one morning and, as he put it, stayed for two years.

Wickham offers a compelling portrait of Elizabeth's life. He described Tilty as a dreary little house, and Elizabeth as living in a frightful mess with all her children underfoot. It was rigorous to a degree, the heating inadequate, and water had to be drawn from the well—Fred the miller would arrive every afternoon at tea-time to give the well four hundred pumps. It was always muddy because of the pigs living in the farm just past the front gate. When he was there, Wickham had a studio behind the house off the garden, and Elizabeth had a bedroom studio upstairs lined with books. The children weren't allowed in the library/sitting room where Ruthven Todd's Blake collection filled the shelves. It was unclear what Elizabeth lived on, but her life was dictated by domestic rounds. The two older children went to Thaxted County Primary School and the two younger were at home. She rarely went to London and seemed to have little work. There were sometimes others staying, including Wickham's son, whom it seems, was briefly deposited on Elizabeth by Wickham's former wife in his absence. Wickham also brought his Bechstein to Tilty, and gradually discovered that Elizabeth could play the piano, though she didn't take it seriously.

But Wickham adored Elizabeth. It was, he said, always great fun to be with her. Though they were lovers, Wickham was always aware that they never shared a room: "Sex went on everywhere, in the pantry, on the Bechstein, in the drawing room, but we never shared a bed."[1] In a curious way, theirs was a detached life, he commuting to London to work, she at home with her children who were never aware that he was anything but an intermittent boarder. They went about seeing friends, and travelled to Paris together, yet they remained essentially separate.

Wickham was fascinated by Elizabeth's relationship with her children. He found it extremely physical, indeed sensual, and took to making sketches of her, beautiful nudes in which babies crowded over her body. Elizabeth delighted in the physical aspects of motherhood, and she was wonderful with her children. In an old photograph taken by Wickham, they are gathered in the barn around a small wooden table. It is painted with flowers and the children's names are on the corners in Gothic script so that it looks like a piece of Balkan folk art. On top sits a seven-branch candelabra. The children are playing with balloons and a hand-made toy farm. Life was frugal. Elizabeth was not a strict mother but there were rules. One of the childhood moments that sat in her daughter Georgina's mind was of a family picnic when she and her siblings were fighting over candies. Elizabeth took the candies from them, and threw them in the river. "These sweets were meant to give pleasure," she said. It was an indelible lesson.

Though Wickham was in love with Elizabeth and had suggested marriage, he gradually realized that this was not the basis of their relationship. She might speak of desire and amusing each other, but she would never use the word love—it was a word to be used economically. Wickham gradually understood his was the role of itinerant lover. Not without a certain animus, he remarked that Elizabeth "liked all her men to be temporary. Indeed she forced that upon one. She wasn't given to living sensibly. One did what one did as it came along, responding to circumstances. She took all kinds of risks, and was a very generous spirit, though she was not conscious of it."

During Wickham's stay at Tilty, it was announced that Louie was coming to visit. The whole scenario became rather ridiculous. Wickham remembers that he had to be tidied up, put in a different room and made to look like a paying guest, as Elizabeth wasn't about to admit to her mother that she had a man in the house. The house was cleaned and painted and the children remembered waiting for Granny with great trepidation. Ironically she never arrived. As the train eased into Dunmow station, unable to see because of her failing eyesight, Louie descended onto the platform while the train was still in motion and promptly broke her hip. She spent the rest of her visit in hospital. Wickham felt that Elizabeth was frightened of Louie, still dominated by her, though one might see that from Elizabeth's perspective, there was not much point after so many traumas in adding the damning fact of a lover to the sins her mother held against her.

Elizabeth remained an enigma to Wickham. He could not understand her obsession with Barker whom she loved to talk about, though she seemed quite aware that there was no hope to the relationship. She would get Wickham to read Barker's books and give him endless versions of *By Grand Central Station*, always describing the situation and elaborating it in "snapshotty" ways. He could only conclude that she needed a painful drama. She often complained of boredom; nothing was happening to her. If one could keep the elation going, everything was fine, but as soon as there was a hitch, any dullness or tediousness, she would immediately collapse in recriminations.

He felt she needed another great fire, some incendiary thing to get her going. She needed a terrible drama so that she could emerge and shine as the wonderful person who could transmute it all to poetry. George had provided that and she had written *By Grand Central Station I Sat Down and Wept*. Wickham felt there was no one else for Elizabeth but Barker: once she had dedicated herself to him, she had done it completely.

After more than two years the relationship ended. Wickham concluded that while Elizabeth found him attractive, she did not find him interesting. She wanted a poet. "She was ruthless in her quiet way. She just turned me out. I was no longer useful; I could be dispensed with." But he also added that she was quite right. "I just said too bad and buggered off." The truth was Elizabeth didn't want to hurt Wickham and discussed with Didy Asquith how to end the relationship. She finally chose the only route she knew—she assumed the end as an accomplished fact. But there was an incident several friends, including Didy, reported. Barker did visit while Wickham was at Tilty, and though Wickham remembered the occasion as being friendly, Barker's vanity was piqued. Intuiting something was going on, in a fit of jealousy he ripped up Wickham's photographs of the children. It hurt Elizabeth terribly, since it felt as though he were destroying her children. Elizabeth could never confront Barker with her lovers nor be candid to others. Later when her daughter asked her about George's accusation that she had affairs, she replied: "George is so unjust. It's all lies." Elizabeth saved none of Wickham's letters and never mentioned him in her diaries. There are very few photographs of him at Tilty. Among Elizabeth's albums are to be found occasional photos where a male face has been cut out. Georgina would explain the strange censorship in the albums as Elizabeth's attempt to avoid George's wrath.

In the early 1960s, Wickham found himself in California and looked up Jean Varda. On Varda's boat *The Vallejo* in Saulsalito, the two discarded lovers discussed Elizabeth. In the post-mortem, they concluded that "she was one of the most sadly botched individuals and could have been absolutely marvellous. She should have married George or anybody, made reason of her life. Instead of which she sketched her life. I could never imagine what she was trying to do, except bring up the children, I guess."

But Elizabeth had never been interested in making *reason* of her life. To counter a profound insecurity, she had crafted a rage of will. She had made an intimate symbiosis between love and writing, between the man and the work. She had turned her determination to the securing of the demon lover. That year she wrote the poem: "I'd Rather Marry a Young Man" with the lines "But only a devil in the bed/Satisfies a woman's need/Only archangels understand/The less as well as more than human."[2] She was still trying to puzzle out what came after romantic ecstasy; how, like Lazarus, to resurrect herself. "I am the obsessional type: which type are you?" she asked. "If you are the butterfly type you will never forgive my intensity." She was in fact writing a little, but Wickham was never invited into the world of her work; she hid any evidence of it. That year she wrote "Song: The Singing Summer Streets":

Nothing dies, it bursts to birth
Before the requiem is half done,
Before the suitable tears are shed
Or the mourning of the underbred
Nags out its course, the death is dead.

The sighs shoot into the loud trombone
It blows so hard it shakes the earth.
The flowers in a breathless rush break through;
If one has collapsed, then out spring two,
Insatiable for things to do.

It is unnecessary to atone
For sin: he is the losing one;
With all his conjuror's cheap disguise
No geese fly north because of his lies,
No cause is lost, and nothing dies.[3]

She wanted desperately to move on, but she was still stuck. She was a single mother with four children. She was poor and needed work to support her children and possibly to distract herself in the face of her absconding lover. In the inevitable insecurity that is the territory of the writer, she needed emotional support for whatever writing she could manage to do. Isolated, she had no one to tell her whether she was on the right track. The poems she was writing were stilted, Barkerian in acceding to a tradition of rhyme that he could handle marvellously but that constricted the great organic rhythm of her sentences. She was still censored by what she later came to call "the maestro of the masculine." Mostly she succeeded in keeping her turmoil at bay. But Michael Wickham remembered an odd gesture Elizabeth had. Every time she read a book she would nick the pages with thumb and fingernail, making little crescent-shaped indentations and perforations along the edges of the pages. One could always tell when she'd read a book. "Perhaps she didn't do it continuously," he remarked, "but any time distress arose she'd be perforating her way all down the page."

In 1949, Elizabeth approached *House and Garden* and asked for a job on staff. She was hired as a sub-editor at five hundred pounds a year with fifty pounds' dress allowance, and this, added to her Canadian allowance, which was now one hundred and fifty dollars a month, meant that she was suddenly financially secure. She was to become Features Editor before she left in 1951. She used to say that her value to the magazine was that she could write grammatical, readable sentences with verbs in them, but the truth was, while few articles were attributed, she wrote half the magazine. The signed pieces: "Homemakers of Tomorrow," "Why Always the Piano," and "This Christmas You Can Enjoy Your Guests" were light fare, and she wrote fast. It must have felt good to be back in public life among adults, but she still had the children to think of.

In an address Elizabeth gave at the Royal Society, Burlington House, in 1950 called "Design Begins in the Nursery,"[4] we get a glimpse of the real side of single-parenthood. She speaks as an expert who has been "in unmitigated contact with four children, not to mention borrowed ones, over a period of nine years

. . . it's like being out in a hurricane." At the end of the day, "after the noise had died down; the mess, the confusion, the obstreperous clashing of personalities, the urgent needs that can't wait for a minute, all the exasperating and maddening demands are stilled," one tends to romanticize children. She asks that the designers remember the nature of the creatures they are designing for. Children are tough, indefatigable, noisy, messy, destructive, full of insatiable curiosity, with the energy of jet engines. Don't discipline their energy out of them with rules you can't enforce, she advises. Cheap (parents are poor), durable furniture is what's called for. Tables that could be jumped off of, stacked as confidently as circus tumblers, floated in the millstream as boats, unpainted so that the parent could indulge her sentimentality, would be best. From this sketch it's clear that it must often have been wildly fun to be a child at Tilty Mill. Elizabeth would not allow the designers of furniture to forget the "J. M. Barrie" world of childhood.

House and Garden relieved Elizabeth's financial worries, but it meant the children had to be sent to boarding school. She found a progressive school called Pinewood, in Hertfordshire, where the children were weekly boarders. Elizabeth lodged in London and came home weekends to Tilty. The solution had its costs. Elizabeth felt she was missing the childhood of her babies and her ambivalence is caught in a brief vignette. One Sunday as she was at the train station, leaving her children on the platform, Bashie [Sebastian] turned to her and said: "Mummy, in school the mistress says God doesn't have a body. But how can that be? He must be just arms and legs."[5] On the train to London she found herself crying and bracing herself to head back into her world of dashing, childless, career friends. However, she was confident at least that her children were at a good school; she herself had been to private school. Though they might be illegitimate, she could give them a good education.

But Pinewood was not all she thought it to be. The Australian novelist, Elizabeth Jolley, was matron of Pinewood in 1949. Every weekend, Elizabeth would come to collect her four children with a Swiss au pair called Rosemary. To Jolley, she always looked handsome and efficient. "She worked very hard and seemed to me to be a wonderful mother, very fond of her children, devoted." Jolley remembered the children as very sweet, with gentle eyes, well-behaved and intelligent. But Pinewood, though it may have had a reputation as progressive, was bleak. It provides the backdrop to Jolley's novel *My Father's Moon*, and though she admits to having heightened things she recalled the school as a "sad place, many of the staff and children were there because of domestic troubles—divorce was not easy then, single parents had to manage as best they could."[6] The school setting was beautiful: an old estate with rambling woods, sand pits where the children played, and gardens of roses, but the huge lawns remained uncut, and inside, life was humdrum—children in their endless rows of beds, "the smell of ordinary life missing." The two women who owned the school ran it on a shoestring; it was understaffed and there was never enough food. "The children are unhappy . . . They are hungry all the time," Jolley writes in her novel.[7] Elizabeth's son Sebastian did not remember being unhappy at Pinewood, but he did remember being hungry. The one to whom the cost was highest may have been little Rose, who was then only three and a half.

As soon as Christopher was born Elizabeth had started, much to her mother's annoyance, to set aside money in order to send him to Eton. Louie's response had been rather brutal: "This talk about sending your boys to Eton sounds to me quite ridiculous. In the first place, the world has changed & the kind of education which Eton gives would be quite useless to boys who are going to have to fend for themselves. Besides, by the time your boys are old enough to go, there may not be any Eton as such. Anyway the whole idea is one of snobbery and quite unsuitable."[8] It wasn't snobbery on Elizabeth's part, but rather the determination that her children wouldn't suffer from her choices—they would have the best education she could offer—the private school.

While working in London, Elizabeth picked up her life in Soho. She had made her first appearance there in 1947, descending like a bombshell, as beautiful as a movie star. She wasn't liked by all, of course. Caitlin Thomas remembered her vaguely as one of the Fitzrovia crowd [the insiders' name for north Soho]: "a rich girl, thrilled to be among the poor people, which I always thought a stupid attitude because I would like to have been rich."[9] By the early fifties Elizabeth had become a Soho personality.

For those who went there in the late forties, Soho was a refuge against the grey uniformity of London. It was a place where the rules didn't apply. Though many called it a state of mind rather than a place, the heart of Soho was to be found between the four parallels of Wardour Street, Dean Street, Frith Street, and Greek Street. Its inhabitants delighted in its history, dating back to the fourteenth century. It had always attracted iconoclasts: Casanova attended the first nightclubs in Soho in 1760; Mozart and Canaletto lived there, as did De Quincy, Hazlitt, and Karl Marx. Soho was a home for refugees, for the Greeks fleeing the Turks in the 1670s, followed by the French, Italians, Cypriots, and Chinese. In the late 1940s Soho still had the integrity of a village. It was a pleasant backwater, a place where there were numerous pubs within walking distance of each other, and drinking clubs that were entitled to open in the afternoon, with a backdrop of delicatessens, off-licences, small shops, and restaurants. Each pub or club had its own style and collected its regulars. While they included the famous or soon-to-be-famous like Dylan Thomas or Francis Bacon, there were also the local eccentrics, spiky and occasionally irascible, who established their territory and became local legends. Elizabeth remembered Mrs Stewart who arrived punctually at the Wheatsheaf at six each night, with evening papers and alarm clock to do the crosswords, and told stories of her days in Paris when she'd known Joyce and Hemingway, which always ended: "And there they were, my dear, staggering about just like you and the rest of the young fellows are doing today."[10]

Elizabeth took to Soho in the afternoons when work was slow or in the evenings. She had her favourite spots, which included Muriel Belcher's club, the Colony Room on Dean Street, the York Minster also on Dean Street, run by Gaston and called simply "The French," the Wheatsheaf in Rathbone Place, Wheeler's restaurant where one went for oysters, and the jazz clubs, like the Mandrake Club or the Metro. Elizabeth had not been a drinker. By her own report she trained herself to drink at the age of thirty-five—to have the company of people as a bulwark against loneliness.

Elizabeth loved Soho. It was a place where people were accepted on their own merit. If they had any character or flair they could find themselves included. In an obituary she wrote about Muriel Belcher, she identified the rogues and rascals who came to the Colony Room. The two thousand or so members included "painters, writers, tinkers, tailors, sailors, editors, art editors, cartoonists, singers, African chiefs, burglars, strippers, composers, dress-designers, lords, landowners, lawyers, accountants, whizz-kids, barmen, publishers, poets, barrow-boys, advertising people, and unclassifiable people," a motley lot for whom Muriel's club supplied an irreplaceable element in their lives. Though it was just a small shabby room with a bar, when Elizabeth tried to define why people were addicted to Muriel's, she suggested, tentatively, that they had in common "a certain kind of nervous system; or the kind of good manners that recognizes and respects another's hangover or sexual hangups; a lack of pomposity (you can't reply pompously when greeted by 'Hello, cunty'); a capacity to let the delights of the moment take over, and *soar*. Perhaps, even, an innocence." Muriel made you feel "safe"; she could relax the shy, inhibited person. She made you feel sexier, more in the know. It was liberating; you dared to be yourself. Elizabeth thought of Muriel as an artist and it moved her that her art was applied to the touchingly ephemeral. To the art of "cross-fertilizing" people, she brought pain and discipline, and she did it with wit. She could say to a shy homosexual: "Meet Sue. She's had more pricks than you've had hot dinners."[11] Evenings would end in bacchanalia.

Elizabeth always delighted in the touching vulgarity, the joke that breaks the heart. She loved the cocky affirmation, life crude and indomitable rising against all odds. Indeed she was more of a romantic than was George Barker, signing on with the impudent, the outcast, the derelict and the delinquent saints. She called Soho innocent, perhaps in the sense that it only attracted artists and eccentrics and was proud of its impecuniousness. The rogues and rascals demanded the right to go against the rules that kept those less adventurous within the bounds of safety. One did not live to be cushioned against the future. Elizabeth believed that a true life staggered between the gutter and the Ritz. And she had an insatiable appetite for people; she gave a great deal to feed loneliness.

Perhaps what joined Elizabeth and the people of Soho was the sense that life wasn't, after all, safe. You can find some comfort against the black holes, but you can't hide from them. You bashed on regardless, scattering your rats. The artists she found in Soho she loved for precisely that reason. Like her, they were people driven by some voracious appetite they couldn't fathom.

There was an ethic of generosity. When you had money you spent it; when you didn't, without embarrassment, you cadged a drink. Francis Bacon would show up in his wealthier days and the champagne would flow and the wit whirl while Muriel sat back looking like Bacon's painting of the Pope. Elizabeth knew everyone, from Lucian Freud, Francis Bacon, Craigie Aitchison, Frank Auerbach, John Minton, the Roberts, Isabel Lambert, the Bernard brothers, Paul Potts. They were all there, to be counted on.

Soho, of course, had its down side. It could be bitchy, the mannerisms insincere, and the drinking ferocious. And one watched there the delighted relish with which many casualties, like John Deakin, David Archer, or John Minton, pursued their own self-destruction. Soho could also be a dangerous addictive escape. There were many who felt that the energy that went into the life-style drained and eventually destroyed the work.

One might say Elizabeth lived two lives: the responsible one of the single mother supporting four children at Tilty Mill; and the Soho life of the writer "scattering her rats." For all her bohemianism, she worked hard. As well as working with *House and Garden*, she did freelance work for *Vogue*, where, occasionally, her children appeared as models for children's clothes. She had no time left over for actual writing.

The only significant literary moment for her in these two years was the publication in 1950 of George Barker's *The Dead Seagull*. It could have been nothing other than a massive blow. Elizabeth always spoke about the book reluctantly, but, ironically, when it was reissued in 1965, it was she who reviewed it, along with the poem *The True Confession of George Barker*, in *Queen*. She describes Barker as that "seriously and mysteriously underrated and unfashionable poet," and comments that *The Dead Seagull* had had a "happy life" since it was published fifteen years previously, recommended by the Book Society and pretty warmly praised. "Yet the novel to me at least seems to be merely the raw undigested material of the poem—brilliant in flashes like gold in the prospector's pan; but the poem is totally successful and an extremely impressive achievement."[12] Those were careful and parsimonious words, given that it would have been impossible not to have seen a cruel version of herself in Barker's book. The fascinating thing is to imagine what was in Barker's mind as he wrote the book, and in Elizabeth's as she read it.

It is rare to find two literary records of the same experience from the perspective of a male and a female writer, for it cannot be denied that while both books are "fictions," they are poetic transmutations of autobiographical experience. What both writers have done is to find a mythological basis to the same encounter. And we see how divergent those two perspectives are. Barker's book is so full of vitriol that it makes one feel that the male and female minds are mutually exclusive.

Barker was so compelled by the relationship, which in his case had lasted seven years, that he felt the need to write about it, to transform it into the basis for a meditation on obsessive love. The book reads like a kind of meditational exorcism. There is a code, coined by critics, called the biographical heresy that insists that a book is an artifact, never to be traced back to its roots in real experience. But one might say this is part of a larger conspiracy, a conspiracy that caught Elizabeth Smart. The literary world Barker came from was essentially a male world, where everything fed the imperative of the male poet to write. He could find the support from peers and from wives because there was a traditional role for the male poet, a vision of the magnitude of his work. And in his books, he could explore uncritically the myths that set that in motion. One cannot read *The Dead Seagull* without tracing it back to the people who engendered it, because then one can see, with fascination, how reality is woven into myth. One can only wonder how powerful the archetypes are, how deep the demons go, that two people of the magnitude and imagination of Elizabeth Smart and George Barker could remain trapped in their separate solipsisms. Barker has caught something of the real Jessica and the real Elizabeth here, how both gave themselves in service to the myth.

The narrator of Barker's novel is a writer (poet) exploring a relationship in retrospect. Barker begins by admitting his plot is trite. Recounting how a benevolent marriage is destroyed by a passionate affair, the story makes its claim on our attention by exploring the nature of love. The vitriol that threads the text can only be identified as disgust with the sexual and one thinks again of Barker's bifurcated universe: man involved with the metaphysical ideal; woman assigned the lower world of the relational. This disgust sabotages belief in the virtues of love. "Hitherto," the narrator says, "I have believed in love." But he has now come to discover that we are caged in the "locked and barred box of zoological sex"; nature, "the imperial multiplicator," claims us for her "nine-tiered purposes, to reproduce ourselves"; destiny never worries her. The narrator has a dream that he describes as illuminating "my positively albigensian attitude to the viciousness of human reproduction. I simply dreamed that I had become hermaphrodite."[13]

What is most fascinating about *The Dead Seagull* is that beneath its intellectual surface lies a profound and complex misogyny. It was something Elizabeth recognized but that she could never quite believe. Still puzzled, she could write at the age of sixty-four: "Voices. George said he left the Catholic Church (as a practitioner) when he noticed the congregation was 60% women (or was it more?). How he despises us. Why?

Or hates? Or fears?"[14] Perhaps because women have so censored their own resentment, it takes a long time to believe that
a man, while externally, ostensibly, and actually loving
women, could at the abstract level and as the ground to everything, also feel contempt.

Often we look for a complex explanation, when the simple
explanation is at least the place to begin. The way the women
around him acted, Barker was invited to sustain his myths. Yet,
one cannot help but feel that the wit and bravado and intellectual display of *The Dead Seagull* masks an extraordinary fear.
Michael Asquith, Didy's husband, and Barker often went
drinking in the mid-forties, and Asquith remembered endless
discussions about *The Dead Seagull* as George agonized over
it. It seemed significant to him that the working title for the
novel was "The Smile on the Face of the Tiger": Elizabeth was
the tiger and Barker the lady at risk of being swallowed.[15] In
their conversations, Barker seemed obsessed with the devouring aspect of love: he feared he and Elizabeth would end up
consuming each other and he withdrew. She, for her part, could
not take his fear seriously.

The novel is written ostensibly in 1945 about incidents that
happened thirteen years previously. The narrator is a poet who
has married a childhood sweetheart, older than he. Called
Theresa, she is pregnant through their nine-month marriage.
Barker has caught the relationship exquisitely. It is not the relationship of adults. They are essentially innocent, like children
in German folk tales; but the marriage is haunted by the illegitimacy that engendered it. As the woman turns inwardly
towards the child, the narrator stands by amazed at the biolog-
ical imperative of maternity, how a woman seems to be taken
over, her individuality focused only in her body, or her mind
absorbed, almost consumed, by the growing child. But the poet
seems to revile woman for her willingness to be nature's instrument. Her fulfilment in the child is so perfect that all else is
forgotten: "It is for this simple reason that I cannot help
suspecting that the woman exists in a lower category of
spiritual consciousness. I wish to god I could be fobbed off

from the omnipresence of evil by merely fulfilling my function as a father."[16]

Beneath the metaphysical rationalizations—Barker was not a lapsed Catholic for nothing—is of course a banality: the narrator's sense of his own entrapment. The woman has defined herself as the husband's pale appendage (Henry Miller could refer to Jessica cryptically as Barker's consumptive wife) and holds on ruthlessly. She has little identity other than as saint and martyr, at night downcast by the bedside, praying for their forgiveness. But the poet is sensitive to destiny. He cannot understand why this woman has tied herself to him since his character dooms him to destruction. Beneath the love, he feels contempt.

Theresa's very sainthood dictates her own martyrdom. "In the house of your love, my dear wife, there was that marvelously appointed room of forgiveness . . . but were you aware . . . that an anticipation was its tenant?" The logic is Catholic. One sins because there is confession. A wife who confronts every crime with forgiveness asks for more crimes. The narrator even seems fascinated by his own capacity for deception. He no longer knows when he is lying to himself and his deceptions exercise on him the compulsion of multiple mirrors. The wife's self-abnegating protective love is destined to be rebelled against. And we get a shrewd glimpse of the woman's psychology: the poet is the victim of Theresa's demand that he save her from the emptiness she feels. To the man with whom she senses an umbilical, telepathic connection, Theresa can say: "When you are not with me I am . . . empty and absurd." One can imagine those words in Jessica's mouth. And it is a familiar female dilemma: what is the initial emotional and cultural training that a woman feels she needs to be invented by a man? Sadly, in the predictable nature of the human story, one can see Barker's side of it. Jessica could never match his complexity. And no one has the right to expect to be invented by another.

But Elizabeth Smart was a different matter entirely. She was as much a mythographer as Barker. Into *The Dead Seagull* marches Marsden Forsden. The name is curious; perhaps Barker liked it because his narrator could think at first its bearer was a man. Elizabeth, in Barker's vision, was as monstrously monumental as he, and as hermaphroditic.

Marsden is meant to have been Theresa's school chum. The poet has never met her, as Theresa explains, because she has carefully kept her friend away from her home and precious possessions (as she calls the poet). Marsden is too intense, and too beautiful to trust. Theresa explains that she was always an eccentric creature and used to have literary ambitions that have likely evaporated. Her father had sent her around the world with an aunt. She had the misfortune always to have a little too much money. Theresa warns the narrator to be kind to Marsden; otherwise she would fall in love with him.

Barker gives Marsden the characteristics of Elizabeth. She carries two pamphlets: "The Wild Flowers of the Netherlands" and "How To Sin in San Francisco." She postures in a calculated way that the narrator finds ineffectual: "I hate animals; I feel so like them. Let's have a brilliant conversation. Do I look beautiful?" To which Theresa replies all of her does since Marsden's breasts have slipped from her gown. She is restless and imperious and expects the world to follow her whim: "Let's go for a walk. . . . Let's go for a retreat," as she turns querulously to ask: "But does the cut worm really forgive the plough?"[17] It is a rather shrewd, if cruel, parody of Elizabeth. Marsden arrives with a Greek, Jean Theokopolos (whom Barker calls an aging erotomaniac and who is a somewhat thin disguise for Jean Varda). Barker dispatches him rather expertly. Asking for wine, Theo remarks that he loves Mediterranean wine. "I find that I accrue a whole architecture of *mauve* satisfaction when I drink wine." To which the poet replies: "From *white* wine?" Barker could always be funny, at his own and others' expense. It was one of his most seductive characteristics.

Marsden sets about brazenly seducing the poet (which of course isn't hard to do), explaining that she has had hundreds of dreams about him. "It was your book. When I read it I sat down and wrote one exactly like it." She had gone to dozens of parties hoping to meet him. "Oh why, why, why, why, were you never there!" and in a seizure of petulance rolls over on her belly, inadvertently exposing her nakedness under her frock. The poet responds: "I experienced the same sort of hypnotized revulsion that I imagine might have excited me if I had awakened and found a mermaid in bed beside me."[18] (One might imagine that among the blows Elizabeth might feel in reading this book, the claim that her book was an imitation might have been among the worst.)

The poet sees himself as a willing victim as he follows the scenario the fates have dictated. Marsden leaves with a cryptic and perhaps intentionally ludicrous command: "Come." (The poet will later say: "Every time I sneeze, I conceive a child.") It is then that the title comes into play. On the beach, the poet finds a dead seagull, and sees in it the parallel of his wife's virtues. He lays his hand on the breast in which the symbol of the heart had broken and says, "Gull the bitch." It is a mad and brilliant moment.

All the vitriol of years is in those three words and the novel cracks open. For, of course, the narrator means the two women. He reaches down into an atavistic core and damns them both. They are both aspects of the one great mother, the devouring female Hera/Aphrodite who want him for their own purposes and would swallow him whole. It is an annunciatory vision. Between the amoeba and the skull is "the umbilical of the eternal maternal," the gallows on which the male hangs. One remembers the two women, human beings scattered with their babies and scrambling for money in a real world and it is hard, for a moment, not to hate literature, or at least the permission literature and its myths can give. Barker could say they asked for what they got and in a sense by playing the roles society assigned to them they did. In their dependence they were pinioned to him, even though they held their own ropes.

The Marsden Barker has created does bear resemblance to Elizabeth in that she is a conundrum he cannot understand. For a man sexual passion turns most easily to sexual revulsion. Marsden is not a person, she is Pig-woman, Circe, who has made him her prey and he looks back at the passion in the dishevelled bed in retrospect as a sty with the odour of hell. She is soulless, "as incapable of sin as a tigress," a magnificent animal without moral principle: "whatever she wanted was right." (One might say that the difference between her and Barker was he recognized whatever he wanted was wrong and he got it. He would "rehabilitate the dignity of the unforgivable.") She is the randy bitch tearing his life to shreds, powerful because he is greedier and randier. Marsden's is the face of every painter's mistress, an exquisite face masking orgies of egotism in which the devotee finds "dynamos that slowly cut him to pieces." And he writes: "My love, you have been loved by every man since the beginning. My love, you will be abandoned by every man until the end."

And the plot moves as if dictated. The child dies, and the wife lies dying as Marsden stands by not in tears but with a face livid with sexual desire. As she utters, with demonic elation, her sentence—that she is pregnant with his child—the wife dies, cursing.

Certainly this is an orgy of emotionalism that would seem like a parodic Greek tragedy were it not, against all odds, true to Barker's psyche and sustained by the power of the writing. Barker's misogyny was focused on the mother. One remembers the mythological great mothers who were voluptuous, devouring creatures dangerous to their sons. And thinks of Big Mumma, the loved facilitator; she had devoured Barker's father. Barker ran from the mother.

The extraordinary thing about Elizabeth Smart was that Barker was half right. Elizabeth had played the Circe, pursuing Barker with a fierceness that was almost unprecedented. And she used all her female sexual power to get him. She could be hard to be with, so intense that one had the idea she used up all the oxygen in the room. But had she been simply this, she would have survived better, perhaps even as a writer. She might have been Barker's twin, able to subordinate everything to her own dictates, to her own ego as a writer. But like a mad gambler, she had gambled everything on the man. Elizabeth was an original combination, indeed a schizophrenic combination. She had the determination to ruthlessly pursue what she wanted, but what she wanted, the child, the lover, distanced her from the self.

Barker ends his novel, predictably, alone, with his ghosts. When he explores his own revulsion at sex, he admits that he is terrified by its mindlessness. The sense of dramatic urgency that impels one to achievement disappears. (Elizabeth had recognized the same phenomenon in her own novel, how love obliterates all private ambition, the woman being overpowered by voices of blood each time she rises to speak, and love compels her to adore being devoured, filling her heart with images of unborn babies.) Barker would not be devoured. He wanted to be alone. The narrator confesses that he sleeps with "a misery that is not entirely miserable, with an unrest that is not wholly distressful; for the misery of it is shot through with penances and expiations and the unrest, sometimes, takes on a tortured attitude of flagellatory exculpation." Barker would later repudiate the novel, saying he had composed it in a week and it was simply an exorcism. Yet, it cuts to the bone. Barker preferred to be in the mire of his own emotions. That's where the poems came from. Torture was the necessary state. An emotional torture where, however, real life was taken care of by a real woman. Barker was never to be without a woman. Conversely Elizabeth was alone, a state that he found amazing that she could bear. But the truth was that for Barker no woman was completely real. His last wife, Elspeth, could say rather sadly but resignedly, "I don't think any of us really existed for him. He was in love with the muse."[19]

Elizabeth obviously genuinely loved Barker, and also felt that her life was given greater importance because of him.[20] Once she had loved to the level of the archangels as she had put it, at the dizzy level of "the less as well as more than human." It was her pride and distinction. It had a quality of omnipotence and she was still unable to pull that love back into herself. Even George Barker's revelations in *The Dead Seagull* could not sabotage that. Elizabeth would take another eight years to free herself from Barker. Her stamina was indeed almost monstrously magnificent. Barker himself would say that "Elizabeth was slightly disbalanced in her obsession with me."[21] But when she did finally release Barker from her projection, she could encounter him as a human being rather than as a myth, accepting her own responsibility in the long drama. The extra-ordinary thing is that she was never bitter. In *The Assumption of the Rogues and Rascals* she could finally recognize such passion as an essential route to the self, not to be repudiated but to be transformed into a different kind of love, from Eros to Agape. The only anger she found was in the cruel sexual bargain: if she had a motive for resentment, it was simply that she had four children to bring up alone.

For Elizabeth, Barker remained for a long time seductive and irreplaceable. There was no man as witty, as intelligent, as passionate and one might say as slippery as he. And Elizabeth felt he was a great writer. Once we love someone, and Elizabeth did love, it is hard not to count them in our lives. And one thinks of Louie by whom she had been betrayed at the deepest level so many times. Could she exist without the idea of fidelity that gave her being motive? As her childhood nightmare made clear, even as the neck elongated to snake-like proportions, she could save the other by loving enough.

It was like Barker to produce along with *The Dead Seagull* what is probably his best work. In 1950 he published *The True Confession of George Barker, Book One*. It is a witty and outrageous sequence and displayed all his gifts: a spry naughtiness, a robust sexiness, a verbal cunning, the irascible edginess of the satirist. Barker was always the bard. Bits of the sequence were read on the BBC's Third Programme and roused the House of Lords to call it "gilded filth." The persona Barker creates is that of the Villon poet, the Orphic criminal. The poem is funny, outrageous, irreverent about everything from the poet himself to all institutions, from marriage to sainthood. The human story is a black comedy of caterwauling egoists. Behind our masks we hide a face of fear no love can console. " . . . Our state/—Insufferable among mysteries—/ Makes the worms weep . . ."[22]

Barker had received an Arts Council bursary and was by this time living in the south of France with Cass. Didy Asquith sent Elizabeth reports on Cass, whom she said was twenty-four, pretty, though without flair, and without staying power; she had literary ambitions and was working in film. "Whether or not she has the stability to continue without demands or showing nervousness, I don't know." "She can't win." Didy brought out photos of Elizabeth's children and reported George asking: "Who is this one? Is it Rosie?" He chose some of Didy's photos to keep, not wanting the professional ones, which Didy took as a dig at Wickham since they were his photos. Didy assured Barker that Wickham was just a family friend, a good father substitute. They joked about a prince, Prince Antoine Bibesco who had fallen madly in love with Elizabeth and wanted to turn her children into princes and princesses. Barker said he thought it better not to see the children, and that Cass minded about them since he'd been talking in his sleep about Christopher. They spoke elliptically of Elizabeth whom Barker said was a good and noble woman. Didy assured him that he could never love wholly like that again, to which there was no reply. The conversation had all the pain of a post-mortem after a severance. But Didy assured Elizabeth she was the one. George could talk of Jessica nicely and rationally, but the mention of her name sent him green and turned "his face into a saint's when he remembers you as you are and not his phony fantasy." Still, she added that George had spun on her in fury, asking: "She's not still on to me is she? If this is all a frame-up to get me to go back!" Didy replied that Elizabeth concluded they were better apart, but that she would always be "on to" him; "She will never not be." George responded that Elizabeth was a romantic; she had invented it all, being in love with a poet who would never make any money, but she was nice. With all of her "worldly success," she'd get "detached."[23]

In 1951, Elizabeth was able to sublet 1 Rossetti House in Flood Street, a flat belonging to Sir Caspar John whose father, Augustus John, she had met at Scarlet. She was delighted to be able to move the children to London but soon began to have trouble there too. By June, John was writing to her that the landlord was shocked to find there were four children as well as adults occupying his flat. He complained of scratches on the paintwork in the hall and pencil drawings on the walls; the flat was being defaced and turned into a second-rate tenement. He insisted that Elizabeth should go.

Sydney Graham, the Scottish poet, shared space in the flat when he was in London, and it seems that a love affair began. The letters Graham wrote to Elizabeth from his home in Norwich or while he was on several literary tours in the United States are compelling. This was clearly a dialogue between two writers. Graham was a poet who was proffered by those who admired his works as another Dylan Thomas. He shared Thomas's temperament. Dressed as a rule in blue-grey tweeds, he was sturdy of build with a snub nose and protuberant grey-blue eyes. He was prickly, competitive and a frequent visitor to Soho. Elizabeth completely caught his imagination. When he was in the U.S., he could complain of wanting to escape from this "Elizabethless" place. It seems to have been impossible to love Elizabeth without turning her into a legend. She over-whelmed him and the letters become flights of rhetoric, poems.

That May and June, Graham was staying at Rainthorpe Hall, Norwich, where he was given room and board and a place to work by the dowager owner, in the name of his art. At lunch the subjects were Kenya and the fun of guns and safari. He wrote to Elizabeth to maintain his sanity. He was reading her novel, he said, and was astonished: the book set up an extraordinary commotion, a heart-hurt, in his breast. He found himself in the state of romantic ecstasy it described. He was afraid someone would steal her and declared poetry was the only way he could bear the torment of being with her and without her. The affair gave him tremendous creative energy and he found himself inventing his own subjective myth of Elizabeth. What was she that she so fertilized his imagination, turning him into a Joycean pun-artist? She had become his "verb"; he was "Elizabethed," awash in love.

Graham spoke to Elizabeth as a writer/lover and encouraged her to get back to her writing, and she did in fact complete a new story that year that she published in Marguerite Caetani's *Botteghe Oscure*. She must have been deeply blocked, as he resorted to harangues to get her started, complaining that she must at least make the attempt. He reminded her there were tricks to start writing, and that she had many subjects: her time in France, or Ireland, or the "Woman's Lot." He begged her not to be plagued by domestic disaster. He could even share with her his doubts about his own writing, the sense that assaults any writer at moments, when he descended to the hopeless fathoms where he felt untalented and a fraud. But Graham was a professional with only one preoccupation and had the confidence of the sustained writer. He could resurrect himself by tricks, waiting for the real work to come.

The last love letter from Graham, equally excited, equally obsessed, was in January 1952, from New York where he was on a poetry tour with Kathleen Raine. How the relationship ended will never be known. Elizabeth never spoke of Graham to friends or family. It was probably a conventional ending to a romance, with each returning to their own real lives, Graham to a good marriage, Elizabeth to job and children. There was no acrimony, rather a tender nostalgia. Elizabeth was to become equally fond of Graham's wife, Nessie. One might wonder if Elizabeth, having been through the triangular relationship once, wouldn't go through it again. Or perhaps she didn't want to use another as an escape route, since by her own admission she hadn't solved the conundrum of George. However the relationship ended, it did not, in any radical way, resurrect Elizabeth's image of herself as a writer.

How Princess Marguerite Caetani came to write to Elizabeth asking her to submit work is unclear. Caetani was a brilliant editor and in the pages of *Botteghe Oscure* managed to collect most of the British, American, French, and Italian writers of importance in the forties and fifties before they became known. Elizabeth's name had probably surfaced among her many contacts. "The Assumption of the Rogues and Rascals" appeared in 1951. It is based on a trip Elizabeth took to France with colleagues from *House and Garden*, and would appear as part five, virtually unchanged except for paragraphing and punctuation, in the novel she would publish by that name sixteen years later. Perhaps one could say that it is an astonishing testament to the consistency of Elizabeth's feelings that it could fit so well there. It was also a confirmation of the way she wrote: each piece of writing crafted like a poem.

"The Assumption of the Rogues and Rascals" gives us a sense of Elizabeth's state of mind at this time. It is more an elegiac poem than a story. And as always, while the root is autobiographical, she has compacted her experience so that she manages to create a paradigm: a woman's bemusement at life's diminishment: "I cannot bear the lilac tree now. Even while I look it goes brown. Before I have taken the path across the field it will never be summer again."[24] Against the young woman of *By Grand Central Station*, so fierce in her demanding passions, stands the older woman, now thirty-eight, totally appalled by her self-censorship. "I've stopped, at its ardent, obstreperous source, every hopeful passion, every complete desire, with its attendant, demanding impossibles. There's no 'That and it's all over.' Nothing is ever over. I've watched a rogue marry and die, decay and betray, and silently lie and deny. What is under my treacherous scum of a surface? Pressed below into unbelievable obeisance, lie malformed, undernourished wishes, starved, ill-treated, under a social smile."

The claustrophobic sense of entrapment is extraordinary. The love passion is seen and dismissed as only a "myth-preservation in the teeth of the hideous facts. For one hour only, rising to the occasion. Then, lapping, lowering, devouring, like all the wolves in every child's nightmare since the beginning of time, will return the moment of aloneness to be BORNE. No. No. No. It is not possible. It is not bearable. It isn't a pretty picture." There is a double meaning in "borne," of course, which Elizabeth understood. The appalling fact is that one discovers after great passion has died, one is essentially alone. The dilemma becomes how to be born from essential aloneness. When asked by the Canadian novelist Katherine Govier why there was no man to replace Barker, Elizabeth replied that Govier hadn't read *The Assumption of the Rogues and Rascals*. What did she mean by that? She refused to elaborate, but one imagines that she meant one grand passion is enough and not repeatable.

Elizabeth makes a trip with her office colleagues to France the basis for a kind of allegory. The people she is with have sought safety; they keep themselves to themselves, never giving nor receiving. They live professional lives—doctors, dentists—taking their vacations in the south of France and squabbling over money. Elizabeth implies that money is never an objective fact. It is a metaphor; how we use money is a measure of our emotional security. Those who hoard are those who cannot risk life, who cannot give, who seek a petty control in the face of life's largeness. They sit in "their cage of grievance, in seemly mourning for lives laid down a long long time ago." Anaesthesia, however tempting, is not a solution.

"All right," Elizabeth concludes, "the price of life is pain. But the price of comfort is death and damnation. Histrionics are not necessary, either. Nothing specific is necessary. Not even one rogue with any particular name. Not one rascal." The rogues are the ones among whom there "is still enough love." Elizabeth would not hide in pain. She would continue to gamble, to risk her life. She would make a long spiritual discipline out of her aloneness.

Two years later in 1953, *Botteghe Oscure* published a second story, "A Simple Statement."[25] Among the many threads that weave the story one constant is the need to write, to get a "furious weapon." The cost to Elizabeth of not writing was enormous since it was for her, as it is for any writer, the vehicle to shape the chaos. But hers was not self-serving self-pity; there is a deeper sympathy for the way life seems to exact submission in its forward frenzied push to impose its working conditions on us all.

Into the story her old ghosts surface. There is herself as a child "lying stiff on one elbow like a frozen prayer" in the burning autumn woods: "Mother mother my soul's on fire." Louie's dictum is the voice of the mothers: learn to arrange the flowers and take some interest in the house. Granny Baldwin appears in her maudlin self-pity: "I won't be here to trouble you much longer." It is the long line of mothers again who exact conformity. From the verandah of the Barge the child can hear Bob Devlin's saxophone with its wail of desperation:

"There perished an early pioneer, born in the wrong place, in the wrong time, without a furious weapon." (Devlin was a Toronto musician who owned a cottage at Kingsmere and was a constant subject of gossip since he drank.) Devlin's wail from the past often came to Elizabeth as an image in which she could see herself.

What was the problem? It was to be "CORNERED." "All your children on one ocean raft." "The womb's an unwieldly baggage. How to stagger up with such a noisy weight." How Elizabeth maintained her equilibrium is amazing. She could see the poison below the surface massed for attack, and could feel the alluring pull of oblivion: the "powerful and beneficial blackness [that each night had] me on its mind." Yet she did not see herself as unique, just one of the "worried burdened" of whom life, with its spur of necessity, demanded service and serviceability. She offers a funny and blackly comic summary of plot:

> Once upon a time there was a woman who was just like all women. And she married a man who was just like all men. And they had some children who were just like all children. And it rained all day . . . In the end they all died. Do you insist on vulgar details? Mere gossip? Loathsome gluttony? Chapter one: they were born. Chapter two: they were bewildered. Chapter three: they loved. Chapter four: they suffered. Chapter five: they were pacified. Chapter six: they died.

Years later, Elizabeth loved to read this passage in public readings. It cut to the core. And how then do you survive life's script? By a rage of will. "Like this: pray; bang your head; be beautiful; wait; love; rage; rail; look, and possibly, if lucky, see; love again; try to stop loving; go on loving; bustle about; rush to and fro. Whatever you say will be far far less than the truth." Refuse dismay and battle on regardless, which is what Elizabeth did. Indeed, Elizabeth believed the only response to life was "ecstatic surrender" since life has a will stronger than yours. "It is not for you to know." She would always ask of herself, "Can't I possibly be a bit braver?"

The astonishing thing is that Elizabeth shouldered her burdens and did plough on. She had the temperament, which surfaced in her writing, of one who should have gone over the edge, broken down as perhaps did Sylvia Plath. She lived on a vertical plane, where ecstasy or pain could deliver themselves like shafts shattering the moment. And yet she accepted the shapelessness of life as a great life-giving bog and she followed its dictates, keeping her children on her ocean raft.

Love, she now understood, was a working condition, "a simple swept table to begin a meal upon." She had her children, she had lovers; but she would not again live with a man. One remembers an earlier comment she had made on her first escape to Mexico, ecstatic to be free and not to have to hear: "the loud ticking of a man's psyche beside me." The focus of her life would be her children and the work required to maintain them, until she could return to her writing. Meeting another's needs in the on-going intimacy of relationship was something she decided to forgo. But because Elizabeth herself was one of the walking wounded she was accessible to those she felt were hurt. Perhaps this was the core of the great generosity recognized by those who knew her. It often meant that she collected waifs and could be used by them. But she also collected remarkable people and in circumstances that went against "COMMON SENSE."

11   Bit George's Lip

The world is too small. I get tired of playing the guitar,
of knitting, of walking, and bearing children. Men are
small, and passions are short-lived. I get furious at
stairways, furious at doors, at walls, furious at everyday
life which interferes with the continuity of ecstasy.
            Anaïs Nin
            House of Incest

In her effort to keep her household in order, Elizabeth always
needed people to look after Tilty Mill while she was in London.
In the summer of 1951, she was evicted from the flat in Flood
Street, and needed a new plan. The best solution was to return
the children to Tilty and put them in day-school at Thaxted. For
a year they lived at home and then went off again to various
boarding schools. After all the hassles with minders, she
thought she had found permanent sitters. Two of her friends in
Soho, the painters Robert Colquhoun and Robert MacBryde,
were desperate for a place to live. Elizabeth was desperate for
a nanny. Inviting them to Tilty seemed to be a convenient way
to make everybody happy. It was a typical Smart gesture.

The Roberts were genuine Soho characters; they would fit
Elizabeth's label of rogues. They had come out of the Glasgow
School of Art, and after prizes and scholarships to Italy and
France had found their way to London just after the war. They
were an inseparable couple and perfectly matched: Colquhoun

roughly handsome, rather awkward and inarticulate; MacBryde with the "mobile rubber features of a clown or perhaps of some sophisticated, disillusioned, rather tired French cabaret artist."[1] They had a tempestuous relationship laced with the kind of ferocious jealousy that characterizes an indissoluble union. Colquhoun was the more gifted painter. In fact George Barker, who had taken the Roberts with him to Italy in 1949 to see the puppet plays at Modena and the Palio at Siena, was to call him the only true genius he had ever known.[2] Colquhoun had become famous shortly after the war, and the Roberts' studio at 77 Bedford Gardens became a meeting-place for the artists and painters of the emerging generation, including Dylan Thomas, John Craxton, Francis Bacon, W.S. Graham, and George Barker. But by the fifties the whims of fashion had changed. Neither of the Roberts could sell his work; they fell into penury, and often had to cadge a drink. They had become the despair of clubs and pubs, including Muriel's.

The Roberts stayed at Tilty from 1951 to 1954. The children had fond memories of them, but they had ambiguous virtues as nannies. They ran the house well, perhaps because of MacBryde's ingenuity. He could improvise anything, such as ironing clothes with a heated teaspoon. He was a first-class cook, and would get up early to do his housekeeping, cleaning up, and lighting the fire. The Roberts took care of the children, sewing and mending for them and looked after the garden. The children all remembered one incident when the Roberts clearly wanted some peace. MacBryde, always full of tricks, was doing the washing up and turned and said: "By the way I was phoning up TIM [which was the way you phoned to get the time] and in the background I could hear somebody say that an airplane has come down near Tilty Abbey. It's full of sweets." In a mad dash the four were off over the fields in search of it. Christopher remembered how convincing the story had been. He could only recall one night when the Roberts failed to appear, having got stuck in a pub in Thaxted. The children marched across the hills in a little band to see a local neighbour. She sent them back home and so Georgina, by then nine, put their beds in one room and they sat and waited until the Roberts appeared. Georgina also remembered Colquhoun making costumes for them for a fancy-dress party to which they went as England, Ireland, Scotland, and Wales. They all recalled the Roberts era as a wonderful time: they ran wild, and had total freedom.

But the weekends were another matter. The Roberts mostly drank on weekends. "Nobody," Elizabeth said, "had any money for anything else." When the children were put to bed, the party that ensued could be wild. Graham might be there, or George Barker or Soho friends like Paul Potts. The evening would start well with Colquhoun reciting Shakespeare and MacBryde singing songs from Robert Burns, but it would often degenerate into argument, MacBryde accusing Colquhoun of dandling with the "la-dies." The Roberts would fight and throw things at one another, always missing, and sometimes things went through the windows, which Elizabeth minded since she had the trouble of finding the repairman. Elizabeth would come in to assure the children there was nothing to worry about. In the morning they would surface to find the furniture broken, lamps smashed, or bedclothes thrown through the window. In retrospect Georgina believed that the most traumatic part of those nights was the feeling that something orgiastic was going on just beyond your sight. It was mostly being alone and afraid and not being able to communicate with the adults.

Elizabeth's decision to invite the Roberts to look after her children was, of course, extraordinary, but she thought the children could take it, that they would understand there were more important things to care about than whether or not the kitchen was smashed when you came down to breakfast. Elizabeth had been so smothered by conventionality that breaking it was itself a virtue. She felt that the midnight chaos at Tilty was a normal part of life. Georgina remarked that her mother never had sharp knives in the kitchen because she thought somebody, any normal person, might pick one up and stab someone. That, she thought, was one of the facts of life. Anyone of any interest had a dark side, though Elizabeth was forced to keep her own tightly under wraps. It was a curious ethic. If you were to know life you had to be willing to have people punch you in the nose and burn your house down. The price of genius was chaos.

But Elizabeth loved the Roberts*. She felt they were much maligned; people who didn't know them only saw them drunk. In fact, the Roberts were Soho casualties. In his last years Colquhoun almost achieved a comeback when he was invited to give a retrospective showing at the Whitechapel Gallery on the condition that he contribute new work. Sober and industrious, Colquhoun painted, and the two left London for a well-earned holiday. While they were away, thieves broke into their studio and mutilated or stole most of the canvases. What impressed Elizabeth was that Colquhoun smouldered with a fine anger rather than bitterness and MacBryde retained his sense of the absurd. Perhaps Colquhoun shared Elizabeth's tragic vision of life. Of his canvases Wyndham Lewis wrote: "There is a grave dug behind all his canvases of a certain kind," particularly in the canvases of "elderly women, poor, bloodless, grieving and without purpose," which were, perhaps, a memory of his childhood.[3] After Colquhoun died of heart disease in MacBryde's arms in 1962 (he had been working on a drawing of a man in space, dying—drawing in effect his own death), Elizabeth gave MacBryde a haven at her London flat in Westbourne Terrace where he had a little room off the landing. Sebastian remembered that one could often hear him weeping quietly behind his door. When he left they found twenty-five bottles of pee under his bed. He died in Ireland, hit by a car as

---

* The Roberts' tenure at Tilty Mill House occasioned much gossip. Ruthven Todd claimed that the Roberts had pillaged the collection of valuable books and paintings he had left at the house. He did not blame Elizabeth, who he felt had tried to prevent the "rape" of Tilty. See Ruthven Todd, *Fitzrovia & the Road to the York Minster or Down Dean Street* (London: Michael Parkin Fine Art Ltd., 1973). Elizabeth always insisted it was Todd who neglected to collect his books. Todd had also faulted on the rent, and the bailiff would have carried off the books, had not Michael Wickham stepped in to pay back rent of one hundred pounds. Some books were sold to cover the debt. Elizabeth wrote of the books: "Ruthven had more than thirty years to get back his books, which were a continual worry and responsibility to me." (Letter to Richard Latona, October 16, 1980, NLC: Box 35.) A second rumour about the Roberts, is, however, accurate. When they left Tilty, they owed one thousand pounds to the local pub, which Elizabeth ended up paying.

he staggered from a pub. Elizabeth was loyal; she never said a nasty thing about the Roberts.

In January 1954 Elizabeth took a full-time job copy-writing for Crawfords Advertising in High Holborn. She moved the family briefly to her single room in Coptic Street where she stayed when she was in London. Her children were now aged 7 to 12½ and were at various private schools. She kept up her freelancing, moonlighting for other agencies. She was also doing the occasional article, interview, or book reviews. Elizabeth was to say she often held down three jobs at once. She never stopped wanting to write although, as she put it, she couldn't write anything publishable: "Anyway, living the way I did kept me living in the present." In fact, she was constitutionally unable to put writing before human needs. The cost was enormous:

> Love. Children. Earning a living. Friends. Drinking. Pushed too far to do too much. Silent years. Desperate from hating. Desperate anxieties. So many levels. On one, it's a thin deep line straight to the point. On others up & down to deal with distractions.[4]

As always Elizabeth worked her way into people's imaginations. A close friend, Maria Kroll, who worked in the art department remembers the impact Elizabeth had on Crawfords. The fashion department was run by Margaret Harpenden, a great character: powerful, gifted, rich, and quite modern. Her clients were meant to be impressed by the fashionableness of all they met. Elizabeth dressed in a rather "alternative" bohemian way, before the phrase to describe it was invented: a combination of Oxfam and gypsy, although, according to Kroll, she looked like a great beauty rather like Candice Bergen. Because Elizabeth didn't carry the part of the fashion expert, Harpenden instituted a dress allowance of one hundred pounds a year, ostensibly so that all could look smart. Yet it was really to dress Elizabeth. The tradition stayed long after Elizabeth's departure. Kroll remembers that Elizabeth bought a coat.

Kroll felt that Elizabeth enjoyed the work. She was tremendously professional. Though she might look untidy, she was organized and accurate, wrote fast, edited quickly, and rarely rewrote. She delighted in fashion, having, as Kroll put it, no class inhibitions, and thought of fashion design as an art form, though touchingly ephemeral. Elizabeth used to describe how she'd go down to the fashion department to see the models when she later worked at *Queen* magazine. "I adored them and I admired them so much," she said. "They were wonderful girls. They were totally inarticulate and they could hardly write. But they had this brilliant feeling for what was coming next . . . I'd ask them what was the new idea and find they actually had one."[5] At Crawfords Elizabeth wrote copy for every firm from Yardley through Mary Quant, and Kroll believed that, with her tremendous originality, Elizabeth actually helped to redirect the course of what was to become British fashion in the early sixties. She worked very hard. A list of contracts completed in three weeks could include as many as eighteen jobs. Her bills were high and she needed the work. It was costing about 1,200 pounds a year for school fees, apart from her own and the children's living expenses.

Elizabeth moved like a dervish and Kroll found her deeply compelling. "There was a very great humour and a bravery about her. She was never bitter and always generous."[6] But it was the contradictions that made her fascinating. "There was a black side to it all." Kroll called her a cagey lady, cagey altogether. Though she knew her well she never knew how old she was. While at Crawfords, Elizabeth had two face-lifts; Kroll felt it was a strategy that had to do with "wishing not to fear age." Elizabeth insisted it was a pragmatic strategy. To keep a job in fashion one had to pretend one was younger than one was. Her drinking had become heavier. She often started the day below par and needed something to get her going. She was never without a cigarette and was the first person Kroll ever knew who sniffed glue, before the notion was known. She could often be found at her desk with her nose in a huge jar. Because she worked so quickly, she would take the afternoon off to go to the clubs in Soho. She still spoke glowingly of

Barker and Kroll felt that in a sense she had to live up to her book; she couldn't betray the memory.

Kroll felt that Elizabeth's genius came from her innocence. A great ingredient of genius is the retention of the capacity for a childlike receptivity and openness. Elizabeth seemed raw to the quick. However obligingly and giftedly she worked at Crawfords, she really wanted to write and, tragically, she didn't. All the writing she did was a particular distraction from writing. She was extremely disciplined but she did not have the writer's ruthlessness. Every claim seemed to supersede the claim of writing. Kroll, as a close associate, felt there was almost a death wish in Elizabeth in those years. "Was it possible that Elizabeth was living out George Barker's doom?" she wondered.

But it was perhaps simpler than that. The choices Elizabeth made early dictated the shape of her life. For all her romantic extremism, in the life she lived she could depend on no one but herself. Barker was not there to offer support. She was a single mother who maintained four children, and the conundrum was simple. To keep her children she had to work. To work she kept them in private school. She was both father and mother, and there was no time for feeling, the kind of feeling necessary to writing. Elizabeth would sustain her professional life until 1966, when, abruptly, she retired to Suffolk on a writer's grant. When she could finally say, "The children are off to seek their lives with bundles adequately packed,"[7] she could abandon twenty years of mopping up and take a look around.

Elizabeth had to leave Tilty Mill in January 1955 when the landlord sold the property. Though she had met Todd several times in his trips back to England, he never collected his books and she had to hire two lorries to have them transported to the new home she had found at 9 Westbourne Terrace in Paddington, which she took on a seven-year lease at five pounds a week. With its crumbling exterior, it was a typical rundown London flat on two and a half floors, but Elizabeth made it charming and very relaxed. Her own room, the sitting room, was lovely, with three enormous windows and two large fireplaces at each end, both of which she'd light. Here she kept her bed, covered in the familiar paisley spread, a writing desk, Todd's books, and a couch for visitors.

Elizabeth's life was very social. She had numerous friends in Soho as well as professional friends. She continued to meet Barker when he came up to London—he was still living with Cass. The editors of *X* magazine, Patrick Swift and David Wright, would meet at her flat in the beginning of the sixties to do interviews, and Elizabeth sometimes offered her drawing room as a sort of office where they would hammer out their editorials. The artist Craigie Aitchison recalled being interviewed there by Paddy Swift, and Elizabeth wrote their words down, including the bits from the pub where they adjourned afterwards. Christopher's memory, spoken with animus, was that she had been treated like a secretary making the coffee. The painter Frank Auerbach remembered her coming into The French one evening, having made thirty pounds in a couple of hours writing advertising for Jaeger fashions; they went back to the Westbourne flat, and, though the pipes were frozen, she produced food and drink. He, being penniless in those days and unable to get home, had fallen asleep on a bed and awoke to find a pound note in his pocket. "This happened two or three times. She deemed it a matter of course to make sacrifices for artists," said Auerbach.[8] Over the years there was often somebody in residence, including Robert MacBryde, Mrs Watt's son Sholto Watt, John Deakin, Michael Asquith and his second wife, Hase, or Anthony Cronin and his wife.

In September 1957 Elizabeth found herself accompanying George Barker to Paris, after Cass had left him. Michael Asquith remembered that Barker was so shaken by the novel experience of actually being left by a woman—Cass had apparently absconded in the middle of the night through the back garden with Barker's younger nephew—that he proposed to Elizabeth, though she again turned him down.

That December 15 at Westbourne Terrace, Elizabeth recorded in her diary the cryptic entry "Bit GB's lip." Georgina remembered the incident. "Mother always said she was in love with George for nineteen years. The last time they lived together I remember coming downstairs and my mother sitting in bed with a black eye and George was gone. I asked 'Where is George?' She replied: 'He's in the hospital having his lip sewn up. I bit him.'" It was the boys' sports day at the King's School, Canterbury, and she and Elizabeth went all over Edgware Road looking for a black eye patch because Elizabeth refused to wear a pink one.

Barker's last wife, Elspeth, received both Barker's and Elizabeth's versions of the incident, though she tended to believe Elizabeth's. Barker was in a state. Cass having run off somehow compounded with the death of his mother in 1957. For days he had been violent and unpleasant and was drinking a lot. Elizabeth was tired. It had gotten so ghastly that she said she wore her motor-bike helmet when he was around, which provoked floods of fury. One evening he'd come home drunk with his pub friends; they'd fought and he'd managed to grab her. Elizabeth was possibly for the first time really frightened and she bit back, as hard as she could. She was particularly acrimonious about the pathetic men who had sat there drinking her wine and then watched her being strangled in her own house. When she bit George, they suddenly leapt up and rushed for an ambulance to take him to hospital. Barker's version was that he had no idea why she did it. It was jealousy. He'd strolled in and was having a pleasant drink when suddenly this fury out of hell was clinging to his upper lip. Elizabeth told the novelist Katherine Govier: "I wasn't cross. I just bit down and"—she made a spitting motion—"felt this flesh."[9] She had bitten through the lip. Barker would say in retrospect: "It was great fun when she bit my lip. Since then I've affected a moustache. Alcibiades had nineteen love wounds."[10]

Whatever occurred that night, December 15 seems to date the end of Elizabeth's romantic engagement with Barker. She had been in love with him for nineteen years; she described it as the type of love "when you shiver and shake and it's pain at the same time knowing it wouldn't work. Then it turned into another kind of love. You want nothing from the person. You love them whether they're there or not but you certainly don't want them to come and live with you."[11] She always insisted that, from early on, she realized the relationship wasn't going to work. Though Barker proposed several times, she never accepted. "He was a marvellous man, absolutely super, but not a husband." In retrospect, she would say "I think I needed somebody like him . . . really . . . I don't know . . . really terrible in a way. Cut down to size, a little bit too small for my actual size but I think it did me a lot of good."[12] Elizabeth could add: "I think I chose suitably for me. I would have turned into a nasty literary hostess, I expect, or something awful. And I would have been very spoiled."[13] What had stalled her, she insisted, was that even when the price was too high and she knew she deserved more, George would appear at her door with a joke, and she couldn't refuse him. It was his humour "that absolutely slayed me. No, George I cannot fault. I tried to. Can you imagine how long I tried not to be in love with him? But I think he's wonderful."[14]

She wanted to live intensely, not safely or comfortably, and needed the edges, where the real person came out. Her "propaganda," as friend Hase Asquith felt, was not about love but about children, and there she could be ruthless. "Children are the important thing if you are a woman and you didn't need a man fulltime for that." Asquith could say: "She knew certain things about life that very few people know. They're hard to explain. She just knew what mattered and what didn't, what it was all about, especially from a woman's point of view. She knew about suffering and generosity, about giving and getting back and that the only thing that mattered were people."[15]

The next year Barker met his fourth wife, Didi Farrelly (the family always spoke of wives to define Barker's long-term relationships, although he was still legally married to Jessica), and went to join her in the U.S. Didi was something of a literary hostess. Her first husband had been connected to the Beat scene and her expensive home on the east side of New York became a stopover for poets. Jay Landesman, who was later to become Elizabeth's publisher, was at the time seeing his play *The Nervous Set* through Broadway. He remembered long nights at Didi's with George Barker, Ginsberg, Corso, and Orlowski. One image from those nights was indelible: "Barker leaning against the mantelpiece and the Beat poets at his feet because they thought he was the end, their god. George bent down toward Ginsberg with a cigarette in his hand, and said: 'Light me, Jew.' It was uproarious, perfect George and they loved it."[16] Elizabeth was not to see George for the next year and a half; her diary contains a cryptic reference: "Didi's first G.B. baby, 8th December 1959." Barker was to have three sons with Farrelly.

As she continued writing advertising copy, Elizabeth kept her hand in publishing. With Agnes Ryan in 1957 she published *Cooking the French Way* (Paul Hamlyn), a sophisticated cookbook that stayed in print for years. The buried humour in it is amusing: in a recipe for hog's head Elizabeth advises that if you can't find a whole hog's head, take half. In November 1958 she contracted with Barrie Books to write a biography of Marie Stopes, the pioneer campaigner for birth control. Her portrait would have been entertaining, for Stopes was a fascinating character, something of a religious monomaniac who believed God had instructed her to establish her clinics, and Elizabeth initially found her outrageousness amusing: she loved to remark that Stopes was technically a virgin when she wrote *Married Love*. Though she kept copious notes, and started a correspondence with the Stopes estate, Elizabeth never finished the biography. It was due April 1, 1959, an impossibly early date. In October her publisher Jane Bunting wrote asking her to please buck up and not be self-conscious and indulge in perfectionism. Clearly she knew more than anybody else about Stopes, and she wasn't, as she claimed, starving under a handicap but had exceptional advantages, not the least of which was that she could write.[17] The publishers wrote again in March 1960 to cancel the contract, and asked her to return the fifty-pound advance in convenient instalments. What is interesting about the incident is that it illuminates Elizabeth's vulnerability. Bunting felt that Elizabeth abandoned the project because she had lost her nerve as a writer, although it is also true that the more she found out about Stopes, the more she despised her hypocrisy.

12   This Unendingly Square-Rooted Globe

Contrary to most creative women of our time, I have not imitated man or become man.
    Anaïs Nin
    Diary of Anaïs Nin

To arouse a desire to create is difficult; to kill that desire is extremely easy.
    Constantin Stanislavski
    An Actor Prepares

One of the odd phenomena that has characterized our culture—sociologists usually lay the responsibility on the shoulders of the Victorians—is the curious dispassion we have for children. There is nothing remarkable about bringing children into this world: it is women's work, valuable of course, but to be done in private, and certainly it carries no kudos. From childhood, Elizabeth was an eccentric in the great value she ascribed to maternity. From the age of ten she "collected" babies—there were those scrapbooks and those "baby" letters from friends. Jane had called it a compensation impulse that had to do with the emotional parsimony in Louie's house; babies were a softening influence. But it was also more than that. In that episode long ago when Elizabeth had run away from home and had saved her mother's life and the city of Ottawa by blowing out a match she found in the street, she had thought of the friends she would bring on her journey. One was her cat, Mrs Felix, with her kittens in the padded box with the strange smell and the bloodstains. It was the mystery of birth that fascinated and she wanted, even then, to understand Mrs Felix's "tender motherhood." For Elizabeth all other occupations seemed what she called "flibbertigibbet by comparison with the act of birth. Love and all its flimsy fancies are rolled under this mighty event, rolling all before it: crushed like straw conceits."[1] "This is work!" she would say. If a friend were caught in the familiar dilemma of wanting a child with an unwilling lover, she would always counsel: "Have a baby!" It was dangerous advice, since few had her strength to keep going. It had to do with her great reverence for nature. One might call Elizabeth's attitude to nature mystical, but it was not esoteric. Life was the "roll of matter heaving into heaven in its long painful individual way." How could one, as a woman, forgo the mystery of the child?

Elizabeth Smart was as passionate a mother as she was a writer. She delighted in her babies. In a "Children's Record Book" she kept complete records of the births: the length of the umbilical cord, the weight of the afterbirth. The amazingly strange mystery of birth had to be carefully recorded. She noted when her children first smiled, when they were weaned and what they ate, when they walked, their first words: at seventeen months Sebastian used to say "Am gonna tell George"; Rosie was talking fluently at two with words like "bulldozer" and "traitor." She noted the complicated trail of domiciles, of schools, of medical histories. She loved words and had her children write little illustrated autobiographies by the time they were thirteen.

Of necessity the narrative of Elizabeth's life as a writer includes her children, as, one might say, the narrative of George Barker's life would not. Each of them had remarkably different temperaments and their strategems for survival, as in all families, had something to do with where they came in the family. Georgina was the eldest and her portrait of the Smart household in retrospect is fascinating. To call the world Elizabeth created bohemian would imply a predictable self-consciousness. It had rather the peculiar combination of freedom and conventionality that in some ways characterized

Elizabeth herself. There was no place for cant and social hypocrisy, but there were the private schools and an underlying ethic: "In the order of beings, poets were gods."[2] Georgina believed until she was sixteen that the definition of the poet was he who leaves. No one expressed any recrimination against the absconding poet. It was, one might say, a professional hazard.

Georgina was a shy child and by her own account used camouflage as a protective device. She grew up somewhat intimidated by the household, though she insisted that her mother never presented herself as anyone important–"She was just our mother. She wasn't the poet; George was"–Georgina found her so intelligent that, as a child, she always felt uncomfortable asking the banal ordinary questions: one was afraid of betraying one's stupidity. "You can't help, if you're the child of such a person, feeling insignificant and terribly small next to an extraordinary mind." And there was the myth of these extraordinary parents, "not a burden exactly but difficult to live up to, people saying all the time how wonderful she was." George had little to do with the children growing up, and Georgina remembered him as being mostly absent: "He did not turn up at Christmas and birthdays. He came when he felt like it. He had nothing to do with our daily life. He was just someone we waited for with great excitement." Georgina recalled pinching ten-shilling notes from his pockets when she was kissing him good-night and giving them to her mother. When she asked Elizabeth why George didn't live with them, the reply was always: "Ask him."

In 1956, Elizabeth sent Georgina to Legat, a Russian ballet school, not particularly sound academically and somewhat pretentious. Georgina set out for a career in dance. There was cachet among the schoolgirls in having a poet father, while it was a little disconcerting to have Elizabeth show up at the boarding school, as she was wont to do, with her hair dishevelled and wearing gumboots and a rain coat. At sixteen Georgina remembered writing herself letters signed by George. In retrospect she felt this was a sign of her resourcefulness.

When she needed him, she just made him up. A poignant entry in her diary of 1958 reads:

> I am training to be a ballerina . . . I am not wasting my time. I declare I am not wasting my time. I have a wonderful and terribly talented papa (I call him this because it describes him perfectly although to his face I call him George). He is a very beautiful poet. He writes poetry that even the best critics call "divinely inspired." The most wonderful thing about Papa is that he is the only man over 30 I can abide. . . . I love him. I respect him. He is my father. My mother has always a difficult time. Poets are terrifying people to live with. They rush off at odd moments and are neither seen nor heard of for months. Then lo and behold they suddenly appear on the threshold as though nothing has happened. They treat everyone else as though they hardly existed but are merely there to help their own inspirations. They are erratic, mad and so emotional. I adore one special poet.[3]

Georgina first discovered her mother as a writer when she was seventeen and read *By Grand Central Station I Sat Down and Wept*. She had fallen madly in love with a married painter, and she remembered crying and nodding "because of the unknown to be experienced." The book became a reference point, an admonition that the aspiration was total awareness. She would later write: "Can't read one sentence of your book without bursting into tears, but no more moods. It's so exhilarating to suddenly feel above the slough of despond where these hideous sentiments ferment. I'm just so happy to be me and so must let you know how glad I am that you ever sat down anywhere."[4]

At nineteen, Elizabeth sent Georgina to study at the Sorbonne and the letters she wrote back attest to the intensity of her attachment to her mother. In the midst of writing an essay on Montaigne's search for a philosophy of death and answering Christopher's letter in French just to snub him for his steely wit, she writes: "I love you not because you are my mother, but because you are you." She considered her mother her closest friend.

In the autumn of 1962, she was working as a dancer, touring Canada in the *Gilda Review,* a comic show centred around a French Canadian female impersonator. Everyone was "professional and dedicated" she wrote to Elizabeth, "although by some standards the show's a trifle crude." She added that she had told one old customer: "Culture is a pretentious interest in aestheticism." "It doesn't really sound funny now but coming from what he imagined was a pathetic little stripper, it made everyone roar." When she was in Ottawa, Louie gave her Elizabeth's "The Collected Works of Betty Smart." She loved it, and found herself laughing hysterically at the patty de faw graw sandwiches, and crying "because you were an adolescent too and everything seemed suddenly unbearably sad."[5] Later she went to New York to look into acting school, but eventually settled in London in a career in publishing.

This is not to say that there were not difficulties in her relationship with her mother. There could be tremendous fights as only two women of strong temperament could have. She would often throw at Elizabeth the accusation that she had been abandoned in her first year in the name of her mother's passion, that she had been confused in her notions of romantic love by her mother's romanticism, or that Elizabeth hadn't set clear boundaries for Rose. Georgina was remarkably like Elizabeth, a fine strength masking vulnerability. She inherited her mother's candour, her humour, and the generosity with which she took on other lives.

In retrospect, Georgina understood how complicated her mother had been. She recognized that she was deeply, deeply shy. Often she felt the freedom her mother affected was theoretical, and indeed perhaps a reaction to her own mother's prudery. Though she had been the author of *By Grand Central Station,* like most women of her generation, Elizabeth was timid about sexual candour. It embarrassed her. She managed to offer her daughter the facts of life in the back of a taxi. "Oh by the way I have something to tell you" and Georgina pretended she understood the way a child will when she realizes the adult is squirming. Occasionally Georgina felt as if she were Elizabeth's mother, since Elizabeth had to be evasive and secretive about her own sexuality and propounded the myth that she had no physical needs. None of the children ever knew about her lovers. When she went to her mother for advice about her first grand passion, Elizabeth told her to think of him as though he were a man in a book. In the matter of sexual passion, she didn't know how to help her daughter. She who had been so controlled by her mother was afraid to say anything that might be wrong or intrusive. She was reticent and her vision of woman was contradictory: a woman had to be soft, vulnerable, and passive, and yet she herself was fiercely independent.*

Looking back Georgina understood that Elizabeth's ego as a writer was undernourished and starving, though she didn't allow her daughter to see it. She seemed so powerful, it was impossible to conceive of her as someone who needed sympathy and encouragement. Yet Georgina was able to do what her mother had always asked, to walk powerfully into her own life. Eventually giving up publishing, she moved to Cornwall with her husband and children and devoted herself full-time to painting. She understood that Elizabeth's message had been subtle: it was lived rather than articulated. For Georgina, Elizabeth was, without cant and with great humour, the spirit of love. She could always be counted on.

As soon as she could afford it, Elizabeth sent her sons to The King's School, Canterbury, one of the best private schools in the country, the kind of place characterized by matins service and evensong. Christopher took on the persona of the sober and stoic one in the family. He could write that at The King's School, he was getting on all right except for the floggings, and, though he got a slight concussion at rugger, it wore off. He was brilliant at sports and won all the trophies. For his tenth

---

* Elizabeth told Katherine Govier that, in the fifties, she had desired "a gentleman to keep her in matches, and to strike them. She learned to fill her own coal bucket in Chelsea . . . but it didn't come naturally: she only wanted 'to be possessed, stamped all over.'. . . When men are mean all she wanted was to make them comfortable—'I'm a bit whorey that way,' she says." (Govier, "That Smart Woman.")

birthday, George bought him a developing kit and camera at the chemist's, initiating the passion that was to become his career. His letters home are full of solicitude for Elizabeth, and occasionally cutting about George, who by 1960 had moved to Rome. "Will he be back for Christmas? Then again he usually says he will be and we don't see him again for six months."[6] The children were always aware that money was scarce and their letters contain poignant lists of how they spent their shillings. Sebastian could write: "It's thoughtful of you to send me a soap box as most parents don't." All the children hated to burden their mother with requests for money, but whenever anything was wanted badly enough the money came through. Contemptuous of money, Elizabeth refused to allow it to become an issue. She was her father's daughter. Christopher remarked that "if you asked for something that mattered to you, she'd say, we'll do it, we'll get it organized, and she did."

The Barkers were certainly not the poor boys at private school and their schoolmates were never aware that there might be anything eccentric about their background. While she went by the name of E. Smart at Crawfords, Elizabeth called herself Mrs Barker at The King's School to protect the boys from what would have been an horrendous position at prep school—being thought of as bastards. For all intents and purposes as far as the children were concerned, she and George had been married and divorced. "We always said separated," Christopher remarked. "That was the way we were led to understand it, though mother in fact never said as much."[7] Christopher only understood the true dimensions of the relationship years later when he read *Necessary Secrets* and *Autobiographies*. "Elizabeth would never have dreamt of casting aspersions on George."[8] As schoolboys at King's, the young Barkers longed only for respectability: to be like their school chums. Maria Kroll remembered being amused once when the boys turned to Elizabeth at home and said: "Can't we have sheets?"

The truth was that Christopher hardly remembered George as having been part of the family. He had to begin his search for him when he was nineteen. In 1962, on the way to joining

Elizabeth and the other children who were vacationing in Hydra, he went to see George in Rome. He had no idea he was going to visit one of the other Barker families. No one had told him that Didi had three sons. It was a staggering discovery. Christopher found George charming, marvellous, just the ideal father he had always wanted. But the dark side also surfaced in sudden bizarre moments of anger. George turned on Christopher for using the word "plebs" and spat accusations of public-school snobbery. They talked of the separation of Elizabeth and himself, and while George spoke of Elizabeth as wonderful—crossing the Rockies by train, the dining-car table covered with glasses and the way the light hit the glass and sparkled out of her face—yet he could not resist justifying himself. Elizabeth had gone off with Michael Wickham when his back was turned. Christopher knew that, indeed, she'd been left in the lurch.

Christopher obtained a scholarship to study English at Princeton in 1963 but after trying academia briefly, turned to a full-time career in photography. He too only gradually understood that his mother was a writer. At about fourteen he became aware that she had published a book, but it was presented as some funny little book. He felt she belittled herself. "She was the scrubber and the bearer of children. She wasn't the poet; that was left to the great and mighty like George." Yet he also understood that Barker had been perfectly made for what Elizabeth was seeking: "like a spider in a net, waiting, absolutely hand-made to what she needed right then and the rejection of her ridiculous background. She never let the bad side of George get to her." Elizabeth was very keen that Christopher not reject his father since his mode in adolescence was accusatory. Her lesson was to transcend bitterness: "She always talked about the kaleidoscopic nature of George's character, as though it were a detective story and it was going to go on forever and she'd never get to the bottom of it. Many floundered on the rock of George." Christopher was puzzled. On the one hand, Elizabeth was fiercely independent and yet, with George, she played the little woman. "George liked the company of men; at parties Mum encouraged this—the men talking together was sacrosanct; the women were the handmaidens dashing about. Her coquettish side was stimulated by George's machismo." It was staggering to Christopher that "great as she was, she could fall into such an old-fashioned role." Christopher could see the profound hunger that smouldered under her carefully constructed carapace. The vulnerability was enormous.

Sebastian was a more tumultuous personality. He enjoyed the years at The King's School and, scholastically gifted, obtained a scholarship to study animal physiology at Corpus Christi, Oxford, and worked as a research assistant in the Royal College of Surgeons. But he soon gave up academic work to turn to poetry. At the age of eighteen, when he was going to Oxford, he wrote to George about poetry and got an immediate response. As he put it: "At eighteen I first became apprised of his intelligence. He opened to me completely. I had a father. He has never let me down since. He never took any cognizance of any socially or spiritually accepted standard. He had gone his own way, lived his own life. He was there."[9] Sebastian published his first book of poetry at the age of twenty-nine. The reviews were very good, but, ironically, he had to brook accusations from friends of unconscious imitation of George. He wrote in anger to Elizabeth: "What my pub-crawling friends fail to realize is that I had to acquire a father late in life—from the age of 18 in fact and that this tends to be not quite so natural as having one from the year dot. It is greatly to my credit that I have not spurned his image but am attempting to absorb him into my bosom. What do they know of their fathers?"[10]

It took Sebastian longer to recognize the poet in Elizabeth. In the early seventies he remembered a night with his poet friends, Robert Pollet and other "heavy young literati among them." Elizabeth came downstairs with a pile of her poems in her arms, and in their youthful arrogance they tore them to shreds. But soon Sebastian was to realize how desperately Elizabeth needed support. He was to become one of the catalysts that ensured that *The Assumption of the Rogues and Rascals* saw the light of day.

It was Rose who was the tragic figure in the Smart family. Those who knew her intimately remembered her as bright, funny, with a lively delight in anything new, and yet somehow doomed. Elspeth Barker would say: "It was absolutely something within her; from very early she was learning how to destroy herself."[11] Rose had inherited the excess of both her parents. Hers was a spirit that could not easily accommodate the world, and several factors seem to have been motive springs for her temperament: a profound lack of self-confidence that made her exceedingly unforgiving of herself, a deep and irreverent anger at the way the world functioned that led her to choose its eccentric edges, and a humour and gutsiness that kept her battling until her death at age thirty-five. Elizabeth preserved her daughter's diaries and in them we see the torment that was Rose's life.

Rose was sent to Legat to study ballet at age six. She was a good student, often in the top quarter of her class. The school report at age eight speaks of her as very talented with outstanding capacities for ballet and remarkable imagination. Her surviving diaries begin in 1960. The diary of any adolescent tends to be introverted and rather maudlin, and yet Rose's is more poignant than most. She had just transferred to a new school, giving up ballet. She was lonely and vulnerable and missed her family:

1960

May 17: Why am I me? Why is everyone in the world hostile towards each other and if something isn't going to be nice to England, England doesn't respond. . . .

Oh I am so so depressed. I wish there wasn't such a thing as war. Why, oh, why, do countries have to quarrel so much? It never does anyone any good . . . I am not afraid of death, but I am afraid of the war, all those poor innocent people getting killed, and the first thing I think about when I think of war is my mother & family. I love them all so dearly. I would waste away if I new [sic] any harm had come to them . . . Please *some thing, some body,* get my mind of [sic] war and death. I want to go to school nearer home, so that at least I can see Mommy more, be near her and know she is safe. George is a maneiak [sic] not ever being with Mom at all or giving her any money what so ever. I hate him. No, I don't hate him. I am angry with him. . . .

July 17: I wish my father would be like a father. He never pays for anything, he just doesn't seem to realize he has a wife and four children who need money to live. I don't see how he can expect us to love him although I still do, but I can't say I always speak highly of him. I hope I see him next holidays. Oh I wish he didn't drink. I love Mommy so much, I hope I'm like her when I grow up, I mean the way that she is so gentle and loving & kind, not in the way of jobs though, because I want to be an actress, and I know Mommy will let me be one if I really want to.[12]

Rose was a beautiful adolescent—with a creamy Irish complexion and a Renoir physique, but at ballet school the pressure had been to be thin. Feeling inadequate and vulnerable, she desperately wanted to distinguish herself. She explained to Georgina years later that she started taking drugs, specifically speed, at school because she felt she was too fat. Rose was to become an addictive personality: always obsessed with food or slimming, with drugs or quitting drugs. She could find neither the will nor the discipline to break through; she felt she had nothing to hang on to.

In January 1961, Elizabeth became seriously ill. For months she dragged herself about until the illness was diagnosed as hepatitis and she was forced to bed. Michael and Hase Asquith were living at Westbourne Terrace at the time and explained that Elizabeth stayed in bed that year, doing her advertisement copy from her sick room. She was so frightened by the ordeal—she must have been thinking of the lives that depended on her—that she actually managed to give up drinking and smoking. At her wit's end, she felt unable to cope. Rose was the major problem: she had begun to rebel, and was always in trouble at school. When Elizabeth tried discipline—even going so far as to lock Rose in her room those nights she was home at the Terrace and tried to slip out—it did not work. Jane wrote from the U.S. that a possible solution might be for her to take Rose off Elizabeth's hands. They could try a U.S. school. Rose wrote in her diary: "Gosh, I feel so lonely, I wish I lived in America. I am going to try and persuade Mommy to let me go to school there . . . the best rock n' rollers, actors, actresses and political members etc. are American."

Rose was sent to High Mowing School in Wilton, New Hampshire. It was not entirely a success. There were altercations with Jane, who felt Rose lacked discipline. The academic reports were good, but Rose was finally expelled from High Mowing for pulling down the American flag in a graveyard. She returned to London after a year and was sent to private tutors, "Miss Dixon and Miss Wolfe," in Westminster. The following summer, at the age of sixteen, Rose became involved in a disastrous love affair with a man twice her age. Sebastian remembered Geoff as brilliant with a sense of the absurd that reached levels of hilarity, and yet he was a man who had found no outlet for his talents and was driving a taxi. Rose was too young, Sebastian would say, to understand the ruthlessness that disguised an essential weakness. She loved Geoff and perhaps had set her mind on saving him. In mid-December 1963, Elizabeth wrote ominously in her diary: "Rose [age 16] left home." The whirlwind that was to take Rose down its tracks had begun.

Elizabeth was exceedingly nervous about her youngest daughter, but with her usual stamina, she barged on, accepting a full-time job at *Queen* magazine in January 1964. And the truth was this was an exciting time. London in the 1960s had changed. Wartime England and its legacy in the fifties was over; things had loosened up. With style, flair, and creativity, London initiated the sixties revolution. There was Carnaby Street, the Beatles, and the new British film industry; there was Tony Richardson's *Tom Jones*, and Antonioni's *Blow-Up*. And according to Bob Johnson, now production manager at *Harpers & Queen*, who shared a cubicle with her at *Queen* in those days, there was Elizabeth Smart whose writing at the magazine helped to change literary journalism in Britain. *Queen*, he said, had a younger attitude to art and literature, within the context of fashion, and Elizabeth had a sixth sense for change.[13] "I can feel it happening," she told the novelist Jill Neville in 1964, "a new mood in the air." "She was partly responsible for promoting the new mood that became the Swinging Sixties," said Neville. At *Queen* she "wrote many of those words that amused us when London magazines crackled with the electricity of a jaunty, saucy decade."[14] *Queen* was an old magazine that had been going for at least 120 years, but it had recently been bought by a new editor, Jocelyn Stevens, who wanted to make it zippy and tremendously modern. It became *the* magazine of the times. It was not simply a fashion magazine, but rather was written in the style of *Vogue* in the 1920s and had the same impact. It attracted the best writers and articulated a new lifestyle. It was the magazine that counted. Elizabeth used it as a vehicle to encourage new writers she felt mattered. "She was enormously encouraging to any writer she thought had talent," novelist Margaret Drabble has said.[15]

Elizabeth described her sequence of jobs at *Queen* as sub-editor, fashion writer, literary editor, and associate editor. Though much of her work was anonymous, her remarkable reputation came as book reviewer for the arts section: "Queen's Counsel." Her column appeared twice a month from January 1964 to October 1966 and could cover as many as fifteen books (this in addition to freelance copy-writing and the occasional contract at Crawfords). Bob Johnson described Elizabeth's working methods: "She would come in in the morning and light up a cigarette and take a swig of gin. She chain-smoked Gaulois." Once Johnson remembered saying to her: "Just put the box in your mouth and light the box." And he recalled her taking what she called "brilliancy pills" to keep going. "In the absence of anything else she would grab a can of Cow Gum. She's the first person I ever heard of sniffing glue. But she was professional to her hair-roots." While she wrote the book-review column, her main job was laying out fourteen pages of fashion, writing intros, and making the captions fit. Her friend and colleague Ann Barr, now a freelance journalist, could say: "Her pages were like concrete poetry. She was the highest paid copy-writer in London. No one could shoot fashion copy as fast as she; she could come up with titles with a snap of the finger, and at *Queen*, her word was God."[16] One of her reviews begins: "There are bags under my eyes this fortnight from the books I've been kept reading till dawn, and dawn, as you may have noticed, is getting later every day. Groggy but undaunted I rise to recommend."[17]

Soon, Elizabeth was having an impact. Margaret Drabble remembers that when Elizabeth reviewed her early novels in *Queen*, it was wonderful to be acknowledged by someone of such stature. "I liked the idea of her: colourful, she went her own way and was independent. She was much loved. She was unorthodox and was already a cult figure. I had read *By Grand Central Station*."[18] Elizabeth reviewed every genre of book: fiction, poetry, science, sociology, natural history, travelogue, and sentimental romance. Her standards were high and her model of excellence in writing was Samuel Beckett. But there is a sub-theme going through the reviews that is fascinating in retrospect.

Elizabeth occasionally used *Queen* to battle against what she perceived to be the male establishment's refusal to give attention to women's books. That this was a preoccupation can be seen in a list she wrote in 1960 of all the women writers she could think of, as if to convince herself of their numbers—there were over one hundred including the dead, the living, and those out of the country. In one column called "Shelving the Question," she confronts the difficulty of ranking books in terms of their goodness or badness, and explains that she follows the idiosyncratic principle of determining their value by deciding where she would place them on her bookshelves. She explains she delights in strict, and sometimes insulting arrangements of books that she changes constantly, "rather on the hostess's principle of seeking piquant juxtapositions." All books need suitable companions on either side. But the women, she explains, she has recently segregated, departing from the hostess principle: "I did this in a fit of pique one day, having listened week after week, until it was the last straw, to men, mostly Irishmen, declaring that women were incapable of creating works of art. And, although it is worrying sometimes not having Sappho and Jane Austen and St Teresa elsewhere to keep the balance, it works out very conveniently, since arranging books has also physical considerations of height and length, and the girls on the top shelf fit very neatly into the space available to them, while the up-and-coming girls can expand downwards indefinitely, being lifted or lowered as others come challengingly along."[19]

This was still the mid-sixties. Though Simone de Beauvoir's *The Second Sex* had been published in France in 1953 and was translated into English in 1957, it would take time for her ideas to percolate through the culture. Before Kate Millett or Germaine Greer had begun to articulate the issues of feminism, Elizabeth was discussing the problems of women writers in her column in *Queen*. She chose humour and pique rather than anger, for she was not a feminist. What she loved in the feminine was the sexual and she always felt it would be risked by stridency. On one occasion she complains of the attention given to James Bond. He "goes on and on to greater glorification. Academic characters write serious apologias for him . . . People even *protest* against him as if he were an outrage instead of an outlet. . . . But what about the equivalent female emotional phenomena that just get called trash, and are dismissed with an indulgent smile? No ladies trailing clouds of culture come forward . . . to sing the praises of their soothing gooey balm . . . I don't see any reason why woman's great throbbing subconscious shouldn't be catered for without a sneer. It is *catered for*, of course. It's the sneer I object to." She recommends several sentimental romances and adds: "Now isn't that the kind of thing bound to make you feel better at once in a world where true love and desirable coincidences are so thin upon the ground that you're lucky if a loved one turns up for an appointment? Doesn't . . . even the goo play a part in making you turn with relief . . . to the nappies and dirty dishes, and the monstrous but tangy people who are your own loved ones?"[20]

In a powerfully affirmative review of Jean Rhys's *Wide Sargasso Sea* and Christine Brooke-Rose's *Such* she begins by quoting at length Southey's famous letter to Charlotte Brontë: "Literature cannot be the business of a woman's life," commenting that "Luckily, Charlotte wasn't snubbed. And luckily it gets harder and harder to snub gifted girls, though the more gifted, the harder the slogging, usually."[21] She concludes that the reason Rhys has been neglected and has only a small, if ardent band of fans since she started publishing in the late twenties, is that she was "ahead of her time in both style and mood." One could say the same of Elizabeth.

In reviewing Edna O'Brien's *August Is a Wicked Month*, she begins:

> Don't listen to a word any man says about it and if you are a man yourself then for goodness sake isn't it time you got to know a bit about women? The greatest deceit, or is it sleight-of-hand, that women have been practising on men is in the careful camouflage of the workings of their minds, or emotions, or the inextricably blended mixture of the two—perhaps necessary for a workable slavery but not really nice, is it? You could argue that it's better not to know—like about the maid's bedroom in Victorian times—but if so you won't know which way the wind's blowing either and it might be an even iller wind that's blowing you even less good. . . . If you believe in free speech and include women in, it's not sporting to wince when they're too direct or to insist that they refrain from speaking *their* truth.[22]

In February 1965, one year after she joined *Queen*, Elizabeth took up the issue of women writers in a three-page column called "Is There a Woman in the Book?" It is astonishing to see that Elizabeth anticipated not only the arguments but the women writers who would become important to the debate that would follow at the end of the decade.

I see a phenomenon: women talking; women daring to tell the truth about themselves; women being intelligently articulate. Surely this wasn't always so? In the great folk tradition the cleverest women smiled and said nothing: it was against their own interests to speak; and anyhow who was there to listen?

"Men hate clever women," "Be good, sweet maid, and let who will be clever." And besides, women were so busy. Can it be irrelevant that Jane Austen, Christina Rossetti, Emily Brontë, Emily Dickinson and Virginia Woolf had no children? Or that only Virginia Woolf had a husband?

Yet they had enough energy and application to travel and entertain, to be rulers' and kings' mistresses, scholars, campaigners, reformers. They were even tellers of rattling good yarns and unforgettable children's stories. But that's a rather different thing from speaking unmasked straight out of deepest experiences.[23]

She complains that it has not been easy to counter the taunt: "What have women ever done?" In Auden's five-volume *Poets of the English Language* there are only five women. And yet she proposes the "treacherous observation" that the kinds of novels that are appearing are the beginning of something exciting. "There have been at least half a dozen excellent ones in the last year, far more, and more pulse-quickening, than the men have given." She reviews Paddy Kitchen's *Lying-In*, a novel written in the first person during the nine days in hospital after child-birth, describing it as candid, truthful, funny, and moving. "Surely a book like this couldn't have been written thirty years ago? Djuna Barnes's *Nightwood*, though not at all like this or any other book, was the lone pioneer of the kind of thing I'm talking about. But not everyone agrees with me. In fact many strenuously disagree."
    She goes on to catalogue the comments of women writers on whether they take umbrage at the label "woman writer." From the confusion of responses it is clear how raw and fresh the issue is. Brigid Brophy says: "I don't really think there's such

a thing as a woman. There's no psychological difference. Femininity can be put on like a wig. Some women set out to write a book and you find they have deliberately left female fingerprints all over it. But good writing has nothing to do with sex." Sylvia Bruce remarks that it is more difficult for a woman to get her work taken seriously. The worst label is "sensitive woman writer." Stevie Smith dismisses the phrase as a bit of journalese: "The sooner [it] is burnt the better." Susan Lund thinks the phrase will die out but comments bitterly that women writers are always looked down on.

Still there were women on the other side of the debate who affirmed the term. Veronica Hull insists there is a difference between men and women writers. "While women have to lead such different lives from men, and spend so much of their time looking after children and others, obviously they write differently." And she compares British women writers with their French counterparts. "*The Mandarins* could not have been written here. Women are allowed to be more serious and objective there. Here there is resentment and fear." Cressida Lindsay likes the term. A lot of women try to write like men and that is a mistake. "But writing is a masculine thing to do: it demands effort and isolation. I think the effort of it *is* masculine." Margaret Drabble thinks the term is inevitable but doesn't mind it since writing novels is one thing women are just as good at as men—"historically, Jane Austen and all that. They write different types of books." Margaret Forster finds the term flattering: "It's an achievement to keep a house, look after children and write too." Paddy Kitchen ends the debate by saying that she is pleased to be a woman novelist but that her books are not *for* women. "The most intelligent comments come from the men. There are areas of experience that women can write about better. . . . Novels should be based on social reality with moral/ethical considerations." And Elizabeth concludes simply: "So much for the thorny subject of women writers." But of course it was not so much. Elizabeth, in *The Assumption of the Rogues and Rascals*, had to puzzle out for herself the most painful and complex part of the debate. Why was it so impossible to find the confidence to speak "unmasked straight out of deepest experiences"?

One of the costs to Elizabeth of journalism was that it didn't help the writing. She rarely complained directly, but how she felt becomes clear in her novel *The Assumption of the Rogues and Rascals*. Like many writers, Elizabeth had an amusing habit in her novels of getting her own back in little buried barbs. In *The Assumption of the Rogues and Rascals*, she describes an altercation with her boss at the magazine. As she sits "hot and forgotten, bound to desk and duties, bullied into paralysis," she remembers her boss's response to her witticism: "See what happens to whores. No good words will marry them" to which the boss replied: "'That's not good, Elizabeth. Go back to your sprightly magazine articles and please us better. Don't get above yourself."[24] Ambition cast down. However brilliant she was at *Queen*, Elizabeth was a journalist, and felt she should not think of herself as a writer.

In 1964, when Elizabeth was fifty-one, two things happened that were to demand a profound revolution in her life: George returned from Rome in March with his new wife, Elspeth (her name had been Elizabeth but she changed the spelling), and Rose was now pregnant. Elizabeth might have had her professional life in order, but privately she was plunged into the crashing, excruciatingly intense moil of her personal life with its ongoing everyday realities.

Elizabeth and Elspeth (who was half her age) had been friends in London. While Georgina was absent in America, Elizabeth had adopted Elspeth as her substitute daughter. They had good times and jolly drinks, playing their roles. When Elspeth went off to Rome with her lover Tony Kingsmill, Elizabeth lent her clothes and said she was sending her to her nuptials. But in Rome Elspeth encountered George Barker. She had met him once before at Elizabeth's flat, but then he had been "unbelievably rude." Now, the meeting took.

Elspeth was beautiful, and, though dark-haired, had the same wild, free, sylphlike beauty Elizabeth had had in her youth. Indeed she could have been mistaken for a daughter. Her background was in some ways similar to Elizabeth's. Her parents had run a private school in Scotland where she received an

excellent education. She too had been brought up by governesses. She was rebelliously bohemian and passionate about
literature. When she met Barker she was writing a first novel
and translating medieval Greek ballads. Part of Barker's
courtship technique, she realized in retrospect, was to encourage her, lending her his typewriter as she translated her ballads
afternoons in a Roman garden full of roses. Barker's irascibility and authority she found wonderfully compelling. She, like
Elizabeth, loved his confidence since she lacked it herself. Of
course one night he got totally drunk and told her her transla-
tions were trash, and, being young, she was absolutely stricken
and couldn't bring herself to look at them for years. It was a
scenario of the times, she explained.[25] One wanted to win the
man. That's where the prestige lay, the good talk in that world.
Women did not count. It was a bit adventurous to have good
women friends, and women writers were thought of as
weirdos, disturbed, mad. Elspeth even felt she was cheating if
she read a woman writer.

Elspeth's first child was born at the end of the year. She
always insisted that George was not keen on having more and
more children—he had encouraged Cass to have an abortion.
He made fusses but there wasn't much he could do about it.
When the babies came, however, he delighted in them. Still he
was always in and out, on and off. He left the responsibility for
them (he was to have fifteen children) entirely to his wives.

When George and Elspeth returned from Rome, Elizabeth
was furious. She didn't mind Elspeth having an affair with
Barker but she did mind very much if it was to be something
that lasted. She no longer wanted Barker herself, but she didn't
want someone else to have him, certainly not on her own turf in
London. Didi and her sons had not counted because they were
out of sight and mind and George had been constantly to and
fro from Rome to London. Elizabeth was quite childish in her
jealousy, trying in her way to isolate Elspeth and to lure George
to her side. Once at a publication launch of one of Barker's
books, the photographer chirped: "Now we'll have Mrs Barker
next to Mr Barker" and both women stepped forward. It was a
repetition of a classic scenario. The women became enemies.

When Elizabeth came to visit, as she did on rare occasions, the women would talk coolly and Barker would eventually disappear for long drives in his car. The estrangement lasted six or seven years. It was part of the triumph of these two extraordinary women that they broke the silence and became deeply intimate friends.

In January, Rose was in hospital with the first signs of the liver disease that was to cause her death. On August 29, 1964 (Rose was seventeen), her first child, Claudia, was born. She had wanted the baby and Elizabeth had encouraged her in her wish. She was already seeing a psychiatrist through the Young People's Consultation Centre but Elizabeth believed they could all cope. Rose was soon home. Geoff had been violent, on one occasion breaking down the door of Westbourne Terrace to claim his child. He would commit suicide the next year, a blow Rose could never understand. Elizabeth began to realize that Rose was heavily taking drugs.

It was only in the mid-sixties that London finally acknowledged the existence of a drug subculture and articles began to appear in the *Observer* and *The Times*. One article from 1967 survives among Elizabeth's papers; she must have been trying to understand the phenomenon. The article profiles a young addict, aged nineteen, who, like Rose, had been turned onto hard drugs by a boyfriend. She claimed it was easy to get heroin from your local doctor. One person registered and then the prescription was shared around. By 1967 there were between two and three thousand narcotics addicts in Britain, most under twenty. Even with treatment, the chances of staying off heroin were one in ten. Quoting William Burroughs, an addict for fifteen years, the article concludes: "The client will crawl through a cellar and beg to buy."[26]

The secure home Elizabeth had founded at Westbourne Terrace began to crumble in 1965. She had inadvertently forgotten to renew the lease and now the landlord wanted her out. He felt she wasn't paying the market rate. He sent builders to work on the flat below and, by design, they came up through the floorboards of her flat. With the dust flying everywhere,

Elizabeth moved out. Quickly she found a flat in Great Cumberland Place in a smart area on the edge of Marble Arch. Georgina had the job of moving their things to the new flat, since the others were working, and she remembered people running up to her in the street trying to buy their tatty old furnishings. When she arrived at Cumberland Place, the flat had no electricity. She was sitting amidst the furniture beside a lit candle weeping when the others arrived. She realized it was the end of an era and the flat was only a make-do place. By this time (the children were ages seventeen to twenty-four), everyone had begun to establish their own lives. Elizabeth only kept the apartment a year. In June she was fired from full-time work at *Queen* (the only explanation offered was that someone else had wanted her job). She was back freelancing.

But things did pick up. Elizabeth had also found the Dell, the house in Suffolk that she was to make her permanent home, and bought it for two thousand pounds. It was the only place she actually owned, and she planned it as her retirement home where she could retreat to write poetry. She also found the "Copy Shop," a tiny flat on Peter Street in Soho that was to be her own hideout. She called it the Copy Shop because it was there she went to do her freelance copy-writing.

Elizabeth loved the Copy Shop. It was, according to Georgina, the first sane thing she'd gotten on her own. She loved the district. Peter Street was an old Dickensian street with the houses rather run-down and crumbling. Her flat was at the top of a dark narrow stairwell—Christopher remembered the passageway as lit with swan-necked Victorian gas lights and the walls as rather slimy. In her apartment the walls were bright, the curtains always blowing, and there were invariably fresh-cut flowers. She'd asked the artist Bruce Bernard, who was then an out-of-work theatre scene-shifter, to do the place up. He painted it white with stripped pine, and a shelf in every cranny. It was pure Elizabeth. When the Soho market finished at six P.M., the barrow boys would throw the fruits and vegetables that had gone slightly off into the streets and the big garbage grinders would collect them in the evening. Elizabeth, coming back through the streets of Soho from some smart advertising agency, would pick up the leftovers and make marvellous ratatouilles. She couldn't bear the waste.

Another piece of luck occurred. Panther wanted to publish a paperback edition of *By Grand Central Station I Sat Down and Wept*. Brigid Brophy asked to write the foreword and, identifying it as one of the half-dozen masterpieces of poetic prose in the world, called the book "one of the most shelled, skinned, nerve-exposed books ever written. It is a cry of complete vulnerability . . . transformed into a source of eternal pleasure, a work of art." It was published in July 1966 and reprinted in 1970.

Elizabeth was clearly excited and wrote to her mother that the book was to be reissued. She could never have been prepared for Louie's acrimonious response.

Feb. 22, 1966

Dearest Betty,

It has disturbed me that you should want to republish your book "By Grand Central Station . . ." in which you hold up your father & mother to public criticism. Your father gave his life as a result of our mistakes which he so loyally kept to himself that it resulted in stomach ulcers & death. I include myself in adding to his hurt & have suffered accordingly. My development came very late, but having reached a point where I was conscious of my mistakes I have confessed it freely to you & to Jane, & thought you had forgiven me.

I have realized so completely how limited & stupid I must have seemed to you, but I think you will give me credit for acting from the best motive I understood. I am filled with admiration for you & the way in which you have met life & coped with it & I have never, even when things were darkest, ceased to love you.

In spite of some beautiful poetic writing in your book I am inclined to agree with the New Statesman who a few weeks ago spoke of your book & of George's

"Confessions" as being 20 years out of date. Could you tell me why you should want to revive it when you, yourself have travelled so far since you wrote it? You surely can't have a desire to lower the stature of your father & mother.

I am sorry if my understanding is still at fault. Perhaps you can take time to enlighten me. Always with love. Mother.[27]

Louie was always consistent. Her style was to confess what she described as her errors, insist on her love, and then put her criticism in the mouths of others; resorting to the *New Statesman* was rather ingenious. Her monomania is fantastic. One searches *By Grand Central Station* to find criticism of even the fictional parents depicted, but there are only a few paragraphs recording conventional parents unsympathetic to their prodigal daughter. The strongest aspersion against the Louie-like character, who is a very brief cameo, is: "'Love? Stuff and nonsense!' my mother would say, 'It's loyalty and decency and common standards of behaviour that count.' But her eyes were like medieval wildmen in her head, clutching at her diminishing days that brought them no rest."[28] Yet Louie could demand that her daughter relinquish her book, and, with the usual blackmail, insist on her own loyalty and affection. Elizabeth could write philosophically about it: "She achieved *a little* of the letting go late in life, after 70. But the letter about the book came when she was over 80, still distressed about her image,* the unflattering light she felt it cast upon her,"[29] but she was deeply hurt. Barker's wife, Elspeth, remembered Elizabeth, years later, reading her mother's letter to her in the Dell's kitchen. "Elizabeth wanted so much for her mother just to love her," she would say. Four months later, Louie Smart died at the

---

* According to Charles Ritchie "the publication of *Grand Central* and the accompanying publicity must have been a shock [to Louie] in the days when people *were* shocked." However, Elizabeth had always explained to him that her mother's reaction had more to do with the "Mother–Daughter relationship" than with anything social or moral. "There was certainly, to the end of her days, a bitter sense in Betty that she had been rejected by her mother from childhood" (Letter to author May 11, 1990).

age of eighty-two. The only immediate entry in Elizabeth's diary was: "27 June: Mummy died." Yet, to the end of her life, she would still be digging a grave to bury her.

Elizabeth wanted a launching for her book that no one would forget. "Right!" she said to Christopher, "It's got to be something people will talk about for a long time. I want to do it at the Round House." The Round House was then an old abandoned train turntable shed in Chalk Farm. Arnold Wesker had acquired it and there was talk of it being revitalized and turned into a new arts centre. The launching became the kick-off activity. It was a stunning venue for *By Grand Central Station*, and the invention of the Round House as a theatre. But the question was how to turn its huge empty amphitheatre into a habitable space. Elizabeth comandeered the help of Christopher and his painter friend Ashley, who lived downstairs from the Copy Shop. No one had any money. They found pieces of lathed timber that had fallen off a lorry in Peter Street and drilled holes in them, making them into huge free-standing candelabra that lit the whole cavernous space. Huge buckets were filled with cut flowers and gallons of wine and beer were laid out, with a live band wheeled in on a haycart they'd found out back. The food was a tin washtub full of strawberries with a monstrous jug of cream beside it. The party on July 14 was something out of a Jean Cocteau memorial. It was the time of mini-skirts and long, flowing Indian dresses, and women flitted about looking like sylphs. All the Sohoites came, as well as family and publishing friends, about five hundred people; it was the display of affection that Elizabeth needed. The party went till 2:30 A.M. The next day, cleaning up, Elizabeth said: "People broke a hundred glasses. I know, because I hired them."

Elizabeth stopped all work for *Queen* in November. In fact it was a relief, since she had decided to retire to the Dell and devote herself to writing. But Georgina remembered 1966, after the re-publication of *By Grand Central Station*, as a terribly painful time. To think of Elizabeth was to start crying. Elizabeth felt she had failed her gift, and when she drank, became deeply unhappy. She would speak as though Barker had taken the guts out of her and would lament the cruel sexual bargain: her gift had gone to children and the womb. But there was the Dell and she was determined to pick up her writing after a twenty-year interruption and start again. It seemed auspicious that she was awarded an Arts Council Grant of two thousand pounds that autumn. Yet even this she was not permitted to enjoy completely. She received a letter from an old-age pensioner on the Isle of Wight, addressed "To the Idle Authoress" and railing at the disgusting idea that a government Arts Council grant should be going to a woman who hadn't done anything in twenty years. The letter cut to the bone.

Elizabeth was still isolated and the re-publication of *By Grand Central Station* did little to bolster her confidence. When she had asked her brother, Russel, to give her money for a year so that she could be free to write, he had said: "Oh, Elizabeth, you'll never write another book," and when George spoke of encountering a fan of hers she thought he was pulling her leg. By 1974 she could still write: "Have I really got a fan, even one?"[30] Though the reviews of the book had been good, nothing much happened. While it did establish the book as an underground classic and it slowly became a cult book that *aficionados* hunted down, for years Elizabeth was to make only a few pounds a year from it. Margaret Drabble speculated that the timing was off. Elizabeth had missed the women's movement. "Had the book come out in 1968/69, its impact would have been formidable."

Just when Elizabeth was about to get started, when she had found the environment for writing with the Dell as her retreat, disaster struck again: Rose's life was falling apart. Rose was pregnant with her second child. In early December she was found wandering about in Earl's Court, and was taken to the Mardis Court Hotel with Claudia where she spent a disastrous night, leaving the next day with a clergyman from Drugs Anonymous. She was charged with possession of drugs. She agreed to enter a home for drug addicts, and an injunction was taken out against her current boyfriend who had been supply-

ing her with drugs. Jane was born on December 19.
Immediately after the birth, Rose left the hospital and Elizabeth
and Georgina went to collect the child.

On Christmas Eve, Rose entered Spellthorne St Mary, an
addiction-cure centre, though she only stayed a little under a
month. For Elizabeth, there were expensive nightmare taxi
rides through London trying to track Rose down. Someone
would say they had seen Rose in a remote part of the city and
off Elizabeth would go. And there were the endless rounds of
solicitors and social workers. In the court case that followed in
February, the two children were made wards of the court in
their grandmother's care. Rose then briefly entered St
Bernard's Hospital under the care of a psychiatrist. Elizabeth
now had full responsibility for her two grandchildren.

Rose wrote to Elizabeth describing her life at St Bernard's:

> My account of St. Bernard's is thus: . . . the manner and
> kind of the people herein is . . . entertaining. Constant
> snarling amongst the young "drug addicts" and a bitchy
> word or two for the staff sister. . . . The alchoholics (sp?)
> seem much more civilized, and cheerful, however, they're
> twenty years ahead of me and rather disapproving of
> drug-addicts' ways (being rather aggressive I agree, when
> left alone in their de-drugged world) but personally, I find
> them more re-assuring of my sanity. Ah well, God bless us
> all! I'm in a deroggatory (sp?) position, but I always said
> I wanted the *real* fight not namby-pamby insincere and
> neutralizing coverage of facts. However, there are the few
> obsoletes that make it rather ah . . . boring. . . . I seem to
> be the only one not being put on pills, so perhaps I will not
> be here until Doomsday.[31]

On her release she moved to Peter Street and wrote less cocki-
ly: "Please darling Mummy, I need your confidence in me now.
I know I'm not doing anything harmful for myself. I'll try to
get the children off your hands as soon as I can get it all done
properly." But Rose had no skills, no particular training, and
the question of how to survive was problematic. She began a

course at the London School of Speed Writing, which she found difficult—she was unused to the sheer slog of it. By August she was again picked up for possessing heroin. She wrote to Elizabeth from Holloway Prison:

> I do hope that the shock you probably received when you got my solicitor's letter was not too horrible. I hope you understand why I was adamant about not getting in touch with you first. I bring enough bad luck but to have to bring the news to you always terrifies me as this, especially, seems one time too many. But anyway I implore you don't worry about me. I deserve all I got. . . . McCarthy [her solicitor] probably gave you an explanation of my circumstances. . . . If Spellthorne will take me back again . . . I may also be lucky enough to have the children there too. I hope I am allowed bail. How are lovely Claudia and Jane? Don't visit me if it makes life impossible. It's only depressing for both of us.[32]

The case hit the papers. Rose was sent to Spellthorne for six months, including Christmas and her twenty-first birthday, while Elizabeth kept the children at the Dell.

George wrote from Canada where he was visiting, and said he would phone on his return. Rose was put under therapy and read and worked in the garden. She thought she could make it this time. She wrote to her mother:

> How [are the] children? They're always in my thoughts, and I'm daily preparing myself for the hard task ahead of me in life. *Now* I really don't know where all your strength comes from, unless God is *that* strong. You amaze me . . . I really do hope you don't mind my emptying your serenity. [When I'm released] you can then be a real granny not an active one. I'll bring the children to your house for tea in their best dresses, and we'll talk about the weather and Wordsworth! And then you can go and garden in good faith, while I give them dancing lessons etc. Mad isn't it?[33]

Rose was trying to understand herself. She wrote to Elizabeth that she was beginning to "appreciate the calm and the dull rather than the quick and the dead." The life of drugs was a pointless horror. She would make it this time.

Easy formulas for understanding Rose do not work. She was fierce and wily about the authoritative interpreters, and at Spellthorne she found her psychiatrist marvellous but unable to help. She was pragmatic about drugs. People look for reasons behind reasons behind reasons for someone's taking heroin, but it was rather simple: once you're hooked, it's hell to get off them. There were many and complex factors that determined Rose's temperament. She had a rage for life, and those who knew her loved her for her humour and fierceness. She had street wisdom, but no training as to how to fit in. She could write to Sebastian: "There are times when I feel as though I'm insane but only because of my innate sanity. A high price to pay. I don't know where I belong: probably not even on this unendingly square-rooted globe. Still I am here."[34] Underneath everything lay a radical insecurity, a sense of inadequacy, a conviction that she could please no one; and she had a capacity for loneliness that seemed boundless and unassailable. Released from Spellthorne in March, she moved to London to attend a slimming programme and to undertake analysis at the Marlborough Hospital in St John's Wood. She then moved to Oxford where Sebastian was studying. She was often at the Dell with the children, and in 1969 married, but her life had not essentially changed.

13   Organic Matters

Worm my best beast friend. Mud my first love.
    Elizabeth Smart
    "Notebooks"

Organic matters. Gardening in the rain. Gardening in
the snow. Watching plants grow. Making *something.*
Such a strange non-thing writing. Writers have to
construct an importance, a sacred vocation, not to feel
fiddling. Millions of demons whirl around suggestively.
Cut through. Bash on regardless.
    Elizabeth Smart
    Autobiographies

As long as Elizabeth could remember, it had always been her
plan to find a cottage in the country where she could retreat to
write. Kingsmere had taught her that her imagination was most
alive in the context of trees and earth. It had to do with her way
of seeing: "Glue your eye to a bead & from that small point
spin around & then you'll know what you think."[1] Of plants
she could make intimate friends and learn from them, to the
extent that people almost became obsolete. The Dell was in
Flixton near Bungay, Suffolk. When she moved there permanently at the end of 1966, it was still essentially farmland.
Elizabeth loved her part of Suffolk—bordered on Norfolk
where there was still a whiff of gentry, the country estates taken
over but not yet broken up. To the south were dozens of tiny

villages called "The Saints," with labyrinthine roads lined with thorn and blackberry hedges and forlorn churches; to the west, the River Orwell with its secret inlets where you could catch mullet and crab, and pick samphire on the mud-flats, and eventually reach the coast with its cliff-walks and bird sanctuaries, and ferocious brown sea. Flixton was a sleepy village where you could feel at home in the local pub in gumboots and jeans.

Elizabeth's acre of land, a few kilometres from the village and at the end of a winding road, had been a clay pit in the eighteenth century, once part of a local estate that had been dismantled. The land abutting her property had been turned into a gravel pit and so approaching the Dell was a strange experience, past a moon landscape of gravel mountains, sudden lakes, and strange mining-town machinery. The main house was originally two adjacent cottages that she would eventually connect into one. Inside, the clematis climbed through the windows, the kitchen had a stone floor, a hot coal fire; Elizabeth put up her William Morris print curtains, and covered the walls with books. There was also the Gas House at the back where she collected things—nature abhors a vacuum—things that couldn't be abandoned to a rubbish dump. Its centrepiece was an old three-piece suite in leather. When friends came she'd sometimes light a fire in the Gas House and they'd sit and drink mulled wine. There was also a crumbling shed called the Summer Palace, covered in clematis. To house guests she put in a wash basin and electric lighting, though rats ran through its eaves and over its roof and it was damp. The property was surrounded by a ring of ash trees and was a perfect private retreat.

But if Elizabeth hoped the Dell would stimulate her writing, the problem now was that, at the age of fifty-four, after "fight[ing] off twenty years of mopping up," she found herself with a second brood of children, Rose's two daughters. There was to be no equanimity for Elizabeth. She was wracked by Rose's confusion: "When a child's in trouble, you have the events, the patterns, trying to find a cause or a suggestive turning point."[2] In the end she was always the one to whom the rescue of Rose and Rose's children fell. There was no one else.

Alone at the Dell with Claudia and Jane while Rose was in Spellthorne, Elizabeth found a new way to "bash on regardless." Instead of sinking into the despair that her fate invited, she found a simple, indeed private way to keep her imagination alive. She decided to turn the barren clay acre around the Dell into an exquisite garden. She had always managed to live her life intensely; if she was to be isolated with her grandchildren at the Dell, then she would make it a passionate isolation. With the discipline and skill of a writer she turned the garden into her page.

She later wrote: "The madness struck me in the early spring of 1967. Not suddenly. It came on like a cold or an unsuitable love affair: a few ominous shiverings and tremblings; an obsessive picking-away at the small-print gardening advertisements in the Sunday papers (offering gluttons fifteen flowering shrubs for 12s 6d)."[3] She pursued gardening with the same passionate, disciplined intensity that she had pursued love and writing. From childhood she had loved wild flowers and fungi, for their "secretiveness" she had said, and had found it necessary to know their Latin names and to seek them where they grew. Now she hunted down books on gardening and luxuriated in their names: *Be Your Own Garden*, *The Cultivation of the Rose*, the four-volume Royal Horticultural Society Dictionary. She scoured the second-hand book shops, on one occasion buying ten books on gardening for twenty-six shillings. And there were the manuals, catalogues, and magazines. She studied plants, at night sitting in bed making long, lusty lists of plants and their Latin and colloquial names: she wanted not clematis, but one of each of the two hundred varieties of clematis, or at least to know them personally. In her gardening career she produced eleven garden journals and twenty notebooks of gardening records. Her garden grew so complex that she had to keep daily records of plantings just to remember where she had put what and when.[4] Though she projected a book on gardening, and Peter Owen Ltd was interested, it came to nothing. However, for a short time in 1969, she was hired by Sally Beauman, then Features Editor, to write a column on gardening for *Harper's Bazaar*. Beauman was a keen gardener and thought Elizabeth's columns wonderful: "Elizabeth was the new Sackville-West, I thought," but editorial policy was then determined by the publisher for Hearst, one Marcus Morris, and Morris decided he hated Elizabeth's column; his wife hated the column. *Harper's* readers did not want to read about how to start a garden from nothing by digging up tons of clay subsoil; they had gardeners to do that for them. They wanted pretty descriptions of Lady X's herbaceous borders. Beauman, caught in the middle, asked for cuts to the columns. Elizabeth was acrimonious. Her last column was a vengeful, vivid account of how to construct a proper compost heap. Beauman thought it funny, considering the circumstances, but Morris was not amused and Elizabeth was fired. "Someone bland, upper-class, and irreproachable replaced her, I expect."[5] Beauman understood that Elizabeth was not a woman to whom compromise came easily.

The acre Elizabeth began with was, as she described it, "an old pit shaped like Australia on the map, but three-dimensionally more like a bath-tub with the tapless end bent downwards toward the windy North."[6] Digging down she found old rubbish, bicycle chains, every manner of debris from dead radios to fishpaste jars and inscrutable bits of iron. But this she would turn into a "personal paradise," shaped to a human idea. It would be a place for pleasure, for every age to find interest, calm, and refreshment. She divided it into seven parts, leading unexpectedly into each other, each with a different mood. The parts had names: the Gas House Garden, the Bear Garden (at the centre of which was a statue of a bear), the Magic Circle (a cleared circular space surrounded by trees, with peach and apricot climbing, and branches entwined overhead so that it was completely enclosed and felt like a room), the Heather Hill, the South Point, the Azalea Bowl, and Poet's Corner. It would be a garden for all seasons, with flowers to web the snow and berries that lingered, and with sweet smells even in winter—scents were mnemonic, potent "memory-restorers." The trees and plants were placed to meet the eye like brush strokes. She played games with perspective so that at one point the flowers were miniatures and at the next, giants, and one felt like Alice in Carroll's labyrinth. All plants were welcome: from the elegant to aromatic herbs, silvered moon plants, and what she called the happy-go-lucky self-sowers, like giant hog-weed and Scotch thistle, which were allowed to stay if they were not interfering with others.

The garden was a kind of palimpsest of the layered identities of Elizabeth Smart. Into it she channelled the voracious passion that had always compelled her to create and to turn ordinary pain into beauty: if there was sadness the sadness could be transformed and celebrated. To garden *aficionados* she wrote:

When my avaricious eyes reeled round Notcutts, in their first experience of the instant garden centre—an experience which makes all other distractions, temptations, forbidden fruits and self-indulgences wan by comparison —they lighted lustfully on rhododendrons. So shapely. So large. So important-looking. Noticeable even from far off. Extravagant with their blossoms. Exotic even without. Evergreen. . . . I had to have some rhododendrons. And I did, tottering out to the car weak with their weight and the wild unwieldly emotions that gardening seems fraught with. Like a jaguar (who'd promised not to) biting into the neck of a gazelle . . . Exultant. Shameful. Furtive. Fulfilled. You want those rhododendrons so much you don't care if you kill them. Later, of course, you take intricate care to please them. . . . [I] kept wondering if they were suffering, would collapse after they found out they'd been cheated when their roots went beyond the peat and Sequestrene—you know that look of dismay on a hungry baby's face when its bottle turns out to be too hot and you feel a total betrayer? Especially as I kept buying more, and more; cheap ones, expensive ones, impulse buys, laboriously-thought-out buys, rhododendrons dwarf, medium, tall, early, late. And my plans for them grew more and more ambitious.[7]

Gardening was a love affair. At a moment of intense pain and confusion, it was a physical pursuit of something outside the self. Each plant was exciting: "This falling in love with certain plants is no whimsical joke. The idea of them gnaws away incessantly at you." "If you see even one red dead nettle blooming when nothing else is, you have a bond of affection with it that nothing can break, and I think everything that happens between the last Michaelmas daisy and the first daffodil has double triple quadruple value . . . They mean something is *happening*. The dead earth still lives. And there are times when I find that very very hard to believe."[8]

She loved the mystery of plants birthing, as she had the mystery of human birth. She had not intended her garden to be large, but "she could not stop imagining its endless possibilities."[9] She gardened whole days until sunset, transplanting and rearranging and with joy and despair recording in her journal the life of each plant as it flowered or failed to; and in rather bleak columns recorded the deaths. Yet always the addendum: "Mind reeling with possibilities for the spring."

There were friends who accused Elizabeth of using gardening as a displacement of writing, but they missed the point. Her creation of a garden was an art and her love was genuine and ironic. Gardening was allegorical: the undervalued was the valuable. The idea that weeds are described as weeds and flowers as flowers was ludicrous. She would say, amused: "These weeds are flowers because I define them as such," and the garden became a spiritual discipline. It was absolutely necessary for Elizabeth to be involved in something real, and since her spirit and capacity to write and publish had been supressed in the real world, undefeated, she exercised her imagination on a garden. It provided her the stamina to survive spiritually.

While she took care of Claudia and Jane, hanging nappies on the line, bringing the wood in for the fire, collecting mushrooms or herbs and shelling peas for soup, she gardened. She would note: "Jane pulled up every one of the 36 newly planted Thyme in the W. veg. bed. After despair, I put them in again."[10] The only complaint she made against finding herself with another set of babies was that after the age of fifty-one has a different nervous system. There were times when looking after the grandchildren would get too much and she'd run to the outhouse and scream and scream. When she returned, the children would have a funny look, but knew that granny did these odd sorts of things. As always Elizabeth found a way to reconcile and affirm. The children would not suffer her anger.

One of her plans was to write a book on gardening. Though it was never finished what it was to be is clear from the preface she later composed for her publisher; the allegorical underpinnings are also clear:

> The book is a celebration of survivors. It is about the plants miraculously still with us, the un-man-made amazements that still meet us in fields, in meadows, in hedgerows, in woods, on moors, in vacant plots and deserted yards, in abandoned gardens and bomb-sites, by streams and rivers and canals and lakes and estuaries, in puddles and ditches, round every corner where escape, victory, freedom, triumphant flowering are possible for plants. And plants are masters of survival methods. . . .
>
> The main plot of this book is the season: spring, summer, autumn, winter, the always surprising events of the changing year: birth, maturity, fading, dying; then again, impossibly, resurrection, rebirth.
>
> But there are also a million sub-plots here, the breath-taking escape stories that each plant greets us with by its mere presence. The triumph! The beauty! The cheek!"[11]

And one could add that Elizabeth admired plants, "greedy expedient clammerers," because they never stopped to doubt.

Elizabeth had many visitors to the Dell. The garden was an art work meant to be inhabited. She kept lists of the endless numbers who visited. Whenever she left the Dell, even if for weeks, she never locked the door; all were invited in, the taxi driver with the passenger. It was part of her generosity, her extravagance. "When we brought down a case of wine," Hase Asquith explained, "she would open all twenty bottles at once, not just two as a normal person might, even though there were only three of us. The terrible waste never seemed to occur to her. She never thought of tomorrow. She had a complete trust, as if life would take care of her. I think she was never careful because she wasn't afraid of suffering. Most people are, they protect themselves. She just threw herself into things. It took enormous courage. You see, she died from her heart in the end."

In 1967, George Barker wrote to say he and Elspeth at last had the chance of getting a house in the country. He had been reading *The Times*, a newspaper he usually never read, and in the classifieds had found a notice that a poet with family was required to occupy a National Trust House in Norfolk. Fate had again imposed its coincidences. The Barker house was thirty-five miles from Elizabeth's cottage; George would be a permanent part of her life.

In 1975 Elizabeth staged a midsummer party at the Dell that many remembered as one of the greatest parties of the last fifty years. She lit the paths with burning torches and made great vats of food, including chocolate mousse in a huge barrel. Blankets were placed on compost heaps for beds, and the lucky slept in the Gas House and Summer Palace. The London journalist Ann Barr wrote in the *Observer*: "The rogues and rascals shrieked like hyenas in the night about their loyalty and pain." And George Barker walked around with Elizabeth and declared the garden a poem.[12]

When Rose had got to her feet again and was married and with the children, Elizabeth was already thinking of a new book. She was under pressure for taxes and it became expedient to leave England for a time. Over the last years she had often thought of returning to Canada, but could never find land where she could live cheaply enough. She left for Canada on February 11, 1970. She was fifty-seven; her real intention was to pick up the threads of her writing.

Surely it was no coincidence that Elizabeth's trip to Canada began at Pender Harbour. Arriving in Vancouver on February 20, she went immediately to Irvine's Landing to visit Maxie and also to meet the Canadian writer Hubert Evans. The old schoolhouse that she had once covered with yellow flowers, while waiting for George, was gone, but she visited the hospital where Georgina was born.

Yet she had come to write. She knew she had never lost the impulse: "I always felt guilty not writing"; rather she had lost the habit. To recover this, she required isolation and immediately looked for a cabin like the one she had called "The Pulley" on the mountain she had sold long ago, as if to pull the circle back. She found a cabin in Little Fort on Campbell Lake, sixty-three miles north of Kamloops, and wrote to her children that she had a job watching out for forest fires. She had one room, a bed and table, and lugged her water in buckets from the creek. There, with a stamina that is painful to witness, she began the arduous process of recovering her gift in a notebook she entitled "Second Class Notes." The initial entries are stark. It has been too long. She had to begin from scratch.

> Monday: 23 Feb. 70 Out of my window: tall straight tree trunks; pines. . . . Nearest building a little woodshed, open on one side. . . . Next, the next cabin. . . . Wooded hill beyond. Behind me the stove crackles, the kettle hums.
>
> The table on which I write is about 2 ft by $3\frac{1}{2}$ & covered with shiny cold white. . . . On it a small glass jar full of spruce. . . . These cedars all have leaves that branch upwards only at first, then on both sides. . . . Yesterday I walked for miles & miles, following a trail that had been snowploughed . . . $6\frac{1}{2}$ miles off, 2,300 feet up, 63 miles north . . . [13]

The next day she looked with dismay at all these "ridiculous statistics." What were they for? "Excessive warming up, oiling of the machine, inducements to engine to start?" But she also knew it was better to invade from outside than from within, and she continued to catalogue the flora and fauna. She would walk the lake trail up to the clearing from where one could see mountain all around and where the trail started to go steeply down to the dark forest. It was beginning to thaw.

Ruby-throated kinglets came poking around. She too was beginning to thaw, slowly. She was reading Thoreau's *Walden* and found it mostly marvellous, though irritating on vegetarianism and no tea and coffee; he was twenty-eight, she wrote, when he went to his cabin. She had brought other books that included everything from Hubert Evans' *Mist on the River*, to Emily Brontë's *Gondal* poems and *Pioneer Sketches of the District of Bathurst*. On her walks plant hunting, she took along her camera. There were what she called "waddling days," lethargic days when she was reluctant, unambitious. She tried every ruse to force herself to write, including rhyming games:

> Will [my garden] survive? . . .
> Scratch scratch clear a patch
> Leave it a minute. The weeds are in it
> Ouch says the saint as he divests
> himself of the love of created
> objects.
> (Love, says the lizzy
> Chica dee dee dee dee)
> But when he is bare
> & shivering there
> what then? says the hen
> How now my brown cow?
> What is this?
> A cool snow-locked wisdom
> Out of earshot, scream & kiss.
> Calm. Dead?
> A better compost
> than most?

This rhyming is only to tickle my fancy. Fancy. From fancy the imagination & very soon to fancy parts . . . fancy cakes & the unit of plastic excesses. And plastic itself. I'm around for the flowing of the clay & the sweep of the brush & the swoop of the line to the hidden broken cup lying unkillable undecayable in the sand pit . . .

And to herself she said apologetically: "If I babble on this virgin notebook gets decently covered & we're both less embarrassed."

But the exquisite, delicate phrasings of the moment that had always been her gift did begin to return. She had always been able to hear the moment, the inanimate thing, the minutiae of sounds breathing. And one sees with relief in "Second Class Notes" how the alchemy of the image begins to return. She began with what she called wordsnaps, though the film was "only black and white and the camera of limited perspective."

> 4 March: There in the middle [the lake] boomed loudly under me, terrifying me. There were . . . tiny fissures in the hard snow as if someone had dragged a tiny stick along very cleanly and incisively. I hummed to the reeds & cattails near the shore . . . Against the sun the torn bits of birch bark up the trunk of the tree are like luminous inflamed flesh . . .

> 6 March: The mildest day yet. On my window a stalagmite rising from the sill is growing thin. . . . But when I went outside to photograph it, I found it was woven into the mosquito-net screen—so not the miraculous natural engineering feat I imagined. But still a mystery. Why is it? Why there?

And finally on March 9, Elizabeth began to examine the reason for her writer's block. "Melancholy and despondency. Is it [isolation] too much of a good thing? I never did say one needs nobody *ever*. But how to arrange it so that they don't take all; and that some stimulus comes from outside without destroying everything." And she thought of George: "He's given a lifetime to it [writing] with No distractions like love & other people. Or he makes it & them part of his plan." George certainly had his own demons. He sometimes needed drink and speed (easier in the days when drugs were part of the culture and were offered over the counter) and on occasion he would wing out of control. Yet the world or perhaps the world of people he had constructed around him allowed him his moods and his ruthless insistence on the value of his work. He might have had blocks but he never doubted he had something to say. She by contrast always felt herself illogically trembling lest anyone look over her shoulder, even when no "any" was there. How to claim George's authority?

But Elizabeth concluded it had always been like this: "I can remember days at Kingsmere when I was still a school-girl—despair & despondency & the blank page & trying to whip myself up & lash myself into action—settling for any kind of action—a small walk even; learning a few Latin names . . . Am I expecting too much of myself? I keep saying just a little, just the next simple step—plunge off the ashtray if necessary . . . For it's something even *to want*, to want to bash your head against the wall to ease the pain. No pain. No wants. No life." She read a little Vaughan and a few pages of *The Anatomy of Melancholy* looking for useful clues. But what she needed was to know that her subject was worth it: "Only towards the very end of her life did I try to glean earliest memories of my mother. So every day these valuable memories are fading in the memories of the living & the living, unexcavated, are dying . . . dying in my dying memory too." And then how to believe in her right to write it: "What one needs (needs? Wants. One can could must do without it) is acknowledgement of one's own sacred burden—talent, gift—to help to make it real & urgent to oneself." She needed what George had, those few to say yes, of course, yes.

On the 30 of March she left Little Fort to spend two weeks with Maxie and then travelled to Ottawa to visit Russel, his family, and old friends like the Sprys, the Pearsons, the Frank Scotts, A.Y. Jackson, Pegi Nichol MacLeod, and Karsh. But there too she went off to spend time at her brother's cabin in Mont Ste Marie. Jane came up to visit and they went together to Kingsmere. Their father and mother were dead; their sister Helen had died of cirrhosis of the liver in 1958; the Barge belonged to the Sprys. They felt like characters out of a Chekhov play. In June Elizabeth went with Jane to New England. Jane had found her a cabin in Fox Lane, Vermont, where she could again isolate herself and pick up the thread of her thoughts.

She organized the cabin, arranged her books, planted the garden with vegetables, and began again with lists of flowers, edible tubers, the medical application of plants.

> 25 June: longing to avoid the painful concentration. But today, "just living" is lovely . . . nothing wrong, nothing to complain of. Except myself, the old costive self. The goo (if there, if rich) buried so deep . . . Cowardly traitor, criminal negligent, NOW . . . Where's the passion? Where's the pride? What is the message?

There were times when it got so bad she would wake up after dinner and sit with her head in her hands and look up with bleak eyes in a state of pain. She would drink and run in panic from the cabin, losing herself in the woods:

> It's in; it *has* to come out. It's this feeling (would agony be too strong?) that it's *stuck*. Pray for even a stillbirth. What a relief. Does it matter? Does it matter if this tomato plant grows up sickly or askew? It does to the gardener. It does to me. And it should to *every* me. Supposing all the tomato plants & me's grew askew? But that means a purpose, yes, but it's presumptuous to look beyond the immediate purpose. Nosey. Just get on with the job. Yes, the job. Get on. Something very very small. . . .   .
>
> Let me out of this. No. I'll pin you down, I'll corner you, I'll get you to the wall . . .

She read *The Cloud of Unknowing*, she read Jung and Samuel Beckett. And then on July 15, the first of whole sections of what was to become *The Assumption of the Rogues and Rascals* began to emerge. "Philoctetes agonizing on his lonely isle! Just because he stank."

> 15 July: First inkling of a breakthrough. What Bliss. The ferns immediately assume a startling beauty & the sense

of richness permeates through all the woods. . . . The endless opportunities for joy that suddenly take you
unawares, releasing you, like a wild bird into uncaged
freedom. A bonus! . . .

Now I'm at the centre of the world & nothing else matters & everything is all right & a benevolence flows down
over everyone & over every petty preoccupation & idiot-
ic anxiety & irrelevant interruption & the painful paralysis is as nothing & how can it ever have been? And soon,
if I need them, I can summon . . . the thoughts of characters & the little charms of events & the immortal
moments. And if they should prove unnecessary, then
they will be concentrated with a rich epithet, but not forgotten (put me in, put me in!! calls Harry Osborne from
his thin shallow grave. Tell them H.O. was here.) . . .

She knew she had done every possible variation on the theme
of romantic love in *By Grand Central Station*: "Thank goodness that's done. Nothing to say there." What she wanted now
was more difficult. She could say of that kind of love: "I felt
deeply for that foolish suffering long before I knew the useless
details. The details bind one up so seeing & hearing, thinking & delving deep are shelved for puzzles. When people
are floundering in such dilemmas is it likely they'd listen?"
But below the catatonia produced by attention to the business
of living lurked mysteries that shocked one out of preconceptions—from the cruel sexual bargain imposed on
women to one's own insignificance in the great cycle of
fertilization and decay.

But there was the consolation of art as well: "Beckett witty in
his agony"—she could ask: "Where are all those laughs I was
looking forward to being the author of?" Or Bach's calming
vision that raised one's eyes above the raging and the agony to
look at the great mystery of the world. "Beauty and why it
pleases." She had a plot for *The Assumption of the Rogues and
Rascals*, and as with *By Grand Central Station* it was autobiographical, but autobiography reduced to its simplest elements
and, as in a poem, reconstituted in an unrecognizable and

evocative form. She would later encapsulate the narrative for her publisher Jay Landesman:

> This is the story of a person (female) who has been shattered by an experience & is resolved to get on with survival, work, bringing up children, etc. She is consoled by friends, drink, nature, observations etc; she learns compassion for other people; she wants to make something (write something), to capture the past, to encapsulate the present, to make sense of being alive. She tries various other ways of life but finds they won't do. She goes on, and on, and gets a glimpse of a meaning. She is pacified (ie accepts the will of God as some people would say). *Or* it is about being a woman, unprotected. *Or* it is about being alive without telling lies. *NB* But if it were easy to tell what it is about I wouldn't have written it, would I?[14]

There would be many meditations in *The Assumption of the Rogues and Rascals* but the one she discovered at Fox Lane might be called "The Breakthrough" (one of the working titles for the book). What, and one might specifically refer to the woman writer here, caused the blockage or as Elizabeth put it "Whence cometh the catatonic?" She concluded it was not the skill, the craft that the world thwarted, but "the ability to tell the truth." "In the snare of kindness, humanity, sordid expediency . . . the adolescent cocoon of all-absorbing feeling or no feeling & then the whory desire to please, to entertain, to craft the nasty lethal pity." The capacity to tell the truth was warped. The compassion demanded of a woman—so curiously fuelled by self-flattering sacrifice since the only validation permitted was that of service—paradoxically emptied the ego. "Is ego a prick to the muse?" Does one need to be ruthless to write? To start one needs the security, the instigation, the conviction that it's worth doing. In the writer "one sees the monstrous ego pushing on like a toad. Sometimes wonderful, sometimes disgusting is the ruthless push through." How can one have the nerve to insist on the sustenance one needs? One must. Out of these meditations would come one of her best poems written in

1982: "The Muse: His and Hers." But she still had more thinking to do on the subject. On Wednesday, August 5, she packed up her books and her "Second Class Notes" and returned to London.

14   A Bonus

How weary, how worn, how disappointed with me [the muse] is & she had such hopes. But the old girl still hangs on. So don't chastise, teacher, maestro of the masculine, who knows where this trickle is leading or if it is a priming of the pump? I have to trust, to follow the inspiring lead & have faith in inscrutable ways.
Elizabeth Smart
"Notebooks"

Rose gone. "They disappeared at dead of winter." Leaving me with 2 children, 2 peeing dogs. Aye, there's the rub.
Elizabeth Smart
Autobiographies

When Elizabeth got back to the Dell, the poems that were eventually to be published in *A Bonus* came slowly:

Why am I so frightened
To say I'm me
And publicly acknowledge
My small mastery? . . .
Could I stand up and say
Fuck off! or, Be my slave!
To be in a very unfeminine
Very unloving state

Is the desperate need
Of anyone trying to write[1]

"Trying To Write"

Soon the Dell imposed its old rounds. Rose's life continued to thrust its disorders—she was arrested again in 1971 for procuring drugs and in 1972 for possession—and though she had always been there for her daughter, Elizabeth felt a mother's guilt. She often had the grandchildren with her and in 1971 could write to a friend who had expressed interest in her work that she found it difficult to do anything but garden, though it might be easier when the youngest started school in the fall. Elizabeth was congenitally unable to put her own needs first. People came down to the Dell in a constant stream expecting to stay. She would complain that she didn't want them to come and then find herself serving them breakfasts and elegant meals. When Georgina would say affectionately, "You hypocrite," she'd smile and respond: "Yes, I am." She used much energy and time always being there for people, but the effort to turn them away was too costly. Once, at Westbourne Terrace, she had broken out in a rash because she couldn't ask Mrs Watt's son, Sholto, to leave. The habit of welcome was so deeply ingrained she didn't know how to change it, and Georgina often felt that she had learned the hostess habit from Louie. In *The Assumption of the Rogues and Rascals*, Elizabeth would rewrite T.S. Eliot's dictum to "Give, sympathise, entertain. I think: their needs may be greater than mine. I suffer."[2]

Even the garden proved both a delight and an agony. The plants wanted constant attention, sometimes whole days, and she felt guilty if she neglected them: "Has it come to this? I must choose between a thought & the life of a plant?" Drought brought panic. When she was ordered by the Bungay municipality not to water her garden, she ended up sitting on a chair outside, watching her weepy bundle of plants with roots wrapped in cellophane, wondering if they would die. They were living entities, vegetal children, and she felt personal pain.

But diaries can, of course, be deceiving. Often we reserve them for our anguish. Elizabeth delighted in people. There was always Soho, where the spirits of the past ("maybe I even saw De Quincey coming by his kind young prostitute") and of the present entertained one, and vintage lines that could unlock frozen seas would be uttered. She loved the drinkers, the "bum philosophers," like Jeffrey Bernard, to whom she wrote the poem: "Slightly Rhyming Verses For Jeff Bernard's 50th Birthday," though when together they didn't often speak of writing. (Bernard spoke of her as a trouper. "I never thought of her as a writer, just as a remarkable woman."[3] Theirs was an old and comfortable friendship. Elizabeth had gotten him his first job in journalism.) A drinking pal, "Canadian Jo," remembered a time in Soho when they all got very drunk and Elizabeth lay flat out on the grass. An American academic, having been pointed in their direction, came up to Jo and said: "Elizabeth Smart, I've always wanted to meet you." And Jo pointed to Elizabeth on the ground: "That's Elizabeth Smart." She and Jo went home and spent the next day together: "One of the favourite days of my life."[4] There were many friends who could stimulate, like Michael Hamburger, Tony Cronin, and David Gascoyne. There were close women friends, like the remarkable Hetta Empson, the wife of William Empson, in her Hampstead flat that crescendoed into parachutes like clouds on the upper floor. There were always people to count on: her brother, Russel; Bobby McDougal, her old school friend; Grisell Hastings, and more. One close friend was Mary John, the wife of Caspar John who had been there to help Rose in the difficult times and eventually moved into the Dell to help Elizabeth with the grandchildren. Sebastian remembered the two of them walking into his house in Norfolk, Elizabeth with her remarkable intellectual curiosity, her bright little eyes, Mary John in tow. He often felt old and stodgy as they carted him off like a pair of "wild Red Indians." "Elizabeth could always create wonderful situations. The nasty unpleasant experiences didn't stick," he said.[5]

Elizabeth also had a number of lovers over the years. She was the kind of woman other women fell in love with. Georgina thought she went along with it for a bit, but then got angry, more at women than at men, as she felt they invaded her privacy and wouldn't leave her alone. She complained they clung, though she wouldn't admit to having given any encouragement, and Georgina remarked that she didn't know her mother had affairs with women until a couple of years before she died. Ironically Elizabeth had a double standard. She had conventional heterosexual relationships, one with the Israeli poet, T. Carmi, who was the editor of the *Penguin Book of Hebrew Verse*, and twelve years her junior, and with a nuclear physicist, N.W. Perry, whom Hetta Empson hoped she'd marry. But among women she was always looking for someone to take her under her wing. She wanted "some strong devoted person (or 2) constantly at hand saying '. . . You can *do* it!'"[6] but, as she well knew, she "couldn't stand having them around." When they got too close she would feel suffocated. One thinks of her fear of being smothered by Louie. Elizabeth preferred the "contented cowfields of friendship" where no one had any control over her. The other person would invariably feel abandoned. The friendship could end abruptly with Elizabeth saying she wanted to cut all ties and be left alone.*

Elizabeth needed people. Her acrimony surfaced when she felt they interfered with writing. She wanted to confront her writer's block, and in the early seventies often went up to Cambridge to visit her friend Marie Singer, a Harley Street psychologist, who had founded a practice to deal with scientists and artists who suffered creative blocks.

One of the persons who may have understood her block most clearly was her son Sebastian. He remembered sitting one day in the garden at the Dell and his mother turning to him: "Look, Sebastian, I have this writer's block absolutely totally badly," she said. She was writing an article about the painter Craigie Aitchison. He told her to rap away, and he wrote her words down. Then he went into the house, typed it up, and presented it to her. "There you are," he said, and she responded, "You're cheating." "No, I'm not," he replied, "those are your words. I've just typed it up." And she smiled: "You clever bastard."

---

* A female lover of Elizabeth from a later period in her life (she did not want to be identified) did say that she had never encountered anyone who could be sexually aroused by language as could Elizabeth. Her response to language was erotic.

What Sebastian did was call her bluff. He knew she was blocked over something non-essential, complaining of not writing. He had outmanoeuvred her. "She had to face up to the fact she was a writer."

Sebastian's understanding was movingly precise:

> The reason for her block is very simple but very difficult to catch. Familiarity breeds contempt. George first of all, then children, the next-door neighbour etc. The very necessity of respecting the life obviated and made ridiculous the writing. Because she was such a great respecter of the spirit and the life, she immediately put herself down and elevated these people and so she couldn't write because her own spirit annihilated her. George was aware of this but he wasn't going to help her. She had to work it out for herself. I don't think many writers could have suffered as badly as she did. The first book was so marvellous, written in white heat, passion. The second had to be gotten together, and the material was recalcitrant. She was a perfectionist, far too ready to annihilate herself. But she was also the proudest of people, the first to recognize her successes.[7]

And, one might add, Elizabeth, like many women, had allowed what she called the "teacher, chastiser, maestro of the masculine"[8] to occupy her psyche and was only now dislodging him. That figure was embodied in Barker whom she had loved, and whose opinion she respected completely. She suffered from the belief that he was absolutely correct, invulnerable. Only in the seventies, as she recovered her own authority, did she come to see that his judgements, while perhaps brilliant, applied only to himself. That exorcism was completed in the poem "The Muse: His and Hers." When it "popped out" in January 1982, as she put it, she was rather taken aback by the bitterness it expressed.

> His pampered Muse
> Knew no veto.
> Hers lived
> In a female ghetto.

When his Muse cried
He replied
Loud and clear
Yes! Yes! I'm waiting here.

Her Muse screamed
But children louder.
Then which strength
Made her prouder?

Neither. Either
Pushed and shoved
With the strength of the loved
And the unloved, . . .

Guilt drove him *on*.
Guilt held her *down*.
(She hadn't a wife
To lean upon.) . . .

Those gaps! It's decades
Of lying low;
Earth-quaked, deep-frozen
Mind askew. . . .

This test-case woman
Could also be
Just in time for
A small cacophany,

A meaningful scream
Between folded womb and grave,
A brief respite
From the enclave.[9]

In 1975, Elizabeth, for a brief moment, again found a champion. Patrick O'Connor at Popular Library wanted to bring out
the first American mass paperback edition of *By Grand*

Central Station. Though she was already long finished with the novel, Elizabeth was thrilled. She wrote in her diary: "The heady stuff of praise, recognition, sets me restless & all atremble. Time to emerge out with some work . . . A daily discipline. The sheer boredom of covering pages will lead to a stroke of a shape, a flash of a way out so that there can be an end of this desperate want, a lulling of the urge to speak, a pacification of the frustrated voice."[10] The American paperback sold well, but Popular Library did not ask for a new book.

Despite all the mystery around blockage, one of the most brutal truths is that a publisher is a crucial part of the equation. Elizabeth had not had a publisher to nurture her and affirm the work, and when she did find one, whether Tambimuttu or later Jay Landesman, she had, as she put it, the distinction as a writer of watching each of her publishers go bankrupt. She was cut off. She was known to the large houses and respected, but until now they hadn't sought her out. One can wonder whether the productivity of a writer like Virginia Woolf had much to do with having her own press, Hogarth Press. Or closer to home, Barker had a publisher, Faber & Faber, to count on. As his son Sebastian put it, "He could give everything to poetry. He could do what he bloody well liked as long as he produced a poem every so often, and of course it attracted women because the published poet does. He could live in America, in Italy because he had the great umbilicus."

In her diary Elizabeth listed with pride the reviews *By Grand Central Station* received. She particularly noted the attention of Canadian critics, George Woodcock and William French, and her underlinings of Woodcock's perceptive review are fascinating. She noted that he called the book a minor classic, read and treasured by a few cognoscenti, rather in the same way as Malcolm Lowry's *Under the Volcano*. Woodcock insisted they had not been wrong "in London in 1945 when we thought it a remarkable book, one of the few successful pieces of sustained prose lyricism to be produced in our time or any."[11] She also seems to have noted with approval his remark that Ottawa surfaces in the book as "a place cold in heart as well as in climate, hypocrisy's native land." Elizabeth wasn't interested in the business of literary reputations but in the simpler idea that someone was listening and had understood. That was the necessary catalyst.

Encouraged by the attention, Elizabeth continued to work on her new book. Sebastian remembered one day at the Dell in 1976, sitting with his mother in the garden. He was writing *On the Rocks*, his third book of poems, and in a state of nervous tension he said something like "Love is stronger than death." He wanted to understand the pain after love: "Is it a lifetime's absence of love that one feels, an absence that was only apparently obscured? Or is it the absence of a single ordinary individual whose apparent presence only occupied a portion of one's years?" His mother became very modest and little-girlish as she often did when feeling shy, and replied that she had once been in the condition where she understood such things but time had passed and she was older now. She took Sebastian round to the shed where she kept her papers and, at the cost of much courage, said: "By the way, I've got this manuscript. Perhaps you'd like to look at it. Perhaps you'd like to help me." It was a characteristically delicate response since what she offered was the first draft of *The Assumption of the Rogues and Rascals*, her cagey response to Sebastian's question. Part of the manuscript was printed, part in typescript, and part hand-written. Sebastian was excited. He read it and made notes, and assured her the essence was there. It cohered.

The cost to Elizabeth of trusting her own instincts after years of damming them up was enormous. She wrote in preliminary notes:

> What I want to write about is there—naturally not shaped and known, but only mathematically calculated from the force with which it breaks out on a necessary opportunity. Women, children, Home, and the 97 positions of the Heart, lying low. Well camouflaged, functioning as urgently as ever under the platform upon which is enacted unimportant everyday affairs . . . It is false & ridiculous to listen to fools advising me to think of other people & their positions, to invent characters & imaginary towns &

situations for them. I don't want the scope of the world laid out like the largest newspaper, no, but squeezed dry & compressed & reduced to its minimum but most potent. I shall just *have* to be brave & go ahead in all my embarrassing obsessions & my heavy, red-nosed self-examination. It would be despicable. Wouldn't it? (Would it? convince me, in any case I am trying to convince myself) to speak generally of Woman & to apply a weak crating of all I know. . . . [12]

And yet, at an intuitive level, Elizabeth knew exactly what she wanted. The novel was crafted like a poem. By January 1976, she had thirty-two small sections, most of one to three pages, some of ten, which she shaped and juggled until she had discovered the right rhythm—a book of twelve sections that moved through a series of what one might call meditational stages from "After the War" to "Pacification." Part of Elizabeth's problem of confidence was that she was writing in a new form and she knew it. She insisted that her publisher call her books prose books. "[They] are *not* novels or novellas. They are short but that is their right length, the length they have to be, and I don't see why they *have* to be put into the old categories. What would you call Alice in Wonderland? Tristram Shandy? The Natural History of Selbourne? The works of Edmund Lear?"[13]

Elizabeth's book was neither novel nor autobiography, although she did not shy away from personal reference; as a poet might do, she boldly brought her own name and the names of friends and places into the text. The book is rather a prose meditation on what it is to be mother and writer conceived in language of great poetic intensity. The tradition of fiction, as it were, ghettoizes reality, turns it into story; Elizabeth instead distils under great pressure lived moments, again as a poet might, to probe them for meaning. If Virginia Woolf insisted women writers needed a different syntax, Smart might insist that they needed to shatter the safely constructed boundaries between fiction and reality. Her meditation is an effort to tell the truth about what it means to be alive, and to be a woman, so that the references are not confessional but are real moments offered as litmus tests fixed in time. Given the orthodoxy of attitudes towards fiction, it is a brilliant risk.

We are invited into the exquisite spectacle of a mind musing, turning the chaos of detail into sense. The narrator is a woman who has stepped from passion, "the mad moment, . . . the electric revelations that caused the soul to seize up," into reality. "The womb's an unwieldly baggage. Who can stagger uphill with such a noisy weight?"[14] At the age of sixty-four, after bringing up four children and two grandchildren, and thirty-two years after the publication of her first book, Elizabeth could fairly ask to examine "the cruel sexual bargain." With humour and with bitterness she looks at the phenomenon of the absconding male: "Adam delved and Eve span. / In their sorrow they brought forth children. / But in Adam's absence, Eve has much to do." So much meaning is distilled under pressure that the revelations come in flashes. She writes: "Men find this loophole out of salvation. Women are cornered into it. They can't desert with all their children on one ocean raft." The irony of being cornered *into* salvation is what Elizabeth wants to grasp—to be closer to the mystery that begins with the Herculean labour of birth, and continues at the cost of passion being pressed into unbelievable obeisance, in the name of other lives, without even the slightest parole. "So between worry and action the faces of women fall away." What becomes of the shelved desires in the years of mopping up? When the body is old and the ego has flown where does the strength come from to survive?

It is a spiritual discipline. "It is the roll of matter heaving into heaven in this long painful individual way." The book describes the individual agony of a woman who is a mother and writer, responding to the furious dictates of mutually exclusive disciplines. And the writer recognizes: "It takes pain to burn through time, to turn a spot on the wall into the centre of the world, now and hereafter." And her only solution is magnificent acceptance: "In the meantime, get a furious weapon. A rage of will. Rise above your turmoil. Exert yourself a swirl above the most you can exert yourself. . . . Everything physical dies but you can send a mad look to the end of time. You can manipulate the bright distracting forever-escaping moment."

In the core of *The Assumption of the Rogues and Rascals* is an extraordinary moment that Elizabeth entitles "A Strange Dream." One might see it as an encapsulation of what it was to be Elizabeth Smart, a poet, with the sensibility of a Dickinson or a Tsvetayeva, metaphysical in temperament, assaulted by strange gods, requiring the force of the whole soul to "hold on quaking":

A strange dream happens, and keeps happening when times are worse.

There was a small domestic castle, brushed over pale orange plaster inside, with small unsteady spiral staircases of stone leading down to cellars that were happy, but full of lonely anguish.

Outside in the beech woods, when the leaves were small and calligraphic, loped a troupe of half-grown boys like deer, with bodies the colour of sunlight on bracken, and black eyes, and thick straight hair. They were light-footed, swift, and evasive, but when a soft moon hung on the edge of the horizon, they came stampeding towards the stone castle as if they were all hooved.

I stood upstairs at a window and prayed that this galloping herd would not crash into the walls. They veered to one side, and their sound grew fainter until the woods appeared safe.

Safe, but apprehensive. That evil orange swelling moon hung expectantly. The overgrown maple bushes on either side of the muddy track stirred ineffectually. . . .

They came. With savage grace and royal silence, careering with a cruel panther purpose. Oh their wild terrible untouchable beauty! . . .

And the dream ends:

O Mother, this body is your house, inconsolable, anguished, dark, mysterious, and happy. If I can bear this

onrush, this excruciating pain and ecstatic fear, it will be a
castle I can hold. . . .

To be Elizabeth Smart was not easy. It was to be "inconsolable,
anguished, dark, mysterious, happy." Writing was not a casual
exercise in plot. It was costly. It was visionary—the wild
youths came in their savagery and royal silence to attack, even
if the attack brought ecstasy. She hung on, quaking, and waited
for the message.

Even as she wrote, she embroiled herself in doubt. She continued to question whether a woman could "tangle with art"
and not repudiate being a woman? "Is not her true creativity
(i.e. having babies) the most creative thing possible anyhow?"
"An aspiration to art *has* to be mean, selfish, oblivious of other
people's screams, sufferings."[15] For her writing always involved guilt: "Now, now comes the moment, when, if ever, I
must throw myself away, use all strength (capital), time (all
that might remain), eschew compassion, consideration for others' troubles, home, garden, rumours & tumults, to rush, tread
roughshod, forget irrelevancies . . . shut out the noises, children's cries, dog's damage, fires going out. Lord, Lord, give
me strength, ruthlessness, tenacity of purpose." But it was her
very capacity to live the dichotomies that gave her her great
originality as a writer. With four children and grandchildren,
she was able to write books that sent a mad look careering into
eternity. One might add that the bifurcated life Elizabeth Smart
was forced to live as mother and writer will probably not be
repeated in the same terms. Some of the social prejudices and
preconceptions—her own among them—that fenced her in,
have been shattered. It would be hard to be so alone again.
There are structures of support now, both practical and emotional, and the example and company of other women writers
as grounds for confidence, proving that the womb is not unten-
able baggage. And it would not be so easy to displace one's
genius on a man. But it is also dangerous to use her as an example. No matter what, Elizabeth Smart's life would have been
painful, since her aspirations were high and she would always
feel she hadn't done enough. As with any writer, this was the

price of her gift. "What I'm making is a *real* place for language in my life since I must put up with it anyway. I want to be respected by those who are dead. I want to sing & make my soul occur."[16]

Isolated as she remained, the gathering together of her poetry was also an agony. Her essential shyness undermined her. But by 1976 she put together a manuscript she called *A Bonus* and took it up to London to her friend Jill Neville, who was then book critic for *The Sunday Times*. Neville left the manuscript on the kitchen table, and there her friend Jay Landesman found it. As he read the poems he asked whose they were. When Neville replied they were Elizabeth Smart's, Landesman said: "They're terrific. They should be published." Perhaps knowing Landesman, Neville replied shrewdly: "You publish them." Landesman countered that he was not a publisher (though he had brought out a book by his wife) and that Elizabeth, with her name, could get any publisher she wanted, but Neville assured him that Elizabeth didn't want to deal with a big publisher; she was shy about her talent and wanted the personal contact of a small press. She added that Landesman could get the rights to *By Grand Central Station*. To Landesman the prospect of publishing both books was too thrilling to resist. They phoned Elizabeth. Polytantric Press, which Landesman ran from a small office off the canals in Maida Vale, was in substance invented to publish Elizabeth Smart. "It was Elizabeth who got me into the game and I had a good time for the next five years." An inveterate iconoclast, Landesman loved the idea of Elizabeth. He thought of Elizabeth and George as forerunners of Jack Kerouac's *On the Road*, completely breaking with conventional moral codes; but Kerouac had done it in the fifties when it was easier. "Elizabeth and George did it in wartime, that's the exciting thing. They were in pajamas when the rest of the world was in uniforms."[17]

Landesman was American, a playwright and entrepreneur, and had been an impresario of a nightclub in New York. He was also known for publishing and editing *Neurotica* magazine, an underground literary magazine in the U.S. in the forties and early fifties. He was something of a character himself and fitted comfortably into the tableau of rogues and rascals. He encouraged Elizabeth and treated her with flair, arriving on the occasion of each publication in a Rolls Royce, in white gloves, with roses and champagne. And he was a good promoter.

He brought out *By Grand Central Station* in hardcover in June of 1977. He convinced W.H. Smith, who were the major British distributors at the time, to handle the book and there were good write-ups in the *Bookseller*. Smith's promised to make a big show of it, but in the end took only nine hundred copies. Landesman distributed the rest of the two thousand copies printed, and the book sold out.

In August he published *A Bonus*, and sold out the first run of two thousand copies. Then he made a deal with Tom Maschler, director of Jonathan Cape, to distribute a reprint of three thousand copies. Maschler admired Elizabeth and agreed to do this, though Cape had never distributed other authors' books before. The decision was not altruistic because Maschler obtained an agreement from Landesman to co-produce Elizabeth's new book. *The Assumption of the Rogues and Rascals* came out in the spring of 1978 under the combined imprint of Jonathan Cape and Polytantric Press. The book trade was delighted to see the name of Elizabeth Smart again; she won the comeback of the year award: "Elizabeth Smart is Alive and Well and Still Writing" was the invariable theme.

Elizabeth may have been shy about promoting her work, but she was meticulously professional about publication. She insisted Landesman use the American edition of *By Grand Central* rather than the British one for printing, since she had been able to make a lot of corrections to it and had given it the extra spaces it needed. She suggested he use her endnotes, which Popular Library had rejected on the grounds they would lessen the appeal to a wide public. They identified the buried quotations in the book and "would add a page or two for thickening." The notes identified quotations or echoes of everyone from Rilke, Blake, Shakespeare, Milton, the Bible, to Dorothy Dix. They also noted the musical references—from Bach, Mozart, and Purcell to "Chattanooga Choo-Choo" and "The Logger's Song"—"I see you are a logger / And not just a common bum / For nobody but a logger / Stirs his coffee with his thumb."[18] When she sent Landesman the corrected typescript of *The Assumption of the Rogues and Rascals*, she insisted it was important to have lots of spaces between the parts and between paragraphs: "As in music, the spaces are as important as the notes."

There were good reviews of *The Assumption of the Rogues and Rascals* but a number of the influential ones were brutal. Auberon Waugh brought out a review simultaneously in *The Evening Standard* and *The Statesman* entitled: "Heroine in a Terrible Mess!" He quoted Elizabeth's words: "What's it all about? What's it all for? No story, no characters, no memory of people, places, things," and commented:

It's true that her book has no story or characters. The heroine is not remotely interested in anyone else, and she can't be bothered to remember people, places, or things in the course of this terrible concentration on herself . . . The answer to her agonized questions . . . is surely that Miss Smart wishes to exhibit herself. . . . The most endearing thing about her is that she seems to be under no illusions [that she is not a complete mess]. If the spectacle of a young woman so obsessed with her emotions is likely to revolt, the spectacle of an older woman still wallowing in them 30 years later will scarcely be found more appetizing.[19]

Waugh found that some of the writing was successful, but one was disproportionately grateful for those parts because the rest was so badly written, and he chastized her for errors. Quoting the excerpt that ended "Leave the washing-up and take a look around," he concluded: "I really think she should get the washing-up done."

Elizabeth was angry at Waugh's review, but stoical: she felt he hadn't understood the book. It was an *ad hominem* review by Sebastian's friend Robert Pollet that hurt and Sebastian wrote to her consolingly: "If George Barker in all his glory can't knock you off your perch, and he can't, Robert Pollet in a seizure of red brio certainly won't."[20] Jeremy Treglown's literary mugging in the *New Statesman* was also brutal. Over dinner in a Greek restaurant in Charlotte Street, Sebastian told Elizabeth that Treglown should be challenged. She declined, but for ten days Sebastian felt she was like a person "kicked in the teeth and bloody on both sides of the road." Still, she was tough; she could override it.

And she had her defenders. Tim Dooley, a friend, wrote in *Aquarius* that, because of the way the novel was treated by reviewers, the book needed less a note than a public defence, and he pointed out the misogynistic nature of most of the attacks. Quoting the narrator's sentence "The spectacle of a young woman so obsessed with her own emotions revolts me" he commented: "Studiously avoiding the word young, some of our most fastidious male critics have echoed this statement as a judgement of the author's work, simultaneously revealing their own thinly disguised horror at the possibility of immodest self-expression from a woman." The book is "too alive and too fresh to be injured by the carpings of the mean-minded and the smug."[21] Ironically, the phrase "The spectacle of a young woman obsessed with her own passion" was a quotation, one of the barbs Elizabeth buried in her novels. A Canadian journalist (whom she did not identify), having been told she was the most interesting Canadian in London, had looked her up and then dismissed her, and she was throwing his words back at him. In the small world of British reviewing, it was these words that returned to haunt her. Yet she put on a brave front and only complained that Dido's cry was heard; why not hers? "No one says: what a fuss those Aegean girls make about sex."[22]

Sydney Graham wrote to her to say that *Rogues and Rascals* was a great book, better than *By Central* "meaning no harm, Miss." He saw that she was writing at her best and wondered what she was going to do now that she had put out another book "thrilling and special" that would not fit into the world.[23] What she did was propose another book to Jay Landesman, her gardening book. The truth was, Elizabeth was having fun. For years she had not known how to define herself. Though she always thought of herself as a writer, it had been difficult to describe herself as one. She would say she had written only "one book and a short one at that." When *By Grand Central Station* had disappeared so quickly, she "couldn't feel that it had ever happened, and therefore never thought that anybody read it." "I thought I might say I was Sebastian Barker's mother—he writes, and reads—and that explains you. People want some explanation and you have to have something ready to give them."[24] Now she was a three-book writer. She kept a thorough list of all reviews (for the three books there must have been over eighty). She was suddenly in demand for radio interviews and readings. The readings were terrifying, "like sitting in a gas chamber" (she'd never read before), but she was good. She accepted invitations to read her work at The Poetry Society, at universities and on the BBC and was interviewed about *Rogues and Rascals* by Malcolm Bradbury on BBC East TV. *By Grand Central Station* was dramatized for BBC radio; an adaptation by Geoffrey Sherman appeared off-off-Broadway in New York; she received a request from Jane Wells to set it to music; and she resurrected a jazz version of "Grand Central Station Blues," with its marvellous mock-chorus: "Boo Hoo Hoo Hoo / Choo choo choo choo/ Wish I could lose/ Those Grand Central Station Blues." In a triumphant riposte, *Rogues and Rascals* was issued in paperback by Panther in February 1980. And finally, Elizabeth Taylor Mead of Metropolis Pictures bought the film rights to *By Grand Central Station*. Though Elizabeth didn't want a film made, Mead, finding her life imitated it, had fallen in love with the book and was able to persuade her. Mead took out three options and bought the rights in perpetuity, though she could never get the film off the ground. When Elizabeth saw the script by Roy Battersby she detested it; it was a disaster. She wrote to a friend: "Roy's so Non-Visual, with reams of unsayable poetry, plus out-of-period obscenities & banal exchanges like trying-to-be witty schoolchildren." When she and Christopher read it together, they found themselves laughing hysterically in all the wrong places. "O dear, isn't it sad," she added. "So many people who seemed to love the book keep trying (& succeeding) to destroy it. My book seems to drive people's wits astray. I don't know why."[25] The whole incident was painful and disturbed her relations with Landesman who had encouraged her in the project. She felt he had invaded her privacy. "I sold them the rights to my book," she said. "Not to my life." But with the 17,000 pounds she received, she was able to remodel the Dell.

In fact, Elizabeth had begun to eclipse Barker as a public literary figure. On a number of occasions she and George, or she, George, and Sebastian were invited to read together. The press was curious about the family dynasty and not always kind to Barker. Frank Delaney organized a writers' conference in Glasgow in the summer of 1980 that was to feature Elizabeth and Barker forty years after the affair that had occasioned their novels. The reviewer in the *Glasgow Herald*, John Fowler, reported that Barker "pulled the rug" from under the carefully orchestrated event when he claimed that he was not the man described in *By Grand Central Station I Sat Down and Wept*. "Indulgently he dismissed Ms Smart's book as 'Just carfuffle, what you could read in any woman's magazine' and contended that it expressed not her love for him but for the English language. Ms Smart, unperturbed by this unexpected turn of events, read out some purple passages with considerable force, and Mr Barker was eventually persuaded to read an excerpt from his book *[The Dead Seagull]*, which demonstrated why hers became a best seller and his remains out of print."[26] The animus in the review is evident in that the reviewer has misread Barker; what he meant was, if the plot was conventional, the glory of the book was its language. Elizabeth would have understood. But it is true that Barker didn't mind scoring points of wit, as when he described *A Bonus* in an interview with the novelist Julian Barnes as the writing of the "imperial clitoris."[27] He had made a career of irascibility. When he was asked by John Goddard what he thought of *By Grand Central Station* he replied: "The best thing since *Wuthering Heights*. And I hate *Wuthering Heights*. Women don't have souls."[28]

Barker, in fact, reviewed *A Bonus* for the Catholic magazine *The Tablet* under the pseudonym Anna Cryon. The review, if not the pseudonym, was affirmative:

For these verses are declaration of a positively terrifying innocence, both of the mind and the heart. They do not pretend, and this is their innocence and their honour. It is Elizabeth Smart's gift to be able to walk about not only naked but actually divested of five or six of her seven protective skins. These poems are like secrets disclosed in the dreams of the imperial womb.[29]

But privately Barker's opinion was not so affirming. He wrote on the back of his review copy that there was a great deal of concerned protestation in these verses and quoted: "The lady doth protest too much etc." He was thinking of the poem about male fruit. Beside the poem "Blake's Sunflower" he noted that the business of apologizing to men who have not been hurt was a shocking specimen of female vanity. Blake, he assured Elizabeth, would not have minded. And beside the poem "Trying to Write" he complained that he did not understand why it was necessary to be in an unloving and unfeminine state to write. He might have been right but it was the maestro of the masculine speaking. Barker could have no idea how he threatened Elizabeth; he forgot he was dealing with someone with only one protective skin.

These last few years, with the encouragement of people actually reading, understanding, and praising her work, Elizabeth wondered if she could bash on regardless. She was not interested in companionship, at least not continuous companionship, and sought isolation at the Dell in order to write. And, often, she was isolated; the only way out of the Dell was the moped her family had given her for her sixtieth birthday, which meant braving the elements and in winter sometimes putting the bike in the warm kitchen to get it started. It had taken her nearly a year to realize she was free. But she was in her mid-sixties, poor, and her actions restricted: "no car, no money, no clothes, no figure, no beauty, no energy. Still, I could rearrange things. A good piece of life to lay out as I like."[30] She wrote in her diary and gardening journals, and contemplated writing an autobiography. She read her old journals, old stories, and was fascinated and even surprised to recognize her early mastery.

She was feeling old, feeling she had waited too long:

> Frail treacherous body. How did I ever get through? I want you [body] to get me somewhere in a hurry & offload my heavy festering mind that's fragile, perishable & just beginning to rot with delayed delivery. What vindictiveness! You did your job but now you take your revenge, less and less tender . . .
>
> Nobody else is coming to live in you when I collapse. . . . Stop that racket. Settle down. Make, as you well know how to do, a little euphoric time. You always had precedence over my poor patiently waiting, frustrated mind. Heart bangs on. Aggrieved drummer."[31]

While she continued to write poems (she would publish a pamphlet called *Ten Poems* in 1981 and *Eleven Poems* in 1982), she jotted notes for her autobiography. Culling long-remembered moments from the past, she realized she had to start with what she came to call her "Mother Book." "I'm tangled up in the various layers of the Mother thought. From pretty and superficial to deep, ugly, murderous," she wrote in 1979. "The smug mother love walking around so self-congratulatory, so sure it won't be shot-at. Sacred, known to be sacred, scaring the jeerers, touching the toughies, committing acts of super-egotism under the guise of unselfishness, and with the approval of the world."[32] The battle was so fierce that both family and visitors remembered how sleep had become an agony for her. At night you could hear her grinding her teeth and screaming "Mother, Mother."*

> I am 63. I still scream, cry out at night; heard throughout the house, through several walls, still wrestling with infantile anguishes & anxieties.

---

*When I visited Elizabeth Smart at the Dell cottage in 1979, I too, heard her cry "Mother" in her sleep.

Long ago, 40 years or more, a beautiful young woman was tender towards me, took me into her mind, her life, her bed, and I thought she had laid my mother's ghost.

But no. Faceless memory breaks through the decade's discipline. All the carefully collected consolations are scattered, shattered by the eruption of the sense of the first fatal separation.

But we had a wonderful childhood.

So, this is the dangerous adventure. I fear the giant waves, the icebergs clashing cruelly in a lifeless landscape.[33]

Elizabeth was clear that, as always, she wanted not to speak of her individual mother, but of the mysterious persistence of the mother archetype that seems so buried in the psyche it takes a lifetime to dislodge. It was "an unresolvement," a poison, a thorn, that gets expressed when the poison gathers to a head.

Love (i.e. George) was worked out, done, resolved, to the last painful echo dying away, a metamorphosis into an impersonal unpossessive love. I never cry out in my sleep for *him*. Sometimes ("when memory recurs") there's regret, a piercing poignancy for what might have been. But no. That is done. With those ingredients that was all that could be made ("I did me best when I was let.") . . .

So dig a grave & let us bury our mother; but not before we've murdered her.

(My poor daughters, my poor daughters, *please* do the same to me.)[34]

Elizabeth tried to solve the mystery—why Louie would use every weapon at her command to get her way about George, about her book, about her movements: how a mother could love with a passionate intensity that would kill for a child's safety, and yet not *see* the child or help it to be itself, but rather hinder it or destroy it rather than let go. Rats and mice and hedgehogs, by contrast, let their children go with a realistic grace. She remembered Louie's scenes of hysteria and crying, of pacing up and down on the verandah at Kingsmere, wailing in her uncanny voice, "I'm going insane!" or moaning as she lay soft and whale-like on the bathroom floor. She had tried to analyse that fear, that need for control that "ruined five people's lives," as rooted in sexual fears hidden in her leatherbound Emerson.

But the impact on herself is what she wanted to understand. "I went on loving her—if this is love. If what a child feels for the mother is love. If it isn't love, what is it? Later, whatever it was joined to a passionate compassion, a protective pity, that tied one in ropes, constricted movement, even thought." Elizabeth's book would have been about that more profound mystery, the introjection of the parental archetype that sabotages until resolved, the way the deep psyche is occupied by a living drama where the inflated characters are more grotesque than the vulnerable human beings they represent. Elizabeth could more or less forgive *her* mother; it was *the* mother who must be murdered and buried; it was the passionate relationship, longer-lingering than the most passionate sexual love, that had to be understood. It had sabotaged her confidence, stayed her hand, when she wanted to "manoeuvre selfishly in the untried name of art."

The plumbing of the mystery was excruciatingly painful: "Down into the well, my dear, to explore these murky waters. Are they undrinkable? Can anyone wash in them?" Elizabeth was frightened of her mother. She knew she had been betrayed. The passionate love her mother had created with her sentimentality was continually bartered. It was the golden cup: each time she reached up, it was withdrawn a finger's breadth. It created a tremendous desire to be loved, too profound to be evaded. As Elspeth Barker said: "The spectre of your mother is always standing in your head one way or another. Elizabeth was always trying to prove to her mother that she could be loved."

Elizabeth continued to keep notes and to refer to her "Mother Book," but it was never to be written.

Elizabeth did everything she could not to repeat her mother's errors. Indeed, that very effort may have created too vast a permission. She felt she too had failed. "I've been as erroneous as all other mothers—yes, alas. In fact, what I knew, my passion about such matters was a hindrance; a TOO MUCH."[35] Yet, had *she* failed?

It was true that Rose in the seventies continued to flounder. In 1975 Rose was living in a squat in Cornwall Terrace in London with her two children. For a while it had been lovely, almost a co-operative, but the government was turning the squatters out and she did not know whether she would be out on the street the next night. She wrote in her diary:

> I'm beginning to get frightened here. . . . The insecurity and fear that I feel are often too much to cope with by myself, so I score some gear . . . [but then] I have added the insurmountable anguish of guilt. . . . I completely despise the terrace. The people here are ghosts & demons. Most of the people left are junkies. . . . Atmosphere death-like. A junkie's paradise. Another person's grave.[36]

One part of Rose knew why she took drugs: it was taking one's chances that attracted and perhaps there was a feeling that one had gone the whole way while others took out "their brains, hearts and genital parts before they went to bed at night."[37] You could get blocked and stay in control. For a moment you felt free, before everything closed in on you. And then of course you came down and it was all an evil spell. She went in and out of disastrous relationships, struggled in the condition of being an unmarried mother and wondered if, for the good of the community, single-family difficulties could be shared and absorbed rather than isolated as they are in the welfare state. She felt that her life was being indefinably stolen from her without protest. She could not believe that all would turn out for the best. "What best. It's a bloody, gruesome and painful climb just to get to the top of the hill—not the mountain. . . . hopelessness. I'm not at all happy. I don't think I ever have been, well not since I was under six."[38] Her psychiatrists suggested she try writing, but she had not the discipline. Often she returned to the

Dell with her children. At first the isolation would feel idyllic, but then with time to reflect, the insecurities would set in. The drug-induced swings were horrendous:

> With my encyclopedic badness for a part, it doesn't make remembering a rose-tinted dream. In fact often these nights I have weird and horrible visions as I'm trying to go to sleep. Sort of interwoven with and embellishing my life. Perhaps to someone who knows, say, the chronological events . . . that have occurred to me the last eight or nine years would say—"Oh yes, rather eventful . . . very unusual," but to me they were ghastly and I cannot forget any of them. I have known the emotion of true, utter fear too many times not to respect and abhor it. I truly do sometimes wonder at the quite remarkable fact that I still am, considering the none too few times that I have been near to death.[39]

Elizabeth tried everything, from tolerance—allowing Rose to bring some of her night characters down to freeload—to criticism of Rose for her self-pity. Often Rose felt the Dell was a trap not a retreat—humiliating to crawl back to the womb. And she would lash out at Elizabeth accusing her of total unawareness, thinking she was the only one who suffered. "It's sad that despite having written such a great book, she is totally completely out of touch with life." And the conundrums that Rose could get herself into in anger were poignant, indeed tragic. "It's as if I'm supposed to accept the responsibility for all the things that make E. suffer. If I weren't here she'd have nothing else to do."[40] But the tragedy may have been that Elizabeth and her daughter were too alike; feeling far too acutely for easy survival. If Elizabeth was neurasthenically sensitive, she could not protect her daughter from this; Rose wrote: "Less pressure from people to be something that I'm not . . . If you're oversensitive of what people think of you, it eats at your sanity and strength of purpose. And worse still you know at the back of your mind that this pressure is half self-inflicted."[41] Had Elizabeth been able to read Rose's diary (or indeed had Rose read hers) it might have helped, for Rose's life often seemed a demonic parody of her mother's. But in the end, Rose lacked one essential thing Elizabeth had: discipline, the discipline, one might speculate, that can come from the father. In extremity, Rose always returned to Elizabeth, assured that she was there. She also had the support and love of her brothers and sister and of George and Elspeth, but nothing could pull Rose through. Neither family nor professionals could soothe her.

In 1975 a strange bequest came through. Elizabeth's old Ottawa friend Donald Buchanan had died in 1966 and left part of his estate to Rose. For a long time, the bulk of the money was held in trust while certain conditions of the will were satisfied, and it remained a mythical idea. But in October 1975, the money arrived and Rose had 18,000 pounds to reshape her life. She immediately bought a house in Cambridge, and decorated it lovingly, making a home. It took one and a half years before boredom and isolation set in, she got into debt, and the house was sold. In 1978 she moved to Ireland with her new boyfriend, a classical composer. She liked Ireland, the children were happy, but there was no work and housing was impossible. While she managed to get off drugs, she was still taking Veganin, a popular over-the-counter painkiller, but in large doses, and she was drinking. She returned to Norwich. In December of 1979 she was ill in hospital, with an infected kidney. On February 21, 1980, her third child, a son, was born. "James, my beautiful son," she wrote.

In the last few years of her life, Rose often went to Bintry to stay with Elspeth and her father, whom she now considered one of her closest supports. Elspeth delighted in her humour, her love of the new, but she felt Rose was a doomed spirit. "It was something absolutely in her which you could predict from the age of fourteen. You sought for words—lack of confidence—and watched as she attached herself to men. At first you thought she wanted to rescue them and then you realized she wanted to learn from them how to destroy herself."[42] At the end Rose was living in a mean little council house on Magpie Road in Norwich with her baby and daughters, now teenagers. It was the busiest street in town and the house for the blind was on the same corner, the blind tottering around among the speeding cars. Her life had shrunk to a pinhead. The last time Elspeth went to visit, Rose was not at home and she found her in the pub huddled in the corner with a blanket over her and a bus-driver boyfriend sitting next to her, also comatose; they looked like two people at the very end of the world. Rose had said: "People do really want blood for their money; true to mercenary politics, blood-money takes not only the blood but the life, the soul of the victim."[43] As she had written to Sebastian, she didn't know where she belonged in this unendingly square-rooted globe.

In March 1982, Rose was rushed to the intensive-care unit of King's College Hospital. She had been looking ill and a friend insisted she visit her doctor. She died on the 20th. The cause of death was listed as bronchopneumonia and paracetamol overdose. "Death by misadventure." Earlier doctors had missed the fact that Rose's liver had deteriorated beyond repair. She had been taking so much Veganin, that her liver finally failed. Everyone came to the hospital—Georgina, Sebastian, Raewyn (his girlfriend), Christopher, George, Claudia. They waited throughout the day, knowing it was hopeless. Rose never recovered consciousness, though she kept trying to free herself of all the tubes, and the nurses complained they couldn't treat her because she wouldn't lie down properly. Claudia screamed and everyone cried. That night they returned to Georgina's and had a kind of wake—Georgina remembered: "We sang and we cried. . . . It was a tragic end but we were a family."

Both Elizabeth and George were in a state of shock and Elizabeth had to be supported at the funeral. Dozens of friends wrote to her of their love for Rose. Afterwards she went to stay with George and Elspeth at Bintry. Elspeth remembered she was like a little child, following her about when she was hanging out the washing, needing to be told what to do and how to do it. "What shall we do now, Elspeth?" "We'll have lunch." "Those few days something strange happened. She needed the treatment one gives a little child: a lot of love and hugging and little rests, and tiny things to eat—two fish fingers with a bit of parsley on top. It was terrible. At night she'd sob for Rose and have horrendous dreams screaming for her mother." Elspeth felt a bottomless pit had opened. And yet, after a few days, Elizabeth had the energy and stamina and courage to pick herself up again.

Elizabeth felt a devastating failure over Rose. When others tried to assure her there was no blame, she wouldn't allow them to dispute with her. She had failed and it was necessary to face it. She wrote in her notebook:

Do I want to, can I face my own pain alone now? Shock keeps horror at bay. Hands off. Distanced by mist & pride & drink & friends & necessities like food, babies, fires. The strong hostess Discipline (hostess? hostages?) but until I do nothing can happen such as a healing reality, the next thing. A new pain will arrive. Opener, more unprotected than the worst one, the last one (cocooned in shock) a flowing, a bleeding, a sweeping (a letting go?) but this must be borne alone. . . .

So the pain sits still, crouching, heavy, occupying all my inside, always, all the time, whatever my outside does.

—Dear God, thank you for the great gift of alcohol given to us miserable sinners in our need—a BLOW, a tremendous failure. To bring somebody into the world & not be able to explain the point of it. Great capacity for pleasure, no capacity for pain. Great strength, pride, but no knowledge of cause & effect. The morning after the night. Unprotected against "the long bitterness of life." The mean, the ungenerous. But why couldn't I have told her what I knew, about her, about life—No I stuck to my own [illegible] in an effort maybe to save myself. Ignoring for me, shame, torment, failure, a vague love is not enough. *Make actions urgent, its nature clear*! This I failed to do. And she suffered, cried for help, suffered, & still loved on. Was bewildered, found it too painful. Died.

Where, if anywhere, do a mother's responsibilities end?[44]

In July 1982 she wrote in her notebook: "Rose died!" and composed the poem that had been germinating for months.

> Unstoppable blossom
> above my rotting daughter
> Under the evil healing
> bleeding, bleeding.
>
> There was no way to explain
> the Godly law: pain.
> For your leaping in greeting,
> my failure, my betrayal,
>
> shame for my cagey ways,
> protective carapace;
> blame for my greeting leaping
> over your nowhere place.
>
> Spring prods, I respond
> to ancient notes that birds sing;
> but the smug survivor says this is *after* the suffering,
> a heavenly lift, an undeserved reward.
>
> Your irreversible innocence
> thought heaven now, and eternal,
> was surprised, overwhelmed
> by the painful roughly presented bill,
>
> the hateful ways of the ungenerous.
> But, loving the unsuspecting flower
> could love urge bitchiness
> as a safe protective covering?
>
> O forgive, forgive, forgive,
> as I know you would,
> that my urgent live
> message to you failed.
>
> Two sins will jostle forever, and humble me
> beneath my masked heart:
> it was my job to explain the world;
> it was my job to get the words right.

I tried, oh I tried, I did try,
I biked through gales,
brought hugs, kisses,
but no explanation for your despair, your desperate Why.

With its smile-protected face
my survival-bent person
is hurtled on by its nasty lucky genes,
its selfish reason,

and greets the unstoppable blossom
above my rotting daughter,
but forever and ever within
is bleeding, bleeding.[45]

On Rose's gravestone, Elizabeth and George had carved the simple memorial: "O Rosa Mundi Floreas in Caelo."

15 Non Omnis Moriar

Waiting for sixty years
Till the people take out the horses
And draw me to the theatre
With triumphant voices?
I know this won't happen
Until it's too late. . . .
　　　　　Elizabeth Smart
　　　　　"Trying to Write"

Like a white stone in the depths of a well,
One memory glimmers within my soul.
I can't, I don't want to fight its spell,
Joy and pain together make up its whole.
　　　　　Anna Akhmatova
　　　　　"Summer 1916, Slepnyovo"
　　　　　Translated by Lyn Coffin

With the publication of the North American edition of *By Grand Central Station I Sat Down and Wept*, and the two new books in 1977–78, Canadians had begun to discover Elizabeth Smart. Young writers like Katherine Govier and Susan Swan went to visit her at the Dell. In 1979, Denis Deneau of Deneau Publishers, Ottawa, met Elizabeth at a London book fair and suggested he would like to bring out the first Canadian hardcover edition of *By Grand Central Station*. Also that year, at a poetry festival in Cambridge, she met Margaret Atwood and the poets Seán Virgo and Patrick Lane. Lane, then writer-in-residence at the University of Alberta, asked if she would be interested in coming to Edmonton as writer-in-residence. She had said yes and thought no more about it, but the offer duly arrived for the academic year beginning in September 1982. She wrote to Govier in November 1981: "I've been doing lots of poetry readings & going up to London & elsewhere & attending any parties that I can get myself asked to. Fresh-fields-and-pastures-new time, I guess. Which makes Canada come at the right time." When she was invited to read at London's Canada House, she again wrote: "Aren't all these events amazing as I nudge up to 70?"[1] She was excited by the prospect of returning from exile.

With Rose's sudden death in March, Elizabeth thought of cancelling the Edmonton adventure, but her children advised her to go. They felt she needed to get away and insisted Rose's children would be taken care of. George and Elspeth had applied for legal custody of Jane, who was fifteen, and Claudia, then seventeen, wanted the two-year-old James to live with her and her boyfriend. The trip to Canada seemed auspicious in the process of consolidating what Elizabeth always called her "independent writer's life."

Elizabeth arrived in Canada on August 31. It was "a bit scary," she told Govier, "but everyone seems warm and friendly." It is hard to imagine how fragile she was, mourning her child. She had left the Dell, her garden retreat, her family, all her supports. What did she have in her mind? With bravado she told a CBC reporter before she left: "I know I'm going to love them all . . . but I'm going to try not to love them too much. I'm sick of love, I'm sick of responsibility. And as I'm nearly seventy, it's just about time to be irresponsible again . . . I'm not suited to it. I'm not a responsible person."[2]

Immediately there were problems. She had thought that Edmonton would be rugged, surrounded by a wild nature, the nature she had loved in childhood. She found herself instead marooned at the university, without transportation, amidst what she considered "hideous . . . buildings, muddy parking lots, trim, unwitty parklands," and roads that were wide and uneventful. She was expecting to have to correct the excesses and temptations of an ego trip, since she had been led to believe there was a lot of interest in her work in Canada, and to have to keep people from eating up her time. Instead she found an unbearable loneliness. Few asked about or seemed interested in her work. She was expecting to write her "Mother Book." This was to be her last chance; she had made the courageous gesture of cutting herself free. She wrote jottings in her notebook.

The first problem was that Elizabeth was given accommodation in a high-rise apartment. Most writers need an environment that reflects the psyche—Elizabeth loved a physical space that declared its attachment to people. The places she had invariably chosen were always a battered record of the psyches that had occupied them and she would turn them into something warm, lovely, an oasis in the chaos. In her high-rise apartment she felt cut off. "I'm trapped in a limbo here, in a padded cell . . . I prowl around my thick carpeted rooms, blank, caged. Turn on the radio—TV—get disgusted. O God O God."[3] One day, venturing down into the ravine, she found wild mushrooms and felt happy "to have twigs tearing my hair & a whiff of the wilderness."

More important, she had had expectations of excitement and yet found herself alone, endlessly, in her "unreflecting" apartment or her spacious office, hour after hour. Soho was her venue, where the people shared her nervous system; drink was not a civilized sip; it oiled the big resolving tensions and moved one to the edge of desperation where she felt the insights came. This was "the Bible Belt, the Suspender Belt" where she suffered the shock of what she called alcoholic coitus interruptus. She knew there had to be a pulsing human life somewhere, but she couldn't find it. People were cautious and she was dismayed by their kindness. It seemed somehow wrong, a tinge of the insult, to be dealt with kindly; she had the feeling of being a chore. She watched welling up within her the kind of neediness she had known as a child of twelve.

Sept. 12

To Think! I was going to enrich their lives & I find myself
poverty-stricken. A desert within, a desert without.
Needing *them*—if only they'd take pity on—where can I
find it—where is it hiding—the passion & the life.

Instead of the garden, what? (I'd hoped for the Wild)
Instead of friends? (Kind acquaintance? very different)
Instead of big resolving tension drinks? (a civilized sip,
stopped before one gets anywhere?)
Why this is Hell—& how shall I get out of it?[4]

The chairman of the writer-in-residence committee that year
was Professor Sara Stambaugh, herself a published novelist
who had written about the Mennonite culture. For Stambaugh,
securing Elizabeth for the post had been a coup, bringing
national attention to the university. Warm letters had flashed
back and forth, and Elizabeth had immediately identified
Stambaugh as the buddy she always needed, the woman close
to her own age who could stand between her and the world,
who would take her under her wing. But their meeting proved
a disaster, as Stambaugh described it:

A week or so after she arrived, I took her to the University
Faculty Club with a favourite creative writing student (at
my own expense, of course), and Elizabeth got skunked. I
had given her a bottle of scotch when she arrived, but I
subsequently learned that she didn't like scotch. That horrible evening she drank everything in sight and mainlined
martinis and house wine until she lapsed into incoherent
babble and made passes at both me and the undergraduate
male student. We finally poured her into her apartment,
difficult as it was as the ending of a very unpleasant and
disturbing evening.

After that I avoided Elizabeth (to her apparent surprise).
I might add that others in the department also attempted to

befriend her and had comparable experiences, so that she seldom received a second invitation. Luckily Alice VanWart (to my joy) took her over, though how she managed Elizabeth remains one of the mysteries of life.

. . . A person like Elizabeth is better to read about than to cope with in the flesh.[5]

Elizabeth loved to shock and be outrageous in the face of prudery, which may have explained the passes, but she was devastated by the response she had elicited. She couldn't bear to be disliked. Writing to Christopher at the end of September, she spoke not of the incident, but of her loneliness:

At first I was rather shocked & appalled by it all & by my total isolation, but gradually I begin to adapt. Being unused to academics & their quiet ways, I was confused at first. No where except the faculty club with always the same professors. We sit at a round table with jugs of beer on it from 4 to 7 and then all go home. But I am beginning to make a few friends & they ask me to their places. The river is beautiful & has a ravine on either slope left wild with trees turning yellow & a green golf course at the bottom. Often I walk to the university over the high level bridge trying to keep the level-headed insouciance of my Sioux ancestors. Incidentally there's lots of red Indians & Chinese among my students.[6]

Elizabeth did gradually discover allies. There were the drinking pals who met in the faculty club Friday nights; the odd faculty member like Greg Hollingshead; Jacqueline Dumas, owner of Aspen Books, who would later write her first novel and dedicate it to Elizabeth; the local bookstore crowd; and Alice VanWart.

Perhaps VanWart gives the clearest picture of Elizabeth's reception at the university, a picture corroborated by others. The previous year VanWart had decided to write a long chapter of her Ph.D. thesis on Elizabeth Smart. When she proposed the topic, it proved to be problematic. Who was Elizabeth Smart? Was she a Canadian writer? Her books had never been published in Canada. Then suddenly, at Patrick Lane's instigation, Smart was to be writer-in-residence. The thesis was approved. VanWart felt the university wasn't much interested in Smart. "Nobody knew who Elizabeth Smart was, nobody had read her books. Elizabeth had walked in with great expectations and it soon became apparent these weren't to be met and the disappointment set in."[7] Elizabeth wrote in her diary, "Only 2 people have mentioned my work." She was indeed as far from an ego trip as it is possible to be.

VanWart first met Elizabeth in October at an evening party arranged for her at Aspen Books and was astonished by the shy, awkward figure she struck. Elizabeth always felt vulnerable in a public context: "before the world, people not friends, alien attitudes, the treacherous smiling habit-locked enemy, to be placated at all costs." The conversation turned to her book and she asked to read VanWart's thesis. VanWart had the office next to Elizabeth's and, taking her courage in her hands, she dropped in. When Elizabeth read the draft chapter, she declared it the best thing that had been written on her work, an illumination to her; it was a great relief to have someone discussing the work rather than the legend of the love affair between her and Barker. Though ironically she had helped to create the legend, it had become a camouflage that distracted from the real writing. On the desk was a pile of manuscripts. When VanWart asked what they were, Elizabeth replied offhandedly they were her journals. Denis Deneau, who was in the process of publishing *By Grand Central Station*, had suggested she collect and edit them, but she was afraid to let them go. She asked VanWart to take a look and let her know what she thought. VanWart was astonished by their beauty. They told a history relevant to Canadians, and recorded the evolution of a masterpiece that was not the spontaneous product of an adulterous love passion, as the legend had it, but a work that emerged slowly out of an apprenticeship directed by a love of the craft of language. VanWart said the journals must be published, and Elizabeth would later ask her to edit them.

VanWart was the closest friend Elizabeth was to find in Edmonton. She moved Elizabeth with her candour and

Elizabeth came to see Rose in her. She too did not fit in at the university. To get away from her apartment Elizabeth would often spend weekends at her place, which was filled with plants and light. There were long quiet Sundays of reading and talk of literature.

By late fall, Elizabeth's isolation was broken and she had more than enough work on her hands. Deneau Publishers brought out the new hardback edition of *By Grand Central Station* in November, the first Smart book to be published in Canada. There were suddenly promotional interviews on television and radio, articles in newspapers and magazines, and invitations to read across the country. In the process, Elizabeth was able to meet most Canadian writers, and was also madly reading hundreds of Canadian books. She had reunions with her sister, brother, old escorts, school friends, long-lost cousins, and old family relations, was on literary boards and panels, and was guest speaker at annual banquets and convocations.

On November 30, she was invited to read at Toronto's Harbourfront. Katherine Govier and her husband, John Honderich, drove her to the reading. Elizabeth loved to call him "O Superb Honderich" because one evening when she and Govier had returned home late, he had a dinner of chili ready for them and Elizabeth couldn't believe a man would do such a thing. Approaching Harbourfront, they saw ELIZABETH SMART flashing on the Queen's Quay billboard. To tease her Honderich said: "There's your name in lights, Elizabeth," and drove past it three times so that she could relish it. As she got out of the car, she picked up a huge sack she had brought and slung it over her back. The sack contained books by young Canadian writers: by Joy Kogawa, Robert Zend, Seán Virgo (her own were not among them), and Elizabeth handed them out saying: "Here you must read this. It's simply marvellous" as if she were sharing some fabulous secret. The books must have cost her a great deal. The novelist Susan Swan remembered that night: "It was breathtaking, that kind of generosity and sense of service to beautiful language. To me that was the best of her; what she represented in my own hagiography of

Elizabeth Smart."[8] But in the car later, Elizabeth seemed sad, plucking at her hair desperately, muttering lines from the "Ancient Mariner": "Alone, alone, all all alone."

Like many writers, Elizabeth wanted to be loved for her work. She never lost her essential rawness. When she was asked to be judge of the Alberta Poetry Yearbook, which involved reading 1600 poems from across Canada, it was painful. She wrote in her journal: "1340 had to be rejected. I felt like a murderer. It *hurt* for *every* one spoke to me. Everyone had something important or funny or sad or brave or wonderfully observant to say & I heard it. I can't do it. It's impossible. (Judge not that you be not judged)"[9] This was not affectation. She meant it.

Elizabeth had a great impact on those who admitted her into their lives. Soon she had droves of students bringing their manuscripts for comments. VanWart watched from her next-door office. She had seen other writers-in-residence at work, but she felt none were valued like Elizabeth; there was a magic she offered that had something to do with the way she convinced one that one mattered to her as a human being. Sara Stambaugh was also to say that though "socially she was impossible," "Elizabeth did well by the students and in her professional capacity was a good Writer in Residence."[10]

Still, the public perception of Elizabeth Smart was otherwise. That autumn marked the seventy-fifth anniversary of the University of Alberta. Writers were invited from all over the country, and Elizabeth, as writer-in-residence, was in the spotlight. A faculty member, Diane Bessai, gave a party at the time, which Alice VanWart remembered. That night the writers were elbow to elbow. Suddenly VanWart became aware that everyone was talking of Elizabeth Smart. It was said that Elizabeth was making a spectacle of herself. Though VanWart had not seen her all night, she eventually found her sitting alone on the couch in the library, drunk and talking to herself. When VanWart asked her if she wanted to go home, she replied that she had no way of getting there. VanWart drove her to her apartment and received a lecture about constipated Canadians who knew nothing of bacchanalia. No one understood her. She should have expected this since it was the reason she had left Canada in the first place and nothing had changed. And she turned on VanWart, accusing her of being symptomatic of her countrymen.

VanWart was miffed and went into her office the next Monday to confront her: "So you think I'm an uptight Canadian?" Elizabeth looked at her squarely and said she didn't know what she was talking about. VanWart learned the first lesson about Elizabeth Smart. There were two kinds of drinking. The first was for pure pleasure. Elizabeth could write in *The Assumption of the Rogues and Rascals*: "The evening rises and rises. Crescendo! Con brio! Anguishes and anxieties whirl away up into a loud Dionysiac chorus, and the moment hangs like a golden bursting ball. Yes. Those were the days when we razed sacred temples with Dionysius egging us on."[11] But drinking was also a defence against shyness. In both cases the pursuit was catharsis. Things jar; they are talked about when you are drinking and there's a certain licence you're allowed, but you are not expected to take anything personally, nor to talk about it again.

VanWart invited Elizabeth to dinner and, over vodka, the ice was broken and the real friendship began. Elizabeth called her Rosie, and spoke of her own life; how the thing that had really crushed her was Rose's death. She had decided to come to Canada because she needed to get away from it, from family, from England, from the memory. At one point she cried on VanWart's shoulder: "Rosie, Rosie, you must forgive me." She felt a mother's guilt and could not be placated.

Elizabeth remained bitter about what she felt was Edmonton's judgementalism. In February she wrote a letter in her diary. There is no salutation and to whom she was apologizing is unclear, but it might have been to Edmonton itself: "I'm truly sorry for any unease I may unwittingly have caused you. . . . I am baffled as to how anything that I said or did at any time may have been misconstrued. . . . My desire to communicate, to talk, may make me prod a bit, perhaps too roughly, too precipitately. I must have been very clumsy on the occasion on which the misunderstanding occurred. Please forgive me."[12]

She may have been thinking of the Stambaugh incident, as she came to think of it, for it festered and she could not dismiss it. It angered and humiliated her to think of Stambaugh accusing her of making a pass at her, as the story surfaced in her conversations later in Toronto. She could hardly have been bothered by the implication of lesbianism—she spoke openly of her early novella *"Dig a Grave and Let Us Bury Our Mother"* as about a lesbian affair. Alice VanWart concluded that what hurt her was the withdrawal of affection from someone whom she had identified as an ally. One might speculate that after George, Elizabeth had sorted out her feelings about men. Women were more problematical. It was not unusual for Elizabeth to abandon long-standing friendships with women in acrimony at some incident.

When she tried to analyse the incident she concluded: "But it all comes down to this: I still can't say I am I. Though secretly & far within, my mute self-confidence is fat & fed & content to wait it out. They'd get . . . regret . . . but maybe I less. I guess it's the vision of the seas of boiling blood where we're all tossed together that they are lacking. Their cozy caged insecure serenity. A lack of realizing that there are terrible things that can squash you down." And then after a break she added with her usual cockiness: "Even if you don't want a penis for personal use, you want to see them rising triumphant around you." She may have been angriest with herself for taking such criticisms to heart, for she concludes: "Stop the whoring charm & grim faced into the next phase. Denying smiles. To the enemy placatory gestures. It's time to abandon the gigantic camouflage. It was never meant to be a covering that lasted to the end."[13]

That February she wrote a letter/poem to George Barker on his seventieth birthday:

Remember:
Seventy is sweeter
than seven & twenty
when we met & didn't miss.
So I send you a kiss

for Feb 26th
from far far far away
where—topsy-turvy
incomprehensible place,
drinking & thinking
are mad words
not to be done in public.[14]

But Elizabeth did have another life that was rather tender and amusing. She suddenly found herself being courted by a prominent Edmonton judge, retired, in his eighties and virtually blind, whose name by coincidence was Barker and whom she called Bark. Bark courted in the old style with roses and brandy; he had a wonderful sense of humour and he could "take a drink." Elizabeth was having a good time and, with friends, they would go off to picnics and he would read her Shakespeare's sonnets under the trees. But Bark was a serious courter and, while Elizabeth was fond of him and treated him affectionately, she had no intention of taking on the responsibility of a partner.

Elizabeth's year was winding down. She was asked to write a formal report on the year, and she made suggestions as to how to improve the position of writer-in-residence. First the job should be given a higher profile. An initial reception should be held and she listed the invitees: beginning with the press, radio and TV, the film world, and ending with all faculties at the university, especially History, Anthropology, the Social Sciences: "Let the engineers rejoice in metaphoric connection, let the social workers meet the English language and its exponents; let them desire Dostoevsky who might throw light on their problems, let the dentists say 'They flee from mee that sometime did me seek.' It concerns thee, O Canada."[15] She also suggested that, since the university owned many old houses, one should be set aside for the writer. It should contain comfortable old furniture and bookshelves already supplied with the classics and reference books. The writer needed to be able to have spontaneous gatherings, to give informal readings, and play stimulating literary games. "All writers . . . seem to have and to like the same kind of living place—a place with a lived-in look, a place for casual comfortable encounters . . . a place where people with poetry on their minds could drop in and talk."

She wrote to Christopher at the end of March that she had decided to stay in Canada. She hadn't got much writing done, what with the streams of students and reading all over the place. "I do *so* want to get another book done," she said.[16] Recommended by Alice Munro and Michael Ondaatje, she was awarded a Canada Council grant to write for a year, and decided to move to Toronto.

At the end of June, VanWart helped her to pack up her books and mail them to Toronto. At a farewell party not many, if any, of the faculty appeared, though the students came, as did Bark, and Jacqueline, and others who had been close. As she was leaving the next day, VanWart asked her how the year had been and she replied: "I never felt so lonely, so unloved in my life. I was out of my depth."

Elizabeth arrived in Toronto at the end of June and, through friends, found an apartment on Lowther Avenue in the Annex district of downtown Toronto. It had belonged to the novelist Ian Adams and was exactly the kind of place she loved, a third-floor walk-up attic flat in a crumbling Victorian building. The musician Milton Barnes lived downstairs. She had the apartment painted white, ordered bookshelves built by a local carpenter, and furnished it from the Nearly New until it looked like her old Copy Shop. Every Saturday she went out to prowl the yard sales along the streets of the Annex and finger the wares: books, clothes, dishes for twenty-five or fifty cents, lamps, furniture, iron pots, TVs. She loved the yard sales. "Sometimes they make lemonade," she wrote Christopher, "and it's a partyish kind of thing." Still she felt rather lost. Everybody was kind, but Canada was a foreign country. "I think I'd understand Hungary or Finland better."[17] She asked Christopher to thank his wife for keeping an eye on Rose's grave.

The real problem for Elizabeth lay with Toronto. It is a curious city for artists in that there is little of a mixing-world. There is no place where the painters meet the writers; or the film-makers meet the journalists; little of the London literary party or pub scene that she was used to. The bohemianism of Queen Street was different and belonged to a younger generation. Elizabeth desperately missed Soho, her neutral ground for easy gathering where some kind of connectedness could be established, something to release things within. "The way they drink, or don't drink, seems particularly confusing. The word alcohol is never mentioned unaccompanied by the word problem."[18] Despite her seeming indifference to so-called bourgeois conventions, Elizabeth felt judged for her drinking. She told friends that a number of high-profile Canadian writers had taken her aside and talked to her about her "alcohol problem."[19] To counter her sense of aloneness, she sought out people with her own edgy desperateness.

She wrote in her diary:

> The fragile vulnerability because of the Rose blow —welling up into any vacuum in piercing detail & making so many words, sights, situations excruciating—And now it becomes more & more difficult to speak of this, which at first & for a while, I could naturally, sadly but not so sadly that it embarrassed the listener. Pain crouches everywhere, in ambush, as I totter unprotected, by. Which makes any plan to stand wobbly.
>
> Which makes lying down in sobriety dangerous. Which causes panic. So I stuff books in.
>
> Held together by safety-pins. (Visible in snaps—a face tortured but determined, held-close, incommunicado—until? some kind of deliverance . . .)[20]

That year she had no teaching commitments. In early August she got down to writing, but it was the same tortuous process: "A-muse-ment. Muse yourself." "It will come. Have faith. . . . Think. Explore catharsis. Coddle *and* crack whip. Do not answer questions or think about them as asked. Take in only what's needed! A leaf. A continent. A black hole." And she took as her theme: All I know about why I write. "My poor blind passion welling up & forced by expediency to hold its tongue—Is this an appalling innocence (naked naivety)? They say it is so. With blush and frisson, it reflected back so passion crouched. But squashed, fights feebly back. It can't not. (Says a sudden deep insight.) The message is like the one in the genes. It *can't* be dissipated. Oh flagging prizefighter lurching from the bloody corners. There's game for you! To examine this toddering passion? What, whence, wherefore, whither."[21]

But Elizabeth found she couldn't work the way she'd expected to and the atmosphere of the Lowther apartment began to feel heavy with disappointment.

Elizabeth's life in Toronto was intensely social. Bark came to visit from Edmonton. The novelist Susan Swan, who used to drop in to Lowther for a drink before her classes at George Brown, remembered Judge Barker as a kind of Dutch uncle, with his pockets full of dollar bills; though he had lived a conventional life, he was a wonderfully free spirit. The three of them would talk of going on a tour to visit the cemeteries of the soldiers in the First World War, and Bark would ask Swan to talk Elizabeth into marrying him. When Bark proved insistent, Elizabeth ended the relationship, kindly it seems, and explained to friends: "What would I say to him [he was in his eighties] when we got to the altar and he said 'Till Death do us part.'?"

In October Elizabeth decided to audit Northrop Frye's course on the Bible at the University of Toronto, perhaps as a way to spark her writing for she kept scrupulous lecture notes.[22] Determined to promote her books, she started travelling across Canada, giving public readings and interviews. Again she found herself living the legend of Elizabeth Smart. The reading circuit in Canada is arduous; she constantly had to explain herself. It was amazing that, at seventy years of age, she was up to it, but the astonishing thing about Elizabeth Smart was her indefatigable energy. She would march off in her black velvet jacket and black pants, often a flower in her lapel, on her feet scruffy running shoes or little black Chinese slippers held on

by elastic bands over white socks, and with candour and fierceness covering the shyness she could often move her audience to
tears. She seemed small, but never old. Her hair was the same
dusty blonde it had always been, cut carelessly now, and she
had an amusing gesture of raking her fingers through it whenever embarrassed or amused and saying, "Good God!" Though
her face was Audenesque, lined and lived-in, she had not lost
the old radiance she had had in youth. She was a presence. In
the well-known photograph by John Goddard, one can see it.
She still had the nerve to take up a Lauren Bacall pose, orchid
in the lapel and a cigarette dangling from her lips.

One of Elizabeth's triumphs should have been reading in
Ottawa. She had been back before, but now she came as a fêted
Canadian writer, and the book that her mother had effectively
kept out of the country had been published by an Ottawa publisher. But she found Ottawa had changed. The world she had
once shocked was no longer shockable. The gracious life of the
diplomats, however limited, had been replaced by the bland
world of the bureaucrats. In England Elizabeth had often
dreamed of Ottawa: in the dream she would find herself floating above Lake Kingsmere. Below her she could see
Mackenzie King's estate and all his ruins. But not her family
cottage nor the leaf houses. Her own past was missing. She discovered the world she had loved as a child had "grown into the
nightmare I had always dreamed about." It had disappeared.[23]

When people in Toronto weren't having parties for her,
Elizabeth gave them herself. Indeed, people were a necessary
protection against the black hole. An evening on Lowther
would begin with a superb meal, a rack of lamb or sole bonne
femme. People would be required to recite poems by heart, and
were expected to know the old songs like "The Logger's Song"
or limericks: "What a position the lady physician was in when
we got there. Legs in the air." One forgot her age and so was
caught off guard when she would suddenly sink and disappear
into the bedroom as the party went on. And it was not unusual
for her to become suddenly sad and complain that no one had
been there for her and one was at a loss as to how to comfort

her. There were those who felt her need at such times was rapacious and somehow frightening. But no matter how late the party, she was up at eight A.M. the next morning if required, to attend the Canadian Authors' breakfast as guest speaker or some such function. Her old sense of responsibility was always there to be counted on.

The poet Judith Fitzgerald recounted a poignant incident. After a party, she stayed to help clean up. Elizabeth was sitting in the corner finishing off the scotch when it suddenly occurred to her that she wanted her journal. With amazing acuity, considering the state she was in, she began to search for it. It was clear she had a number of secret hding places where she kept it. She felt carefully behind the books on the bookshelves. It was not there. She went to a pile of books and counted down twelve and lifted the stack. It was not there. She felt her way through a box of sweaters under the bed, and then along the left edge of the mattress. Then she pulled back the sheets and found it. She sat down and, with an anxious intensity, asked Fitzgerald's advice about how to fill out the Canada Council form to request her second instalment. She was terrified of doing it wrong. That Elizabeth, though living entirely alone, had still arranged numerous hiding places for her journal struck Fitzgerald indelibly.[24]

Elizabeth kept up the effort of writing but the resistance was painful. She might walk to her balcony to tend the potted plants she had carefully collected or to look at the tree of paradise that flourished in the front yard. Or she would sit at her desk overlooking Brunswick Avenue.

Every morning when light reflects in the West (can't see the East) the unsquashable urge arises, wobbling its unseeing hopeful head about. Is this the day? at last? now?

It's embarrassing to harbour such a worm; to go so unclothed among the gossiping of the concrete world—a slow organic matter moving over the plastic palaces in a ridiculous search for an unknown destination.

But this happens most days of the week.

Disobedience (What a well-packed portfolio this word is) . . . Indefatigable it is, & must be, this poor blind passion welling up every dawn for seven long, bumpy decades. Again & again. Wearily, patiently circumventing the obstacles (casually or malignantly or without thought) laid in its way. When stunned . . . lying doggo, shocked or asleep, till the weather turns clement, & the winds drop.[25]

In Toronto, Elizabeth felt something desperately important was missing, but she couldn't put her finger on it. She felt terribly exposed. And, though she had what seemed a great deal of attention and intimate friends, she felt neglected. VanWart as editor of her journals commented that there was a curious pattern to Elizabeth's life. When she was in one situation, she always wanted to be in another. Wherever she was, she was thinking of being somewhere else. If in London, she thought of the Gatineau Hills. Nothing, place or person, could quite measure up. On January 2, she wrote in her journal:

Lonely & bored. Unstimulated. Blank. Reading, sleeping, eating, a brisk but destitute walk & becoming boring too. . . . Complaining, explaining but not being able to explain. Getting fat, lethargic, hopeless, like an unloved child. Sorry for myself. For the first time ever. I don't know *where* to go. I don't know *what* to do. I feel trapped & caged. Nobody's the least bit interested in me. (me as me, me as other.) They're not even interested in my being interested in *them*. Polite is all. If that. A tiresome kindness for them, for me. The telephone never rings.[26]

Friends could not help. She was feeling old, invalidated; perhaps she had come too close to her roots, to her mother's country, because an old self-disgust surfaced:

The shameful balking of my waddling body, its greedy seizing of cheap comforts. Betrayal. A shame. A secretness so deep it can't emerge. . . . Avoiding. A void.

Where's courage then? It's still impossible to say I'm me. Why don't I want to drink with myself since there seems slight hope of speaking to anyone, or being understood —except in a general way. Am I lonely? I don't know. I've just assumed most people want support & applause. Maybe this is arrogant. No. It just seems so. Well I could withdraw, absent myself. Eschew. . . . Would this do too much violence to my nature? I'd hate to be hated. I just couldn't stand it. . . . What a lot of pain. Was most of it unnecessary? I could have cut through. Why didn't I have the courage to know what I know? I did but I thought it best to lie low. Now. Now. But things get serious. I could sit here for another decade. Enclosed. Soothed. . . . Old age & death. . . . Only I felt my duties SO LATE. A thing not done. . . .

I still long for interruptions. Death sweeping close, so mean. The useful passions useless. I must get back to my nest. . . . Does my brain collapse? Well, it only sat frozen, & shivered—had nothing to say except I mind.

Elizabeth was a magnet who attracted people. At a party there could be over a hundred people lining every inch of available space in the house. She held the imagination: Michael Ondaatje would write a cameo of her in his novel *In the Skin of a Lion* and she would turn up in a story by Katherine Govier. Perhaps the only people she failed to enamour were feminist writers. In the middle of writing an article "In Praise of Canadian Men," Susan Swan invited a number of Canadian women writers to her mother's house in Forest Hill to talk about men and love. Elizabeth came with Katherine Govier. All sat in a circle and the conversation travelled from person to person, with an emphasis on the need for men to learn sensitivity and tenderness. When Elizabeth's turn came, she looked at the women and said coyly: "Well, you know, girls, if you make too much noise, it won't rise." This was complete heresy to the young feminists and the evening abruptly ended, but in retrospect Swan could say:

We had wanted to make her into our feminist champion of literature and love and deeply lived life, and she had successfully evaded being put in that kind of category because a lot of her feelings about life and sexuality were contrary to the feminist doctrine of that time. I see, looking back, she had a point. She had come to Toronto after the broadest sweep of the movement in the seventies and unfortunately to some extent the women's movement had ended up reinforcing the division between what were traditionally seen as male and female virtues. I think she was trying to say that the traditional female virtues were pretty good and that eroticism came out of having breasts and a womb, out of being able to have children, and to surrender sexually to a man. She wanted to celebrate erotic passion and female sexuality and that was something feminist writers at that time were frightened of looking at.[27]

Swan mused that Elizabeth's misfortune had been, as always, to be ahead of her time, and ahead of the men of her time. As she had told Swan, she realized in retrospect that George Barker had been afraid of her. He had always thought of her as a rich woman from America, and she found that very hard to understand. That he could have seen her as a powerful figure when she had not felt powerful in that sense at all! "There was that sad, wistful sense in Elizabeth's voice of 'He didn't really see me for who I am.'"

That spring, the actress Nancy Beatty approached her with the idea of doing a one-woman play of *By Grand Central Station*, and Elizabeth gave her time generously. There were long discussions as Beatty discovered the complexity of the book: Elizabeth didn't see the book as a lament, didn't want the actress to go overboard with a tortuous current of emotion. It was not all anguish; it was adventure: "How many miles to the gallon to Babylon?"[28] Elizabeth gave Beatty a list of musical allusions in the book, and Beatty was to discover they were not decorative but deeply structural. As she listened to Purcell's opera "Dido and Aeneas," Beatty could see how the cackling women in the opera, happy at Dido's abandonment, became the cackling neighbours in Pender Harbour. And the language was so complex that the only way to discover the underlying emotion when she was rehearsing was to lie down on her back and intuitively feel her way through the text as the moods shifted in a half-line and the emotion ran through her like a river. She discovered the landscape and words were the characters. The myths were real. "Psychologists can look at them, since they're ever looking at myths to explain human behaviour, but Elizabeth had studied them. All the gods and archangels of the novel were personal acquaintances she lived by. And I remember when she talked of Chaudière Falls in Quebec, there was no division between her and the country. She was the country. The power of doing *Grand Central* was that you were talking about a continent. This woman inhabited it." If others found Elizabeth difficult, Beatty remembered her as strong, steady, generous. "She always brought me flowers. I remember thinking she was this beautiful, vulnerable flower. You had to give it room, to water it, and feed it. She was so shy. It takes great guts to be difficult. The drinking was a way of allowing herself to be difficult. It was like travelling with a mountain. She carved out an existence from the heart."[29]

Elizabeth also worked that spring with Harold Redekoff on a music script that she called "Balletic Ballad of Canadian Art" for four voices—piano, flute, and other instruments as desired. Clarke Rogers of Theatre Passe Muraille, with Michael Ondaatje and Alice VanWart, who was visiting briefly from Edmonton, decided to host a special evening for Elizabeth at the theatre in April. A friend, Mary Canary, made a film of the reading and later of Elizabeth at Lowther Avenue being interviewed by the Irish writer Patrick Hynan.

Over the year Elizabeth had much attention, but she was bitter about Toronto. In part, she felt snubbed by the well-known writers and literati. They were "professionals" too busy with their lives to want to really know her. Many turned away because they found her too demanding. Stimulation lagged, and towards the end and still insatiable, Elizabeth was often so lonely that when no one rang—she did not herself often call, not wanting to impose—she would walk down to the doughnut shop on the corner of Bloor Street and Walmer Road to sit into the small hours of the morning. She liked it there because she found people with her own edgy desperation. There the bag ladies were allowed to sit for hours nursing a coffee. They called her Betty. Like another poet, Gwendolyn MacEwen, for whom at another time the same doughnut shop was a refuge, Elizabeth understood pain. Among those who were out of work, homeless, or alone, she found company. After she had left for England, one of the *habitués* phoned Alice VanWart who had by then moved to Toronto and taken over Elizabeth's apartment. The call began with a litany of sexual expletives. When VanWart asked whom the caller wanted, he replied: "Betty." When it was explained that Betty had moved back to England, he cried out: "But she can't have. I paid her." It is a measure of Elizabeth's generosity and outrageousness that, without being judgemental, she would have helped out a lost soul, and allowed him the dignity of paying.

There had been talk of Elizabeth taking up the new post of writer-in-residence at Memorial University in Newfoundland. She had loved St. John's when she had visited on a reading tour and seemed excited at the prospect of living there. But the appointment became the focus of departmental squabbles as it was felt by some that the first appointee should be a Newfoundland writer. The offer was rescinded and she was asked to put her name in a competition. She told Katherine Govier: "I can't at my age be in a competition." She felt that at seventy-one, and given that this was her country, she shouldn't have to go through that. She'd given Canada her best shot, and somehow it hadn't paid off. She didn't really want to return to England; and yet all her other options had disappeared.

A number of friends collected at Lowther to say goodbye that June. Susan Swan remembered Elizabeth at the airport in her running shoes and an old raincoat "looking like a wacky grandmother who had just taken LSD or something, because she had such incredible energy. As she dodged through the people, I had a sense of all of us feeling guilty, that we had failed her somehow. I had a premonition I wouldn't see her again. It was as if she had exhausted Canada. She had come back hoping for

a lover's welcome and it hadn't happened." Elizabeth returned
to England, to her family, to her garden, to her nest. She hadn't
written the book she'd hoped to write. She told Georgina that
she had expected returning to Ottawa to stimulate her. It hadn't.
It had just silenced her.

Once back, Elizabeth discovered it was a relief to be in
England and to pick up the threads of her life. There was Soho.
She would dash up to London to stay at Christopher's flat in
Marshall Street, and would be there three or five days before
disappearing back to the Dell for weeks. She had a ritual.
There'd be long talks and the place would fill with blue
smoke—she smoked Gaulois for serious smoking and
Marlboros when she was being healthy. Suddenly at five P.M.,
it was *l'heure d'apéritif*, the magic hour she so loved. She'd
wickedly rub her fingers together and say "Let's have a drink."
They'd go to The French. On a good day it would be a half-pint
of bitter, which she'd nurse, and it would set her up perfectly,
and there'd be the good humour when she'd turn to a friend and
call him affectionately: "You rubbishy person." But if she was
really thirsty, it would be a vodka—she used to say if you don't
like the taste of alcohol you drink vodka because it has no
taste—then you knew that the magic hour was going to collapse and fold on itself and there'd be no evening. She might
tear her hair and turn on you and say: "Would you come if I
called?" Christopher remembers that sometimes, at night,
when she was fast asleep, you could still hear her grinding her
teeth and screaming "Mother." But in the pubs there were
friends who knew the pain that Elizabeth was nursing. At the
Colony Room, where Ian Board had replaced Muriel as owner,
among the regulars were Marsh Dunbar and Graham Mason. It
was fun, with wit bristling over the surface of a genuine tenderness, and a code of generosity with everyone buying rounds
as the drinks came fast and furious. One of the things Elizabeth
must have loved is that you couldn't get by on reputation. It
wasn't who you were or what you did but whether you were up
to the wit. At The French she would talk gardening with the
owner, Gaston. And there were Bruce and Jeffrey Bernard,

though if you wanted to visit Bruce you went to The French and to see Jeffrey you went to the Coach and Horses for the two hadn't spoken in years. Or there was Craigie Aitchison who loved to tell the story of a taxi ride with Elizabeth and George to Clapham. "All the way down Whitehall, George pointed out the architecture to me. 'You know, Craigie, that was built by Christopher Wren, that was torn down by Napoleon.' I didn't know a thing about architecture and was swallowing it all up, and Elizabeth said: 'Don't listen to a word. He knows nothing. He's making it all up to impress you. That's not Christopher Wren, that's so and so. The Houses of Parliament was somebody else.' She kept saying to George: 'You're talking nonsense.' Finally as we got near Clapham she said: 'Thank goodness there's nothing here. He can't point out any more lies and rubbish to you.'"

Alice VanWart had finished editing *In the Meantime7* while staying on Lowther Avenue that summer and it came out in the autumn of 1984. Elizabeth was pleased. She was also working with Andrew Ford on "Cabaret Songs and Interlude." And she advised Christopher on the selection of poets for his book *Portraits of Poets*, a remarkable book that was to draw considerable attention. "Mom always had to be encouraging," her son said. But it was to her garden that Elizabeth gave most of her creative passion.

When Alice VanWart visited Elizabeth in July 1985 to consult her on the manuscript of the early journals, *Necessary Secrets*, she was moved to see Elizabeth in her own context, in her various roles. Elizabeth had her grandchildren with her. She apologized profusely, knowing VanWart had come to work, but explained that Georgina had had the opportunity to go to France and hadn't gotten away in so long and etc. Elizabeth was slower now, and for the first time one noticed her age. The days were ritualized—hot and beautiful and also tranquil. The first thing Elizabeth did in the morning after tea and a little reading was to visit her plants in her seven gardens. Journal in hand, she'd check each one in turn and make notes on their various states of well-being. It was arduous: something had died, something had come up, something needed replanting. She treated them like living beings, like children. This one was naughty, that one pushy, that one a thriver. In the afternoons they would all get into Elizabeth's little Citroen and drive to Bungay and buy plants, or books on gardening, often ten at a time. Elizabeth was still obsessive. The garden was a life force. She said to VanWart: "You can't get any more elemental than this." Or they would drive to the river pond where VanWart would swim with the children and Elizabeth would read on the bank, or write in her garden journal. At night they would all crawl into the big bed and watch TV. VanWart felt totally and wonderfully subsumed into the tranquil harmony of the house. Two evenings there were parties, when the Barker clan collected and they'd be cooking dinner for twelve or fourteen. In the two and a half weeks VanWart was there, they never actually got down to the journals. Elizabeth would always promise—this afternoon—but when the time came she would grow suddenly impatient, and say to VanWart that she didn't remember the past, it was all so long ago. VanWart could only acquiesce. She would not disturb Elizabeth's harmony. She felt that Elizabeth was absolutely at peace with herself; there was no grief. When Elizabeth took her to the Bungay station, VanWart had the terrible feeling she wouldn't see her again.

Elizabeth had returned to an old spiritual discipline as she toiled with the elemental powers. As always, it was absolutely necessary for her to be involved in something real. Her son Sebastian visited her at the Dell that summer:

I wasn't expected at the Dell. I surprised her. I found her in the garden and saw how she really was. Terrible beads of sweat on her forehead indicating a heart problem and that she hadn't long to live. She was over in the flowerbed at the face of the Dell tending to the flowers. She was working. She didn't know that anyone was there and I was only a few paces away. I suddenly became aware I was treading on intimate privilege. I looked at her and saw an old woman wandering around in her garden passionately trying to work out the answer. What she was supposed to do; how she was supposed to be inspired. I saw somebody working 150%, a spirit working. No answers and yet perfectly in tune with the earth. It was very difficult for me to say hello. Perhaps I should have walked away at that moment. She looked up—beads of sweat, this passionate face—a sorrow at the non-understanding of anything and yet simultaneously a knowledge of what she was doing. She turned round and said "Hello" but I wouldn't have been surprised had she said: "Who are you?" But she gave me the immediate hook she always gave into her affections. She had to do that. She did it out of reflex. It was almost as if she had to snap back into her body. She had been musing, thinking in the most serious form. I felt privileged to see such an immortal life. And for her to turn round and make it easy for me to come to her! I respected her compassion for me. We went inside and did what we always did.[30]

The doctors had told Elizabeth she had fuzzy arteries and she must quit smoking and drinking. But she had always made her pact with the rogues and rascals. In retrospect it was clear to her family that she knew she was dying and had decided to do it with dignity. She made peace with each of her children. That Christmas she gave Georgina a bottle of perfume called Poison. It was a private joke. There had been tensions between them. Elizabeth had been worried about Rose's youngest child and would have provided a home for him had not Georgina insisted on doing so. Though Georgina had herself been ill, she loved Elizabeth too much to allow her to assume that responsibility again, but Elizabeth's refusal to demand from her sons and their wives had irked. Now, Elizabeth offered perfume, and they laughed and said it would never be bad again. She talked at length to Christopher on those smoky afternoons. And she went with Sebastian to visit the retreat he'd built in Greece.

Three weeks before Elizabeth died, the Barker clan collected for the wedding of one of Rose's daughters, Claudia. As Elspeth described it, it was a hilarious time. The wedding was held at the registry office in Norwich. Millions of Barkers trouped in and took all the chairs in the church so that when the groom's family arrived there was no place to sit and a massive reshuffling took place. When the bride was asked to take this man she suddenly started to vomit and rushed out. She seemed to vanish. The loo was on the far side of the town hall down Kafkaesque corridors miles and miles away. Claudia eventually returned with a nappy clasped to her face. As the Barkers drove out of Norwich, Elizabeth was hell-bent on opening a bottle of champagne. She was in the front and George was driving erratically as he was prone to do. They were afraid that the cork would explode in his face and so they encouraged Elizabeth to aim out the window, which she did, narrowly missing an aging pensioner tottering by. They went back to Bintry and had a jolly party. Elizabeth was in the midst of those she loved and who shared her nervous system.

In mid-February, she went with Sebastian to Greece for ten days. He had built himself a small house just outside the village of Sitochori. It was spring and the nights were already mild. Several nights after they arrived she said: "Can't we go out and see a little action?" She wanted to go up to the café to sit with the Arcadians. They walked the steep rocky road to the village, she with beads of sweat pouring off her face. The café was typical, a small concrete hut where the menfolk gathered around an open fire under neon lights, cracking peanuts and drinking coffee. Elizabeth was the only woman, and, as they entered, one of the head patriarchs, Stathis Politis, sent over a brandy. Elizabeth was delighted and turned to Sebastian and said: "I fancy that one there. What's his name?" And he replied: "He's the head of the church." "Great, I'll have him," she said. And then suddenly serious, she asked: "Sebastian, how did you do this?" for she recognized in the café of Sitochori the presence of the rogues she loved. Going to bed later, she gave her son some wine and demanded he read her the poem *Anno Domini*.

One day they drove into the mountains near a place called Paradiso. The landscape was newly green, the trees coming into flower. There was a shepherdess walking her flock of sheep. They wandered for hours, Elizabeth collecting specimens of plants in her Marlboro cigarette package. She talked of the poets she loved.

Elizabeth was tired. In bed she read flower books, and Sebastian collected flowers and plants from the mountainside and brought them on a tray; she was most delighted by the ones she had never seen before. And she proofread the manuscript of *Necessary Secrets* and was pleased with it. She said to Sebastian jokingly: "If I died would they bury me in that churchyard up there?" But she was so terribly alive, it never occurred to him that death might be close.

Lying there in that small Greek house, contemplating retreat seemed to release memories. "That's when she told me of her life," Sebastian said. She spoke in a different way, willing at last to make value judgements. It was an unloading. She spoke of "The Pulley" of her childhood. "You must understand there's another side to George that's not very good," she said, and she spoke of George allowing her to sell her mountain. She was young and in love and would have given him anything, but he should never have asked. It had been so important to her.* She spoke of whom she loved and why, how she was frightened and proud of her children's love. She loved George's willing-ness to throw himself into life, his capacity to control the moment and create a huge umbrella effect, how he delighted to provoke and play. But she also said that George's ruthlessness had its price, that the ruthlessness must be reflected in the life and in the work because the work doesn't just stand as a palimpsest by itself, unrelated to anything. "There was an urgency of communication in these essential facts."

Elizabeth always admired Barker as what she called "a work-er and a phenomenon." "He goes from the sheepish and shame-faced to the roar of authority."[31] She was angry with him for his treatment of herself and Elspeth, whom she loved, but she never doubted his genius. Almost the first thing she did with

---

* George Barker was affronted that Elizabeth claimed to have sold her mountain for him and vehemently denied she had done so. Indeed, both Jane and Russel believed the mountain was sold in the mid-fifties. Yet in later years, Elizabeth always remembered it this way. One might say that in her mind, her mountain with its "pulley" was a symbol: it was the secret place where she went to write.

any new friends was to offer them Barker's poetry. She believed writers had to construct sacred vocations, with their millions of demons whirling around suggestively. They had to be monsters. How lucky are the "sexy ambiguous poets, self-eating or no."[32] The image she always offered of George was that of a small figure running across a dark plane and a brilliant, gorgeous bird called poetry lands in his arms, and it is all he can do to barely hold on to it and keep running."[33] She wished that she herself had been able to be more ruthless. She accepted Barker as he was and continued to love him in a disinterested way. It had been a great love affair: impossible to live apart, impossible to live together. "I don't remember ever having had the feeling they could have been happy together," Michael Asquith said. "Had George ever given in to Elizabeth, she would have got fed up with him." Sebastian reported that at the end it was lovely to be in their presence. Their minds delighted in each other; there was the coherence of the years between them. It would last twenty minutes or three-quarters of an hour, and Elspeth would step back and allow it to happen. No bitterness or jealousy; they all knew what was going on; it had its own kind of purity. To the end she was unsentimental, unrepentent: "He's marvellous for about an hour," she'd say of George. "If you catch him at the right time." She retained the intensity of emotions that had always been her gift, an intensity that frightened the faint-hearted. She refused to be anaesthesized against the sharpness of life, and did not regret her pain; from pain came the ability to receive joy.*

Elizabeth and Sebastian returned to London. There was one more evening of devouring poetry and wine: Herbert, Vaughan,

---

* Like Elizabeth, Barker has the capacity to penetrate the imagination as a conundrum. Lindsay Clarke, a neighbour of Barker's in Norfolk, has written a novel, *The Chymical Wedding,* in which the central character, an aging poet, is based loosely on Barker. It is a compelling portrait. In conversation, Barker remarked: "Matthew Arnold said: 'Such a price the Gods exact.' It's not invariably the price, there's Chaucer, Eliot etc. But if often is. The Gods exacted a price from me and it's too expensive. The song's not worth the money and vice versa. I saw Ezra eighteen months before he was dead, and he said: 'Everything I did was wrong.' There are many accusations one can bring against people who write verse." (Interview with author, April 29, 1990.)

Traherne, Baudelaire. The last weekend, George, Elspeth, Graham, and Marsh were to come to dinner at the Dell, but the pipes froze and Elizabeth said she was going down to London to stay with Christopher. On March 2, she saw the painter Craigie Aitchison and a young poet, Patrick Cunningham, and they went to an exhibition of paintings at Notting Hill Gate. When her old friends Michael and Hase Asquith arrived late, she dragged them away immediately: "Oh come along, enough of culture," but at lunch she felt ill, was worried about her will, and left abruptly. On the night of the 3rd, she spoke to Georgina by phone and was to come round the next day for a children's party. She went to Soho with Sebastian who said: "Her spirit was as light as a feather."

The morning of the 4th, after she and Christopher had coffee, he left the apartment briefly to see about a job. When he returned, he found her sitting by the phone. The message she had been writing telling him to call so and so, just before the heart attack, was still in her hand. To Christopher came the thought that his mother had known she was dying. "She elected to do it that way. She was not going to be infirm. It was Go. Do it well. Like running on your sword."

Christopher phoned Georgina. She was drinking coffee with a friend and with her help managed to get to Christopher's flat. She was in a state of complete shock. She had been expecting Elizabeth and couldn't help thinking her mother hadn't come to her because she had known what was to happen and it would have been terrible for the children. When Georgina arrived, Elizabeth was still in the chair by the phone. She sat at her feet and found herself staring for what seemed hours. Georgina went out to buy soup. When she returned, it seemed that there wasn't enough for everyone; she turned to her mother and said: "There's none for you." As she heard her own voice it sounded like Elizabeth's. It was the kind of joke she would have loved.

Sebastian phoned George. When Elspeth returned from work, she found George sitting in the den, "stunned like a winter bird, hovering." She went into the kitchen to sit down, and suddenly had a very strange feeling, not of Elizabeth being there but of her having just been there, for a moment, and as though she had heard her say in that lovely warm way she had about her: "It's all right really." The words were hanging in the air as though Elizabeth had said them and gone. She found herself looking at the snowdrops on the sill lit by the winter sun. "I don't say that everything felt at peace or better, but just that she had illuminated the kitchen for a moment."

The church at South Elmham was packed for the funeral. Some stood. In her obituary notice Ann Barr wrote: "There were people who had known her two years, people who had known her 40. All returned her love. She had encouraged; she had also carried trays upstairs." Sebastian read Henry Vaughan's poem, with the verse that Elizabeth, aged twelve, had written on the first page of her journal:

Then bless thy secret growth, nor catch
At noise, but thrive unseen and dumb;
Keep clean, bear fruit, earn life and watch,
Till the white winged Reapers come![34]

The coffin was taken up the hill to a grave beside Rose's. On the headstone are carved words from Horace: "*Non Omnis Moriar,*" or as George Barker translated them, "I am not entirely dead." There was a party at the Dell afterwards. All the rogues and rascals were there. Her old friend the poet Eddie Linden wept: "She was a mother to me." Elspeth Barker said: "She never did anything despicable. She was a glory to the world."[35]

Notes

Works by Elizabeth Smart

By Grand Central Station I Sat Down and Wept. London: Editions
Poetry London, 1945; London: Panther Books Ltd, 1966; New York:
Popular Library, 1975; London: Polytantric Press, 1977; Ottawa:
Deneau Publishers, 1981.

A Bonus. London: Polytantric Press, 1977.

The Assumption of the Rogues and Rascals. London: Jonathan Cape and
Polytantric Press, 1978.

Ten Poems. Bath: Bath Place Community Arts Press, 1981.

Eleven Poems. Bracknell: Owen Kirton Ltd, 1982.

In the Meantime. ed. Alice VanWart. Ottawa: Deneau Publishers, 1984.

Necessary Secrets: The Journals of Elizabeth Smart. ed. Alice VanWart.
Toronto: Deneau Publishers, 1986.

Juvenilia: Early Writings of Elizabeth Smart. ed. Alice VanWart. Toronto:
Coach House Press, 1987.

Autobiographies. ed. Christina Burridge. Vancouver: William
Hoffer/Tanks, 1987.

Elizabeth's Garden: Elizabeth Smart on the Art of Gardening. ed. Alice
VanWart. Toronto: Coach House Press, 1989.

Manuscripts

The National Library of Canada, Ottawa, holds the great bulk of Smart
manuscripts. There are two collections: The Elizabeth Smart Fonds,
acquired with the assistance of the Cultural Property Import and Export Act,

consisting of eighty-four boxes of material; and the Alice VanWart Collection of Elizabeth Smart, consisting of four boxes. Other manuscript material by or relevant to Smart can be found in the George Barker Collection, the Harry Ransom Humanities Research Center, The University of Texas at Austin, Texas.

End Notes

Abbreviations

NLC   The Elizabeth Smart Fonds, The National Library of Canada
TSC   Elizabeth Smart material in the George Barker Collection, the Harry Ransom Humanities Research Center, the University of Texas at Austin
VWC   The Elizabeth Smart Papers in the Alice VanWart Collection, The National Library of Canada

One: Personal Pronouns

1. *George Barker: Collected Poems*, ed. Robert Fraser (London: Faber & Faber, 1987), p. 3.
2. Interview with Hase Asquith, London, 12 May, 1989.
3. The first traceable ancestor of Elizabeth Smart emigrated from Hertfordshire, England, in 1640 and settled in Billerica, Mass. His grandson, Benjamin Baldwin, had a varied career: he was a soldier in the Revolution, author of a *Genealogical Narrative*, and was known locally as having had a great business talent. He married Ruth Paddock, daughter of Zachariah Paddock and Deborah Freeman. Unless further documents surface, whether there was an Indian connection can neither be proven nor disproven. Source: *John Baldwin, of Billerica, Massachusetts* (Salt Lake Family History Library). Genealogical researcher: Preston J. Owens: Owens Family History Specialities, Utah.
4. Elizabeth Smart, *Autobiographies*, ed. Christina Burridge (Vancouver: William Hoffer/Tanks, 1987), pp. 141–42.
5. Interview with Jane Marsh Beveridge (Smart), Cambridge, Mass., 4–11 July 1988. My account of Elizabeth Smart's childhood is based on interviews with and letters from Jane Marsh Beveridge (Smart's younger sister), Russel Smart, Jr., and Gypsy (Parr) Telfer, as well as on Smart's own reminiscences. Mrs Beveridge has written an account of her childhood, entitled "Four Horses: Sixteen Legs," and generously

allowed me to quote from manuscript.

6. *The Ottawa Citizen*, 26 September 1931, p. 2.

7. *Autobiographies*, p. 140.

8. Interviews with Gypsy (Parr) Telfer, Ottawa, 10 November 1988, and Jane Marsh Beveridge, Cambridge, Mass., 4–11 July 1988.

9. Thomas Seccombe, *Dictionary of National Biography*, vol. 15 (London: Oxford University Press, 1921–22), pp. 364–65.

10. Interview with Russel Smart, Jr., Ottawa, 11 November 1988. Also letter from R. Smart to author, 5 October 1989.

11. Charles Ritchie, *My Grandfather's House: Scenes of Childhood and Youth* (Toronto: Macmillan of Canada, 1987), p. 154.

12. Jean Mallinson, "Interview with Elizabeth Smart," 4 March 1983. Transcription from tape—NLC: Box 74, F 7.

13. Robert L. McDougall, ed., *The Poet and Critic: A Literary Correspondence between D.C. Scott and E.K. Brown* (Ottawa: Carleton University Press, 1983), pp. 111–12. The club was on Aylmer Road; it had a membership of from fifteen to twenty men who met each week "to provide a congenial occasion for the meeting of good minds." Scott was a member.

14. Elizabeth Smart, *By Grand Central Station I Sat Down and Wept.* (London: Polytantric Press, 1977), p. 67. All subsequent citations are to this edition.

15. Elizabeth Smart, *The Assumption of the Rogues and Rascals* (London: Jonathan Cape and Polytantric Press, 1978), p. 66.

16. Ritchie, *My Grandfather's House*, p. 154.

17. *Autobiographies*, p. 165.

18. Interview with Jane Marsh Beveridge, Cambridge, Mass., 4–11 July 1988.

19. Jane Marsh Beveridge, "Four Horses, Sixteen Legs."

20. Elizabeth Smart, *In the Meantime*, ed. Alice VanWart (Ottawa: Deneau Publishers, 1984), pp. 45–46.

21. Interview with Lady Roberta Mason (formerly Bobby McDougal), Retford, Nottinghamshire, 19 April 1989.

22. *In the Meantime*, pp. 49–50.

23. *In the Meantime*, p. 7.

24. *Autobiographies*, p. 146.

25. From "Scenes One Never Forgets," *In the Meantime*, p. 11.

26. Interview with Jane Marsh Beveridge, Cambridge, Mass., 4–11 July 1988.

27. *Autobiographies*, p. 157.

28. *Ibid.*

29. From unused notes for *Dig a Grave and Let Us Bury Our Mother*. NLC: Box 3, F 12, (13 December 1939).

30. NLC: Box 3, File 2 (1937).
31. Jane Marsh Beveridge, "Four Horses, Sixteen Legs."
32. *Autobiographies*, pp. 139–40.
33. Jane Marsh Beveridge, "Four Horses, Sixteen Legs."
34. *Ibid.*
35. Conversation with Senator Eugene Forsey, Ottawa, 18 November 1988.
36. NLC: Box 55, F 34—undated.
37. *Autobiographies*, p. 158.
38. Jane Marsh Beveridge, "Four Horses, Sixteen Legs."
39. *Autobiographies*, p. 180.
40. Elizabeth Smart, *Juvenilia: Early Writings of Elizabeth Smart*, ed. Alice VanWart (Toronto: Coach House Press, 1987), pp. 34–35.
41. *Autobiographies*, pp. 180–81.
42. C.P. Stacey, *A Very Double Life: The Private World of Mackenzie King* (Toronto: Macmillan of Canada, 1976), p. 127.
43. *Samara*, 1923. Available in the Elmwood School Archives, Rockcliffe, Ottawa.
44. *Autobiographies*, p. 140.
45. *Samara*, 1928–29. Available in the Elmwood School Archives, Rockcliffe, Ottawa.
46. *Necessary Secrets: The Journals of Elizabeth Smart*, ed. Alice VanWart (Ottawa: Deneau, 1986), p. 13.
47. Interview with Russel Smart, Ottawa, 11 November 1988.
48. *Juvenilia*, pp. 17–20.
49. *In the Meantime*, p. 16.
50. Letters from Louie Smart, 16 April 1925; 1 May 1925. NLC: Box 15, File 1.
51. *Juvenilia*, pp. 24–26.
52. Interview with Jane Marsh Beveridge, Cambridge, Mass., 4–11 July 1988.
53. Jane Marsh Beveridge, "Four Horses, Sixteen Legs."
54. This is how Mrs Beveridge characterized their relationship in interview with author.
55. Letters from Helen Smart, 5 February 1928; 21 May 1928. NLC: Box 17, F 1.
56. *In Their Words: Interviews with Fourteen Canadian Writers*, ed. Bruce Meyer and Brian O'Riordan (Toronto: Anansi, 1984), p. 188.
57. *Juvenilia*, p. 13.
58. Mallinson, "Interview," 4 March 1983.
59. *Juvenilia*, pp. 46–47.
60. Interview by Peter Gzowski, "Morningside," CBC Radio, 29 November 1982.

61. *Juvenilia*, p. 45.

Two: The Great Sexual Necessities

1. School Yearbook, Hatfield Hall, Cobourg, Ontario. Vol. I, 1930, p. 5.
2. Mallinson, "Interview," March 4, 1983.
3. Interview with Tibs Partridge, Toronto, 26 June 1988.
4. *Autobiographies*, p. 185.
5. Mallinson, "Interview," 4 March 1983.
6. Smart refers to these incidents a number of times, including in *Autobiographies,* pp. 142, 159.
7. Letter from Louie Smart, 19 January 1931. NLC: Box 15, F 1.
8. *In the Meantime*, p. 133.
9. Interview with Sandra Gwyn, London, England, 15 December 1988.
10. Sandra Gwyn, "The Capital: Forsey and Spry: the Grand Old Gents of Ottawa," *Saturday Night*, November 1976, p. 14. Other sources describing this period include R.H. Hubbard, *Rideau Hall: An Illustrated History of Government House, Ottawa* (Montreal and London: McGill-Queen's University Press, 1977); Madge Macbeth, *Inside Government House: As Told by Colonel H. Willis-O'Connor* (Toronto: The Ryerson Press, 1954).
11. Rideau [pseud.], "Ottawa Letter," *Mayfair*, October 1934, p. 40; *Mayfair*, July 1934, p. 58.
12. Shirley E. Woods, Jr., *Ottawa: The Capital of Canada* (Toronto: Doubleday, 1980), pp. 261–62.
13. Katherine Govier, "That Smart Woman," *Fanfare, The Globe and Mail*, 12 April 1978, p. 11.
14. The Graham Spry Papers, The National Archives of Canada, Vol. 84–12.
15. Ritchie, *My Grandfather's House*, p. 155.
16. Interview with Diana Holland-Martin (formerly Didy Battye), Overbury, Gloucestershire, 3–4 May 1989.
17. Ritchie, *My Grandfather's House*, pp. 153–54.
18. Interview with Irene Spry (wife of Graham Spry), Ottawa, 12 November 1988.
19. Graham Spry Papers, Vol. 84–12.
20. Graham Spry Papers, Vol. 5. Correspondence, 1931–1933.
21. Graham Spry Papers, Vol. 21–4. Diaries and Journals, 1931–33.
22. NLC: Box 75, File 3.
23. *Necessary Secrets*, p. 44.
24. *Autobiographies*, p. 153.
25. *Autobiographies*, p. 152; p. 176.

Three: Kissing the Dead Lips of Emily Brontë

1. "Terminal Report," Hatfield Hall, 12 January 1931. VWC.
2. *Autobiographies*, p. 129.
3. Graham Spry Papers, Vol. 5. Correspondence, 1931–33.
4. *Autobiographies*, p. 129.
5. *Necessary Secrets*, p. 11.
6. *Necessary Secrets*, p. 14.
7. NLC: Box 2, File 3, Diary 1933. The first part of the episode is in *Necessary Secrets*, p. 17.
8. *Necessary Secrets*, p. 20.
9. *Autobiographies*, p. 130.
10. Letter to Meredith Frampton, 26 August 1933. VWC: Box 2—"Meredith Frampton."
11. *Juvenilia*, pp. 88–89.
12. *Juvenilia*, pp. 93–98.
13. *Necessary Secrets*, p. 104.
14. The Canadian Women's Institute was established in 1897 as a complement to the Farmers' Institute by Adelaide Hoodless.
15. Mrs Neve Scarborough, *A.C.W.W.: A History* (Yorkshire: John Wadsworth Ltd., The Rydal Press, 1953), p. 8.
16. *Necessary Secrets*, pp. 37–38.
17. *Necessary Secrets*, p. 45.
18. *Necessary Secrets*, p. 38.
19. *Necessary Secrets*, p. 31.
20. *Juvenilia*, pp. 104–5.
21. *Necessary Secrets*, pp. 50–51.
22. *Necessary Secrets*, p. 62.
23. *The Ottawa Citizen*, 27 January 1935.
24. *Necessary Secrets*, p. 59.
25. *In the Meantime*, p. 151. Elizabeth felt that, because people saw her as beautiful, they assumed she was lucky and unassailable. She couldn't be hurt.
26. *Necessary Secrets*, p. 57.
27. *Necessary Secrets*, p. 65.
28. *Necessary Secrets*, pp. 48–49.
29. *Necessary Secrets*, p. 63.
30. *Necessary Secrets*, p. 66.
31. *Necessary Secrets*, p. 224.
32. Ritchie, *My Grandfather's House*, p. 158.
33. *Necessary Secrets*, p. 163.
34. Interview with Marian Scott, Montreal, 18 August 1988.
35. Letter from Frank Scott, 18 October 1950. NLC: Box 36.

Four: The Stifled Moment

1. VWC: Box 3—"My first day at university . . ."
2. *Necessary Secrets*, pp. 78–79.
3. *Necessary Secrets*, p. 79.
4. *Ibid.*
5. *Necessary Secrets*, p. 80.
6. The manuscript of "My Lover John" is available in the Graham Spry Papers, Vol. 42–18. All quotations are from this manuscript.
7. Letter from Jane Marsh Beveridge to author, 12 May 1990.
8. *Necessary Secrets*, p. 78.
9. *Necessary Secrets*, p. 82.
10. *Necessary Secrets*, p. 83.
11. *In the Meantime,* p. 138.
12. *Necessary Secrets*, p. 86.
13. *The Times* (London), Saturday, 17 June 1944.
14. *Necessary Secrets*, pp. 99, 113.
15. *Necessary Secrets*, p. 120.
16. *Necessary Secrets*, p. 167.
17. *Necessary Secrets*, pp. 130, 144.
18. *Necessary Secrets*, p. 103.
19. *Necessary Secrets*, p. 106.
20. *Necessary Secrets*, p. 115.
21. Jessie Chambers, *D. H. Lawrence: A Personal Record* (London: Jonathan Cape, 1935), p. 82.
22. *Necessary Secrets*, p. 136.
23. *Necessary Secrets*, pp. 128–29.
24. *Necessary Secrets*, p. 133. Smart is referring, of course, to Samuel Johnson's *Prefaces.*
25. *Necessary Secrets*, p. 147.
26. Interview with Diana Holland-Martin, Overbury, Gloucestershire, 3–4 May 1989.
27. Letter from Louie Smart, 6 May 1937. Collection of Jane Marsh Beveridge.
28. Letter from Jacques Bieler, 24 April 1937. Collection of Jane Marsh Beveridge.
29. Letter from Charles Ritchie, 16 February 1937. Collection of Jane Marsh Beveridge.
30. Letter from "Bill," 4 March 1937. Collection of Jane Marsh Beveridge.
31. *Necessary Secrets*, p. 112.
32. Letters from I. J. Jay Hermann, 2 May 1937; 15 May 1937. Collection of Jane Marsh Beveridge.

33. Peter Ustinov, *Dear Me* (London: Penguin Books, 1977), pp. 97–100.
34. Interview with Peter Ustinov, Toronto, 21 October 1989.

Five: Dig a Grave and Let Us Bury Our Mother

1. *Necessary Secrets*, p. 186.
2. *The Diary of Anaïs Nin, Vol. 4, 1944–47*, ed. Gunther Stuhlmann (New York: Harcourt Brace Jovanovich, 1971), p. 36. Varda did the jacket covers for a number of Nin's early novels.
3. Henry Miller, *Varda: The Master Builder* (Philadelphia: The Walton Press, 1971), p. 8. Reprinted from *Remember to Remember* (Norfolk, Connecticut: New Directions, 1947).
4. *Necessary Secrets*, p. 173–74.
5. Conversation with Simonette Strachey, Oxford, 9 May 1989.
6. *Necessary Secrets*, p. 191.
7. *Necessary Secrets*, p. 175.
8. Letter to Graham Spry, 22 May 1938. Graham Spry Papers, vol. 42–12, Correspondence 1938.
9. Letter to parents, 4 June 1938. VWC: Box 2—"Parents."
10. Letter from Jean Varda, 10 May 1941. NLC: Box 37.
11. *The Assumption of the Rogues and Rascals*, p. 11.
12. *Necessary Secrets*, p. 178.
13. Letter from Louie Smart, 9 October 1938. NLC: Box 15, F 1.
14. John Goddard, "An Appetite for Life," *Books in Canada*, vol. 11, no. 6, June/July 1982, p. 8.
15. "A Remedy For Stuffed Shirts," *The Ottawa Journal*, 27 April 1939, p. 6.
16. Interview with Muriel Flexman, Cobourg, Ontario, 1 August 1989.
17. Letter to Lawrence Durrell, 15 January 1939. Lawrence Durrell Collection, Special Collections, Southern Illinois University at Carbondale.
18. *George Barker: Collected Poems*, p. 88.
19. Letter from Lawrence Durrell, 15 January 1939. NLC: Box 33.
20. Letter from Louie Smart, 6 June 1939. NLC: Box 15, F 2.
21. *Necessary Secrets*, p. 179.
22. Letter from Lawrence Durrell, (undated: from Athens to New York). NLC: Box 33.
23. Letter from Henry Miller, 20 February 1940. NLC: Box 35.
24. *Necessary Secrets*, p. 181.
25. *Necessary Secrets*, p. 184.
26. *Necessary Secrets*, p. 185.
27. *Necessary Secrets*, p. 196.
28. *Necessary Secrets*, pp. 200–1.

Six: Music and Sappho's Girl

1. Because of this exhibition, it has often been suggested that Smart was influenced by Paalen and the Surrealist Movement. Certainly, she was reading the Surrealists' pamphlets, but she dismissed Paalen as "bound in swaddling bands of pedantic dogma" (*Necessary Secrets*, p. 205). The Surrealists' insistence on the integrity of the sub-conscious may have confirmed her instinct to explore the enigmas of her own psyche, but in her art she left nothing to chance. Her writing was always carefully crafted.
2. *Necessary Secrets*, p. 206.
3. *Necessary Secrets*, p. 217.
4. *In the Meantime*, p. 139.
5. "Dig a Grave and Let Us Bury Our Mother," *In the Meantime*, p. 80.
6. *Ibid.*, p. 48.
7. *The Diary Of Anaïs Nin, Vol. 4*, pp. 58-60.
8. *Necessary Secrets*, p. 205.
9. *Necessary Secrets*, pp. 211–12.
10. *Necessary Secrets*, pp. 212–13.
11. *Necessary Secrets*, p. 232.
12. *Necessary Secrets*, p. 211.
13. *In the Meantime*, pp. 89–92.
14. *Necessary Secrets*, p. 236.
15. *Autobiographies*, pp. 170–71.
16. Letter from Alice Paalen (undated). NLC: Box 35. Translated from the French by author.
17. *Necessary Secrets*, pp. 206–7.
18. *Necessary Secrets*, p. 217.
19. Interview with Joyce Marshall, Toronto, 15 May 1990.
20. Letter from Lawrence Durrell (undated). NCL: Box 33.
21. Melvyn Bragg, *George Barker*, "The South Bank Show," London Weekend Television Ltd., 14 February 1988.
22. Letter from George Barker, 25 January 1940. NLC: Box 18, F 1.
23. *Autobiographies*, p. 46.
24. *Necessary Secrets*, p. 243.
25. Letter from Russel Smart, 26 April 1940. NLC: Box 16, F 1.
26. Letter from Russel Smart, 10 May 1940. NLC: Box 16, F 1.
27. Letter from Louie Smart, 19 April 1940. NLC: Box 15, F 2.
28. Letter from Louie Smart, 20 February 1940. NLC: Box 15, F 2.
29. Letter from Louie Smart, 2 July 1940. NLC: Box 15, F 2.
30. Letter from Russel Smart, 24 March 1940. NLC: Box 16, F 1.
31. *Necessary Secrets*, p. 239.
32. *Necessary Secrets*, pp. 238–42.

33. Interview with George Barker, Bintry House, Norfolk, 29 April 1989.
34. Letter from Christopher Isherwood, 8 May 1940. NLC: Box 34.
35. Letter, 28 June 1940. Quoted from *Autobiographies*, p. 27.
36. *Necessary Secrets*, p. 245.
37. Henry Miller, *Big Sur and the Oranges of Hieronymus Bosch* (New York: New Directions, 1957), p. 59. In this book Miller refers to *By Grand Central Station* as "a very unusual little book, a 'love story,' the jacket says. The romance which inspired the book took place at Anderson Creek when Varda ruled the roost."
38. Letter from Louie Smart, 4 July 1940. NLC: Box 15, F 2.
39. Letter from Louie Smart, 30 August 1940. NLC: Box 15, F 2.
40. Letter from Russel Smart, 14 August 1940. NLC: Box 16, F 1.
41. *Necessary Secrets*, p. 246.
42. Interview by author with Elizabeth Smart, The Dell. Flixton, Bungay, Suffolk, 15 February 1979.

Seven: Oh My Canadian!

1. *By Grand Central Station I Sat Down and Wept*, p. 17.
2. Interview with Alice VanWart, Toronto, 19 March 1990.
3. Bruce Meyer and Brian O'Riordan, eds., *In Their Words*, p. 192.
4. *Autobiographies*, p. 54. Elizabeth Smart quotes George Barker.
5. Interview with George Barker, Bintry House, Norfolk, 29 April 1989.
6. *Autobiographies*, p. 50. Smart always made a distinction between fact and emotional truth.
7. *Autobiographies*, p. 52. Synopsis for the film script of *By Grand Central Station* written by Smart in 1980.
8. Melvyn Bragg, *George Barker*, "The South Bank Show," London Weekend Television Ltd., 14 February 1988. Barker is quoting lines from his poem "In Memory of David Archer, XXXVII," *George Barker: Collected Poems*, p. 588.
9. *Autobiographies*, p. 164.
10. George Barker, "The South Bank Show."
11. David Wright, in *Homage to George Barker*, eds. John Heath-Stubbs and Martin Green (London: Martin Brian & O'Keeffe, 1973), p. 29–31.
12. *George Barker: Collected Poems*, p. 167.
13. Interview with Elspeth Barker, Bintry House, Norfolk, 29 April–1 May 1989. This was how Elspeth Barker characterized the Barker rages.
14. *George Barker: Collected Poems*, p. 531.
15. See Barker's poem, "In Memory of David Archer, XXXVII," which is a haunting confession of the incident. *Collected Poems*, p. 611.

16. Maurice Carpenter, in *Homage to George Barker*, p. 44.
17. Paul Potts, in *Homage to George Barker*, p. 14.
18. Interview with George Barker, Bintry House, Norfolk, 29 April 1989.
19. *Homage to George Barker*, p. 50.
20. Interview with Elspeth Barker, Bintry House, Norfolk, 29 April–
    1 May 1989. See also George Barker, *The Dead Seagull* (New York:
    Farrar, Straus & Young, Inc., 1950). It is possible to see something of
    Barker's version of Jessica in the portrait of Theresa.
21. *Autobiographies*, p. 46.
22. Since Smart had spoken of F.B.I. notes, an application was made
    under the Freedom of Information Act to the U.S. Department of
    Justice, Federal Bureau of Investigation, for information or files about
    Elizabeth Smart. One cross-reference was located (a cross-reference
    refers to a name appearing in the file of another individual, event,
    activity, organization, or the like). Access to the "three pages" relevant
    to the request was denied under subsection (1b) of Title 5, United
    States Code, Section 552. [(Explanation of subsection 9b): (A)
    specifically authorized under criteria established by an Executive order
    to be kept secret in the interest of national defense or foreign policy
    and (B) are in fact properly classified pursuant to such Executive
    order.] A second appeal was also refused with the explanation: "Ms.
    Smart is not the subject of a Headquarters main file but is alluded to
    briefly one time in one file, the subject of which is another individual
    or an organization. The Bureau has processed only the portion of the
    file that pertains to Ms. Smart. This material is classified. . . . Recent
    review has determined that this material warrants continued
    classification under Executive Order N. 12356. This material is not
    appropriate for discretionary release. (Letter from Richard L. Huff,
    Co–Director, Office of Information and Privacy, 21 June 1990)
23. Russel Smart, Smart's brother, thought that Smart didn't actually sell
    her mountain until the mid-fifties at which time the property was sold
    to the National Capital Commission. (Letter to author, 29 June 1990)
24. Though George Barker gave his permission to quote from published
    works, permission was refused for quotation from his letters. In the
    National Library of Canada there are approximately 130 letters,
    telegrams, or notes from Barker to Smart dated from 25 January 1940
    to 31 March 1967. The NLC also holds 12 hardcover notebooks by
    Barker. In the George Barker Collection at the University of Texas,
    72 items of correspondence (some drafts) from Barker to Smart are
    catalogued.
25. Letter from Jessica Barker, 7 November 1940. NLC: Box 63, F 11.
26. Letter from Jessica Barker (undated: Hollywood). NLC: Box 63, F 11.
27. Letter to George Barker (undated: December 1940). Quoted in

Autobiographies, p. 28. Many of the surviving letters by Smart from this period have been published in *Autobiographies*.

28. Letter to George Barker 24 December 1940. Quoted in *Autobiographies*, pp. 29–30.
29. Letter from Jessica Barker, 14 January 1942. NLC: Box 18, File 11.
30. Letter to George Barker, 17 January 1941. Quoted in *Autobiographies*, p. 32.
31. Sandra Djwa, *The Politics of the Imagination: A Life of F.R. Scott* (Toronto: McClelland & Stewart, 1987), p. 196.
32. Interview by Peter Gzowski, "Morningside," CBC Radio, 29 November 1982.
33. Letter to George Barker, 24 February 1941. Quoted in *Autobiographies*, p. 33.
34. Letter to George Barker, 24 February 1941. Quoted in *Autobiographies*, p. 34.
35. *Autobiographies*, p. 170.
36. *Necessary Secrets*, p. 248.
37. *Necessary Secrets*, p. 253.
38. *Necessary Secrets*, p. 251.
39. *Necessary Secrets*, p. 253.
40. *Necessary Secrets*, p. 255.
41. *Autobiographies*, pp. 37–38.
42. Letters quoted in *Autobiographies*, pp. 34–35.
43. Letters quoted in *Necessary Secrets*, p. 262.
44. Letters quoted in *Necessary Secrets*, p. 259.
45. Interview with Russel Smart, Ottawa, 11 November 1988.
46. *Autobiographies*, p. 30. Barker's words quoted by Elizabeth Smart.
47. *Necessary Secrets*, p. 263.
48. Eleanor Wachtel, "Passion's Survivor," *City Woman*, Summer 1980, p. 55.
49. *Ibid.*, p. 55.
50. *Necessary Secrets*, pp. 267–68.
51. *Autobiographies*, p. 153.
52. *Necessary Secrets*, p. 254. Throughout *By Grand Central Station* Smart uses biblical and classical allusions. For a study of the metaleptic structure of the novel, see Alice VanWart, "*By Grand Central Station I Sat Down and Wept*: The Novel as a Poem," *Studies in Canadian Literature*, Spring 1986, pp. 38–51.
53. *Autobiographies*, p. 31.
54. *Autobiographies*, p. 44.
55. Letter to George Barker from F.C. Blair, 19 September 1941. NLC: Box 64.
56. "Moral turpitude" was an offical charge under which an individual

could be refused entrance into Canada. Though a request was made to the Department of Employment and Immigration, and a search was undertaken at the National Archives of Canada, Social Affairs & Natural Resources Records, Government Archives Division, any official correspondence regarding George Barker could not be traced.

57. What file is referred to remains a mystery. A request for all files on Elizabeth Smart under the Access to Information Act was refused under subsection 3 (m) of the Privacy Act, which dictates that information regarding a private individual cannot be released until twenty years after the individual's death. (Letter from R.W. Rapley, A/Director, Public Rights Administration, Employment and Immigration Canada, 7 December 1989.)

58. *Autobiographies*, pp. 71–76. Barker's letter is reproduced in its entirety.

59. *Autobiographies*, p. 148.

60. *Autobiographies*, p. 30.

Eight: How Many Miles to the Gallon to Babylon

1. Smart recorded meeting Anaïs Nin when she reviewed the Stuhlmann edition of Nin's *Journals* (*Queen*, 6 July 1966). Nin never mentions the meeting in her diaries.

2. Elizabeth applied to the American Consulate for a visa for Georgina and was advised: "It will be necessary for you to submit to the Consulate General documentary evidence that you are the mother of Georgina Elizabeth Barker, as well as the consent of the child's father before issuing a non immigrant or an immigration visa." She was of course required to fill in a form with particulars of her marital status, and detailed information about her husband. (Letter from Paul R. Josselyn, American Consulate General, Vancouver, B.C., 4 February 1942) It took the Consulate one month to process the application.

3. *Washington Times*, 5 March 1942.

4. Telegram from Jessica Barker, 6 April 1942. TSC.

5. Letter from Jessica Barker, 4 April 1942. NLC: Box 18, F 11.

6. Letter from Jessica Barker, 9 April 1942. NLC: Box 63, F 11.

7. Letter from Jessica Barker (c/o Mrs Maas), 20 May 1942. NLC: Box 18, F 11.

8. *The Diary of Anaïs Nin, Vol. 3 1939–1944*, ed. Gunther Stuhlmann (New York: Harcourt Brace Jovanovich, 1969), pp. 150–51. Among Smart's papers is a typed manuscript of "erotica." The corrections are in George Barker's handwriting. NLC: Box 57, F 1.

9. *The Diary of Anaïs Nin, Vol. 3*, pp. 175–77.

10. *The Diary of Anaïs Nin, Vol. 3*, pp. 197–98.

11. P. Adams Sitney, *Visionary Film: The Avant-Garde 1943–1978* (New York: Oxford University Press, 1979), p. 84.
12. Spry was working with the Ministry of Aircraft Production in London. See Letter, 18 December 1942. TSC.
13. Letter from Louie Smart (undated). TSC.
14. Letter to George Barker, 15 February 1942. TSC.
15. The Commodore's report on the convoy in which Smart travelled was provided by the Directorate of History, National Defence—CR. Ref. North Atlantic Convoys OPS 1650–239/15.
16. *The Assumption of the Rogues and Rascals*, p. 29.
17. *By Grand Central Station I Sat Down and Wept*, p. 117.
18. Letter from Didy Asquith, 15 February (no year is indicated). NLC: Box 32.
19. Letter from Willard Maas, 18 June 1943. NLC: Box 35.
20. *Autobiographies*, photosection, p. 4
21. *Autobiographies*, p. 79.
22. Letter from Jessica Barker, 7 August 1943. NLC: Box 63, F 11.
23. *Autobiographies*, p. 103.
24. *Autobiographies*, p. 105.
25. *Autobiographies*, p. 104.
26. Interview with Didy Asquith, Overbury, Gloucestershire, 3–4 May 1989.

Nine: Marginal Notes, Never the Text

1. Letter to Louie Smart, 10 October 1943. VWC: Box 2—"Mother."
2. Letter from Louie Smart, 21 January 1944. NLC: Box 15, F 2.
3. Letter to Louie Smart, 4 January 1943. VWC: Box 2—"Mother."
4. Letter from Louie Smart, 14 February 1944. NLC: Box 15, F 2.
5. Letter from Mrs H. Osborne (undated). VWC.
6. Letter to Louie Smart, 3 December 1943. VWC: Box 2—"Mother."
7. Letter to Marie Maas, 5 Dec 1943. TSC.
8. Letter to Louie Smart, 17 March 1944. VWC: Box 2—"Mother."
9. *Autobiographies*, p. 108.
10. NLC: Box 4, F 15.
11. *Autobiographies*, pp. 108–9.
12. Letter from Louie Smart, 22 July 1944. NLC: Box 15, F 2.
13. Letter from Russel Smart, Jr. NLC: Box 17, F 5.
14. *Autobiographies*, p. 112.
15. Interview by Vicki Gabereau, "Variety Tonight," CBC Radio, 11 January 1983. Parts of the interview were published in Vicki Gabereau, *This Won't Hurt a Bit* (Toronto: Collins, 1987), p. 87.
16. Jill Neville, "Something Happened," *Harpers & Queen*, March 1977.

17. *Autobiographies*, p. 112.
18. *In the Meantime*, p. 139.
19. Letter to Marie Maas, 10 February 1944. TSC.
20. Letter to Marie Maas, 9 November 1944. TSC.
21. Letter to Marie Maas, 17 September 1944. TSC.
22. Letters from Jessica Barker, 2 May 1944; 10 April 1944. NLC: Box 63, F 11.
23. Interview with Anastasia Wyatt-Wilson, Alvaton, Kentucky, 7-9 October 1990.
24. *Autobiographies*, p. 113.
25. Letter from Louie Smart, 22 January 1945. NLC: Box 15, F 3.
26. Letter from Russel Smart, 24 February 1945. NLC: Box 17, F 4.
27. Interview with Joyce Marshall, Toronto, 15 May 1990.
28. Letter from Louie Smart, 3 March 1945. NLC: Box 15, F 3.
29. Interview with Sandra Gwyn, London, 10 May 1989.
30. Letter to Louie Smart, 12 March 1945. AVW: Box 2—"Mother."
31. *Autobiographies*, p. 114.
32. Interview with George Barker, Bintry House, Norfolk, 29 April 1989. Friends like Michael Ondaatje and Nancy Beatty remembered Elizabeth having said the first title was "Multiple Images."
33. Letter from *Editions Poetry London*, 21 August 1945. NLC: Box 44. For portraits of Tambi see *Tambimuttu: Bridge Between Two Worlds*, ed. Jane Williams (London: Peter Owen, 1989).
34. Georgina Howell, *Vogue* interview, 1977. NLC: Box 74, F 5.
35. *The Sunday Times*, 20 October 1945, p. 497.
36. *Times Literary Supplement*, 20 October 1945, p. 497.
37. Cyril Connolly, *Horizon*, vol. XII, no. 68, 1945.
38. Letter from Louie Smart, 14 June 1946. NLC: Box 15, F 3.
39. *Autobiographies*, p. 116.
40. *Ibid.*
41. NLC: Box 4, F 13.
42. Letter from Willard Maas, 16 July 1946. NLC: Box 35.
43. Letter to George Barker, 27 September 1946. TSC.
44. Letter from George Barker (undated). TSC.
45. *Autobiographies*, p. 125. Comments by Barker quoted as interpolated text.
46. Letter to Marie Maas, 7 January 1947. TSC.
47. Letter to Marie Maas, 15 February 1947. TSC.

Ten: The 97 Positions of the Heart, Lying Low

1. Interview with Michael Wickham, Wiltshire, 9 May 1989.
2. *In the Meantime*, p. 104.

3. *In the Meantime*, p. 98.
4. Elizabeth Smart, "Design Begins in the Nursery," address to the Royal Society, 1950. NLC: Box 54, F 1.
5. Interview by author with Elizabeth Smart, The Dell, Flixton, Bungay, Suffolk, 15 February 1979.
6. Letter from Elizabeth Jolley to author, 30 August 1989.
7. Elizabeth Jolley, *My Father's Moon* (London: Viking Books, 1989), p. 10.
8. Letter from Louie Smart, 14 June 1946. NLC: Box 15, F 3.
9. Caitlin Thomas with George Tremlett, *Caitlin: Life with Dylan Thomas* (New York: Henry Holt & Co., 1986), p. 5.
10. For a portrait of Soho see Daniel Farson, *Soho in the Fifties* (London: Michael Joseph, 1987); Anthony Cronin, *Dead as Doornails* (London: Oxford University Press, 1986); J. Maclaren-Ross, *Memoirs of the Forties* (London: Alan Ross Ltd., 1965).
11. Elizabeth Smart, "Muriel." NLC: Box 55, F 25. (Proofs for *House & Garden*, 1980).
12. Elizabeth Smart, "Books: SURVIVORS," *Queen*, 2 June 1965, p. 22.
13. George Barker, *The Dead Seagull* (New York: Farrar, Straus & Young, Inc., 1950). All quotations are from this edition. According to Jane Smart, the title refers to a seagull Barker found one day while walking casually along a beach, but it is certainly reminiscent of Chekhov's play, *The Seagull*, with its theme of romantic disillusionment.
14. *Autobiographies*, p. 174.
15. Interview with Michael Asquith, London, 12 May 1989.
16. *The Dead Seagull*, p. 39. A friend of George Barker, Paul Potts, while deeply admiring of Barker's poetry, could say of the novel: "He wrote what is perhaps the worst book ever to have been written by a real artist, in which it is stated throughout that sex is filthy and she whom you do it with dirty. The name of the book, *The Dead Seagull*. One can never forgive Barker for writing that kind of nonsense." (*Homage to George Barker*, p. 14.)
17. *Ibid.*, p. 46.
18. *Ibid.*, p. 61.
19. Interview with Elspeth Barker, Bintry House, Norfolk, 29 April–1 May 1989.
20. Alice VanWart, "Elizabeth Smart: A Reconsideration," *Brick: A Journal of Reviews*, no. 33, Spring 1988, p. 51.
21. Interview with George Barker, Bintry House, Norfolk, 29 April 1989.
22. *George Barker: Collected Poems*, p. 212.
23. Letter from Didy Asquith (undated). NLC: Box 32.
24. "The Assumption of the Rogues and Rascals," in *Botteghe Oscure*,

vol. 8, 1951, pp. 211–19.

25. "A Simple Statement," in *Botteghe Oscure*, vol. 12, 1953, pp. 132–39.

Eleven: Bit George's Lip

1. Anthony Cronin, *Dead as Doornails*, p. 131. For a portrait of the Roberts see also J. Maclaren-Ross, *Memoirs of the Forties*; of their work, Malcolm Yorke, *The Spirit of Place: Nine Neo-Romantic Artists and Their Times* (London: Constable, 1988).

2. Interview with George Barker, Bintry House, Norfolk, 29 April 1989.

3. John Rothenstein, *Modern British Painters, Vol. 3* (London: Macdonald & Co., 1984), p. 169. See also George Barker's eloquent elegy, "Funeral Eulogy for Robert Colquhoun," *Collected Poems*, p. 437.

4. *Autobiographies*, pp. 174, 148.

5. Vicki Gabereau, *This Won't Hurt a Bit*, p. 87.

6. Interview with Maria Kroll, London, 12 May 1989.

7. *The Assumption of the Rogues and Rascals*, p. 115.

8. Letter from Frank Auerbach to the author, 26 June 1990.

9. Katherine Govier, "That Smart Woman," p. 11.

10. Interview with George Barker, Bintry House, Norfolk, 29 April 1989.

11. Interview by Vicki Gabereau, "Variety Tonight," CBC Radio, 11 January 1983.

12. Interview by Nigel Lewis, "Sunday Morning," CBC Radio, 29 August 1982.

13. "Elizabeth Smart" on "The Journal," CBC TV, 24 February 1984.

14. *Ibid*.

15. Interview with Hase Asquith, London, 12 May 1989.

16. Interview with Jay Landesman, London, 10 May 1989.

17. Letter from Jane Bunting, 2 October 1959. NLC: Box 70, F 4.

Twelve: This Unendingly Square-Rooted Globe

1. *The Assumption of the Rogues and Rascals*, p. 31.

2. Interview with Georgina Barker, Looe, Cornwall, 22–25 April 1989.

3. Private notebook, in the possession of Georgina Barker.

4. Letter from Georgina Barker (undated). NLC: Box 19, F 3.

5. Letters from Georgina Barker, 16 November 1962; 6 October 1963. NLC: Box 19, F 1 & 2.

6. Letter from Christopher Barker, 8 November 1960. NLC: Box 20, F 2.

7. Interview with Christopher Barker, London, 26 April 1989.

8. It was not Elizabeth's style to cast aspersions on anyone. In the privacy of her diary, there are almost no derogatory remarks about

acquaintances and friends.

9. Interview with Sebastian Barker, London, 12–13 May 1989.

10. Letter from Sebastian Barker. NLC: Box 21, F 1.

11. Interview with Elspeth Barker, Bintry House, Norfolk, 29 April–1 May 1989.

12. Diary of Rose Barker. NLC: Box 22, F 2.

13. Conversation with Bob Johnson, London, 5 May 1989. Not all agreed. Sally Beauman, Features Editor at *Harper's Bazaar* at the end of the sixties, felt the influence was overstated. "Of her literary standing, yes, there was no doubt—*Central Station* is a wonderful book and I think ES would be a good reviewer/literary critic—but by the seventies I would say, sadly, that her influence was very peripheral, being overtaken (as Happens) by all those gossipy anecdotes that accrue to make little legends—the drinking being, presumably, a factor in that, together with the writer's block." Letter to the author, 19 June 1990.

14. Jill Neville, "Something Happened," *Harpers & Queen*, March 1977.

15. Letter to author from Sylvia Bruce, 21 June 1990.

16. Interview with Ann Barr, London, 8 May 1990.

17. Elizabeth Smart, "Books: WOTALOTIGOT!" *Queen*, 20 October 1965, p. 50.

18. Conversation with Margaret Drabble, London, 25 April 1989. In 1968, Drabble published a speech called "Women Novelists" in the *National Book League Periodical*, which was a fascinating effort to predict the future of the novel. She noted the vast increase in the effort by women to deal with the literature of childbirth, contraception, abortion and copulation. "The voice of the emancipated woman is raising itself in fiction," she wrote. "Men have always written about sex, of course, and in four-letter words too . . . but women until now . . . have been less vocal." But the problem was how to find an erotic language. "Nobody could dismiss the achievements of the linguistic pioneers, and yet at the same time we have the poetic, evocative, powerful work of Elizabeth Smart, whose book *By Grand Central Station I Sat Down and Wept,* which used, to describe the experience of love, the language of another century—the language which she describes, specifically, as the language of love."

19. Elizabeth Smart, "Books: SHELVING THE QUESTION," *Queen*, 30 June 1965, p. 14.

20. Elizabeth Smart, "Books: GOO," *Queen*, 16 June 1965, p. 15.

21. Elizabeth Smart, "Books," *Queen*, 20 October 1966, p. 26.

22. Elizabeth Smart, book review, *Queen*, 20 October 1965, p. 50.

23. Elizabeth Smart, "Books: IS THERE A WOMAN IN THE BOOK?" *Queen*, 24 February 1965, p. 17.

24. *The Assumption of the Rogues and Rascals*, p. 83.

25. Interview with Elspeth Barker, Bintry House, Norfolk, 28 April–
    1 May 1989.
26. *The Observer*, 12 February 1967, p. 21.
27. Letter from Louie Smart, 22 February 1966. VWC: Box 2—"Mother."
28. *By Grand Central Station*, p. 67.
29. *Autobiographies*, p. 165.
30. *Autobiographies*, p. 149.
31. Letter from Rose Barker, 20 February 1967. NLC: Box 25, F 1.
32. Letter from Rose Barker, 26 August 1967. NLC: Box 25, F 1.
33. Letter from Rose Barker, Christmas card (undated). NLC: Box 25, F 4.
34. Letter to Sebastian Barker, 5 January 1977. NLC: Box 25, F 8.

Thirteen: Organic Matters

1. *Autobiographies*, p. 167.
2. *Autobiographies*, p. 149.
3. Alice VanWart, ed., *Elizabeth's Garden: Elizabeth Smart on the Art of
   Gardening* (Toronto: Coach House Press, 1989), p. 13.
4. *Elizabeth's Garden*, Preface.
5. Letter to author from Sally Beauman, 19 June 1990.
6. "The Paeony Affair," *Elizabeth's Garden*, p. 19.
7. Elizabeth Smart, "Lusting After Rhododendrons," *Harper's Bazaar*,
   p. 12. NLC: Box 61, F 14.
8. *Ibid.*, p. 17.
9. *Elizabeth's Garden*, Preface.
10. *Elizabeth's Garden*, p. 38.
11. Letter to Jay Landesman, 6 September 1978. In the possession of Jay
    Landesman.
12. Ann Barr, "Mourned by the Rogues and Rascals," *The Observer*, 23
    March 1986.
13. VWC: Box 2; all quotations are from the 1970 journal "Second Class
    Notes."
14. Letter to Jay Landesman, 18 February 1977. In the possession of Jay
    Landesman.

Fourteen: A Bonus

1. Elizabeth Smart, *A Bonus* (London: Polytantric Press, 1977), p. 19.
2. *The Assumption of the Rogues and Rascals*, p. 76.
3. Conversation with Jeffrey Bernard at the Coach and Horses, London,
   21 April 1989. The poem is quoted in the successful dramatization of
   Bernard's life, "Jeffrey Bernard Is Unwell," by Keith Waterhouse,
   which starred Peter O'Toole as Bernard in the first production in 1989.

4. Conversation at The French with "Canadian Jo," London, 21 April 1989.

5. Interview with Sebastian Barker, Toronto, 9 December 1989.

6. *In the Meantime*, p. 139.

7. Interview with Sebastian Barker, Toronto, 9 December 1989.

8. NLC: Box 12, F 1 (1982).

9. *In the Meantime*, p. 25.

10. VWC: Box 2 (1975).

11. George Woodcock, *The Globe and Mail*, 1 November 1975. NLC: Box 74, F 1.

12. NLC: Box 51, F 2.

13. Letter to Jay Landesman, February 1977. In the possession of Jay Landesman.

14. All quotations are from *The Assumption of the Rogues and Rascals* (London: Jonathan Cape and Polytantric Press, 1978).

15. *Autobiographies*, p. 183.

16. NLC: Box 11, F 1 (1976). Elizabeth is paraphrasing W.S. Graham's poem "What Is the Language Using Us For?" from *Implements In Their Places*, (Faber & Faber, 1977).

17. John Goddard, "An Appetite for Life," *Books in Canada*, vol. 11, no. 6, June/July 1982, p. 9.

18. Literary references list in NLC: Box 50, F 14; musical references list in Box 11, F 1.

19. Auberon Waugh, "Heroine in a Terrible Mess," *The Evening Standard*, 7 March 1978; *The Statesman*, 4 March 1978.

20. Letter from Sebastian Barker, 9 May 1977. NLC: Box 21, F 1.

21. Tim Dooley, *Aquarius*, No. 11, April 1979.

22. *Autobiographies*, p. 169.

23. Letter from W.S. Graham, 24 April 1978. NLC: Box 33.

24. Philippa Toomey, "Elizabeth Smart Is Alive & Well & Still Writing," *The Times* (London), 15 March 1977.

25. Letter to Katherine Govier, 28 November 1981. In the possession of Katherine Govier.

26. John Fowler, *Glasgow Herald*, 30 August 1980.

27. Julian Barnes, *New Review*, vol. 4, no. 37, April 1977.

28. John Goddard, "An Appetite for Life," p. 9.

29. Anna Cryon, "Secrets Disclosed," *The Tablet*, 26 March 1977. Smart identified Anna Cryon as G.B. in her list of reviews from 1977–79 (in the possession of Jay Landesman), as did the editor of *Aquarius*, Eddie Linden.

30. *In the Meantime*, p. 141.

31. NLC: Box 11, F 1 (1976).

32. *In the Meantime*, p. 133.

33. *Autobiographies*, p. 170.

34. *Autobiographies*, p. 170–71.

35. *Autobiographies*, p. 188.
36. Rose Barker Diary. NLC: Box 28, F 1.
37. Rose Barker Diary. NLC: Box 23, F 14.
38. Rose Barker Diary. NLC: Box 23, F 3.
39. Rose Barker Diary. NLC: Box 23, F 3.
40. Rose Barker Diary. NLC: Box 23, F 9.
41. Rose Barker Diary. NLC: Box 23, F 3.
42. Interview with Elspeth Barker, Bintry House, Norfolk, 29 April–1 May 1989.
43. Letter to Sebastian Barker, 5 January 1977. NLC: Box 25, F 8.
44. NLC: Box 61, F 3.
45. *In the Meantime*, p. 111.

Fifteen: Non Omnis Moriar

1. Letter to Katherine Govier, 2 November 1981. In possession of K. Govier. To bolster Smart's sense of Canadian interest in her work, Govier had approached Toronto's Coach House Press with the idea of publishing an edition of Smart's poems under the title "A Scratch on the Bark," though the venture came to nothing.
2. Interview by Nigel Lewis, "Sunday Morning," CBC Radio, 29 August 1982.
3. *Autobiographies*, p. 195.
4. *Autobiographies*, p. 196.
5. Letter to author from Sara Stambaugh, 6 June 1990.
6. Letter to Christopher Barker, 28 September 1982. In the possession of Christopher Barker.
7. Interview with Alice VanWart, Toronto, 19 March 1990.
8. Interviews with Katherine Govier, Toronto, 4 June 1990; and with Susan Swan, Toronto, 20 June 1990. See also Ken Adachi's perceptive profile of Smart: "'Conformist' was years ahead of her time," *The Toronto Star*, 4 December 1982.
9. NLC: Box 12, F 1.
10. Letter to author from Sara Stambaugh, 6 June 1990.
11. *The Assumption of the Rogues and Rascals*, p. 80.
12. NLC: Box 12, F 2 (13 February 1983).
13. NLC: Box 12, F 1 (20 November 1982).
14. NLC: Box 12, F 2 (February 1983).
15. NLC: Box 54, F 2.
16. Letter to Christopher Barker, 31 March 1983. In the possession of Christopher Barker.
17. Letter to Christopher Barker, 10 November 1983. In the possession of Christopher Barker.
18. *Ibid.*

19. Letter to author from Aviva Layton, 9 July 1990.

20. NLC: Box 12, F 1 (October 1983).

21. *Ibid.*

22. Though Elizabeth spoke of Frye's course to others, she chose anonymity in his class. He did not know her by sight and she, perhaps being shy, did not approach him. When he was informed she had attended, he was "very sorry" not to have met her personally. It would have been fascinating to hear the author of *The Great Code* speaking with the author of *By Grand Central Station* (Letter to author from Northrop Frye, 21 June 1990).

23. Roy MacGregor, "Poet's History Baffles the Bureaucrats", *The Toronto Star*, 27 March 1983. The title of MacGregor's article refers to Elizabeth's financial situation in Toronto. As a repatriated Canadian citizen, she was entitled to an old age pension, but Health and Welfare insisted on signed affidavits from those who had known her in her youth. "They want to know where I've been every minute for the last 69 years," she said. "Which is rather silly because I don't know myself." But she said she loved being called a senior: "Never a prefect, never head girl, but now I'm a *senior.*"

24. Interview with Judith Fitzgerald, Toronto, 15 March 1990.

25. NLC: Box 12, F 1 (October 1983).

26. NLC: Box 12, F 1 (2 January 1984).

27. Interview with Susan Swan, Toronto, 20 June 1990. Elizabeth said to John Goddard: "It's a natural feeling to want to have a baby when you're really in love. Every woman feels it and I think men do too when they're really involved. A woman is a man with a womb, that's what the word means. It's not a man without something, it's a man with something and that something is a womb. I wanted these female experiences." (Goddard, "An Appetite for Life," p. 10).

28. *Autobiographies*, p. 175.

29. Interview with Nancy Beatty, Toronto, 6 April 1990.

30. Interview with Sebastian Barker, London, 12–13 May 1990.

31. *In the Meantime*, p. 138.

32. *Autobiographies*, p. 156.

33. Comment by Elizabeth Smart to author. Among Smart's papers preserved by Jay Landesman is a calendar called "Great Love Affairs," ed. Pamela Mosher (San Francisco: City Lights, 1982). The lovers range from D.H. and Frieda Lawrence to Dylan and Caitlin Thomas. Elizabeth Smart and George Barker belonged among their number.

34. Henry Vaughan, "The Seed Growing Secretly," read at Memorial Service, St. James's Church, Piccadilly, 3 July 1986.

35. Ann Barr, "Mourned by the Rogues and Rascals," *The Observer*, 23 March 1986.

Index